Learning to Teach Modern Foreign Languages in the Secondary School

Learning to Teach Modern Foreign Languages in the Secondary School has established itself as the leading textbook for student teachers of modern foreign languages in the UK. It is also being used in many other countries. The practical focus of the book is underpinned by a theoretical perspective, and readers are encouraged to develop a personal approach to modern foreign language teaching. Relevant statutory frameworks are also taken into account.

This fully revised third edition has been thoroughly updated in line with recent policy and curriculum changes. And, with the recent increased emphasis on teachers as researchers, and the alignment of many PGCE courses with Masters level criteria, reference to important concepts and theoretical positions has been strengthened but the main focus remains on professional practice. Additionally, a new chapter discussing the findings of research on Second Language Acquisition and Foreign Language Learning has been added. Other chapters cover a wide range of relevant topics, including:

- Teaching methods and learning strategies
- Teaching in the target language and developing cultural awareness
- The teaching of grammar
- Differentiation and assessment
- The use of ICT in modern foreign language teaching.

Each chapter features: an introduction offering a brief contextualisation of the topic; objectives identifying what the reader should know, understand and/or be able to do having read the chapter and carried out the tasks in it; discussion of the most important issues with reference to their application in the classroom; tasks inviting the reader to relate content to work in school; a list of annotated further readings.

The book has been designed to allow the reader to 'pick and choose'; specific topics and chapters don't need to be read sequentially. Examples are given in French, German and Spanish but most are transferable to other languages. It will prove an invaluable resource to MFL student teachers and their mentors and tutors.

Norbert Pachler is Reader in Education and Co-Director of the Centre for Excellence in Work-based Learning for Education Professionals at the Institute of Education, University of London, UK.

Ann Barnes leads the Secondary PGCE programme at the University of Warwick, UK, and co-ordinates the MFL strand.

Kit Field is Professor of Education and .... University of Wolver-hampton, UK.

Related titles

Learning to Teach Subjects in the Secondary School Series

Series Editors
Susan Capel, Marilyn Leask and Tony Turner

Designed for all students learning to teach in secondary schools, and particularly those on school-based initial teacher training courses, the books in this series complement *Learning to Teach in the Secondary School* and its companion, *Starting to Teach in the Secondary School*. Each book in the series applies underpinning theory and addresses practical issues to support students in school and in the training institution in learning how to teach a particular subject.

Learning to Teach Modern Foreign Languages in the Secondary School

Third edition

Norbert Pachler, Ann Barnes and Kit Field

Routledge
Taylor & Francis Group

LONDON AND NEW YORK

To Benjamin, James and Daniel

First published 2009
by Routledge
2 Park Square, Milton Park, Abingdon, Oxon, OX14 4RN

Simultaneously published in the USA and Canada
by Routledge
270 Madison Avenue, New York, NY 10016

Routledge is an imprint of the Taylor and Francis Group, an informa business

Typeset in Bembo by RefineCatch Limited, Bungay, Suffolk
Printed and bound in Great Britain
by TJ International, Padstow, Cornwall

British Library Cataloguing in Publication Data
A catalogue record for this book is available from the British Library

Library of Congress Cataloging in Publication Data
A catalog record for this book has been requested

ISBN 10: 0–415–43241–3 (pbk)
ISBN 13: 978–0–415–43241–2 (pbk)

Lesson plan → ps. 96

Contents

Introduction to the series

This, the 3rd edition of *Learning to Teach Modern Foreign Languages in the Secondary School*, is one of a series of books entitled *Learning to Teach [subject name] in the Secondary School: A Companion to School Experience*, covering most subjects in the secondary school curriculum. The books in this series support and complement *Learning to Teach in the Secondary School: A Companion to School Experience* (Capel *et al.* 4th edition, 2005), the best-selling, generic textbook which has been designed to help student teachers learn to teach. These books are designed for student teachers on different types of initial teacher education courses and in different places. And it is hoped that they will be equally useful to tutors and mentors in their work with student teachers. In 2004, the second edition of a complementary book was published, entitled *Starting to Teach in the Secondary School: A Companion for the Newly Qualified Teacher* (Capel, *et al.*). This book is designed to support newly qualified teachers in their first post and covers aspects of teaching which are likely to be of concern in the first year of teaching.

The information in the subject books does not repeat that in *Learning to Teach*; rather, the content of that book is adapted and extended to address the needs of student teachers learning to teach a specific subject. In each of the subject books, therefore, reference is made to *Learning to Teach*, where appropriate. It is recommended that you have both books so that you can cross-refer when needed.

The positive feedback on *Learning to Teach in the Secondary School*, particularly the way it has supported the learning of student teachers in their development into effective, reflective teachers, has encouraged us to retain the main features of that book in the subject series. Thus, the subject books are designed so that elements of appropriate theory introduce each element of the teaching and learning process. The material is interwoven with tasks designed to help you identify key teaching and learning issues and apply these to your own practice. Although the basic content of each subject book is similar, each book is designed to address the unique nature of each subject.

We hope that, whichever initial teacher education course you are following and wherever you may be following that course, you will find this book useful and that it will support your development into an effective, reflective teacher. Above all, we hope you enjoy teaching modern foreign languages.

Susan Capel, Marilyn Leask and Tony Turner
January 2008

Illustrations

FIGURES

TABLES

Abbreviations

A	Advanced
ACCAC	Curriculum and Qualifications Authority for Wales
ALL	Association for Language Learning
AO	assessment objectives
APL	accreditation of prior learning
AQA	Assessment and Qualifications Alliance
ARG	Assessment Reform Group
AS	advanced subsidiary
AT	attainment target
ATL	Association for Teachers and Lecturers
AVCE	Advanced Vocational Certificate of Education
CA	conversation analysis
CALL	computer-assisted language learning applications
CBLC	Certificate of Business Language Competence
CCEA	Council for the Curriculum, Examinations and Assessment
(C)DA	(critical) discourse analysis
CEDP	career entry and development profile
CEF	Common European Framework
CILT	National Centre for Languages
CLIL	content and language integrated learning
C/LMSs	content/learning management systems
CLT	communicative language teaching
CORI	concept-oriented reading instruction
CPD	continuing professional development
CSR	collaborative strategic reading
DCFS	Department for Children, Families and Schools
DELLS	Department for Education, Lifelong Learning and Skills
DENI	Department of Education for Northern Ireland

DES	Department of Education and Science
DfEE	Department for Education and Employment
DfES	Department for Education and Skills
DR-TA	directed reading and thinking activities
DV	digital video
DVR	digital video recorder
EAL	English as an additional language
EBR	employment-based route
EC	European Community
EdD	Education Doctorate
EFL	English as a foreign language
ESL	English as a second language
ESOL	English for speakers of other languages
ETR	experience-text-relate
FL	foreign language
FLA	foreign language assistant
FLL	foreign language learning
FTE	full-time equivalent
GCE	General Certificate of Education
GCSE	General Certificate of Secondary Education
GOML	graded objectives in modern language
GTCE	General Teaching Council for England
HEI	higher educational institution
HMI	Her Majesty's Inspectorate
ICT	information and communications technology
IEP	individual education plan
INSET	in-service education and training
IRF	initiation, response, feedback
ITE	initial teacher education
IWB	interactive whiteboard
KS	Key Stage
KWL	know, what to know, learned
L1	first language/mother tongue
L2	second language/English as a second language
LA	local authority
LMS	learning management system
LTS	Learning and Teaching Scotland
MA	Master of Arts
MEd	Master of Education
MFL	modern foreign languages
NACELL	National Advisory Centre on Early Language Learning
NAGTY	National Academy for Gifted and Talented Youth
NALA	National Association for Language Advisers
NALDIC	National Association for Language Development in the Curriculum
NC	National Curriculum
NCC	National Curriculum Council

NFER	National Foundation for Educational Research
NLS	National Literacy Strategy
NLSfE	National Language Strategy for England
NNS	non-native speakers
NQF	National Qualifications Framework
NQT	newly qualified teacher
NS	native speaker
OCR	Oxford, Cambridge and RSA Examinations
Ofsted	Office for Standards in Education
OHP	overhead projector
OHT	overhead transparency
PA	personal assistant
PGCE	Postgraduate Certificate in Education
PhD	doctor of philosophy
PoS	programme of study
PPP	presentation, practice and production
PSHE	personal, social and health education
PVR	personal video recorder
QAR	question–answer–response
QCA	Qualifications and Curriculum Authority
QTS	qualified teacher status
RSS	really simple syndication
SEN	special educational needs
SENCO	special educational needs co-ordinator
SLA	second language acquisition
SMSC	spiritual, moral, social and cultural
TBL	task-based learning
TDA	Training and Development Agency
TES	*Times Educational Supplement*
(T)EFL	(teaching) English as a foreign language
TL	target language
TSI	transactional strategies instruction
VCE	Vocational Certificate of Education
VLEs	virtual learning environments

Introduction

CAVEAT MAGISTRA!

Teaching modern foreign languages (MFL) with the aim of helping pupils achieve some proficiency in a foreign language and enjoy their MFL learning can be very rewarding. Trying to widen the horizons of pupils as to how people in foreign countries communicate with each other and live is an exciting challenge. An MFL teacher can be the catalyst for developing curiosity in young people about foreign cultures and people, and for broadening their horizons and helping them overcome any negative stereotypes they might hold. Through their MFL learning experience, pupils may also gain a better understanding, and a different perception of themselves.

Among many other things, as an MFL teacher you need to be imaginative, creative, patient, outgoing, enthusiastic and very well organised in order to be successful. Teaching is a highly complex task; teaching MFL, in our opinion, even more so. It requires, for example, the management of pupils, the classroom and resources, interpersonal skills, subject and professional knowledge and the ability to empathise with young people. MFL teachers need to plan well, regularly try out new ideas, cater for the needs of and differences in individual pupils, make learning challenging and enjoyable, assess pupils' learning regularly and effectively, evaluate their actions constantly and adapt to an ever changing educational context.

There are a number of challenges facing MFL teachers, which you need to be aware of when starting your course of initial teacher education (ITE) as these can have a profound impact on your work, for example:

- the status of MFL in society and the media in the UK;
- the perception of MFL being a difficult subject among pupils, parents and more widely;
- the importance for pupils of memorising as well as the ability to recall a large number of linguistic items;

- the importance for pupils of understanding and being able to use new linguistic structures to generate (unique) utterances;
- the comparatively limited opportunities for real-life use of MFL skills in the UK;
- the highly conceptual nature of the subject matter;
- the need for good general communication and social interaction skills;
- the use of the target language (TL) as the main means of classroom instruction and interaction;
- the constraints resulting from pupils' invariably limited linguistic means in the TL compared with their conceptual understanding, world knowledge and cognitive development aged 11+.

Becoming an effective MFL teacher requires a commitment from you to keep up with new developments in the field as well as your willingness to engage in continuing professional development and to challenge sometimes deeply held personal views on what constitutes effective MFL teaching.

ABOUT THIS BOOK

Our perspective on MFL teaching and learning is based on our own experience of teaching pupils, university students and student teachers; on the research and scholarship we are engaged in; on in-service education and training (INSET); on continuing professional development (CPD) provision; on curriculum development work; on dialogue with colleagues nationally and internationally as well as reflections on the ideas expressed in the scholarly work of practitioners and researchers. Consequently, the aim of the book is to help you progress in your professional development by providing stimuli for discussion, reflection and evaluation of a wide range of good practice.[1]

In this book we aim to address the perceived tension between theory and practice. The book is not intended as a prescriptive set of rules on how to teach, nor as a collection of 'tips for teachers', but instead as a framework for MFL teaching based on an understanding of pertinent theoretical issues, possible approaches, strategies and examples to help you learn to teach MFL effectively.

The book is primarily aimed at MFL student teachers on a programme of ITE and it is underpinned by one main premise, namely, the need for an aspiring MFL teacher to develop a personal approach to MFL teaching. While the content of MFL teaching is prescribed in many ways in the form of statutory frameworks and requirements as well as examination specifications, the 'art' of MFL teaching lies in choosing the most effective, and appropriate methods to develop in pupils the relevant knowledge, skills and understanding about the TL and culture(s) and maximise their learning. This is why the ability of MFL student teachers to make personal professional judgements is so important. MFL student teachers learn a lot from observing and working with MFL teachers in schools and/or teacher educators during the course of their ITE. This book aims to support this learning process.

We hope that the book will also be useful to mentors and tutors who work with

MFL student teachers and provide an overview for them on some of the most important issues MFL student teachers have to cover during their ITE.

The text is designed to allow you to 'pick and choose' chapters and refer to specific topics rather than reading the book from cover to cover. Each Chapter features the following sections:

1   Introduction: offers a brief contextualisation of the topic.
2   Objectives: identify what you should know, understand and/or be able to do after having read the chapter and carried out the activities in it.
3   Discussion: the most important theoretical, conceptual and practical issues of a topic are investigated with reference to their application in the classroom, and activities, inviting you to reflect on the content of the chapter and relate it to your work in school, are included. Wherever possible, you should record your work on the reflection activities in a personal 'journal', (e-) portfolio or blog as these reflections can yield very useful evidence against the qualified teacher status (QTS) standards. Wherever practicable, you should try to discuss findings with peers and your colleagues as well as your higher education institutions (HEI) tutors.
4   Summary: emphasises the key points in a chapter.

Individual examples in the book are given in a modern foreign language, French, German or Spanish, as these are the main MFL taught in secondary schools in the UK. Most of the examples, we hope, are transferable to other languages.

While it is intended that the content of the book applies across the range of MFL taught in secondary schools, this book is primarily concerned with general methodological considerations. No systematic discussion of pertinent, language-specific issues can be provided in the space available, for example, how to address the possible difficulties pupils may have with the correlation of the spoken and the written word in French, the inflectional tendencies of the German language and its comparatively flexible word order or differences in scripts/alphabets/writing systems. These issues may occasionally be touched upon in the practical examples given. For language-specific issues, other resources and publications should be consulted.

A book accompanying the current title called *A Practical Guide to Teaching Foreign Languages in the Secondary School*, also published by Routledge (Pachler and Redondo 2007) offers a number of practical examples and we refer to it throughout this book.

Because of the many differences particularly in teaching methods, the issues involved in post-16 MFL teaching are dealt with separately in the Epilogue. Our primary concern in this book is with teaching MFL at 11–16. In the Epilogue we examine some of the most important issues concerning MFL teaching at post-16, but do not attempt to cover this complex area in detail. This is done in a separate, complementary book edited by one of the authors of the current title, Norbert Pachler, entitled *Teaching Modern Foreign Languages at Advanced Level*, and published by Routledge in 1999. Also, a number of the issues raised in this book are examined in greater detail in another complementary book edited by another author of the current title, Kit Field, entitled *Issues in Modern Foreign Language Teaching* and published by Routledge in 2000.

We have restructured some of the content of the book in line with suggestions received from student teachers, colleagues and reviewers. All the chapters have been updated and amended, and chapters focusing on information and communications technology (ICT) and assessment have been substantially rewritten in the light of recent developments and research. With the increased emphasis on teachers as researchers, and the alignment of many Postgraduate Certificate in Education (PGCE) courses, at least in part, with Masters level descriptors of the National Qualifications Framework (NQF), we decided to include a separate chapter on findings from Second Language Acquisition (SLA) and Foreign Language Learning (FLL) research and their relevance to practice. As part of the process of updating all chapters, we have included references to new insights gained from research, personal professional experience and background reading.

All websites cited in the book were available as of 31 August 2007.

THIRD EDITION: CHANGES TO THE STATUTORY REQUIREMENTS

In this third edition of *Learning to Teach Modern Foreign Languages in the Secondary School*, we take account of important recent changes to the statutory requirements governing the teaching and learning of MFL in the secondary school since the book was first published in 1997 and subsequently revised in its second edition in 2001. These include the KS3 MFL Framework, the publication in 2007 of a new MFL National Curriculum for England to be statutory from 2008, changes to examination requirements at GCSE and GCE A level, the introduction of the National (KS3) Strategy, the findings of the Dearing Report (2007), new Standards for Qualified Teacher Status (from September 2007) and the accompanying Standards for practising teachers.

For ease of reference and space we refer to the statutory framework for England only throughout the book. This should have a negligible impact for readers training and/or working in other parts of the UK and elsewhere as they can easily substitute references to the statutory requirements for England with those applying to their own contexts. References to the statutory requirements for England tend to be used for contextualisation and exemplification purposes of generic principles and frameworks.

NOTE

1   In order not to make the style of the book too unwieldy and to avoid formulations such as 's/he' or 'his/her', we use the feminine form generically when referring to nouns like 'the pupil', 'the teacher' or 'the mentor'. Only the term 'MFL department' is used in this book when referring to teams of MFL teachers although schools may also be organised on a faculty basis, etc.

1 Modern foreign languages in the secondary school curriculum

INTRODUCTION

In recent decades both the teaching and learning of modern foreign languages (MFL) in secondary schools in the UK have witnessed a number of important developments. second language acquisition (SLA) and foreign language learning (FLL) research have offered new insights into the processes governing FLL and have suggested various implications for approaches to teaching (see Chapter 14). Teaching methods have come and gone out of fashion and there have been considerable innovations in the field of educational technologies. In addition, many changes have occurred in the wider educational context, including legislative requirements and entitlements.

In recent years, in part because of the possibilities afforded by the internet to do so timely and relatively cheaply, UK governments have been very active in providing guidelines and frameworks for MFL teachers to support them, particularly in England, but also, increasingly, to prescribe what and how to teach. In 2002, the government published a National Language Strategy for England (NLSfE) (DfES 2002a) which contained far-reaching decisions about the future of MFL teaching and learning by making its study in KS2 (for pupils aged 7–11) an entitlement as well as by discontinuing the requirement for pupils to study a foreign language at KS4 (for pupils aged 14–16). All of these impact on pupils' learning experiences.

In this chapter, we consider the rationale behind teaching and learning MFL in the secondary school and give an overview of the statutory framework and other policy documents governing MFL teaching and learning. The focus is on England as it is 'blessed' with a wide range of initiatives and attendant guidance and exemplification documents.[1]

With the introduction of MFL into the primary curriculum, the discussion of when, why and how to teach foreign languages is becoming more nuanced and differentiated. Pedagogical approaches need to be, and are being, developed that are appropriate for younger learners. This book, while making references to policy developments in the primary field, will primarily focus on the secondary age range.

OBJECTIVES

By the end of this chapter you should:

- be aware of the rationale and purposes of MFL teaching and learning in the secondary school curriculum;
- have an understanding of the developments in the curriculum Key Stages 2–4 and post-16, in particular, the NC MFL Orders, the GCSE criteria and the KS3 Framework for MFL;
- be aware of developments in the field from the Nuffield Languages Inquiry (2000) until the findings of the Dearing Report (2007).

MFL IN THE SECONDARY SCHOOL CURRICULUM – RATIONALE AND PURPOSES

The rationale and aims for the study of MFL in the secondary school curriculum are very similar throughout the UK and elsewhere.

One important reason for the study of MFL as part of the secondary school curriculum is the recognition that it has an important role to play in terms of contributing to the personal, social, cultural and general linguistic development of pupils in preparation for their adult lives, both for work and leisure. This was explicitly reflected in the 1999 version of the NC MFL Orders:

> For example, MFL provides opportunities to promote:
>
> - *spiritual development*, through stimulating pupils' interest and fascination in the phenomenon of language and the meanings and feelings it can transmit
> - *moral development*, through helping pupils formulate and express opinions in the target language about issues of right and wrong
> - *social development*, through exploring different social conventions, such as forms of address, through developing pupils' ability to communicate with others, particularly speakers of foreign languages, in an appropriate, sympathetic and tolerant manner, and through fostering the spirit of cooperation when using a foreign language to communicate with other people, whether other learners or native speakers

- *cultural development*, through providing pupils with insights into cultural differences and opportunities to relate these to their own experience and to consider different cultural and linguistic traditions, attitudes and behaviours.

(DfEE/QCA 1999: 8)

The wording of the rationale for the study of MFL in the school curriculum may have changed since then, yet the general principles have remained fairly stable.

Still very important in our view is the provision of what Eric Hawkins calls an 'apprenticeship in foreign language learning' (Hawkins 1987: 282), the development of a foundation in pupils for future MFL learning by arousing in them a curiosity for and an interest in learning (about) foreign languages and cultures. As such, the study of MFL 'exposes learners to new experiences and enables them to make connections in a way which would not otherwise be possible, and this in itself deepens their understanding of their mother tongue' (DES/Welsh Office 1990: 3).

In addition, MFL learning, like other subjects of the secondary curriculum, can be seen to be very valuable in teaching young people important transferable skills such as working with reference material, e.g. dictionaries, and other skills such as (inter)-personal skills, study skills or problem solving, equipping them for their working lives and providing them with the skills base required by employers. Indeed, the 1999 version of the NC MFL Orders listed a number of opportunities for promoting so-called key skills through MFL:

For example, MFL provides opportunities for pupils to develop the key skills of:

- *communication*, through developing their awareness of the way language is structured and how it can be manipulated to meet a range of needs, and through reinforcing learning in specific areas such as listening, reading for gist and detail, and using grammar correctly
- *application of number*, through talking and writing about the time and measures in the target language, and carrying out conversions about distances and currency
- *IT*, through using audio, video, satellite television and the internet to access and communicate information, and through selecting and using a range of ICT resources to create presentations for different audiences and purposes
- *working with others*, through developing their ability to participate in group conversations and discussions
- *improving own learning and performance*, through developing their ability to rehearse and redraft work to improve accuracy and presentation, and through developing learning strategies such as memorising, dealing with the unpredictable, and using reference materials

- *problem solving*, through developing their ability to apply and adapt their knowledge of the target language for specific communication purposes.

(DfEE/QCA 1999: 8)

MFL learning can be seen to be instrumental in preparing pupils for life in present-day multicultural and multilingual Britain and Europe and, indeed, in the world in an age of increased globalisation. MFL have a valuable contribution to make to the wider school curriculum in terms of cross-curricular themes but also as a focus for extra-curricular activities. The former is exemplified in the 1999 version of the NC MFL Orders, the latter is examined in detail in Chapter 8:

For example, MFL provides opportunities to promote:

- *thinking skills*, through developing pupils' ability to draw inferences from unfamiliar language and unexpected responses, through enabling pupils to reflect on the links between languages, and through developing pupils' creative use of language and expression of their own ideas, attitudes and opinions
- *financial capability*, through knowledge of different currencies and exchange rates
- *work-related learning*, through opportunities to cover work-related contexts within the topic of the world of work.

(ibid.: 9)

Without wishing to overemphasise a vocational rationale for FLL here, it can be noted that from a national economic point of view and in the current context of competitive international economic activity, the UK, as a trading nation, urgently needs a workforce with competence in MFL (see e.g. DES/Welsh Office 1990: 4). When wanting to sell goods to customers abroad, the fact that English is the international lingua franca is not sufficient. The business world is in the process of globalisation both in terms of businesses increasingly operating in an international context and in terms of multinational companies establishing themselves firmly in the UK. Pupils might well find themselves one day in a work situation requiring them to operate in a modern foreign language in the UK. It could, indeed, be argued that it is this national economic concern that has become more important than any other in justifying the place of MFL in the secondary school curriculum. The global market is forever evolving, however, and perhaps pinpointing which *language* will be economically valuable for pupils and the country's economy is rather difficult. It could be argued that the learner developing confidence in foreign language learning and competence in language learning strategies, enables the learner in the future to use these attributes when learning a language needed for specific purposes. After all, learning Mandarin or German now does not necessarily mean that it will be that language which is required for that particular pupil in later life. Equally, the fact that revenue from tourism makes a major contribution to the country's gross national product, should be an important incentive to study MFL.

A 1987 Her Majesty's Inspectorate (HMI) discussion paper proved to be very influential in laying the foundations for the current rationale for MFL teaching and learning for England. It influenced the so-called Harris Report (DES/Welsh Office 1990), which even now still provides a useful point of reference and delineates the following purposes for MFL teaching in the secondary school:

- to develop the ability to use the language effectively for purposes of practical communication;
- to form a sound base of the skills, language and attitudes required for further study, work and leisure;
- to offer insights into the culture and civilisation of the countries where the target language is spoken;
- to develop an awareness of the nature of language and language learning;
- to provide enjoyment and intellectual stimulation;
- to encourage positive attitudes to foreign language learning and to speakers of foreign languages and a sympathetic approach to other cultures and civilisations;
- to promote learning of skills of more general application (e.g. analysis, memorising, drawing of inferences);
- to develop pupils' understanding of themselves and their own culture.

(DES/Welsh Office 1990: 3)

These purposes for MFL teaching and learning in the secondary school build largely on the *tenets of communicative language teaching* (CLT), which has been the prevailing approach to MFL teaching since the 1970s. Its most important characteristics are briefly summarised by Johnstone (1988: 12):

- an increase in the amount of foreign language used for everyday classroom and personal purposes;
- the introduction of functions (asking for, offering, refusing, etc.) and general notions (food, hobbies, time, travel, etc.) as constituents of a language syllabus, in addition to grammar, vocabulary and situations;
- a gradual move beyond course-books as sole or even principal determiners of the language syllabus and towards the use of authentic texts and other personalized inputs selected by teachers and pupils themselves;
- an extension of group, paired and individual activity, to complement whole-class work;
- the gradual introduction of information-exchange based on role-play and simulation, and to a lesser extent of practical skills activities . . . and of communication games;
- the introduction of assessment, in many cases related to graded objectives, for purposes of 'diagnosis' and of 'formative evaluation'.

A detailed discussion of CLT and its implications for MFL teaching methods can be found in Chapter 3 (see also Pachler 2000a; Barnes 2007; Kramsch 2006).

The emergence of CLT to some extent went hand in hand with the inclusion of MFL, predominantly French, in the curriculum of many comprehensive schools, which were established in the wake of the reform of secondary schooling from the mid-1960s onwards. The move away from grammar translation towards communication skills is a reflection of the wider range of ability and motivation of pupils studying MFL: 'None of the foreign language teachers down the ages . . . ever had to face the challenge that we face: they never met, in their classes, more than a select minority of quite able learners' (Hawkins 1994: 109).

As a consequence of the widening in the ability and motivational range of learners in the 1980s, a large number of MFL teachers began to focus in their work on graded objectives, i.e. short-term, achievable learning targets that were assessed at regular intervals with a view to enhancing learners' motivation and their sense of achievement. These objectives mainly centred on language skills required for communicating in seemingly authentic situations.

Prior to the introduction of the GCSE in the mid-1980s, a sizeable number of pupils studying MFL from the age of 11 tended to opt out at 14, leaving in the main the more able and better motivated pupils to continue their study of MFL to 16. The number of pupils entering for GCSE examinations and achieving grades A$\star$ – C rose steadily from the introduction of the GCSE. Implicit in this growth is a widening of the ability range of pupils studying MFL. In response to pupils 'voting with their feet', the 1999 NC Orders made it possible for those pupils to be 'disapplied' from MFL:

- who make significantly less progress than their peers: they are able to study fewer NC subjects in order to consolidate their learning across the curriculum;
- who have particular strengths and talents: they are allowed to emphasise a particular curriculum area by exchanging a statutory subject for a further course in that curriculum area;
- for whom wider work-related learning is deemed desirable than is possible alongside the full statutory requirements: they are able to carry out extended periods of work experience, etc.

This invariably devalued the status of MFL and the government finally decided that from 2004 a foreign language was no longer to be compulsory at KS4. Instead of 'languages for all', MFL became an *entitlement* at KS4, i.e. learners had to have an MFL as an option, but were not compelled to choose one. This has led in recent years to a rapid, and worrying decline in the number of pupils continuing with a foreign language after KS3 (see http://www.cilt.org.uk/research/languagetrends/2006/ks4.htm but also Macaro 2008) and resulted in the Dearing Report (see below). It also led to a requirement being introduced for schools to set a target for take-up of MFL at KS4 between 50 and 90 per cent and appears indirectly to have led to the inclusion of MFL results at 16 in school performance tables from 2009.

The decision – in response to a resolution passed in 1988 by the European Community – to include a *European dimension* in the school curriculum provided a set of *guiding principles* deserving of the attention of MFL teachers (see also Capel and

Pachler 1997: 263–7). MFL can be seen to play an important role in realising the objectives identified in this resolution:

- to strengthen in young people a sense of European identity by emphasising the value of European civilisation and the foundations on which the European peoples intend to base their development today, that is in particular the safeguarding of the principles of democracy, social justice and respect for human rights;
- to prepare young people to take part in the economic and social development of the Community and in making concrete progress towards European Union, as stipulated in the Single European Act;
- to make them aware of the advantages which the Community presents but also of the challenges it involves in opening up an enlarged economic and social area;
- to improve their knowledge of the Community and its Member States in their historical, cultural, economic and social aspects and to emphasise the importance of cooperation between EC Member States and with the rest of the world e.g. initial and in-service teacher training/exchanges.

(Central Bureau 1993: 4)

In 2005, the DfES published a document on how to develop the *global dimension* in the school curriculum which provides some useful guidance across subjects and key stages. It sets out the following eight concepts through which a global dimension can be understood:

- *global citizenship*: gaining the knowledge, skills and understanding of concepts and institutions necessary to become informed, active, responsible citizens;
- *conflict resolution*: understanding the nature of conflicts, their impact on development and why there is a need for their resolution and the promotion of harmony;
- *social justice*: understanding the importance of social justice as an element in both sustainable development and the improved welfare of all people;
- *values and perceptions*: developing a critical evaluation of representations of global issues and an appreciation of the effect these have on people's attitudes and values;
- *sustainable development*: understanding the need to maintain and improve the quality of life now without damaging the planet for future generations;
- *interdependence*: understanding how people, places, economies and environments are all inextricably interrelated, and that choices and events have repercussions on a global scale;
- *human rights*: knowing about human rights including the UN Convention on the Rights of the Child;
- *diversity*: understanding and respecting differences and relating these to our common humanity.

(DfES 2005: 12–13)

Task 1.1 Aims of learning MFL for your learners

What are your own personal aims in teaching MFL to your pupils? Some possible ideas could include:

- communicating in the specific foreign language;
- 'learning how to learn' MFL more generally;
- opening cultural 'doors';
- becoming an independent language learner.

You will probably have more, and your ideal may well be a combination of these.

How, at this stage of your initial teacher education, do you envisage enabling these aims to become reality when teaching your learners? If possible, discuss your ideas with teachers in your placement school, or your tutor or fellow student teachers.

Table 1.1 outlines the situation regarding MFL in the secondary curriculum in maintained schools in England at the time of writing. Primary (Key Stages 1 and 2) are not featured in the table as MFL are currently not compulsory before Key Stage 3 but by 2010 MFL will be at least an *entitlement* at Key Stage 2, and the Dearing Report

Table 1.1 The state of MFL in the secondary curriculum in maintained schools in England

Year 7 *Levels 1–3	Year 8 *Levels 4–5	Year 9 *Levels 5–7	Year 10	Year 11	Year 12	Year 13
Key Stage 3 (KS3)			Key Stage 4 (KS4)		post-16	
Compulsory for all pupils			From 2004, MFL have been an *entitlement* (NB: not an 'option')		Not compulsory	
• National Curriculum (NC) • Programme of Study (PoS) (*content*) • Attainment Targets 1–4 • Levels 1–8 (*assessment*) • Teacher assessment at end of Key Stage • Optional: assessment through ASSET languages[a] • Non-statutory: KS3 MFL Framework (DfES 2002a)			• GCSE (full or short course), or Certificate of Achievement, or Language Units (*assessment*) • Other approved qualification • Optional: assessment through ASSET languages • Specialised diplomas (the exact role that MFL will play as an option in these is yet to be determined, but see http://www.cilt.org.uk/14–19/diplomas.htm for the latest information)		AS level	A level
					IB (International Baccalaureate) Optional: assessment through ASSET languages Other, more vocational, qualifications, or MFL as part of a wider qualification	

Note: [a] ASSET Languages (http://www.assetlanguages.org.uk) is the assessment scheme for the Languages Ladder and is being developed by Cambridge Assessment through OCR and Cambridge ESOL, as part of the National Languages Strategy.

(2007) recommends it will be *compulsory*. Look at the Qualifications and Curriculum Authority (QCA) (http://www.qca.org.uk) and the National Advisory Centre on Early Language Learning (NACELL) websites (http://www.nacell.org.uk/) for more information and see Hunt (2007). The QCA oversees all the qualifications offered by Awarding Bodies and issues obligatory specifications and criteria to which Awarding Bodies must adhere with the qualifications they offer. The QCA ensures that any qualifications offered do indeed meet the requirements. There is some choice for schools, therefore, for example between two qualifications in French, which may vary in the details of assessment, but which will still meet QCA criteria.

With the 2007 NC (http://www.qca.org.uk/libraryAssets/media/MFL_KS3_PoS.pdf), there is no longer a requirement for schools to offer at least one EU language. They can now select a language based on their (local) needs such as Mandarin, Japanese or Arabic, etc.

THE NUFFIELD LANGUAGES INQUIRY (2000)

The Nuffield Languages Inquiry (2000; http://www.nuffield.org/language/), was set up to investigate what foreign language capability the UK needed, to what extent present policies and arrangements met these needs and what strategic planning and initiatives would be required in the light of the findings (see Grenfell 2000, for some thoughts on this). The final report of the inquiry, which drew on evidence received from a wide range of individuals, organisations and specialist consultants, noted that '[capability] in other languages – a much broader range than hitherto and in greater depth – was crucially important for a flourishing UK' (Nuffield Languages Inquiry 2000: 5). Sir Trevor McDonald and Sir John Boyd, the joint chairmen, pointed out that:

> The UK has no automatic monopoly on political or economic success. In a world of alliances and partnerships we need to understand where others are coming from. In a competitive world we cannot afford to be without strong and complete skills: no skills – no jobs. The need to strengthen our children's literacy, numeracy and technology skills is clear and we support it. Side by side with these should go the ability to communicate across cultures. It too is a key skill.
>
> (ibid.:4)

The main findings and proposals of the inquiry included the suggestions that languages be designated as a key skill, that there should be a national languages strategy and that a languages 'supremo', who works with government at raising the profile of languages, be appointed. Other suggestions concerned early language learning, about which non-statutory guidance was included in the 1999 NC MFL Orders, a foreign language requirement for university entry and certain designated vocational qualifications and the establishment of a national standards framework for describing and accrediting language competence.

In Section 4.2 of the final report (see ibid.: 44–9), challenges and obstacles in relation to languages in secondary schools were identified and respective recommendations made.

Challenges and obstacles

- The range of languages is unbalanced.
- Qualifications are inflexible.
- Continuity is at risk.
- There are defects in curriculum organisation.
- Courses provide a poor foundation for future learning.
- Public examination results are below average.
- Boys achieve far less than girls.
- New technologies are not used effectively.
- Good opportunities are being wasted.
- A more positive climate is needed.
- A more co-ordinated approach to teachers' professional development is needed.

Recommendations

- Create a new balance and diversity of languages.
- Keep language learning for all up to 16.
- Recognise progress through graded awards.
- Introduce modular accreditation.
- Review curriculum content and examination syllabuses.
- All schools should maintain active international links.
- Review and reinvigorate the Foreign Language Assistant Scheme.
- Offer incentives for schools which create bilingual sections.
- Boost the use of technology.
- Government and business should promote languages as a key life skill.

The report came to the conclusion that the UK was doing badly:

> We talk about communication but don't always communicate. There is enthusiasm for languages but it is patchy. Educational provision is fragmented, achievement poorly measured, continuity not very evident. In the language of our time, there is a lack of joined-up thinking.
>
> (ibid.: 5)

THE NATIONAL LANGUAGES STRATEGY FOR ENGLAND (NLSfE) (DfES 2002a)

The Nuffield Report resulted in the National Languages Strategy. It is crucial as a student teacher that you keep yourself abreast of rapid changes taking place in the field of MFL as a consequence of ongoing changes in national policy and strategy. The NLSfE, *Languages for All: Languages for Life* published by the DfES in 2002 had three main aims, and is an example of one such important document:

- to ensure MFL in KS2 as an entitlement from 2010;
- to establish a national recognition system in languages;
- to improve language teaching and learning.

Fundamental to these aims are a number of ongoing and future developments, including:

- KS3 MFL Foundation Subjects framework (piloted 2002–03, rolled out 2003–04);
- KS2 MFL framework (draft piloted 2004, published 2004–05);
- National Recognition System (piloted 2004, published 2004–05, now administered by ASSET languages).

Since the Nuffield Report was published, the situation for languages has moved on considerably, but arguably not necessarily in a positive direction. Some of the recommendations arising from the report and the languages strategy have resulted in positive action. For example, there now exists a graded assessment 'ladder', albeit still in development at the higher levels, managed at present through ASSET languages (see e.g. Jones 2007). Primary foreign languages is definitely on the agenda, with a prospective date of 2010 for all KS2 pupils to be learning a foreign language, and various support material has been published and made available, such as the KS2 schemes of work and KS2 framework. In other areas, progress has been less evident. The decision that languages at KS4 should no longer be compulsory from September 2004 has resulted, as noted above, in a worrying decline in learners choosing a foreign language after KS3. Our reasons for making reference to these problems in this book are simple: clearly, we don't do so in order to put you off from choosing MFL teaching as a career. Indeed, well-qualified candidates for initial teacher education are increasingly in short supply. Nevertheless, we believe new entrants into the profession need to be aware of the challenges facing them. Only then, we feel, will they be able to make their commitment count fully. However, viewed from another perspective, the current systemic weaknesses in MFL teaching and learning provide ample scope for ambitious graduates to make a significant difference at various levels and enjoy a rewarding professional life.

THE DEARING REPORT (2006/07)

Partly at least in response to the perceived and actual decline in MFL take-up at KS4 and the attendant concerns on the part of politicians, educationalists and the business community, the Education Secretary commissioned a review of the national languages policy in 2006. Lord Dearing's remit was to examine what could be done to encourage 14–16-year-olds to study GCSE or other language courses leading to a recognised qualification. Lord Dearing's interim Consultation Report (Dearing and King 2006) and a summary were published on 14 December 2006 and the Languages Review final report was published on 12 March 2007 (Dearing and King 2007).

Among the recommendations, backed by government, were:

- MFL to be compulsory at KS2 from 2010.
- A three-year blueprint of fresh measures to secure a renaissance of languages in secondary schools, including establishing an Open School for Languages, introducing more engaging courses and assessment and expanding training opportunities for secondary teachers.
- Making secondary school courses more engaging and accessible and developing alternatives to GCSE for a range of learners and creating more opportunities for overseas visits and work experience.
- Using the Languages Ladder more widely to record and reward progress in the four skills of learning (listening, speaking, reading and writing) and counting points gained through assessment in performance tables.
- Launching a National Teachers Research Scholarship scheme for languages, enabling teachers to work together with other experts to develop their pedagogy.
- Improving teaching through a range of support – including training secondary school teachers to work in support of their primary colleagues – and helping good teachers share their skills with others.
- Greater support for those who want to study community languages and offering a broader range of languages, such as Mandarin and Urdu.
- No return to compulsion at GCSE but strengthening instead the message to schools that they should have a benchmark of 50–90 per cent of Key Stage 4 pupils studying a language.
- Language indicators in the school achievement and performance tables to measure take-up and attainment at 16.
- More personalised learning, with informed classroom assessment of every child's language learning near the end of KS2 to inform teachers at KS3, enabling a smooth transition between primary and secondary school teaching.
- A review of the present GCSE to maintain the level of challenge but to better engage teenagers.
- Active use of 'Immersion Courses' to help pupils manage transition from primary to secondary and to help catch-up at KS3 and more focused learning in KS4.

- Steps to increase the number of Specialist Language Colleges from 300 to 400.

At the time of writing it is too early to gauge the impact of the Dearing Report, but it is to be hoped that its recommendations will breathe new life into MFL in England. For a discussion of the Dearing Report, see Pachler (2007a). Some of the points listed above have already been addressed to some extent at the time of writing: GCSE is being reviewed, a new KS3 curriculum has been proposed and preparations for KS2 MFL appear to be well underway in many schools.

Task 1.2 Producing a display for a Year 9 Options Evening

Imagine your placement school is in the process of organising an Options Evening for Year 9 pupils and their parents. The head of MFL wishes to produce a display for pupils and parents pointing out the benefits that can be gained from the continued study of MFL. Which arguments would you include in the display that could appeal to pupils and parents?

THE MFL NATIONAL CURRICULUM ORDERS FOR ENGLAND

In the remainder of this chapter we move from policy and initiatives to discuss the statutory framework and guidance governing MFL teaching in England. We are only able to provide a brief overview here and you are encouraged to consult the current Orders as well as accompanying guidance material, available online at http://www.nc.uk.net/, for more details. In 2007, the QCA issued a new national curriculum (http://www.qca.org.uk/libraryAssets/media/MFL_KS3_PoS.pdf) which updates the 1999 MFL Orders and is to be implemented for Year 7 in 2008. Further information is available from http://www.qca.org.uk/curriculum.

Even if you do not intend to teach in England, you will find the conceptualisation of the MFL curriculum offered by the QCA, be it in the 1999 Orders or the 2007 version, instructive in thinking about what the curriculum should look like. If you teach in England, you will find that you will need to be thoroughly familiar with the Orders as they are an integral part of the knowledge base expected of a newly qualified teacher and they are the basis for all the work in MFL departments for pupils in KS3. Help with schemes of work is available at http://www.ncaction.org.uk/subjects/MFL/.

The National Curriculum is minimum and statutory, i.e. schools in England must adhere to the National Curriculum in Key Stage 3, but this should not be constraining.

In the main, pupils study one foreign language and can often – typically from Year 8 or 10 onwards – opt for one additional language, or exceptionally more, provided their school has a diversified MFL curriculum. In theory, the statutory requirements apply only to pupils' first, that is their NC language, but in practice schools tend to offer all MFL in the curriculum on this basis.

The statutory orders give clear indications of what pupils should be taught in the programme of study. The 1999 Orders placed greater emphasis on pupils' knowledge of language and skills than previously, and grammar was mentioned explicitly. The Orders also include level descriptions for the attainment targets (ATs) to ensure consistent judgements about pupil performance.

When the NC Orders were first developed in the late 1980s, the Graded Object-ives in Modern Language (GOML) National Co-ordinating Committee submitted a paper to the MFL working group advising the government on the design of the NC MFL Orders, which featured the following objectives for MFL pupils:

> [S]econdary school foreign language learners . . . should be able to operate at their own level of intellect and maturity as:
>
> 1   a person abroad
> 2   a host to, or interpreter for, a foreign national in the U.K. in everyday situations in work and leisure
> 3   a consumer of publications and broadcasts from abroad
> 4   an active participant in collaborative work in a multilingual environment.
>
> (Page 1989: 75)

The fact that these objectives, by and large, found inclusion gives some indication how deeply current thinking is rooted in communicative language teaching (CLT) (see also Chapter 3).

The 1999 NC MFL Orders consisted of a programme of study (PoS) as well as four attainment targets (ATs). Teaching should be based on the programme of study, not on the level descriptions. Progress was upwards through the levels and horizontally through the different contexts. A judgement on pupils' achievement was made by the teacher at the end of KS3.

The 1999 programme of study included detailed items under the following headings:

1   Acquiring knowledge and understanding of the target language.
2   Developing language skills.
3   Developing language-learning skills.
4   Developing cultural awareness.
5   Breadth of study.

In addition to the PoS, the NC features four ATs, namely:

- listening and responding;
- speaking;
- reading and responding;
- writing.

The ATs, which each consisted of eight levels of increasing difficulty plus a description for exceptional achievement, set out the 'knowledge, skills and understanding' that pupils are expected to have by the end of Key Stage 3:

> Each level description describes the types and range of performance that pupils working at that level should characteristically demonstrate. The level descriptions provide the basis for making judgements about pupils' performance at the end of key stage 3. At key stage 4, national qualifications are the main means of assessing attainment in modern foreign languages.
>
> (DfEE/QCA 1999: 38)

THE PROGRAMME OF STUDY AT KS3 (QCA 2007b)

In 2007, the QCA published a new curriculum (http://www.qca.org.uk/library Assets/media/MFL_KS3_PoS.pdf). The factors motivating the overhaul of the NC Orders include an attempt to make the curriculum more intrinsically interesting for pupils, for example, through different approaches to teaching and learning, less prescriptive and more flexible, for example, through personalisation, as well as more in tune with the world of work. The new programme of study is also underpinned by the *Every Child Matters* agenda (see http://www.everychildmatters.gov.uk), the policy adopted by the government aimed at ensuring all children receive the education and care they deserve (see also Chapter 2).

The programme of study of the new Orders stresses the importance of enjoyment as a prerequisite for progress and achievement as well as the contribution of language learning to mutual understanding, personal fulfilment and global citizenship.

The key concepts of the new PoS are:

- linguistic competence;
- knowledge about language;
- creativity;
- intercultural understanding.

In addition, the following key processes are identified:

- developing language-learning strategies;
- developing language skills.

In more detail, the PoS offers the following specifics:

1   *Linguistic competence:*

   (a)   Developing the skills of listening, speaking, reading and writing in a range of situations and contexts.
   (b)   Applying linguistic knowledge and skills to understand and communicate effectively.

2   *Knowledge about language:*

(a)   Understanding how a language works and how to manipulate it.
(b)   Recognising that languages differ but may share common grammatical, syntactical or lexical features.

3   *Creativity:*

(a)   Using familiar language for new purposes and in new contexts.
(b)   Using imagination to express thoughts, ideas, experiences and feelings.

4   *Intercultural understanding:*

(a)   Appreciating the richness and diversity of other cultures.
(b)   Recognising that there are different ways of seeing the world, and developing an international outlook.

5   *Developing language-learning strategies:*

Pupils should be able to:

(a)   identify patterns in the target language.
(b)   develop techniques for memorising words, phrases and spellings.
(c)   use their knowledge of English or another language when learning the target language.
(d)   use previous knowledge, context and other clues to work out the meaning of what they hear or read.
(e)   use reference materials such as dictionaries appropriately and effectively.

6   *Developing language skills:*

Pupils should be able to:

(a)   listen for gist or detail;
(b)   skim and scan written texts for the main points or details;
(c)   respond appropriately to spoken and written language;
(d)   use correct pronunciation and intonation;
(e)   ask and answer questions;
(f)   initiate and sustain conversations;
(g)   write clearly and coherently, including an appropriate level of detail;
(h)   redraft their writing to improve accuracy and quality;
(i)   reuse language that they have heard or read in their own speaking and writing;
(j)   adapt language they already know in new contexts for different purposes;
(k)   deal with unfamiliar language, unexpected responses and unpredictable situations.

The programme of study also contains detail on the range and content of study and curriculum opportunities.

1   *Range and content:*

The study of languages should include:

(a)   the spoken and written forms of the target language;
(b)   the interrelationship between sounds and writing in the target language;
(c)   the grammar of the target language and how to apply it;
(d)   a range of vocabulary and structures;
(e)   learning about different countries and cultures;
(f)   comparing pupils' own experiences and perspectives with those of people in countries and communities where the target language is spoken.

2   *Curriculum opportunities:*

The curriculum should provide opportunities for pupils to:

(a)   hear, speak, read and write in the target language regularly and frequently within the classroom and beyond;
(b)   communicate in the target language individually, in pairs, in groups and with speakers of the target language, including native speakers where possible, for a variety of purposes;
(c)   use an increasing range of more complex language;
(d)   make links with English at word, sentence and text level;
(e)   use a range of resources, including ICT, for accessing and communi-cating information in the target language;
(f)   listen to, read or view a range of materials, including authentic materials in the target language, both to support learning and for personal interest and enjoyment;
(g)   use the target language in connection with topics and issues that are engaging and may be related to other areas of the curriculum.

MFL teachers are expected to develop the above by offering specific opportunities, such as use of ICT and authentic material, and by drawing on a range of contexts, such as those afforded by learning about different countries and cultures.

A significant change from earlier versions of the NC Orders lies in the expansion of the list of languages available for study to include Mandarin, Urdu or Arabic depending on local needs and circumstances. It is also important to note that the NC Orders are characterised by a set of underpinning values (self, relationships, society, environment), a personal, learning and thinking skills framework, as well as four curriculum dimensions, which are meant to provide a context and focus for work within and between subjects, namely:

•   a global dimension;

- enterprise;
- creativity;
- cultural understanding and diversity.

Thus, many of the issues introduced in this chapter are included in the new proposals, although the tangible results of the new PoS are, of course, yet to be determined.

TEACHING MFL AT KEY STAGE 3 (YEARS 7–9)

You must learn and assess all four ATs. Pupil achievement in each AT must be recorded and detailed records kept by you. Level descriptions denote the level of performance in each attainment target. Certain level descriptions were written in order to enable most pupils to achieve level 5/6 at the end of KS3 in line with other subjects. At the end of KS3, you must report to parents on pupil achievement (in prose), according to the levels (schools decide whether to report on each AT or overall). This element of KS3 assessment has been compulsory since July 1997. There are no SATs involved: performance at the end of KS3 is teacher assessed.

By way of a brief summary, the NC can be said to promote the development of an ability in pupils to use the target language (TL) in a variety of real-life contexts on the basis of some knowledge and an understanding of linguistic and cultural aspects using authentic materials and Information and Communications Technology (ICT). However, given the very limited amount of time – rarely more than 70 minutes a week – and the often adverse conditions of MFL learning, expectations of what can be achieved need to be realistic:

> Learners at beginners level should be able to take part in simple transactions and conversations, often featuring simple and familiar language and contexts; their pronunciation will be intelligible, their knowledge of language forms limited and largely implicit; while able to communicate meaning, their ability to produce grammatically correct language will vary.
>
> (Pachler 2000b: 513)

The list of statements contained in the PoS can be seen as an assortment of good practice and is widely endorsed by MFL professionals. The loose structure does, however, mean the NC is very much a framework for teaching rather than learning, requiring from MFL teachers considerable skill and professional judgement in ensuring grading, sequencing and progression (see Mitchell 2003, for an interesting insight into progression in the National Curriculum). Also, in comparison with curriculum frameworks in many other countries, there is very little guidance on content, although there are explanatory notes and examples. To compensate, the NC is supplemented at Key Stage 3 by non-statutory schemes of work and optional tests and tasks, available at http://www.ncaction.org.uk/subjects/MFL/, which – if followed by departments as they stand – could be highly prescriptive.

During Key Stage 3, the majority of pupils are expected to work within levels 3–7 and at age 14, i.e. at the end of Key Stage 3, the majority of pupils are expected to attain at levels 5/6.

Task 1.3 Carrying out lesson observations relating to the NC Orders for England

Observe a number of MFL lessons of a class of your choice focusing on the coverage of the PoS. Choose a number of the PoS statements and observe through which activities they are covered. Table 1.2 gives some examples based on the 1999 MFL Orders.

Table 1.2 Carrying out NC-related lesson observations

No.	PoS statement	Activity
4b	communicate in the target language individually, in pairs, in groups and with speakers of the target language, including native speakers where possible, for a variety of purposes	• practice of new vocabulary through identification of cards in a game of 'pairs' • structured role play for buying food with instructions provided on cards in diagrammatic form • survey to identify most popular food • open-ended drama – pupil 'A' tried to sell as much food as possible to pupil 'B', who had a limited money supply • sending an e-mail to a pupil in the TL country comparing results on a class survey
4g	use the target language in connection with topics and issues that are engaging and may be related to other areas of the curriculum	• communicating real information about their own lives • speculating on a current news item • learning (e.g.) geographical content via the TL

TEACHING MFL AT KEY STAGE 4

MFL are no longer a *statutory requirement* subject at KS4. They are a *statutory entitlement*, i.e. schools must offer MFL in KS4 and set a target for take-up between 50 and 90 per cent of pupils on the roll.

The lack of content specified in the NC can be seen to lead to GCSE specifications overshadowing the NC PoS at Key Stage 4 and, as a consequence, to a considerable amount of teaching to the test.

The offer can, but need not be the GCSE. For details on available qualifications, see http://www.dfes.gov.uk/qualifications/ and http://www.openquals.org.uk. As mentioned earlier, the 'languages ladder', ASSET languages, provides scope for alternative assessment and accreditation, particularly if pupils' attainment for individual language skills may be more appropriate than for all four as at GCSE. There are also developments to make these assessments available 'when needed' rather than working to a fixed timetable. This clearly represents a move towards more personalised assessment.

The GCSE is governed by specifications issued by the relevant government body, the QCA, on the basis of which awarding bodies develop their qualifications. The latest version available at the time of writing could be downloaded from http://www.qca.org.uk/qca_11999.aspx (see also the QCA MFL subject homepage at http://www.qca.org.uk/qca_7351.aspx). Although new GCSE criteria were proposed in 2007 (see below), new grade descriptions were not included. The criteria published in 2000 set out the following grade description for Grade C (QCA 2000b: 4):

> Candidates identify and note main points and extract details and points of view from language spoken at normal speed. The spoken texts include past and future events. They are drawn from a variety of topics which include familiar language in unfamiliar contexts.
>
> Candidates develop conversations and simple discussions which include past, present and future events, involving the use of different tenses. They express personal opinions and show an ability to deal with some unpredictable elements. Although there may be some errors, they convey a clear message, and their pronunciation and intonation are generally accurate.
>
> Candidates identify and extract details and points of view from authentic and simulated texts, drawn from a variety of topics and which include past, present and future events. They show an ability to understand unfamiliar language.
>
> Candidates express personal opinions and write about a variety of topics, both factually and imaginatively, including past, present and future events and involving the use of different tenses. They use an appropriate register. The style is basic but despite some errors the writing conveys a clear message.

Grade descriptions for Grades A and F are also available.

Task 1.4 Familiarising yourself with the latest GCSE Criteria and GCSE specifications for MFL

Obtain a copy of the GCSE specification used by your placement school. In your opinion, how well does it test the requirements in the NC PoS?

New draft criteria for GCSE were published by the QCA in June 2007. Like the new NC programme of study, the draft criteria are informed by wider developments in education, including Every Child Matters. To exemplify this change, as well as the links to the new PoS (see above), the aims of the new criteria are as follows.

GCSE specifications in modern foreign languages should encourage pupils to:

- derive enjoyment and benefit from language learning by following a coherent, satisfying and worthwhile course of study;

- develop understanding of the language in a variety of contexts;
- develop knowledge of the language and language learning skills;
- develop the ability to communicate effectively in the language;
- develop awareness and understanding of countries and communities where the language is spoken;
- recognise that their linguistic knowledge, understanding and skills help them to take their place in a multilingual global society and also provide them with a suitable basis for further study and practical use of the language.

One area of contention in recent years has been the perceived inappropriate, transactional content at GCSE level. The new criteria seek to address this criticism, as well as to reflect other educational developments as follows.

GCSE specifications in modern foreign languages must set out contexts and purposes that:

- are of relevance and interest to pupils;
- correspond to pupils' level of maturity;
- reflect, and are appropriate to, the culture of countries and communities where the language is spoken;
- relate, where appropriate, to other areas of the curriculum.

The criteria also specify there must be an element of choice for the pupils and that grammatical structures and vocabulary, as well as rubrics, should be specified.

The new GCSE criteria allow some flexibility of weighting for the four assessment objectives (AO), which were previously equally weighted. Each AO can now count for between 20 and 30 per cent. The assessment objectives are:

AO1   understand spoken language
AO2   communicate in speech
AO3   understand written language
AO4   communicate in writing.

At least 10 per cent of the total marks for AO2 and AO4 and at least 10 per cent of the total marks for the subject must be allocated to knowledge and accurate application of the grammar and structures of the language prescribed in the specification.

TEACHING MFL AT KS2

The teaching of MFL in primary schools is currently an issue of great debate within the MFL community. From 2010, MFL will be at least a statutory entitlement at KS2 (Years 3–6). This marks a huge change in the curriculum. It is still to be ascertained exactly how all primary schools will provide this entitlement, given issues such as teacher subject knowledge competence and confidence, transition and continuity challenges from KS2 to KS3, and, indeed, which language or languages should be on offer at KS2 taught as a 'discrete' language or whether there should be a broader-based menu of language tasters and language learning skills. For a discussion of possible options, see e.g. Driscoll (1999), Sharpe (2001) and Hunt *et al.* (2005). It is certainly the case that MFL at KS2 is seen by many decision-makers as a potential solution to the declining numbers of learners continuing with a language at KS4 (see, for example, the findings of the Dearing Report 2007), yet the potential dangers are clear: if MFL are not taught well at KS2, then learners may already be experiencing disaffection by KS3. The diversity of models currently in use for MFL at KS2 leads one to conclude that continuity of language, progression and assessment may be distinct challenges in the near future.

KS3 NATIONAL STRATEGY AND THE FRAMEWORK FOR TEACHING MFL (2002)

In recent years there has been a growing awareness that KS3 needs to be challenging and successful for learners, building on previous achievements and reinforcing where necessary. That is why the government introduced the KS3 National Strategy and MFL framework to supplement the National Curriculum with the aim of helping teachers to become more effective and helping pupils to improve their learning.

The KS3 National Strategy had four overarching key principles:

- *expectations*: establishing high expectations for all pupils and setting challenging targets for them to achieve;
- *progression*: strengthening the transition from KS2 so that pupils do not 'fall back' in Year 7, and ensuring good progression in teaching and learning across KS3;
- *engagement*: promoting approaches to teaching and learning that engage and motivate pupils and demand their active participation;
- *transformation*: strengthening teaching and learning through a programme of professional development and practical support.

Its aim, which obviously covered the whole of the KS3 learning experience for pupils across all the subjects, as with the KS2 National Strategy, remains to improve pupils' thinking/learning throughout the curriculum. The KS3 framework for lessons includes an emphasis on objectives, lesson starters, opportunities for pupils to reflect on their learning and associated summaries/plenaries. The KS3 MFL framework produced as part of the overall KS3 Strategy is used by many MFL departments, although it remains non-statutory in schools. It is, however, statutory that student teachers of MFL are fully aware of the framework.

The framework covers Years 7–9 and each year has a focus as follows:

- Year 7: foundation
- Year 8: acceleration
- Year 9: independence.

The framework aims to provide a solid basis for language learning, through five strands as follows:

- words
- sentences
- texts (reading and writing)
- listening and speaking
- cultural knowledge and contact.

For a detailed discussion of the Key Stage 3 Strategy, see Heilbronn (2004) or Stobart and Stoll (2005). Many language departments have used the framework to their advantage and re-evaluated their departmental focus at KS3 and have reappraised exactly what, and more importantly perhaps, how, MFL is being experienced by the pupils.

THE NATIONAL LITERACY STRATEGY (NLS) (1998)

The NLS was first introduced in the late 1990s and is another important policy initiative which has a bearing on MFL, at least in so far as the NLS could be said to be trying to get pupils not to be afraid of metalanguage which clearly links with effective grammar teaching in MFL, i.e. *understanding* and *using* grammar rather than learning chunks unanalytically or grammar with no application. It is very important with the NLS to be aware of potential discrepancies between accepted MFL terminology and NLS terminology (see Turner 2001). Carol Morgan and Peter Neil (2001: 38, 40) summarise the NLS as literacy comprising 11 different skills:

- reading and writing with confidence, fluency and understanding;
- using reading cues;
- understanding spelling and sound systems;
- having fluent and legible handwriting;
- having an interest in vocabulary;
- understanding literary genres;
- understanding non-fiction texts;
- being able to plan, redraft and edit writing;
- knowing a metalanguage (or technical vocabulary) for describing language systems;
- being interested in books;
- developing imagination.

In the NLS, pupils in Year 7 should have learnt the meaning of adjective, conjunction, noun, pronoun, verb, tense, first/second/third persons, adverb, clause, connectives, possessive apostrophe, imperative, preposition, reported speech, subject, active and passive voice. Morgan and Neil note that 10 teaching strategies are included in the NLS:

- drawing attention;
- demonstrating;
- modelling;

- scaffolding (for example, providing writing frames);
- explanation;
- questioning;
- guiding exploration;
- investigating ideas;
- discussing and arguing;
- listening to and responding.

What does it mean for you as an MFL teacher? From your perspective, when teaching MFL, you will need to bear the following in mind:

- In MFL, many of the issues in NLS are already part of the learning process (e.g. reading strategies).
- The main tenets of the NLS (e.g. the emphasis on reading, writing, listening and speaking, and language at word, sentence and text level) are also fundamental to MFL teaching and learning.
- You need to ensure that you are aware of terminology used across the curriculum, so you know what learners already know and are familiar with (this can be problematic, since there are sometimes discrepancies – the important message is to *find out*). The discrepancies appear to arise from different interpretations of grammatical terms in English teaching and in MFL.
- You should highlight KS3 MFL framework objectives as appropriate in your lessons and lesson plans (see the proforma in Chapter 4).
- It is certainly *not* the case that you are expected to teach something 'extra' or new, but that you incorporate literacy (and numeracy) *appropriately* for MFL, e.g. reminding learners of elements they should already know (such as using paragraphs), using strategies for spelling, developing writing frames, and incorporating numeracy skills where possible.
- As with all issues in teaching and learning, just because something *should* be familiar to your pupils through the NLS, you certainly cannot *assume* that it is!

Poole (2002: 213–14) notes the following effects of explicit study of language:

- a greater awareness and understanding of language patterns, structures and rules generally, and the increased ability to identify regularities and irregularities;
- increased awareness of the first, second and third person usage and of polite forms of address;
- increased awareness of tense patterns;
- recognition of prefixes and suffixes;
- increased awareness of the structure of compound nouns;
- understanding of the concept of 'silent letters' (e.g. sept);
- increased readiness to question exceptions to the rule;
- increased readiness among children to notice mistakes and correct each other.

Task 1.5 Links with the NLS

Read through the current NC MFL Order: (1) for explicit and (2) for implicit references to literacy and numeracy. Consider how these might influence your work with pupils.

SUMMARY

In this chapter we have shown that there are diverse educational, economic, vocational and linguistic reasons for including the study of MFL in the secondary school curriculum.

The aims and objectives governing the study of MFL have changed over the years as has the composition of the pupils learning MFL. These developments go hand in hand with changes in society and are a reflection of changes in national educational policy.

In this chapter, the advantages of a broad national MFL skills base were outlined.

Our brief examination of MFL policy and associated initiatives as well as the statutory requirements for England, together with related guidance documentation, strategies and reports, is intended to introduce you to the frameworks governing current MFL curriculum planning, teaching and assessment in secondary schools.

NOTE

1   Due to lack of space, the National Curriculum Orders discussed in this chapter, and used as point of reference throughout the book, apply to England only. Wales, Scotland and Northern Ireland have statutory requirements of their own. For details contact, the Department for Education, Lifelong Learning and Skills (DELLS at http://new.wales.gov.uk/topics/educationandskills/?lang=en), the Department of Education for Northern Ireland (DENI at http://www.deni.gov.uk) or Learning and Teaching Scotland (LTS at http://www.ltscotland.org.uk/mfle/index.asp).

FURTHER READING

Hawkins, E. (1987) *Modern Languages in the Curriculum* (rev. edn.). Cambridge: Cambridge University Press.

This seminal text remains a key reading when considering MFL and their place in the education of school age learners.

Hunt, M., Barnes, A., Powell, B., Muijs, D. and Lindsay, G. (2005) 'Primary Modern Foreign Languages: an overview of recent research, key issues and challenges for educational policy and practice', *Research Papers in Education* 20(4): 371–87.

This article details the current situation with regard to MFL for primary learners and outlines the developments which took place prior to the latest policy initiatives.

Pachler, N., Evans, M. and Lawes, S. (2007) *Modern Foreign Languages: Teaching School Subjects 11–19*. London: Routledge.

This book provides an excellent introduction to some current issues concerning the future of MFL and how it might develop.

2 On becoming a modern foreign languages teacher

(with Ana Redondo)

INTRODUCTION

This chapter sets the scene for your work as a modern foreign languages (MFL) student teacher during your initial teacher education (ITE) course both at higher education institutions (HEIs) and in school experience schools. While the main focus

---

OBJECTIVES

By the end of this chapter you should:

- understand the nature of the competence- and standards-based approach to ITE;
- be aware of the government's Every Child Matters policy and its impact on the role of the teacher;
- recognise the importance of subject knowledge and application, i.e. pedagogical content knowledge;
- recognise the importance of a symbiotic relationship between theory and reflective practice;
- appreciate differences in learning strategies and have started to consider your preferences in terms of teaching styles;
- be aware of possible stages of your development as a student teacher;
- appreciate the nature of your work in schools from two perspectives, your own as well as that of your mentor (and other teachers) you work with.

here is on student teachers following a traditional route into teaching, the chapter – as well as the book as a whole – should, of course, also be highly relevant to you if you are on an 'employment-based route' (EBR) into teaching or, indeed, training to become an MFL teacher outside the UK.

In recent years the work of student teachers in the UK has been subject to a number of fundamental changes. New QTS (Qualified Teacher Status) Standards have applied since September 2007 and it is these Standards to which we shall refer in this chapter. They are available at http://www.tda.gov.uk/partners/ittstandards/. The increase in the amount of time in the past 15 or so years that student teachers spend working with pupils and teachers in schools rather than with tutors in HEIs has been widely welcomed. Nevertheless, the gain in practical experience has created and/or reinforced certain tensions and has necessitated a redefinition of the roles of the key players involved. Although by now reasonably well established, the concept of partnership in ITE continues to evolve.

TOWARDS A MULTI-DISCIPLINARY APPROACH TO MFL TEACHING

The main aim of MFL teaching is to enable pupils to communicate in the target language (TL). The focus of your development as a teacher, therefore, is the pupils' learning, rather than your own teaching *per se*. To be an effective MFL teacher requires a range of skills and knowledge. We posit that there is no single way of MFL teaching and that, therefore, it is important for you to develop a personal approach to MFL teaching against the background of the respective statutory requirements and what we know about MFL teaching and learning from research. In recent years an increasing number of commentators and policy-makers have expressed the need to establish a theoretical framework for MFL teaching. This perceived need relates to the fact that there are many different source disciplines that potentially inform MFL teaching:

> As an applied discipline, language learning obviously needs to be informed by a 'conceptual framework': i.e. by a body of knowledge, drawn from various areas, which both helps to render the teaching experience coherent and provides a basis for evaluating its effectiveness. Without such a body of knowledge, refined into principles for classroom practice, there simply exist no criteria – beyond the weight of custom or fashion – for deciding what is or is not pedagogically effective.
>
> (Roberts 1992: 6)

This observation identifies two key concerns for you: that MFL teaching is an applied discipline and as such inextricably linked to a number of source disciplines; and that these disciplines provide a wealth of knowledge, which allows a better understanding of the teaching process. This body of background knowledge is important but is not sufficient to ensure effective MFL teaching. In addition, there is no single 'recipe' which will work for each group of learners in each specific context at a specific time.

All methodological ideas and recommendations have to be adapted in the light of circumstances.

Neuner and Hunfeld draw attention to a number of disciplines and factors that continue to yield important information for MFL student teachers:

- findings from the field of psychology;
- pedagogical knowledge and research into teaching;
- findings from the field of (applied) linguistics;
- conceptions about the foreign country;
- individual differences of learners;
- previous experience of modern foreign languages learning;
- conceptions about work with (literary) texts;
- specific objectives of learners;
- traditions of teaching methodology;
- methods of mother tongue teaching.

(translated from German; 1993: 9)

To become knowledgeable about and keep abreast with this wide range of considerations requires commitment and enthusiasm on your part. It is an exciting, career-long, quest to expand your methodological repertoire and to be able to see elements of it paying dividends with a particular group of learners. Research, in our estimation, has a very important role to play in contributing to the knowledge base of MFL teachers and it is to this end that we have included a chapter summarising and presenting an overview of relevant insights to be gained from research (see Chapter 14 and also Calvert 2007).

THE IMPORTANCE OF SUBJECT KNOWLEDGE

Subject knowledge is an important consideration for all MFL student teachers. For a detailed discussion, see Pachler *et al.* (2007).

A document compiled by the National Foundation for Educational Research (NFER) some time ago now re-affirmed as one of the central ingredients of effective teaching the importance of *higher* subject knowledge (see Tabberer 1996: 3–4). In the case of MFL, subject knowledge can be seen as a high level of proficiency in the TL good structural knowledge as well as the ability to make effective use of the TL, wide-ranging awareness of the culture(s) of the countries where the TL is spoken, some knowledge of the linguistic theories underpinning the language learning/acquisition process as well as a familiarity with the respective statutory framework and related documents. It also comprises knowledge and the ability to make effective use of Information and Communications Technology (ICT) in the specific subject, i.e. to *apply* ICT appropriately to the benefit of learners of MFL.

For native speakers, there are particular issues which need to be considered. The adaptation of the use of the TL in terms of complexity, speed of delivery, register and tone must be addressed if pupils are to understand and respond appropriately.

Although a key competence to be covered by every initial teacher education course, there is often only little time to focus on personal proficiency in the TL or cultural awareness. Also, there is often only little time to engage with theories of language learning and acquisition. As is the case throughout your teaching career, the onus is on you as an *individual* to maintain a high level of subject knowledge, including up-to-date linguistic competence and cultural understanding. A starting point for this process is often accomplished on an ITE programme via a subject knowledge audit, where you keep a record of your personal achievements and potential 'gaps' in your subject knowledge. Any such gaps in knowledge need to be addressed as early as possible, e.g. a specific grammatical construction, pronunciation issue, etc. You are one of the main linguistic models for your learners and the model needs to be as accurate as possible. This is also the case with structuring lessons, creating resources, etc.; your accuracy in these areas is paramount.

In a study Coleman (1996) highlighted a lack of national standards of linguistic proficiency for MFL graduates. Some observers remain concerned about the impact of a perceived decrease in standards of linguistic proficiency on MFL teaching methodology, particularly the focus on communicative competence. Too little emphasis on structural aspects of the language, they argue, could have detrimental effects on the future of the nation's linguistic potential:

> If these issues were not raised prior to or during A-level, and now have to be postponed indefinitely during the undergraduate course, only to be taken for granted during the PGCE year, then we must assume that a generation of teachers will be coming forward that has never been exposed to or learned certain aspects of German grammar and syntax.
>
> (McCulloch 1996: 15)

In Chapter 7 and the Epilogue, the shift at GCSE and GCE A/AS level towards a detailed prescription of grammatical content is discussed. This shift in emphasis affects the type of MFL education prospective MFL teachers experience but it also demands of student teachers working with advanced MFL learners a high degree of subject knowledge and makes the ability to transmit knowledge about linguistic structures all the more important.

Task 2.1 You as a linguist

Create a brief 'pen portrait' of yourself as a linguist. Include both your first foreign language and your second, if you have one. If you are a native speaker, adjust the list accordingly (e.g. for your second foreign language and/or how you will make your own language accessible). Be as honest as you can in analysing your strengths and weaknesses in the following areas:

- grammar 'rules'
- accuracy (grammar application)
- pronunciation

- range of language
- cultural knowledge.

Work out some initial strategies for how you might address these areas.

Task 2.2 Subject knowledge in MFL

Obtain a copy of an examination specification at GCSE and, where appropriate, GCE A/AS level used by the MFL department at your school experience school for your main foreign language(s). Reflect on how well you feel your first degree course or equivalent has prepared you for meeting the requirements of the specifications in terms of your subject knowledge. Use Table 2.1 to record your reflections.

Table 2.1 Mapping personal subject knowledge against examination requirements

Requirement	Degree course content	GCSE requirement	A/AS level requirement
cultural awareness			
structural knowledge of language			
non-literary topics			
literary topics			
key skills			
other (specify). . . .			

SUBJECT APPLICATION

We have already noted that subject knowledge is essential but not in and of itself enough to being an effective teacher. You need to be able to teach pupils subject knowledge and relevant skills in *appropriate* ways. They need to acquire knowledge in a wide range of fields to be able to do so effectively. You need to apply and use your own subject knowledge and make it accessible and 'learnable' for the pupils. Having the 'knowledge' yourself and trying to 'transmit' it is not enough.

Shulman's (1987, quoted in Bennett 1993: 7) seven categories of knowledge clearly underline the complexity of the teaching process. They are adapted in Table 2.2 and related to the process of learning to teach MFL (although they were not devised for any specific subject).

Table 2.2 Lee Shulman's seven categories of teacher knowledge

No.	Category	MFL relevance
1	**Content knowledge**: referring to the amount and organisation of knowledge in the mind of the teacher. This includes both substantive and syntactic structure of a subject, i.e. the variety of ways in which the basic concepts and principles of the discipline are organised, and the ways in which truth or falsehood, validity or invalidity, are established.	Need to update linguistic competence, cultural awareness/intercultural (communicative) competence and ICT competence on a regular basis.
2	**General pedagogical knowledge**: with a special reference to both broad principles and strategies of classroom management and organisation that appear to transcend subject matter.	Need for an understanding of adolescent development and the relationship between language and learning in general.
3	**Curriculum knowledge**: with particular grasp of the materials and programmes that serve as 'tools of the trade' for teachers.	Growing familiarity with the content and application of the statutory framework and specifications as well as commonly used resources including ICT.
4	**Pedagogical/content knowledge**: that form of content knowledge that embodies the aspect of content most germane to its teachability. It includes, for any given subject area, the most useful forms of the presentation of those ideas, the most powerful analogies, illustrations, examples, explanations and demonstrations. In other words, the ways of representing and formulating the subject that make it comprehensible to others.	Knowledge of and a willingness to experiment with and evaluate different approaches to foreign language teaching including ICT; awareness of relevant background reading and research. Need to expand relevant methodological repertoire which engages various groups of/individual learners.
5	**Knowledge of learners and their characteristics**	Awareness of the existing language skills of learners and of what motivates the individuals within a class; awareness of how current approaches to MFL teaching and learning relate to learning theories.
6	**Knowledge of educational contexts**: ranging from the workings of the group or classroom, the governance and financing of schools, to the character to communities and cultures.	Knowledge of the institutional, local and national context of MFL teaching including policy matters and inspection findings.
7	**Knowledge of educational ends, purposes and values, and philosophical and historical background**	Knowledge of how current approaches to MFL teaching and learning have evolved; awareness of the rationale and purposes of MFL teaching and learning how they relate to the wider secondary school curriculum.

There is much to be learnt in the course of ITE and often only little time is available to focus on subject knowledge. As Shulman's categories indicate, the onus is on subject application, what he calls pedagogical subject knowledge, and the development of your ability to develop in pupils MFL-related knowledge, skills and understanding.

COURSE EXPECTATIONS: THE STUDENT TEACHERS' POINT OF VIEW

Student teachers from a wide range of backgrounds opt to learn to teach MFL. While many elect to train to teach directly after completion of their undergraduate studies or shortly thereafter, others may have followed one or more careers in areas other than education and, for a variety of reasons, have decided that the time is now appropriate for them to retrain. Many others are native speakers of the TL, who may have worked as foreign language assistants. In this chapter, we present two authentic case studies of MFL student teachers. They are drawn from accounts written during a Postgraduate Certificate in Education (PGCE) course. The views expressed are invariably personal and specific to individual circumstances but, nevertheless, illustrate a number of general issues about the process of student teachers' development. The case studies are divided into two sections: an initial statement giving reasons for wanting to become a teacher written before the start of the PGCE course, which are included in this section, and a concluding statement on completion of the course, which can be found at the end of this chapter. Other interesting case study material can be found in Grenfell (1998) and Barnes (2005).

CASE STUDY 1

Initial statement

From the age of 13, pupils are encouraged to investigate career choices, or rather that was the case in my educational experience. At this time no other career option appealed to me in the same way as teaching and the situation has not changed in 10 years. When I ask myself what I want from a successful and satisfying career, teaching fulfils most of my requirements. Teaching allows me to continue to work with my subject interests. I want to work in a team but also with the public, a combination which demands good communication and diplomacy skills. I see teaching as an immense challenge because the potential for rewards, satisfaction and excellence is infinite, but on the other hand failure is unacceptable.

I want to be able to bring or even drag out the best in my future pupils and I am fully aware that that does not mean expecting them all to achieve grade A.

My desire to be a teacher has been reinforced by teaching both English and French (to small groups and individuals) and by the satisfaction that these experiences have brought me. I discovered that I have confidence, discipline and organisational skills which enabled me to teach a language and to engage my pupils' interest. I feel I am able to relate to the educational, personal and social needs of young people and to deal with them within the teaching environment.

I am aware of the conflict between teaching a modern foreign language to enable pupils to pass an exam and teaching it to prepare pupils to use a specific language in and outside of the countries it is spoken.

I am also concerned about the behaviour of today's pupils and the lack of respect they seem to have for each other and for adults. Any improvement, however small, I can make to this situation during my career will give me great satisfaction.

CASE STUDY 2

Initial statement

Unlike a lot of people on this course who seem to have wanted to teach all their lives, the one thing I knew that I was not going to do when I graduated was teach. This was mainly due to my father recommending that teaching was not a profession to go into. As he is himself a teacher, I figured he must know what he was talking about, so I took his advice. I went on to work in a variety of mainly PA, research and sales and marketing roles, none of which ever seemed particularly satisfying or rewarding. I finally decided I had to re-examine what I was after in a career. The result pointed to the fact that I had been avoiding a profession which I secretly thought I might enjoy.

I have not forgotten my own experiences in secondary school, sometimes sitting in a (language) classroom feeling incredibly stupid and panicking because I had not understood what the teacher had been explaining and was too scared to ask. Of course this is a very naive thing to say, but I would like to think that I could persuade pupils in my class not to be afraid to make clear that they have not understood what I have tried to explain. I believe this to be a crucial point in beginning to build a sound working relationship with a class. I am of the opinion that as long as a pupil is making an effort to understand, that pupil deserves the best effort that I can make to help her. I also believe that if that pupil is not making the effort, it is my job to give her a reason to make that effort.

As far as teaching my particular subject is concerned, I am convinced that my enthusiasm for what I have to teach is of prime importance in helping me do my job well. I want to be able to impart this enthusiasm to my pupils, but I can see that this is where the difficulties are most likely to occur. The reason for this is because I have for the majority of my life been taught using very conservative and academic methods. It is all I know and it is what I am most comfortable with at present. To complicate matters further, I am naturally a quite reserved character. So when I see videos of teachers using 'radical' communicative methods, I think 'brilliant!' and then I think 'but I can't do that'. I believe the methods are effective, I can see how they would work, but I am not sure that I am capable of applying them myself. Ideas on how to teach MFL have changed drastically since I was at school, and although it is a change which I approve of, it is also one which I will have to make an effort to adapt to successfully.

On a more general level, classroom management is my greatest worry at the moment, particularly after having seen some classes during my induction week in school. I am aware that with the best lesson plan in the world, if the class is not managed correctly the pupils are not going to learn as effectively as they could.

Planning my work, I do not as yet see as a big problem. I am fairly confident of being able to get straight in my own mind the objectives of a lesson and being able to get from there in terms of suitable activities to meet these objectives.

Task 2.3 Comparing personal and course expectations

The discussion in this chapter so far has highlighted the complexity of MFL teaching and has shown how much there is to be learnt by a student teacher. This task aims to help you decide priorities for your professional development.

1   Reflect on and note how the discussion so far in this chapter relates to your personal expectations concerning the ITE course. In your opinion, what knowledge and skills does an effective MFL teacher need? Also, what characterises a good MFL teacher? What types of behaviour do you think are best avoided by an MFL teacher?

2   What expectations did the two student teachers have initially about teaching? How do their expectations relate to your own?

3   Then, carefully study your course documentation. What expectations are stated in the documents? How do they compare to your expectations?

4   What issues arise from this comparison? What will your priorities be?

Task 2.4 Pupil expectations

When you have the opportunity, carry out a small survey among pupils at your school experience school asking them what characteristics they wish to see in an MFL teacher. Note down positive and negative responses. Are there any differences in your own and the pupils' perceptions?

HOW DO WE LEARN TO TEACH?

The competence-/Standards-based approach to initial (MFL) teacher education

Opinions on how anyone learns to teach vary quite substantially and most agree the process is certainly complex. Some aspects of the research into this process are touched on in the remaining sections of this chapter and include reflection, stages and phases of development and competences/standards. There are what could be termed more 'technicist' models, such as a system introduced in the early 1990s. This was a competence-based approach introduced to ITE in England and Wales, and comprised 'a set of observable and assessable behaviours, a sort of National Curriculum for intending teachers' (Norman 1995: 5). In the late 1990s this was replaced by a Standards-based approach. The Standards have since been revised twice, with the latest version applying from September 2007. This version fully incorporates Every Child Matters into the Standards (see below). Student teachers are required to meet *all* the Standards by the end of their course to be recommended for qualified teacher status. Subsequently, as Newly Qualified Teachers (NQTs), they have to successfully complete a period of induction totalling three full terms (or equivalent for part-time contracts) at the start of their teaching career in order to be entered on the register of the General Teaching Council for England (GTCE) and to be entitled to teach as fully qualified teachers in maintained schools. The induction period, as well as further progression opportunities, are prescribed by further sets of standards.

Since 2000–01 all student teachers have also been required to successfully complete tests in numeracy, literacy and ICT in order to gain QTS. These changes were introduced in a bid to ensure NQTs are able to implement the various government strategies for raising standards. For more details on the skills tests, see the Training and Development Agency (TDA) website at http://www.tda.gov.uk/skillstests.aspx where support material and advice can be found.

A course of ITE should offer the opportunity to track progress towards the standards for QTS. As with many such assessments, meeting a Standard once in one lesson is clearly not sufficient. There exists a need to demonstrate a sustained level of achievement. Some Standards are much broader than others, encompassing a whole professional approach towards teaching and learning, e.g. having high expectations of all pupils. Standards such as these permeate the development as a teacher. Others, such as passing the QTS Skills Tests, are much narrower, in that it is very clear when they are achieved. Courses of ITE will have guidance material and/or systems to help pinpoint where, and how, progress is being made.

EVERY CHILD MATTERS: THE CHANGING ROLE OF EDUCATIONAL PROFESSIONALS

Arising out of the Children Act 2004, Every Child Matters (http://www.every childmatters.gov.uk) is an approach which aims to ensure all children achieve their potential and that all professionals associated with caring for and educating children work successfully together to realise these aims. The five specific outcomes which all children should experience positively are to:

- be healthy;
- stay safe;
- enjoy and achieve;
- make a positive contribution;
- achieve economic well-being.

Clearly, in many cases, professionals involved with children in a variety of contexts will work very closely. From the perspective of a student teacher, there exists a need to be conversant with the approach and content of the government's Every Child Matters policy and to be aware of how roles of professionals are evolving from a perhaps more separate 'education' context to one where you are working together with others not directly involved in education and their expertise is seen as advantageous. As a student teacher you need to be observant and ask questions in your school experience school about this area and, perhaps most importantly from your perspective, work consciously on developing your approach to working with others and in teams (both of which are reflected in the QTS Standards). This can start by, for example, working with teaching assistants or Foreign Language Assistants in the classroom (see Pearson *et al.* 2003; Chambers and Pearson 2004; Cremin *et al.* 2005; Redondo 2007).

Task 2.5 Working with others

Consider the role of a teaching assistant in your classroom. How do you ensure you make the relationship successful for your pupils' learning? Consider the following factors:

- establishing an initial relationship (what exactly are their specific responsibilities?);
- communication *prior* to a lesson;
- participation/role *during* a lesson;
- communication *after* a lesson;
- use of their expertise.

THEORY AND PRACTICE IN (MFL) ITE

The previous section showed that ITE courses are required to assess MFL student teachers in terms of standards, that is, your ability to display certain observable types of behaviour to enable pupils to learn effectively. In order to be able to show these types of behaviour and to ensure pupils learn, as a student teacher you need to develop professional judgement and an ability to reflect, among other things, on your own professional practice and its effectiveness in bringing about learning. This requires practical as well as theoretical knowledge. The relationship between theory and practice is, therefore, an important issue. Many ITE courses now incorporate a Masters element, which in itself demands you to adopt a focus on theoretical aspects of teaching and learning MFL.

Reflection and theorising are increasingly seen as central features underpinning student teachers' development and as catalysts in moving from dependency to autonomy (see e.g. Furlong *et al.* 1996: 32; Roberts 1998: 47–60; Alger 2006).

To find time for reflection on a busy course is not easy. There exists a need to ensure that you evaluate your teaching and pupils' learning effectively. Focusing where possible on pupils' learning, progress and understanding is much more effective from a reflection perspective than the more easily 'fixable' elements of your teaching, although of course these cannot be ignored (aspects such as your own position in the classroom or the modulation of your voice – elements which can have a significant impact on pupil learning, but are not by themselves a solution). As we have already repeatedly noted, the aim of your teaching is pupils' learning, which must, therefore, be the main element you reflect upon. Ask yourself questions such as:

- How well did pupils learn what you intended them to learn?
- What may have impeded/boosted pupils' learning?
- How well did they understand a new concept?
- Did they make progress from previous learning?
- Which groups/individuals were particularly successful/less successful? Why?

Given the number of source disciplines, the perceived level of difficulty of MFL and the wide-ranging literature on its methodology, MFL teaching has substantial theoretical underpinning. The ability to analyse the processes of your classrooms is central to your work as a student teacher:

> 'Theory as intellectual process' . . . is inadequate; what should be offered is theoretical knowledge which may be tentative and to be questioned, but which is also specifically believed 'to be of practical value' and usefully assimilated into the professional development of student teachers.
>
> (Dunne 1993: 105)

The existence of a standards-based model in ITE must, in our opinion, not be seen as bringing theory and practice into conflict with each other:

> The most useful role of theory for the practitioner is to offer a strong constructivist foundation for their activity, and to provide a basis upon which to question the leading fads and rhetoric of the field. . . . The role of researchers, then, is to provide comprehensible input for practitioners, and the role of practitioners is to provide rational interpretation of those ideas for researchers to ponder. Both are locked into a symbiotic relationship that eventually propels the field and advances knowledge.
>
> (Bialystok and Hakuta 1995: 218)

MFL teaching requires practical knowledge including – but going beyond – reflection on what can be observed. That is, practical knowledge, which is predicated on conceptual and theoretical understanding enabling teachers to make deliberate choices at various stages of the teaching process.

Roberts (1998: 54–8) distinguished 11 different purposes for, or types of reflection which remain of distinct relevance for student teachers:

1   to raise awareness of personal images of teaching;
2   to raise awareness of one's personal theories, values and beliefs;
3   to reflect on one's own language learning style;
4   to raise awareness of one's current performance as a learner;
5   to develop the ability to analyse teaching situations;

6   to recall and analyse new and recent learning experiences;
7   to review and access one's own actions in class;
8   to raise awareness of one's routines and their rationale;
9   to test the consistency between classroom events and educational theories;
10   to become able to reframe interpretations of one's practice;
11   to become aware of the social and political significance of one's work.

Reflection can be seen to offer a very useful means of integrating theory and practice and of enabling you to deepen your understanding of your own personal and professional development. However, awareness of the multifaceted nature of the term and the concept is important to ensure the appropriate type of reflection is used for a specific purpose.

For Bevis Yaxley (1994: 26), the process of reflection consists in the first instance of the description of good practice, leading on to articulation of the principles which underpin this practice. This, in turn, leads to the sharing of ideas through open discussion, whether orally or in written form, followed by a process of challenging and justifying professional decisions. The final phase of reflective practice in this model is the close scrutiny and questioning of practice as an independent professional. We would argue that sustained reference to relevant conceptual and theoretical frameworks gained, for example, through discussion with peers, teachers and tutors or engagement with professional and academic literature, is essential in the process (see also Calvert 2007).

Task 2.6 Reflecting on practice

When reflecting on your work on the course (for example, when discussing an observed lesson, or when evaluating pupils' learning), refer to Roberts' types of reflection as well as the research chapter at the end of the book.
  What type of reflection do you tend to engage in? Why?

At certain stages of your course, it might seem difficult to relate what you are taught at university to what you observe in school. For Grenfell, this potential tension in subject methodology between the school experience school and HEI is important in so far as it requires student teachers 'to decide *for themselves*' (1998: 171) and respond practically, intellectually and emotionally. Teachers 'who are simply told what to do and what not to do' are less likely to develop the 'multitude of senses, knowledges and ways of acting . . . required in schools and in classrooms' (1998: 178).

Grenfell (ibid.: 131–44) outlines the following 13 problem areas, or dichotomies, which some of his student teachers experienced:

1   the incongruity between personal views of teaching and those presented on the course;
2   past experience, which has proved to be successful, versus a new approach which has not;

3   the choice between trusting what I know about teaching and learning from
     and trusting what others tell me to do;
4   the need to respond personally to the pedagogic approach versus the need
     to fulfil the course requirement;
5   the ability to criticise versus the ability to do better oneself;
6   to teach by technique versus to teach through individual personality;
7   the need to attend to personal security versus the need to attend to the
     pedagogic needs of the pupils;
8   how can I be a teacher versus how can I be myself?;
9   'I want everything planned so that I know what I am doing' versus 'I want
     flexibility to take pupils' response into account';
10   how far to bring the approach to the particular class versus how far to bring
     the particular class to the approach?;
11   do I use the target language or English?;
12   to teach grammar versus to teach through the target language;
13   who do I turn to with problems?

Task 2.7 Tensions frequently experienced by student teachers

Consider Grenfell's 13 dichotomies. To what extent are they representative of problem areas you have encountered and are facing? Have you been able to resolve them? What strategies did you use? It may be useful to consider these dichotomies at various stages in your programme.

Grenfell also emphasises the importance of the personal theories of school-based mentors. Rather than viewing their practice as behaviours to be modelled and copied, regarding what teachers say and how they teach as being in some ways theoretical 'allows student teachers to be explicit about what they think, and in so doing, objectifying it' (1998: 148). This, Grenfell argues, allows student teachers to change and discuss change as well as 'to develop ways of thinking and acting which allow them to become competent as a teacher in a range of contexts' (ibid.).

Different levels of theorising, to be addressed at different stages of (student) teachers' development and by different partners in the ITE process, can thus be identified.

Stages in the development of student teachers

In the course of ITE, learning takes place at different rates. MFL student teachers undergo a developmental process, which is governed by individual personal differences. One change most MFL student teachers undergo is the gradual shift from a concern with themselves as teachers, as lesson planners and deliverers of subject matter, towards an increasing concern for pupils as learners with individual traits and specific needs.

Based on their work with primary PGCE student teachers, Furlong and Maynard (1995: 73–97) suggest that there are a number of different broad stages of development. These stages are summarised in Table 2.3. None of these developmental models can be seen as inevitable or linear, however. Student teachers develop at different rates of progress according to a variety of circumstances and characteristics. See Barnes (2006) for a discussion of MFL student teachers' concerns, demonstrating that they are indeed concerned with, for example, subject knowledge issues from an early stage in their programmes and that the stages are much less linear than may be implied by some models.

DEVELOPING A PERSONAL APPROACH TO MFL TEACHING AND LEARNING

Gradually, as MFL student teachers become more familiar with the processes of classroom organisation and more confident in interacting with pupils, they begin to

Table 2.3 Stages in the development of student teachers

No.	Stage	Summary
1	early idealism	Student teachers often come to the course with an educational philosophy based on good or bad examples from their own 'careers' as pupils.
2	personal survival	Student teachers can feel quite overwhelmed by their first experience of teaching; they tend to feel insecure and want the pupils to accept them as teachers; they use strategies such as copying the mentor, appraising their initial idealistic view of themselves as teachers and working at gaining and maintaining classroom control.
3	dealing with difficulties	Student teachers start to appreciate the complexities of teaching and gain a basic understanding of certain aspects of the job; many look to pupils for feedback and judge their own effectiveness by how well pupils like them; teaching strategies and classroom organisation become increasingly important and student teachers often try to assimilate the teaching style and methods used by their mentor.
4	hitting a plateau	While having gained certain basic competences many student teachers can lack real understanding; they can often act like teachers but not really think like teachers at this stage.
5	moving on	Student teachers start to think of themselves as professional educators.

develop their own personal teaching style. You need to determine your personal approach to MFL teaching and learning on the basis of:

- the statutory requirements for MFL and their methodological implications;
- the learning styles and individual differences and needs of pupils;
- personal preferences concerning teaching styles;
- the policies and practice prevalent in placement schools;
- good practice described in relevant literature/lectures or observed in MFL classrooms.

The past few decades have witnessed a wide range of approaches to MFL teaching and learning, none of which provided a panacea. In an appendix to his book *Designing Tasks for the Communicative Classroom*, Nunan (1989: 194–6) provides an interesting overview of important language teaching methods. His matrix provides a useful tool for analysing personal preferences concerning MFL teaching and learning.

Many student teachers tend to start to teach in a way they have been or would like to be taught. Below are two activities intended to broaden your perspective and to encourage you to consider other strategies to meet the needs and preferences of pupils in your classroom.

Task 2.8 features a questionnaire (Figure 2.1), which is based on Nunan's matrix. It also builds on Kolb, Rubin and McIntyre's (1974) learning styles inventory. The aim of this task is to guide you towards an understanding of your own preferred learning style and at the same time to make you aware of the principal features of other styles.

In Task 2.9 you can then apply the understanding of learning styles gained in Task 2.8 and start to develop your own approach to MFL teaching.

Task 2.8 Identifying preferred learning styles

1   Read through the questions and statements in Figure 2.1. For each question/ statement, there are four contrasting views. There are no 'right' or 'wrong' responses. You are asked to respond to each question/statement in terms of how it best corresponds to your own personal views. Do not think too hard before responding. Allocate 2 points to the response closest to your views, 1 point to the one ranked second; give -1 point to your third favourite response and -2 points to the response you agree with the least.

2   Transfer your points into the table in Figure 2.2. For the time being, ignore the acronyms at the top of each column, they are explained in Figure 2.4.

3   Then, plot your scores on the grid in Figure 2.3 and join them to make a geo-metrical form. You should end up with a drawing in the shape of a kite. Your preferred learning style is represented by the quadrant, in which the majority of your kite shape can be found. It is defined by combining two of the descriptions in Figure 2.4, which account for the two axes. The graph shows your preferences and strength of feeling.

No.	Questions	Score
1	**Do you believe that language is essentially**	
a	a set of rule-governed structures?	
b	a system which has developed to convey meaning?	
c	composed of a unique rhythm and spirit based around the culture of the country where the language is spoken?	
d	built around correct, grammatical concepts?	
2	**A modern foreign language is best learnt by**	
a	memorisation and forming of good language habits.	
b	listening, reading and then practising.	
c	undertaking realistic tasks, achievable only by use of the TL.	
d	acquisition through constant exposure to and immersion in the TL and culture.	
3	**The primary aim of learning a modern foreign language is**	
a	to achieve a practical command of speaking, listening, reading, writing.	
b	to achieve functional and linguistic objectives.	
c	to provide basic communicative skills as well as essential academic learning skills.	
d	to provide enjoyment and stimulation through access to a foreign culture.	
4	**A MFL course should be structured so that language presented**	
a	is graded in forms of ever increasing levels of difficulty.	
b	is determined by the learner's individual needs.	
c	is based on grammatical items and associated vocabulary.	
d	consists of excerpts from cultural texts.	
5	**The purpose of classroom activities is**	
a	to practise and reinforce correct forms of language.	
b	to engage the learner in communicative tasks.	
c	to allow the learner to respond to commands, questions and clues in her own way.	
d	to build upon structures and language forms learnt previously.	
6	**The learner's chief responsibility is**	
a	to listen, repeat and to respond.	
b	to negotiate objectives and to respond accordingly.	
c	to move towards independence, autonomy and responsibility.	
d	to maintain passive and to allow the materials and activities to determine the nature of learning.	
7	**The teacher's place in the teaching/learning process is**	
a	to act as a model of good TL use and to orchestrate drill practice.	
b	to facilitate through presentation, advice and the provision of authentic, realistic tasks.	
c	to provide comprehensible input and orchestrate a variety of related activities.	
d	to teach, test and to reinforce accurate language forms.	

(Continued)

No.	Questions	Score
8	**In the main the following materials should be used by the teacher**	
a	a coursebook and visual aids.	
b	audio tapes and transcripts.	
c	authentic, realistic materials.	
d	structured examples and related exercises.	

Figure 2.1 Questionnaire

No.	OBH	LMPU	ERP	SGA
1	a =	b =	c =	d =
2	a =	c =	d =	b =
3	a =	b =	d =	c =
4	a =	b =	d =	c =
5	a =	b =	c =	d =
6	a =	b =	d =	c =
7	a =	c =	b =	d =
8	a =	c =	b =	d =
Total				

Figure 2.2 Scoring table

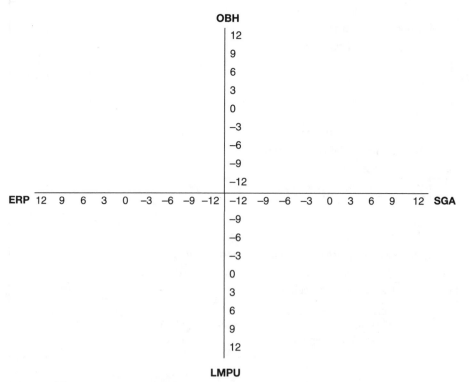

Figure 2.3 Plotting grid

Off-by-heart language learning (OBH)	Learning to manipulate language for personal use (LMPU)	Exposure, repetition and practice (ERP)	Structured grammar approach (SGA)
The content of a course is defined within strict topic areas. Set phrases and key vocabulary are learnt irrespective of their grammatical complexity in order to meet perceived needs and corresponding usefulness in given situations. Learning 'parrot fashion' enables a task to be completed.	Language is learnt through the personalisation and manipulation of language forms presented. Motivation is achieved through realistic and successful communication. The learner is personally involved and takes considerable responsibility for her own learning.	The process of learning is through immersion in the language. Unstructured practice is reinforced through the reactions of others. The learner learns which parts of language work in which situations, thereby identifying and developing positive linguistic habits for herself.	The explanation of grammatical concepts in a logical sequence and the structured application of this knowledge lead to a sound understanding of language structures. This understanding facilitates a sound mastery of linguistic systems.

Figure 2.4 Description of learning styles

Task 2.9 Developing your personal approach to MFL teaching

1   Having identified a preferred learning style, reflect upon the types of learning activities associated with it. What are the implications for your MFL teaching?
2   Then consider activities which will suit other learning styles, for instance, by talking to other student teachers. What are the implications for your MFL teaching?

When planning MFL lessons, try to account for a variety of learning styles. It will certainly not work for your learners if all your lessons are wonderfully tailored to suit you and your preferred learning style(s).

SCHOOLS' EXPECTATIONS AND THE MENTOR'S POINT OF VIEW[1]

The role of your mentor is very important, in helping you develop as an MFL teacher and to progress through the stages in Table 2.3. In order to maximise the effectiveness of the mentor's experience and advice, MFL student teachers need to establish a good working relationship with their mentors and staff at the school experience school. In order to be able to do so it is important for you to gain some awareness of schools' expectations. This section offers advice and guidance from the point of view of mentors, i.e. those experienced MFL teachers, who work closely with student teachers during their time at a school experience school. This includes induction, support in organisational matters, observation of practical teaching, giving advice, guidance and diagnostic feedback, the provision of input on methodology and appropriate approaches as well as, importantly, assessment of practical teaching and target setting.

Why schools and mentors work with student teachers

Schools and departmental teams agree to take student teachers for a whole host of reasons. A study carried out by researchers at the University of Warwick (Barker *et al.* 1996: 57) for the Association for Teachers and Lecturers (ATL) among a representative sample of ITE courses found that subject mentors saw a number of benefits arising from participation in a partnership scheme and receiving student teachers (see Table 2.4).

Table 2.4 Perception of the level of benefit (%: non-MFL-specific)

Benefits	Subject mentors
Professional development	90
Job satisfaction	81
Management skills	76
Curriculum innovation	64
Morale	54
New teaching methods	45
Addition of new resources	42

You need to realise, though, that these benefits to mentors come at a certain cost, for instance, an increased demand on time, workload and administration as often work with student teachers is carried out without receiving any financial rewards or time off in lieu (see Barker *et al.* 1996: i). Having an additional person in the team has a number of implications for the work of a department. This you need to be aware of while in a school experience school.

The role of your mentor

It is important for you to appreciate that *established channels of communication need to be observed*. These vary from course to course and school to school. Your course handbook as well as the staff and departmental handbooks provided by your school experience schools should contain all the relevant information with which you need to familiarise yourself.

At the same time there tends to be a co-ordinating mentor/professional tutor (usually a senior teacher or deputy head) with overall responsibility for student teachers, who works in tandem with subject mentors.

In each department there usually is a named individual, the so-called subject mentor, who often has undergone a training programme with the respective HEI and who is your main point of contact during your stay at the school experience school.

The responsibilities of subject mentors vary from one ITE course to another. However, they typically include liaison with the HEI, giving regular advice and feedback to student teachers regarding their progress and performance against the Standards as well as contributing to their assessment. Subject mentors tend to carry out their duties in consultation with all members of staff in the MFL department, who work with the student teacher as well as the ITE co-ordinator/professional tutor at the school.

It is important for you to be clear from the very beginning what you can realistically expect from your mentor, for instance, how often and when you will be able to meet with her. At the same time you need to be fully aware of your own responsibilities. For instance, in terms of personal organisation you need to appreciate that any necessary equipment and resources in the school or department required for teaching, need to be booked well in advance. Failure to do so might result in you being unable to proceed with a lesson according to plan and cause disruption.

Building a professional relationship with members of staff at your school experience school

Usually you will be asked to observe and work with a number of experienced teachers. The aim is for you to gain as wide a range of experiences of teaching styles and pupils' responses to them as possible. This is an important part of your learning experience during your ITE. It is important that you establish a good working relationship with all members of staff, not just with your mentor.

Working closely with more than one MFL teacher can, on occasion, create certain tensions: you might experience uncertainty as to what teaching styles and strategies to adopt or reject and sometimes advice given by different teachers might seem inconsistent or even irreconcilable to you. You should follow up specific observations made in lessons, which trigger questions and seek clarification as the reasons for employing particular teaching strategies are not always obvious to an observer. In many instances there is more than meets the eye to the way teachers manage their lessons and relate to pupils whom they know well. If any doubt still persists, issues can be raised with your mentor and/or HEI tutor without necessarily personalising them. When seeking clarification in this way you engage in the important process of reflection on practice. This can provide you with an increased understanding of individual pupils and their behaviour as well as teachers' approaches to dealing with them. However, you need to display a professional attitude throughout this process. You need to be acutely aware that some questions you may want to ask might be sensitive.

Any worries or problems need to be resolved in a mature and professional manner by following the correct procedures normally outlined in the course handbook. Remember that not all professional relationships necessarily turn into personal friendships.

In the event of a personality clash, which can occur occasionally, mediation through a third party can help to resolve possible tensions.

Learning from members of staff

You need to understand that you will normally be expected to model your practice on the agreed policies of both the department you work in and the school experience school more generally. Where asked to do so, you need to follow the routines set by members of staff for different groups as pupils can benefit from experiencing continuity of practice and consistency. Often certain variations to set routines are possible, but they need to be discussed with and approved by the member of staff responsible for a given class. Innovation and exploration of new approaches to teaching are exciting, desirable and commendable in a student teacher and, as can be seen in Table 2.4, perceived as a benefit by mentors. They must, however, not upset pupils' well-established routines, which can serve them well in maximising their learning.

Appreciating the range of responsibilities of members of staff at your school experience school

To ensure high quality in collaborative teaching, there is a need for frequent information exchange and discussions between the student teacher and the relevant member of staff.

You will soon become aware that, beside teaching lessons, a typical day of an MFL teacher may include: tidying up the classroom and getting ready in between lessons, doing break and gate duties, attending meetings (at lunchtime or after school sometimes on several days in the week), invigilating detentions (at break time or after school), planning, marking, meeting visitors, discussing work with pupils outside lesson time, running lunchtime or after-school clubs, photocopying, covering lessons for colleagues, dealing with and responding to post record keeping or making and receiving phone calls. Importantly, they also need time for a break, their lunch and socialising with colleagues! Subject mentors often have other responsibilities apart from those for student teachers. You need to respect the busy schedule of (MFL) teachers and observe arranged meeting times.

In the light of these demands and in order to obtain an accurate picture from the beginning of what teaching entails, you need to play as a full a part in school life as possible. This will probably include you staying on after school for staff and departmental meetings, being attached to a form group for registrations, pastoral and guidance time, attending assemblies, attending parents' evenings, performing break duties, contributing to extra-curricular activities or assisting in fund-raising activities.

Task 2.10 Finding out about your subject mentor's daily routine

Ask your subject mentor whether you can shadow her for a whole teaching day (including break, lunchtime and any free periods) and after school to become familiar with her daily responsibilities and duties.

1   In the course of the day list all her duties and responsibilities, note the time of occurrence and their duration.
2   Then discuss with your mentor how representative the day was and which other responsibilities and duties she has on a regular basis.

The student teacher as a role model

From the very start you need to see yourself as an educator not merely as a subject specialist. Your need to take on the wider brief of teachers, which includes concern for your pupils' spiritual, moral, social and cultural (SMSC) development. One way of taking on the full role of a teacher is by displaying a responsible and caring attitude towards pupils. You will often be perceived as a role model by pupils like other members of staff and need to gain pupils' trust and respect both inside and, importantly also, outside the classroom. You need to be acutely aware that pupils observe the behaviour and conduct of those around them carefully and can be duly influenced in their behaviour and/or attitudes towards the subject. When working with pupils, you must never underestimate the formative influence you might have on them!

Visits from the HEI tutor

Schools are used to visits by a whole host of people such as advisers, inspectors, parents or governors, who come for a range of purposes. Departments welcome this but it inevitably adds to their workload. Given that hosting visitors needs to be fitted into an often already tight schedule, visits need to be arranged in advance. Often, your HEI tutor will arrange a visit through your mentor. Should she want to arrange a visit through you, it is very important that you liaise with the relevant members of staff, such as the head of department, your mentor and/or the respective teacher whose class is being observed. You need to observe established procedures such as, for instance, collecting the HEI tutor from reception, where visitors tend to be required to report to be issued with a visitor's pass.

Accepting and acting upon advice

There is a lot to be learnt from the experience and knowledge of (MFL) teachers at your school experience school. Part of their role is to share their practice with you and to advise you on your development as a student teacher and set targets. It is your responsibility to take this advice on board and act upon it. You *need to learn from members of staff* at your school experience school *as well as learn to work with them*. In all your interactions with pupils, colleagues and the school, personal and professional integrity are essential. When something goes wrong, you need to try, together with your mentor, to identify contributory factors and devise possible strategies for improvement.

Invariably, many things will not work out the first time round during your course of ITE. Qualified practitioners strive every day to improve their teaching. No less is expected from those new to the profession. A genuine desire to contribute to a positive learning experience about the ways people from other cultures communicate and live is what is required.

Task 2.11 What is your mentor to you?

In evaluating your own performance and in planning your own future development, you need to consider the place and role of your mentor.
  Identify words from the lists below that:

* represent the role you wish your mentor to take on;
* do not describe the relationship you want with your mentor;
* need discussion with your mentor.

colleague	guide	appraiser
protector	motivator	teacher
consultant	assessor	listener
helper	diagnoser	trusted guide
reviewer	facilitator	counsellor
expert	challenger	critical friend

(Turner *et al.* 1997: 33)

Discuss with your mentor the ways in which she can respond to your needs and promote your development.

BECOMING AN MFL TEACHER – THE STUDENT TEACHER'S POINT OF VIEW

CASE STUDY 1

Concluding statement

Being a teacher turned out to be much different than I expected or rather much more than I expected. I find being a teacher overwhelming as well as being very challenging. Over this year I have developed not only many skills but also as a person. My previous experiences of teaching really did not prepare me for the 'whole school experience'.

After the time spent at my first school experience school I felt that I was ready to be a 'real' teacher and that the rest of the course was simply a formality but beginning again at the second school experience school brought me back down to earth. For the first few days I felt that I was back at the start of the course again which was rather unnerving. The factor which struck me the most was the different ethos between the schools of my first and second placements. The 'feel' of the two schools is amazingly different. In my second school experience school I experienced a pastoral system based on 'Houses' rather than 'Years'.

Throughout this year I have developed in all the competence areas. I have built up a wide range of resources from my first placement for all years which I use to supplement the coursebooks and to add an element of fun to my lessons. My planning and preparation overall have become more efficient and I am more aware of how to approach teaching points and more able to pinpoint areas of teaching which need more attention. My record keeping has become more organised and consistent.

I have now developed my own classroom routines which I intend to improve on when I have my own classes and classrooms. I have drawn these routines and practices from observations made at both school experience schools. Throughout my practices I have built up my use of pair and group work which has helped me to forge better relationships within my groups. My relationships with both pupils and staff have developed well in both placements.

I have chosen five personal targets as a newly qualified teacher: displays, authentic materials, special needs, differentiation and extra-curricular activities. Not having my own classroom as a student teacher I am unable to provide my pupils with adequate and appropriate visual aids around the room. Next year I intend to make my classroom educationally stimulating as well as attractive and inviting. I am looking forward to developing in all of these areas next September.

CASE STUDY 2

Concluding statement

Like most people on the course, I suspect, I feel this year has gone surprisingly quickly. The overall impression I am left with, as the end approaches, is not simply of how much progress I have made, but rather of the realisation of how much more there is to teaching than just 'teaching'! This impression has rollercoasted as I started my practice at my second school, was offered a job there and shown what opportunities are available.

I found combining deadlines for college assignments and teaching quite taxing, partly due to the amount of time which has elapsed since doing my degree, allowing me to get out of practice where essays, etc. are concerned. This did get easier as I became more familiar with the criteria and got used to writing again. More specifically to do with teaching, looking back at my initial statement, I see that certain of my fears did not materialise, while others did in a slightly different shape to that which I had imagined.

My concerns over planning and preparation, for example, proved to be unfounded. Similarly, where classroom management and discipline were concerned, I found I had very few problems, and was if anything occasionally too strict – and this in turn brought about a problem which I had not foreseen, that of being so strict (wanting to keep too much control) that I was very distant from the pupils I was teaching, even to my tutor group. After Christmas, and even more so after Easter, I found that my own self-confidence allowed me to relax and concentrate more on how much pupils were learning, rather than how well they were behaving.

Being aware of pupils' academic abilities not only allowed me to plan more effectively, it also helped me to avoid problems with pupils who would find certain tasks either too easy or too difficult.

Task 2.12 MFL student teachers' point of view

Having read the two case studies, consider the following: did the student teachers' perception about teaching change in the course of their ITE? Can these changes be accounted for by the stages of development described in Table 2.4?

SUMMARY

MFL teaching is a highly complex profession requiring you to understand a number of related disciplines. Learning to teach MFL in the secondary school often features a steep initial learning curve followed by a long process of discovery going beyond the period of ITE into continuing professional development. Teaching MFL is very complex but it can be a very rewarding career.

FURTHER READING

Barnes, A. (2005) 'A passion for languages: motivation and preparation to teach modern foreign languages in eight cohorts of beginning teachers', *Research Papers in Education* 20(4): 349–69.

This article investigates the motivating factors which drive student teachers of MFL to choose to teach.

Grenfell, M. (1998) *Training Teachers in Practice*. Clevedon: Multilingual Matters.

This book is a thorough account of the dilemmas faced by student teachers of MFL as they undergo their initial teacher education.

Roberts, J. (1998) *Language Teacher Education*. London: Arnold.

Roberts' book offers an excellent insight into the development of language teachers and clearly outlines the associated theories and frameworks.

3 Teaching methods and learning strategies in modern foreign languages

INTRODUCTION

> From the survey of approaches and methods . . . we have seen that the history of language teaching in the last one hundred years has been characterised by a search for more effective ways of teaching second or foreign languages. The commonest solution to the 'language teaching problem' was seen to lie in the adoption of a new teaching approach or method. One result of this trend was the era of so-called designer or brand-name methods, that is, packaged solutions that can be described and marketed for use anywhere in the world.
>
> (Richards and Rodgers 2001: 244)

The current perspective on modern foreign languages (MFL) teaching, and indeed the approach which has been acknowledged most widely over the past two decades at least, communicative language teaching (CLT), can be seen as a somewhat eclectic assortment of traditional and novel approaches based on the tenet of the development in pupils of an ability to communicate in the target language (TL) rather than as a prescriptive method of how to teach MFL (see Mitchell 1994: 33). The way in which CLT has been interpreted and understood in the UK has been the focus of a great deal of recent discussion (see, Coyle 1999, 2002; Klapper 2003; Pachler 2000a; Kramsch 2006; Barnes 2007).

> at the micro level, the legacy of a widely-accepted yet narrow interpretation of the so-called 'communicative approach' common to most language learning classrooms, with its prescribed syllabus topics based on 'formulaic' transactional language, inadvertently promoted a reactive rather than interactive role for learners.
>
> (Coyle 2002: 157)

Some of the most disputed areas concern what might be termed 'over-interpretations', such as the virtual absence of any rules or application of grammar, and the supremacy of an (almost) exclusively TL environment where L1 has little or no function. The debate on these contentious areas of course never meant that all language teachers interpreted CLT in similar ways, but that the broad acceptance of CLT resulted in such an approach.

OBJECTIVES

By the end of this chapter you should:

- have developed some understanding of the methodological underpinning of current MFL practice;
- have gained some awareness of the weaknesses of CLT as well as some current and possible future methodological developments;
- have familiarised yourself with a framework for developing the main tenet of CLT, communicative competence;
- have become familiar with some aspects of the field of learning strategies.

Traditional aspects of CLT are the adherence to the model of presentation – practice – production (PPP). This common, but not universally accepted, framework for MFL teaching (see Pachler 2000a) presupposes the need to provide pupils with essential language forms, followed by work on exercises, activities and tasks to enable them to develop effective language habits. The process can be said to be complete when the pupils are able to use and manipulate these language forms to satisfy perceived needs, i.e. to generate language themselves. According to Nunan and Lamb (1996: 46), the PPP model is based on a view of learning as a linear process of understanding, internalising and activating knowledge and that the three stages are characterised by 'a gradual movement from high- to relative low-structure inter-actions (although many production tasks give the illusion of student control)'. At the different stages of the model, the teacher and learners have different roles (e.g. model, facilitator, monitor; listener, performer, interactor) and they feature different activity types (e.g. exposition, information gap, role play) and interaction modes (e.g. whole-class, pair, small group). Nunan and Lamb (ibid.: 46–7) conclude that the PPP model, while simple, is effective and useful for meeting *discrete* language objectives. For more contextualised and integrated objectives, however, more sophisticated models are required. Given the prevailing emphasis on narrowly transactional skills and memorisation of lexical items in the current interpretation of CLT in Britain, the PPP model can be said to possess fitness for a specific purpose (see also Pachler 2000a). There are, however, as alluded to in Chapter 1, developments to make the curriculum for MFL more challenging and engaging, and seen alongside progress in CLIL (content and language integrated learning), there will be a need to develop much more sophisticated and integrated methodological approaches towards teaching the language as learners move from 'learning new words and structures' to 'using language for real expression and communication'. For further information on CLIL, see Pachler *et al.* (2007) or http://www.cilt.org.uk/clip/index.htm.

The change in syllabus design in the 1980s away from a focus on the structural aspects of the TL (as exemplified through, for e.g., O level) to topics supposedly relevant to pupils is novel. These topics tend to centre, on the one hand, on the communicative needs of visitors to a country where the TL is spoken. On the other hand, examination specifications are constructed around so-called functions and speech acts, such as telling the time, how to express likes and dislikes or asking for the way (for a detailed list, see Neuner and Hunfeld 1993: 140–5). CLT, of which language practice through simulation and role play is an integral part, focuses on meaning and the conveyance of personal needs through language.

Most recently, the UK variant of CLT has been characterised by a 'methodological imperative' of maximum use of the TL for instruction and interaction, which is discussed in detail in Chapter 5. The introduction of CLT to MFL teaching in secondary schools can, among other things, be linked to theories and findings of (applied) linguistics as well as the comprehensivisation of the secondary sector and the considerable change in target audiences associated with it.

SOME ASPECTS OF CLT

MFL teaching methodology has been characterised by an emphasis on communicative competence with intercultural communicative competence coming increasingly to the fore (see e.g. the 2007 QCA NC proposals discussed in Chapter 1). This represented a redefinition and broadening of what was deemed to constitute proficiency in MFL learning away from the ability to translate, read and write texts towards an ability to respond, often by way of the spoken word, to aural and oral stimuli. 'Authenticity' of texts and tasks became increasingly important, as did using the TL in 'real' contexts for communicative purposes. The focus was on the ability to use the TL to communicate personal meaning rather than on knowledge about the TL together with an emphasis on active participation of learners and language use outside the classroom (see Mitchell 1994; Pachler 2000a).

In a bid to improve the ability of pupils to communicate in the TL, emphasis has increasingly been placed on the use of the TL for instruction and interaction. As contact with MFL for secondary school pupils invariably comes through language learning, the structured and limited exposure to the TL in a classroom environment, rather than acquisition, subconscious development of language skills devoid of formal explanation, the emphasis on TL use and the focus on 'authentic' material can be seen as an attempt to counterbalance the 'context-reduced' (Roberts 1992: 21) nature of the MFL learning process.

The distinction between language *acquisition* and language *learning* is important in the context of MFL teaching and learning in the secondary school as most pupils are in the main, and for a host of reasons, unable to immerse themselves in the TL and the target culture(s). Eric Hawkins (1987: 99) memorably described the MFL experience of British pupils through the metaphor of 'gardening in a gale'. The limited time available in the school curriculum and the limited exposure to the TL make it difficult for pupils to retain what they have learnt in the classroom when re-entering the world of English outside, as what happens there does not, in the main, reinforce the learning that has taken place in the classroom (see also Barnes 2007).

On the one hand, this fact puts the onus on MFL teachers, among other things, to do the following:

- structure the language that pupils are exposed to;
- select relevant, varied and appropriate material for them;
- provide them with ample opportunities to practise and develop, among others, the skills of listening, speaking, reading and writing;
- facilitate the development of confidence in their own ability;
- develop their cultural and structural understanding.

On the other hand, limitations are imposed on pupils by their learning environment, e.g.:

- the limited amount of curriculum time;
- the limited access to undivided attention by the teacher;
- the lack of exposure to the TL;
- the geographical and emotional distance from the countries and cultures where the TL is spoken.

These limitations make it necessary for MFL teachers to aim to equip pupils with the necessary skills and strategies to learn the TL independently (for some ideas, see Jackson 2004).

For pupils to develop linguistic and communicative competence, the teacher needs to structure the learning environment in a way the pupils perceive to be purposeful. It was with this in mind that local groups of teachers developed clear objectives and defined syllabuses as part of the graded objectives movement in MFL teaching and learning during the 1970s and 1980s (see King 1991; Page and Hewett 1987).

CLT builds on the understanding that the purpose of language is to communicate, and that communication (see Halliday 1975, as summarised in Richards and Rodgers 1986: 70–1) is:

- instrumental (to get things);
- regulatory (to control others);
- interactional (to engage with others);
- personal (to express personal meaning);
- heuristic (to learn and discover);
- imaginative (to create a world of imagination);
- representational (to communicate information).

Pupils need to value the purposes of MFL learning and, at the same time, be aware of what they must do to achieve the relevant objectives. Peter Bimmel (1993: 5–6) identifies the following characteristics of strategic learning:

- setting a goal/an objective;
- devising a plan how to achieve the goal/objective;
- putting the plan into action;
- evaluating whether the goal/objective has been achieved.

These general features of learning are an integral part of the development of competence in the TL. As they are exposed to more and more language, pupils increasingly have to manage the process of learning for themselves. Each pupil is different, will favour different teaching and learning styles and will employ different strategies to manage her own MFL learning.

CLT should place the pupil at the centre of the MFL learning process. Nunan sees the role of the learner in CLT as that of 'a negotiator, interactor, giving as well as taking' (1989: 195). One key feature of CLT is its principal aim of providing pupils with the necessary language and communication skills to use the TL effectively and in a purposeful way. This involves communicating to satisfy personal needs as well as the structuring and sequencing of the learning experience.

Littlewood (1981: 85–95) places CLT in a methodological framework consisting of pre-communicative activities, which he subdivides into 'structural' and 'quasi-communicative' activities, and communicative activities, where he differentiates between 'functional communication' and 'social interaction' activities. Littlewood points out that there are no clear dividing lines between stages of learning. According to him, the learner should be guided from dependence on the teacher and opportunities to use the language in the classroom, to using language alone and in real authentic situations. Pre-communicative activities can involve teacher-centred classroom activities (see Barnes (2007), for some practical work on pre-communicative activities). The teacher selects the content of a unit of work, negotiates learning objectives and organises the presentation of material in a structured way. The quasi-communicative activities are intended to offer opportunities to practise the newly learnt language in situations which can easily be related to real life. Functional communication activities take this progression one step further and are based on the premise that TL use is positively reinforced if it can be seen to work. If the speaker uses language to good effect and she achieves the intended purpose for personal gain, the forms of language used stand more chance of being personalised and internalised. To this end, information gap exercises can be devised for use in the classroom. They involve the transfer of information which is known only to one user through linguistic means. Social interaction activities require the refinement of language use involving more than simply conveying a message, but doing so in a way which is appropriate to the cultural context. Such information gap tasks, however, do not have to be the only 'outcome'. Production and manipulation of the language could, for example, be something creative, e.g. a group outcome, a specific concrete product (e.g. a booklet), or a video clip.

In the UK context, CLT has frequently been characterised by a marginalisation of grammar in the learning process and a diminishing focus on accuracy. This, however, need not be the case. Mitchell (1994: 38–9) summarises CLT in six key descriptions:

1   Classroom activities should maximise opportunities for learners to use the target language for meaningful purposes, with their attention on the messages they are creating and the task they are completing, rather than on correctness of language form and language structure.

2   Learners trying their best to use the target language creatively and unpredictably are bound to make errors; this is a normal part of language learning, and constant correction is unnecessary, and even counterproductive.

3   Language analysis and grammar explanation may help some learners, but extensive experience of target language use helps everyone!

4   Effective language teaching is responsive to the needs and interests of the individual learner.

5   Effective language learning is an active process, in which the learner takes increasing responsibility for his or her progress.

6   The effective teacher aims to facilitate, not control, the language learning process.

A CRITICAL EXAMINATION OF CLT

While CLT has been and continues to be very influential in MFL teaching and learning in the UK, 'it is not *the* panacea of FL teaching' (Pachler 2000a: 38). This section lists some of its shortcomings; for a detailed critical examination of CLT, see Pachler (2000a).

> In the UK developments have led, by-and-large, to a narrow transactional-functional orientation in which pupils are prepared for the linguistic (and non-linguistic) needs of tourists . . . with the emphasis on 'getting by'. On the one hand, this approach is characterised by a heavy emphasis on recall of often random lexical items and phrases derived from narrowly defined, idealised interactions and exchanges at the cost of transfer of knowledge and skills across topics. On the other hand, it tends to ignore the teenage learner's communicative needs and does not allow her to engage in meaningful and realistic interaction, both supposedly central tenets of communicative methodology.
>
> (ibid.: 30)

The following realignments to CLT warrant consideration:

1 *Developing grammatical and discourse competence as subsets of communicative competence:* For Roberts (1992: 27), the main deficiency of CLT is that, contrary to some of its proponents' assumptions, there is a difference between learning a language *for* communication and learning it *as* communication. He proposes a process starting from 'structure' leading via controlled practice to 'function'. In other words, Roberts views the teaching of grammatical forms as a prerequisite for meaningful language use

by reiterating that 'doing is subservient to knowing'. He is concerned that in the MFL context, pupils tend not to perceive the need to communicate in the TL and thinks that this poses a real problem as the 'intention to mean' is a fundamental principle of CLT. While we do not argue for a return to the grammar-translation paradigm here, we advocate an increased focus on grammatical competence and discourse competence, i.e. the inclusion of longer utterances and texts, as subsets of communicative competence. Indeed, the 1999 MFL National Curriculum Orders included an increased emphasis on grammar compared with earlier versions. (See Chapter 7 for a detailed discussion of the role of grammar in MFL teaching and learning.) Without sufficient grammatical knowledge and application, the essential production of language is inevitably reduced and, one could say, impoverished, as is the pupil's potential to work with language in any way independently.

2 *Reappraising the aims of MFL teaching:* CLT, with its transactional orientation, reflected the changes and redirections prevalent when the focus moved to a functional and vocational rationale for MFL teaching and learning. A reappraisal of the aims of MFL teaching and learning towards an educational orientation has been suggested by some commentators:

> [the] primary aim should be, like the primary aim of literacy, to enhance the learner's semiotic system, to help him/her to abstract his/her thought from the contextual prison of spontaneous concepts in order to make language a more autonomous object, of which the learner is more fully aware and over which greater control can be exercised.
>
> (Bauckham 1995: 31)

This would require an increased methodological focus on intellectually and cognitively challenging activities, tasks, texts and contexts (see Pachler 2000a: 35–6). Crucial questions include whether we want learners to know *about* language and/or be able to *use* it appropriately, whether pupils should learn lots of vocabulary and phrases well and/or whether they should be able to apply grammatical rules and patterns in order to generate new language they feel in control of, and whether pupils should be guided almost exclusively by the teacher and their plans for the language learning and/or whether pupils should develop more independent ways of working with languages, for example, through learning and language learning strategies. See Macaro (2006) for an interesting overview of strategies and how their interpretation may be reconceptualised. See also the two-part Special Issue of the *Language Learning Journal* 35(1) and 35(2) in 2007 on Learner Strategies.

3 *Redefining of the notion of authenticity:* We have already noted that CLT can be characterised by syllabus design taking account of topics that are supposedly relevant, namely, ones that centre on the vocabulary and situations encountered by people when visiting a country where the TL is spoken. While adult learners often draw (part of) their motivation from the goal of visiting a foreign country, this is less true for pupils studying the TL at secondary school. Some of the situations presumed relevant for visitors to countries where the TL is spoken, such as making arrangements for train travel, booking hotel rooms, drinking in bars, eating in restaurants, buying petrol, etc., are of limited relevance for pupils, for instance, because of their

different experiences of the world. This raises questions about the 'authenticity' of topics, tasks and material: what are authentic language situations for adolescents? Should more creativity and imagination be incorporated rather than what could be described as the tourist scenario?

Hornsey (1994: 7) suggest that 'plausibility [might be] a more useful guiding principle than authenticity and that for a teacher there are other -ity words that demand attention'. These, in his view, are:

- learnability
- repeatability
- tangibility
- useability
- pronounceability.

Hornsey's suggestions are certainly useful from a linguistic perspective, but the content is still open to debate. MFL teachers working with low achieving and poorly motivated pupils in particular have for many years experimented with tasks that motivate their pupils in a more appropriate way for their specific lives, both locally and from an age context. (See Graham 2002, 2004; Williams *et al.* 2002, 2004, for some interesting work on learners' motivation and to what they attribute their success or otherwise when learning a language.) The change in the notion of 'authenticity', that is, away from situations and material focusing on (the) culture(s) of the TL towards those with more immediate relevance to pupils, i.e. situations and material focusing on using the TL in the UK as part of pupils' everyday experience of life, underpins to some extent the inclusion of vocational contexts in MFL teaching and learning.

4 *Towards 'optimal use' of the TL:* The requirement to maximise the use of the TL by teachers and pupils in earlier versions of the NC MFL Orders can be seen to be at least partly based on the misguided notion that MFL learning is comparable to mother tongue learning (see Pachler 2000a: 33–4). Among many other things, this emphasis on maximum TL use can be seen to lead to interactional classroom dynamics, which are heavily dominated by teachers:

> [whereas] teachers of any subject may tend to tell their pupils 'when to talk, what to talk about, when to stop talking and how well they talked' . . ., FL teachers appear also to prescribe for pupils the very words, even features of words, with which to talk.
>
> (Westgate *et al.* 1985: 276)

More recent versions of the NC MFL Orders move towards what Macaro (2000) calls the 'optimal use' position from a 'total exclusion' or 'maximal use' position in earlier versions. For a detailed discussion of TL-related issues, see Chapter 5. This dominance of the TL in MFL classrooms was found by Lee *et al.* (1998) to be one of the barriers to language learning perceived by many of the pupils involved in their study: pupils had a tendency to feel lost or confused. When learning, clarity for learners as to what they are 'supposed to be doing' is of course of utmost importance. Taken solely from the perspective of the learner, therefore, the TL 'imperative' requires reappraisal (see Meiring and Norman 2002).

5 *Developing intercultural (communicative) competence:* Gerhard Neuner and Hans Hunfeld (1993: 87) note that one of the deficiencies of CLT is its failure to take sufficient account of the specificity of different target audiences. In order to address this imbalance they argue the case for an intercultural approach as an extension to CLT (ibid.: 106–27). As a specific characteristic feature of this intercultural approach, they advocate a didactic concept which fosters comparisons of life and reality in the pupils' own world with that of the countries where the TL is spoken. They warn, though, that this process is characterised by a danger of misunderstanding, threat and incomprehension, which needs careful handling by the teacher. For a more detailed discussion of target culture learning and teaching, see Chapter 8.

Intercultural competence and intercultural communicative competence need to be distinguished here. The former describes the ability to know about and empathise with TL speakers and understand the cultural context in which they live, work and speak, albeit if necessary in their mother tongue or a *lingua franca,* the latter includes in addition the ability to interact in the TL (see e.g. Byram 1997). The 2007 NC Orders, in addition to offering some interesting suggestions on making the content more creative, include specific reference to intercultural understanding:

- appreciating the richness and diversity of other cultures;
- recognising that there are different ways of seeing the world, and developing an international outlook.

Indeed, the proposals for MFL are prefaced by a statement of how important languages are and include the following:

> Languages are part of the cultural richness of our society and the world in which we live and work. Learning languages contributes to mutual understanding, a sense of global citizenship and personal fulfilment. Pupils learn to appreciate different countries, cultures, communities and people. By making comparisons, they gain insight into their own culture and society. The ability to understand and communicate in another language is a lifelong skill for education, employment and leisure in this country and throughout the world.
>
> (http://www.qca.org.uk/secondarycurriculumreview/
> subject/ks3/modern-foreign-languages/index.htm)

6 *Integrating Information and Communications Technology (ICT) in MFL teaching and learning:* Noss and Pachler (1999), in their analysis of the impact of ICT on pedagogy, argue that ICT has considerable potential and that it makes new things possible in new ways. Effective ICT use, they posit, has considerable implications for the role of the teacher and requires fundamental changes to teaching methodology. The successful integration of ICT in MFL teaching and learning is not easy, and involves a number of pedagogical decisions. What are the learning objectives? Can using ICT enable pupils to achieve these learning objectives more efficiently/with more

engagement/in a more authentic manner? Learning should lead the technology: the planning process is easily inspired by new gadgetry and software, and this is not necessarily a problem, provided it is the learning which remains paramount. Teachers also have to acknowledge the world in which most pupils live, i.e. dominated by technology (mobile phones, iPods, chat rooms, etc.). There are debates in the ICT and MFL communities over whether integration is the correct approach. A good website to explore some of these issues is http://www.ict4lt.org. This site has sections on a wide variety of ICT and MFL debates, including teaching using ICT, assessment, etc. Another relevant site, which offers help at different levels of experience, is http://www.languages-ict.org.uk. (Some of these issues are discussed in Chapter 11 and others in Chapter 12; see also Leask and Pachler (2005) and Hood (2000).)

A FRAMEWORK FOR SEQUENCING

On the basis of the discussion of aspects of CLT above we suggest a structured approach to MFL teaching leading to the development of pupil independence. This framework for sequencing, summarised in Figure 3.1, builds on the traditional PPP paradigm and the limitations of PPP identified earlier also apply here. It is important to note that the practical examples given for illustration do not refer to the same topic throughout. Also, they are not aimed at the same level of linguistic proficiency.

Five stages of sequencing:		
Continuous assessment	introducing the topic	Evaluation
	presenting a new language focus	
	practising language forms	
	exploiting the language	
	summative assessment and evaluation	

Figure 3.1 A framework for sequencing

INTRODUCING THE TOPIC

A sense of ownership in and responsibility for the learning process are the first step to autonomy and personalisation. The introduction of a topic can involve the negotiation of appropriate objectives in order to meet individual pupils' needs but should involve the making explicit of objectives, where possible in the TL, but this is not always the most appropriate way, to give pupils a sense of where they are going and why they are being asked to carry out certain activities. Pupils should be aware of the value of a topic and, on occasion, they can be asked to identify key language for themselves. This process of negotiation and discussion enables the teacher to establish her role as a facilitator of the learning process and helps the pupil in adopting an active, participatory role.

One possible strategy you can adopt when introducing a new topic is what Grell and Grell (1985: 105–6, 117–33) call 'to send positive reciprocal emotions'. In order to foster an atmosphere conducive to learning and to motivate pupils to learn, Grell and Grell suggest the teacher might, for instance, try to relate a given topic to personal experiences, tell the pupils something funny or express positive expectations about, show personal enthusiasm for and use a visual stimulus relating to the topic for pupils to comment upon or respond to. Careful consideration needs to be given to whether and how this be done using the TL.

One strategy, based here on the topic of education, which enables pupils to draw on their existing knowledge of the TL and culture and which can be applied to a number of different contexts, is brainstorming (Box 3.1). Though we do not suggest using brainstorming every time a new topic is introduced, we feel it is a good example of a strategy, which allows future learning to build on existing knowledge. Again, careful consideration needs to be given to whether and how this be done using the TL.

Box 3.1 Brainstorming

1   You ask pupils to brainstorm words they associate with the topic in small groups. A nominated scribe notes down all words that group members can come up with. Asking pupils to work within a given time limit can add pace and a sense of urgency.

2   The pupils group their list of lexical items into categories, for instance, buildings, subjects, qualifications, people. Pupils should be encouraged to use the TL and explain contributions to one another.

3   Next you ask the pupils to produce an illustrated guide in the TL on what they feel they ought to know about the topic 'education' for display.

4   Public display of the various guides allows critical analysis of the pupils' work by the teacher through comparison of outcomes of different groups. The emerging gaps in knowledge can be formulated into learning objectives. The teacher's role is to place the content of displays and the learning objectives into a communicative context. This way, through a consolidation of existing knowledge and skills, pupils should be able to experience some sense of ownership of and interest in the topic.

Task 3.1 Communicating lesson objectives

On the basis of lesson observation, how can the objectives of a lesson and a unit of work be communicated to pupils without using English?

Survey a small group of pupils to find out what they think the objectives of a particular lesson or unit of work are.

PRESENTING A NEW LANGUAGE FOCUS: THE PPP MODEL

Having identified objectives and particular linguistic and learning needs, the teacher needs to expose pupils to the language content required. As the teacher you are the principal (linguistic) resource in the classroom and it is your responsibility to select and organise the content into manageable chunks, encouraging the development of the skills of listening, speaking, reading and writing equally. This should be done within a communicative context as pupils need to recognise the short-term and long-term value of these skills. While you need to ensure you give pupils enough time to allow them to familiarise themselves with, as well as assimilate and accommodate, new linguistic items, given the need to progress to higher NC levels, you also need to ensure new words, phrases and structures are used in context and that more complicated utterances are produced as quickly as possible. You can use the PPP model: presentation; practice; and production:

1   *Presentation stage*: needs rigorous focus, use of meaningful context to avoid unnecessary translation into L1.

2   *Practice stage*: needs to be very *structured* – intensive teacher-led and pupil activities (questions and answers, etc.) – need a range of practice activities *before* you can expect pupils to produce and combine/manipulate new language.

3   *Production stage*: needs withdrawal of written/teacher support to encourage spontaneity and independence.

Presentation stage

The presentation stage should include the teaching and learning of vocabulary, phrases and structures (see Field, 2007, for some more practical examples). These linguistic and structural elements should not be taught in isolation from the culture and potential communicative contexts. Visual aids, such as flashcards, the overhead projector (OHP), a PowerPoint presentation (in conjunction with Interactive Whiteboard) or mime and gesture, enable pupils to assimilate words and phrases. Not every item relevant to the topic needs to be taught. Independence in MFL learning requires pupils to use dictionaries, reference material and (contextual) clues to interpret meaning. As a consequence, the teacher needs to ensure that pupils have the skills to carry out related tasks. The aim at this stage is to begin the process of mastering the linguistic forms so that, at a later stage, pupils can draw on these in real communicative situations for themselves. The pupils need to be aware of the communicative potential of language forms.

On the basis of either a lesson you have observed, or a lesson (or partial lesson) you have planned and taught yourself, evaluate how effective the PPP model is in introducing new language items.

Using Figure 3.2, analyse exactly how each phase was effective or otherwise in helping pupils make progress with their learning.

Presenting new language

- Pupils need lots of chances to repeat new language. Just because they repeat a word or phrase, it certainly doesn't mean they know it.
- Especially at the beginning, make sure you plan for this with explicitly writing the presentation question sequence and repetition strategies into your lesson plan.
- Think carefully about how you will use definite or indefinite articles, negatives, etc.
- When presenting language, think about the variety of ways you can repeat (e.g. speed, tone/volume of voice, different groupings, different number of times, repeat only if it is correct, etc.).
- You also need to consider the variety of resources though which you can present language.
- Repetition, yes/no questions, alternative prompts (e.g. is it a cake or a sandwich?), open questions . . .
- You have a huge choice of resources to present new language imaginatively.

Practising language

An important, some would argue *the* most important, phase is practice; yet it is the element often most neglected. Without sufficient practice, pupils will be unable to produce or manipulate new language: class management problems are often very closely bound up with planning (e.g. lack of clarity or suitability) or practice issues (i.e. pupils do not feel confident about the new language and are, therefore, daunted by the production activity).

Break the language learning process into chunks which are easily accessible. Think about what the pupils need to know before they can move on. For example, don't assume they can use the third person because they can use the first, or the negative because they can use the affirmative. Your practice activities need very careful planning.

Producing/using/being creative with language

To create a balance between the more mechanical drilling of language and more creative use of language, think about how pupils might 'play with' the language, use it for more genuine purposes, create new language with the basic elements, incorporate previously learnt language . . .

Figure 3.2 An annotated example of the PPP model

Question-and-answer work is a very important teacher-led strategy in presenting new language, whether the teacher is using simple flashcards, individual pictures on the OHP or an animated PowerPoint presentation. Oliver (1994: 16) notes:

> a major advantage of question-and-answer work is precisely that the teacher, by the careful choice of questions asked, can ensure that learners are helped to move from supported to unsupported use of given linguistic items in a gradual way.

Oliver (1994: 16) proposes the following question types:

- yes/no questions: requiring the pupil to associate a TL word or phrase with meaning;
- alternative questions: requiring the pupil to repeat a word or phrase, to reproduce language using known material;
- negative questions: providing a bridge from reproductive to productive use of language;
- target questions: requiring the pupil to generate (whole-sentence) answers.

The approach exemplified in Box 3.2 is used to illustrate some *basic principles*, with which all student teachers learning to teach MFL should be familiar. It is for this reason that the basic resource of flashcards are used in the first example, despite the myriad of exciting resources available, e.g. through ICT such as PowerPoint and the interactive whiteboard. The risk in choosing such resources to illustrate basics would be that the resource may mask the fundamental message. It is clear that effective use of, for example, presentation software can do a great deal regarding presentation and practice, often in a very stimulating manner. However, the basic principles of the learning process have to remain built in to the use of such resources. (For more ideas on ICT, see Chapter 12.)

Pugh and Murphy (1993: 2–3) show how flashcards and mime games can be used effectively to reinforce new vocabulary (Box 3.2).

Box 3.2 Flashcard games

Teacher/Pupil chooses one flashcard and spins it quickly in front of class. Class try to identify flashcard.

Teacher/Pupil displays group of flashcards. Pupils look away and one flashcard is removed. Class identify missing one.

Teacher/Pupil displays group of flashcards. Teacher/Pupil names all but one of the flashcards. Class identify the missing one.

Flashcards are displayed. Teacher/Pupil names a flashcard and another pupil must point to the appropriate flashcard. This can be played in teams, with winning pupil identifying/removing the appropriate picture.

Flashcards are displayed and numbered. Teacher/pupil names a flashcard and class note the appropriate number. Alternatively, teacher/pupil says a number and class must identify the flashcard.

Teacher/Pupil chooses one flashcard without the class seeing. Class must ask questions to try to identify the flashcard chosen. Teacher/pupil reply 'Non' until flashcard is correctly guessed.

Teacher/Pupil displays one flashcard and makes one statement. If the statement matches the flashcard, class repeats it. If the statement is false, the class stays silent. Class members who make an error are out. Winner is the last person out.

Divide the class into teams. Each team has two chairs labelled: true/false. Teacher/Pupil displays one flashcard and makes one statement. If the statement matches the flashcard, a team member sits on the 'true' chair and vice versa. Points are awarded for sitting on the right chair.

Divide the class into teams. Place a flashcard face down in front of each team member. Against the clock, each team member in turn looks at their flashcard and identifies it. The fastest team is the winner.

The OHP is obviously one alternative to flashcards for presenting and reinforcing new language. It can also serve as a stimulus for language games and as visual support for the use of the TL. For a more detailed discussion of the potential of the OHP, see Tierney and Humphreys (1992). It should be remembered that one aspect of successful methodology in any subject is variety: the growing availability of exciting ICT resources does not mean alternatives should be dispensed with. Sometimes the use of a simple picture or creatively produced visual aid is much more effective for the particular circumstances.

Another possible activity in the context of presenting new language focuses on places in a town. Flashcards are placed around the room. A pupil is blindfolded and spun around. The teacher points to individual flashcards and pupils ask in the TL where individual places in town are, e.g. '¿Dónde está el banco?' ('Where is the bank?'). The pupil who was spun around has to reply by pointing at the correct flashcard and by responding, for instance at a basic level, with 'El banco está allí' ('The bank is over there'). Then, symbols for directions can be presented on an overhead transparency. Pupils repeat and listen carefully. Once pupils are familiar with the new words, short conversations can be presented on a tape. Pupils listen for places sought and directions given. Eliciting non-verbal responses from pupils, such as marking simple plans with the appropriate places, ensure that the vocabulary presented has been recognised in context.

Task 3.3 Presenting new language forms

During lesson observations, note the different resources and methods used by different MFL teachers to introduce new language.

Discuss with pupils to what extent gestures, colours, size, position, voice modulation or movement can help them memorise new language and test out these ideas in your own teaching.

Box 3.3 A PowerPoint presentation

This example, from Niki Overton, PGCE MFL student teacher at the University of Warwick 2006–07, shows selected slides from a PowerPoint presentation used for one lesson with a Year 10 class (Figure 3.3).

Here are Niki's comments on the presentation:

I find PowerPoint a really good tool within the classroom. Not only does it help engage the pupils, with use of colourful images, etc., but it also aids the teaching as it provides a clear structure to the lesson.

The PowerPoint starts with a quick starter activity, where pupils fill in the gaps with the given words in the pool at the bottom. It is always helpful to number things on PowerPoint as this eases the task of going through the answers afterwards. I then outline the objectives and show the title and date clearly.

The slides that follow were included for revision purposes. The vocabulary in the box flies in after the answer is given. This helps recall of vocabulary.

I try to use different shapes to vary the slides and to keep the pupils focused.

The next few slides introduce new vocabulary. Again I have things flying in to keep the interest. I try to find images that the pupils will like, however, one needs to choose images carefully. For example, my Year 10 pupils thought slide 13 was of a boy smoking!

I always try to have answers to listening activities on PowerPoint to hasten the process of going through answers.

The next few slides explain the grammar point and give opportunity to practise. It's always important to use a good, big font so that pupils can read and copy down accurately.

If I am going to do a speaking activity, I will usually have this on the Power-Point to make it clear as to what I expect and to give pupils something to work from. This is especially helpful for the less able learner.

Slide 24 contains the answers to a writing activity, which again speeds up the process of giving answers.

The final slide is a quick game of three in a row which is used as a plenary.

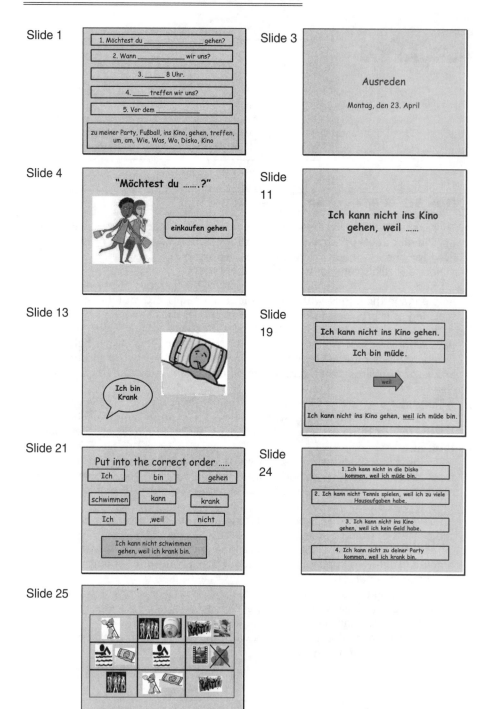

Figure 3.3 A PowerPoint presentation

Practice stage

There is no clear dividing line between the presentation and practice of language forms but, instead, there is a gradual change of emphasis. Practice is one stage in the continuous process of internalising selected language. A behaviourist, habit-forming approach is not necessarily out of place if the pupil is aware of its purpose. Repetition exercises can be effective and it is possible for them to be directed by pupils, provided they realise the value of the exercises and can see the ultimate goal (there is great value in emphasising to pupils *why* a certain activity is valuable in the language learning process: even better if the pupils themselves can identify why a task or activity is of benefit). Although the skills of listening, speaking, reading and writing can be developed independently of each other, this is not advisable as pupils must understand the need to integrate skills in order to be able to communicate effectively. Not to work towards the integration of skills poses the risk of producing 'walking phrase books' incapable of using language spontaneously and of generating their own language in response to stimuli. Coursebooks often provide effective exercises to allow pupils to practise and to experiment with language. Written exercises must relate to the pupils' need to write, listening exercises must contain the type of language which is comprehensible to them. 'Authentic' texts, or texts made to look 'authentic', provide a link between the classroom and the outside world, MFL learning and its use. The traditional, grammar-based approach fell short in this respect:

> One of the major reasons for questioning the adequacy of grammatical syllabuses lies in the fact that even when we have described the grammatical (and lexical) meaning of a sentence, we have not accounted for the way it is used as an utterance.
>
> (Wilkins 1976: 10–11)

Just as the TL should be practised in the context of potential 'authentic' use, it should also be relevant to individual pupils' needs. There is no greater frustration for pupils than practising until the skill, word, phrase, structure, etc. has been perfected and then not enjoying the opportunity of putting it to good use. The teacher needs to provide opportunities for progression beyond what Littlewood calls 'quasi-communicative' activities. Once again, the emphasis and focus should gradually shift to allow for a smooth transition to the exploitation of language.

Useful in the context of choosing effective tasks for practising the TL remains, we feel, Heafford's typology of tasks (1990: 88) despite the fact that the 'value' attributed to activities appears to be determined by unstructured observation of pupils' attitudes to tasks undertaken in the classroom rather than by empirical research. Bearing in mind the point made above regarding pupils understanding the reason for carrying out a particular activity, some of the typology below might be different it the pupils had had an insight into this (Box 3.4).

> **Box 3.4** Heafford's typology of tasks
>
> *Pupil activities of low value*
>
> Choral/individual repetition.
> Reading aloud from the textbook.
> Reading out dialogues/role-plays.
> Translating.
> Copying from board/book.
> Word searches.
>
> *Pupil activities of mixed value*
>
> Doing drill-like activities.
> Pupil–pupil dialogue.
> Receiving grammatical explanations.
>
> *Pupil activities of high value*
>
> Listening to the target language.
> Replying to questions in the FL.
> Asking questions in the FL.
> Engaging in dramatic activities.
> Increasing active/passive vocabulary.
> Reading silently.
> Relating language to social/cultural context.
> Doing written work of an error-avoiding nature.

Class surveys can allow the repetition of simple questions avoiding the possible boredom arising from having to say the same thing to the same person repeatedly. There are many ways in which such surveys might be carried out. Dependent on the class, it may be most appropriate from a management perspective to limit the survey to a small group of pupils sitting together, whereas in a different class, pupils could select e.g. 10 pupils to question. The survey can be differentiated by encouraging the inclusion of an additional question of the pupil's own choosing should they wish.

Pupils often know numbers, but cannot use them at speed. The following activity was devised as part of a bank of active learning strategies by MFL teachers in the New Mills and Buxton area. The purpose of the activity is to practise numbers. Pupils are placed in groups of four. One is the spokesperson, one an accountant, one an inspector and one a researcher.

The teacher explains that she is an auctioneer. She will sell scrabble letters in lots to the highest bidder. The activity usually works best if letters are sold in groups of five or six. The groups of pupils need to consider how much each set of letters might be worth. Points will be awarded for the group that can produce the longest word or the most words in the TL at the end of the game from the letters purchased. Points are awarded for the number of letters purchased and also for money not spent. Each group has 500 units of the foreign currency. The inspector checks that other groups do not overspend, the accountant organises budgets and the researcher helps the spokesperson. After a while, roles within the groups are swapped. To prevent bids of 500 units in one go, groups need to be told that they may only bid in units of 3, which can be changed to 7 or 9, etc. later in the game.

This activity tends to be rather noisy and involves pupils shouting numbers out at great speed. The activity is popular and effective, but does rely on the teacher ensuring appropriate behaviour throughout. Pupils with difficulties in number work might benefit from the use of calculators or other aids.

Task 3.4 Practising language forms

Observe a number of MFL lessons and note the frequency of use of the types of activities listed by Heafford.

Also, find out from pupils how valuable they found the different activities. How do pupil responses compare with Heafford's categories?

Try to ascertain from pupils exactly what they understood to be the purpose of a particular activity.

Production stage

Language should be used in a meaningful way. Opportunities for 'authentic' language use in the classroom are limited. 'Real' communication in the classroom comprises mainly 'classroom talk' and tends to be transactional in nature. This is a valuable part of the process as well as the desired outcome of MFL learning. Pupils need to borrow pens, share books, interact with the teacher. To conduct these transactions and inter-actions in English represents a wasted opportunity and devalues the potential of the TL. You should aim to devise situations where the goal is not achieved unless the TL is used: certainly any language which is known to pupils should be used from that point onwards in the TL (e.g. is there ever a reason to use English numbers once a class has learnt them in TL?).

Individual pupils should be able to use the TL in a way that suits their own needs and personalise it. So-called 'information gap' activities are often used to stimulate communication. Given that pupils progress at different rates and in different ways the teacher needs to tailor activities to suit the individual pupil. Differentiation can facili-tate this process and is discussed in Chapter 9.

Personalisation can be seen to have taken place when linguistic competence is no longer the focus: 'In communicative activities, the production of linguistic forms becomes subordinate to higher level decisions, related to the communication of meanings. . . . The criterion for success is whether the meaning is conveyed effectively' (Littlewood 1981: 89).

Obviously, an approach like this presupposes the adoption of specific roles by both pupils and the teacher. Pupils need to assume responsibility for their own learning through active participation. They are unlikely to display this desirable behaviour trait automatically and will have to be accustomed to working in such a way. In the process of working independently a pupil interprets and generates language 'in terms of what s/he already and uniquely knows' (Dam 1990: 22). As the teacher, you are then no longer merely the source for information, but an advisor, facilitator, consultant and fellow communicator. In addition, you are the assessor, recorder and reporter of pupils' progress.

Figure 3.4 represents the planning of an independent study unit, but also serves as an example for project-based classroom work. The first stage of planning is the identification of an end-of-unit goal. In this case, the goal is to produce an illustrated family tree on behalf of a friend, who must be interviewed to provide the necessary information. The interview and the presentation will be conducted independently of the teacher. This stage is represented by the centre of Figure 3.4. To qualify for this stage, pupils have to prove their ability by completing some tasks. These are represented by tasks inside the second frame. Obviously the tasks are relevant to working independently. If, however, pupils are unable to complete the core tasks, they receive support by being able to attempt simpler tasks, represented on the outside of the diagram. If, for example, a pupil is unable to copy relevant vocabulary and phrases free from spelling errors, she should be encouraged to develop those skills by attempting the word searches and crosswords. Clearly, activities are related to each other and pupils have access to exercises and materials to guide their own development. They may, for instance, choose to focus on particular skill areas. This should give the you the opportunity to monitor individuals' progress.

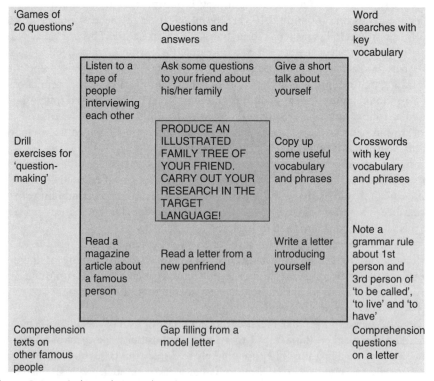

Figure 3.4 An independent study unit

Some pupils will be able to enter the scheme at core task level, others will attempt to do so, but quickly realise the need to step back a stage. Others will choose, or be guided, to enter the process at the initial stage. If accustomed to using dictionaries and reference material, pupils can be given the responsibility to direct their own learning. Those pupils who are not able to complete the core task in the allocated time can do so as part of their homework.

For a more detailed discussion of independent and autonomous learning, see Pachler and Field (1999), Bishop (2006) and Allford and Pachler (2007).

ASSESSMENT OF PUPILS

Assessment, which needs to cover the skills of listening, speaking, reading and writing equally, should not only be seen as coming at the end of the learning process but as an integral part; it should, therefore, be both continuous and summative, both assessment *of* learning and assessment *for* learning, that is, assessment which incorporates feedback indicating how a learner can improve. Pupils do not progress at the same rate in all four skills and they need to be aware of the progress they make. Diagnostic feedback, i.e. the teacher telling pupils (and the pupils finding out for themselves) what they need to do to improve, is an important part of the learning process. Assessment should serve to motivate and inform pupils, but also inform the teaching process and feed into planning and the evaluation of learning opportunities. Assessment and feedback are central aspects of MFL teaching and learning and are discussed in detail in Chapter 10, illustrating how effective assessment can move pupils forward in their learning (see also Barnes and Hunt 2003; Jones and Black 2006).

EVALUATION OF TEACHING

In addition to assessing pupils' achievement, performance and attainment, there is a need for you to evaluate the approaches employed and the tasks and materials used on an ongoing basis, i.e. lesson by lesson. For lesson evaluation from a practical perspective when learning to teach, see also Chapter 4 and Pachler and Redondo (2007). Nunan provides a useful overview checklist for evaluation purposes, which is summarised in Figure 3.5 (adapted from Nunan 1989: 135–8):

LEARNING STRATEGIES

One aspect of MFL teaching, which has received increased attention in recent years, is learner training, i.e. teaching pupils how to learn. Commonly communication strategies and learning strategies are distinguished. Communication strategies allow the learner to overcome a limited linguistic repertoire to ensure communication of meaning takes place. They appear to be more difficult to teach. Learning strategies have been categorised into 'metacognitive' strategies (concerned with managing learning), 'affective' strategies (preparing oneself emotionally and attitudinally for the

Stage	Evaluation criteria
Goals and rationale	Objectives should be realistic, relevant and made explicit to pupils.
Input	Language output must be preceded by input. In order to communicate effectively, pupils must be made aware of the vocabulary, structures and cultural context.
Activities	Activities must be appropriate and devised to facilitate learning rather than to occupy or entertain pupils.
Roles and settings	Pupils must be able to draw on existing knowledge. At the same time they need to appreciate the cultural context of their communication. It is unrealistic to expect pupils to simulate a situation unless they are already conceptually familiar with that context.
Implementation	For real communication to take place, there has to be a transmitter of information and a receiver. Pupils need to use each other to carry out conversations and therefore need training in these roles.
Grading and integration	Tasks should be open-ended so that pupils can operate at their own level. Some require reinforcement, some need to be extended. If the aim is to meet individual needs, tasks must be flexible.
Assessment	There should be a balance between correction of accuracy and the encouragement of communication of meaning.

Figure 3.5 Evaluation of teaching

learning process) and 'social' strategies (pertaining to the interaction with other pupils or language users) (see Harris 1997: 5–6; Ellis and Sinclair 1989: 151–4 and Oxford 1987: 16–21).

The overt teaching – probably initially in English and gradually in the TL – of relevant learning strategies, communication strategies and study skills is advisable and Vee Harris' strategy training cycle seems useful in this context (see 1997: 13–15). It comprises the following:

- awareness raising;
- modelling;
- action planning/goal setting;
- extensive practice;
- fading out the reminders.

Below we consider four areas:

- dictionary use;
- developing the skills of listening, speaking, reading, writing and memorising new vocabulary;

- specific activity/task types;
- study skills.

For a detailed discussion of learner strategies, see the two-part Special Issue of the *Language Learning Journal*: 35(1) and 35(2) (2007).

Dictionary use

Pupils can be encouraged to carry out a wide variety of activities in order to develop dictionary skills. A publication on dictionary skills by Cambridgeshire (1994) implicitly suggested five aspects for the development of dictionary skills. The publication arranged the contents according to the following categories:

- pre-dictionary activities;
- familiarisation with dictionaries;
- using the dictionary to check for accuracy;
- finding the English meaning of words in the TL;
- finding the TL for English words.

Possible activities for developing dictionary skills include:

- identifying the alphabetical order in a list of words;
- familiarisation with the abbreviations used in dictionaries and their meaning/significance;
- word manipulation and derivation work;
- matching exercises;
- word correction tasks;
- identifying the correct meaning;
- prediction of meaning;
- categorisation of words in semantic fields or by grammatical criteria.

For a wide range of useful dictionary activities, see Berwick and Horsfall (1996), Cambridgeshire (1994), Horsfall and Evans (1995) or Pillette (1996), Carduner (2003) and Wingate (2004).

Developing listening, speaking, reading, writing and memorising new vocabulary

One workable classroom-based approach is to break down strategies on a skills basis, that is, identifying strategies that help with the skill areas of listening, speaking, reading and writing as well as other skill areas such as memorising new vocabulary.

Cathy Pomphrey suggests improving pupils' listening skills by raising their awareness of the different factors contributing to successful listening. She does this by administering to her pupils a worksheet/OHT in which she asks them which of the following factors they think could help them, as well as those which would probably not help them improve their listening skills:

- shut out other thoughts;
- think in English;
- keep going, even if they miss some words/phrases;
- listen out for important words and phrases;
- talk while the tape is on;
- guess meanings if they are not sure;
- use clues such as noises, pictures, etc.;
- give up if they miss a word/phrase.

She engages pupils in a discussion on these issues and asks them for any other approaches that have (not) worked for them. Similar lists can be drawn up for other skill areas. For useful examples, see Harris (1997), Rampillon (1989) or Wilkinson (1994). Macaro's work (2001a) provides some very interesting insights into the use of strategies in MFL learning and work by Graham (2003), for example, illuminates some issues with in this case listening. Harris (1997: 7) lists the following strategies for reading:

- Recognising the type of text; poem, newspaper article, brochure?
- Examining pictures, the title, etc. for clues.
- Going for gist, skipping inessential words.
- Saying the text out loud and identifying 'chunk boundaries'; how a sentence breaks down and which parts of it to work on at one time.
- Using knowledge of the world to make sensible guesses.
- Picking out cognates.
- Substituting English words, e.g. 'she something on his head'.
- Analysing unknown words, breaking a word/phrase down and associating parts of it with familiar words, e.g. 'hochgewachsen'.
- Identifying the grammatical categories of words.
- Using punctuation or clues; question marks, capital letters, etc.

Task 3.5 Helping pupils learn how to learn

Devise a list of strategies for a specific group of pupils you have observed or taught with the aim of getting them to think about the following three aspects of language learning by following the examples of Cathy Pomphrey and Vee Harris:

- speaking;
- writing;
- memorising new vocabulary.

Discuss with the pupils whether they deliberately use any strategies.
   Work through specific tasks with the pupils and get them to reflect on how they approach these tasks.

Specific activity/task types

In view of the difficulties a large number of pupils have in completing tasks independently in the classroom as well as when being formally assessed, we also recommend a task-based breakdown of strategies, that is, analysing with pupils the precise requirements of individual types of tasks such as gap-filling or matching answers to questions or selecting words/phrases from a list. This seems particularly relevant in the context of teaching as well as testing and assessment in the TL, which demands increasing familiarity by pupils in how to approach certain types of tasks in order to compensate for difficulties they might have in understanding instructions.

Study skills

Pupils will also benefit from input on strategies concerned more with how to manage and monitor their learning, for instance, setting themselves short-term, achievable targets, keeping vocabulary diaries and revision notes, focusing their learning on areas of perceived weakness, how to go about finding and identifying relevant resources or evaluating the success of their learning. Regular opportunities for reflection on these issues should help pupils become more successful and effective MFL learners. In an account of her experience, Dam (1990: 16–37) discusses the use of a pupil journal, featuring description, analysis and evaluation of their learning as a useful strategy. Harris (1997: 9) suggests the following four strategies for monitoring language use:

- Auditory monitoring: 'Does it sound right?'
- Visual monitoring: 'Does it look right?'
- Grammatical monitoring: 'Is that the right tense, adjectival agreement?', etc.
- Style monitoring: e.g. 'Is that the right tone for a formal letter?'

WHAT DO PUPILS NEED?

We finish this chapter with a number of areas where pupils have highlighted their needs in the language learning process. An important piece of work carried out in a London borough is summarised in the following section by one of the investigators (Lee 2002) on the original project (Lee *et al.* 1998). The findings of this project are significant for positioning where our learners are in their attitudes and approaches to learning MFL and also in highlighting what they need now in order for their potential to be realised as far as possible. Although the work was focused in one particular geographical area, the needs identified by the project are worthy of summary in this chapter and most find resonance throughout this book. The additions in italics are ours and serve to illustrate some themes which may help exemplify how the general finding may be applied to a theme which is familiar, or will become so, to student teachers as you progress through your course and this book, as well as your wider research.

- A sense of achievement and a belief that they can improve *(assessment for learning?)*.
- A realisation that this stems from their own efforts rather than from random external factors *(attribution theory?)*.
- A sense of curiosity about the language they are learning *(engagement/ thinking skills?)*.
- A clear understanding of what learning a language is about, including the terminology involved *(grammar? Learning strategies?)*.
- The ability to know when they are making real progress in it *(assessment for learning?)*.
- The realisation that they are developing skills of language use and language learning and acquiring techniques of mastering new language and applying it in new situations *(learning strategies?)*.
- Goals set for them which are challenging but achievable *(target setting?)*.
- Helpful learning activities which are clearly not assessment tasks *(true CLT?)*.
- Feedback which shows them how to improve as well as indicating their standard *(assessment for learning?)*.
- Active involvement in the work of the lesson *(engagement, motivation?)*.
- A sense, in an appropriate way, of control over their work and progress *(assessment for learning?)*.
- Pupils must be taught effective and efficient ways of memorising new language items *(language learning strategies)*.
- More importantly, however, pupils need to be taught the smaller words and features of a language which do not naturally arise or belong to any topic (what could be termed the 'core' language): essential if pupils are to work beyond the level of the word list or their basic pre-learnt 'chunks' *(application of grammar, independence)*.
- Pupils need to be shown what constitutes a quality response at any level, and how to emulate it *(assessment for learning, target setting)*.
- Pupils need to be taught the precise techniques which they need in order to incorporate, for example, a new language item into known language, and then be given enough time to practise them *(manipulation of language, application of grammar/patterns)*.
- Pupils sometimes need help with and demonstration of basic routines such as how to set out their work, note new language items, etc. *(learning strategies)*.
- A belief that their personal efforts will have no effect on their standard and progress.
- A belief that aptitude for learning a language is something fixed and owned by others, rather than largely an issue of time needed for learning.
- A high level of test anxiety born of a fear that they are always being assessed.
- Confusion over the nature and purpose of what they are doing.
- Praise for doing an easy task with little effort.
- An excessive emphasis on extrinsic sources of motivation.
- Lessons which involve them in long periods of passive working.

- The Modern Languages curriculum and its teaching need to be made much more transparent, so that pupils can see the purposes behind what they are doing both in lessons and over time.
- A much clearer view of what constitutes appropriate *linguistic* progression is needed.
- The teaching should include clear and precisely specified learning intentions.
- A clearer view of pedagogical issues and an appropriate methodology for MFL teaching are needed, linked to an agreed terminology for the various aspects of MFL teaching.
- Pupils need time to master the various aspects of language learning, and more focused help to enable them to apply and manipulate the language they meet.
- The skills of language learning must be fixed in learners early if they are to develop independence later. This includes the understanding of principles which will help them in long-term learning, not simply the immediate problem with a word.

SUMMARY

CLT encompasses a number of different approaches to MFL teaching. These ideas and strategies ultimately aim to develop independent communication by the pupil. Outcomes differ according to the interests of pupils, their backgrounds, their motivation, their perception of themselves and, of course, their abilities. CLT is a methodological framework and you need to determine your own teaching style within it according to personal and contextual factors. Independent language use can be fostered by active participation of the pupil and it is within your professional judgement to decide at what rate to 'let go' (Page 1992), that is, to allow the pupil to be less dependent and reliant on the teacher.

FURTHER READING

Macaro, E. (2006) 'Strategies for language learning and for language use: revising the theoretical framework', *The Modern Language Journal* 90(3): 320–37.

Special issues of the *Language Learning Journal* in 2007 on Learner Strategies 35(1) and 35(2).

This article, and the two issues of the journal, provide an excellent account of strategies in learning MFL and explore the surrounding theoretical debates.

Oxford, R. (1987) *Language Learning Strategies: What Every Teacher Should Know.* Boston: Heinle & Heinle.

The classic text on strategies for MFL learning.

Pachler, N. (2000) 'Re-examining communicative language teaching', K. Field (ed.) *Issues in Modern Foreign Language Teaching.* London: RoutledgeFalmer, pp. 26–41.

This chapter explores the issues surrounding the elements of communicative language teaching and their interpretation and implementation.

4 Observing, planning and evaluating modern foreign languages lessons

INTRODUCTION

This chapter looks at two central aspects of learning to teach modern foreign languages (MFL): lesson observation and collaboration with experienced teachers as well as planning and evaluation.

Lesson observation and collaboration with experienced teachers provide unique opportunities to gain valuable insights into the learning and teaching process as a basis for learning about teaching. They are essential parts of the learning process for you. Our first concern in this chapter is with demonstrating how observation and collaboration can be used to help you develop a personal teaching style.

Our other concern lies with the careful planning and evaluation of lessons and units of work. Planning and evaluation are integral parts of effective teaching and form the foundation for successful pupil learning. Colin Wringe points out that only through planning 'is it possible to see present work in its due perspective and appropriately adjust the emphasis of one's work in the light of what has gone before and what is to follow' (1989: 25–6).

There are many different proformas for observation and planning in use, which include similar features (see e.g. Pachler and Redondo 2007). Many higher education institutions (HEIs) and schools have their own proformas. In order to illustrate the comments made in this chapter we include exemplar proformas, photocopiable blank versions of which can be found in the Appendix. They are not meant to be prescriptive nor do they purport to be the only appropriate or possible way of recording observation, planning and evaluation. They are intended as a starting point for you and need to be tailored to local needs and preferences. The proformas attempt to bring together the most important features of what we perceive to be good practice in these respects.

OBJECTIVES

By the end of this chapter you should:

- recognise the importance of observation and collaborative teaching in learning to teach MFL and be able to carry out lesson observations effectively and professionally;
- understand the importance of planning and evaluation for effective MFL teaching and maximising pupil learning;
- be able to understand the issues attendant to the planning of MFL lessons as well as the construction of outline medium-term, i.e. unit of work plans.

FAMILIARISATION WITH DEPARTMENTAL POLICIES AND DOCUMENTATION

It is important to remember that when you start your MFL teacher education course, you have to be professional from the outset. Your behaviour and attitudes should reflect this professionalism throughout the whole programme, whether in your school experience school or at the HEI. As part of this process, on starting to work as a member of an MFL department, it is important to become familiar with prevailing policies and documentation.

The departmental handbook should contain policies on all relevant aspects of the work of an MFL teacher in a given school, such as the use of the target language (TL), assessment and marking, homework, discipline procedures, staffing and resourcing of the department, organisation of the MFL curriculum, accommodation, teaching methods used, the departmental development plan, extra-curricular activities available to pupils through the department, job descriptions of individual team members and any other information useful to outsiders or colleagues arriving new to the department such as newly qualified teachers (NQTs), inspectors and/or student teachers.

Familiarisation with departmental policies provides important background information for you. It allows reflection on, and learning from the classroom practice observed. Observation of and reflection on why an MFL teacher, for instance, uses certain strategies when giving instructions in the TL might become easier when set against the background of the departmental TL policy. Departmental policies should also inform the planning carried out by student teachers. It is, for instance, important to know that certain procedures for the setting and returning of homework are in place when planning lessons. All such information helps you from a *practical* perspective and also from a *professional* perspective, to maintain a persona which will be effective for your development.

Ask your mentor for a copy of any departmental information, policies and handbooks. Read the information carefully. What has the department set out to achieve? What important general processes and procedures for the conduct of MFL lessons are stated? What policies are in place? What priorities emerge for you as the student teacher from the information you have read?

OBSERVING AND WORKING COLLABORATIVELY WITH MFL TEACHERS

Lesson observation

In her book on observation tasks for the language classroom, Wajnryb makes a very important point:

> Observers need to maintain a sensitive awareness of the potential for vulnerability that inevitably accompanies any observation of teaching. When a teacher opens the classroom door and extends a welcome to a visitor, a basic trust in motive and professional ethic accompanies that welcome. This must be respected.
>
> (1992: 19)

You need to bear this in mind when you engage in lesson observation. Lack of sensitivity to the potential vulnerability of even the most experienced teacher might lead to tensions. The aim of the exercise is not to evaluate critically the practice of experienced MFL teachers against performance indicators; this is the responsibility of their senior colleagues internally or externally from the Local Authority or the Office for Standards in Education (Ofsted). The aim for you is to learn about the complexity of the teaching and learning process and possible approaches/strategies to maximise pupil learning. Data obtained from any lesson observations you conduct should, therefore, be treated confidentially. Figure 4.1 lists the observation etiquette.

In this chapter we describe a systematic approach to lesson observation, which focuses on the gathering of mainly qualitative data, that is, verbal descriptions of certain occurrences during the lesson linked to a small number of observation foci per lesson. The foci for observation change regularly. Brian Parkinson (1992: 20) notes: 'It is a common beginner's mistake to try to capture everything, but you will soon find it impossible to look for more than one or two things in any one observation.'

It is important, though, that observation foci relate to your development needs. Three types of development needs are distinguished here:

1   those perceived by you yourself (which may, of course, be linked to Qualified Teacher Status (QTS) Standards where you feel you need to focus on one or two aspects at a given time);

Please remember 'observation etiquette':

- Ensure the person you are observing knows who you are and why you are there.
- Be aware of the 'background' to this lesson about which you know almost nothing: the relationship built up with the class, the whole range of reasons why the teacher has chosen a particular approach today, etc.
- Few lessons are ever perfect. Please bear this in mind when observing teachers and commenting to them afterwards.
- If you make critical comments on any observation proforma, make sure these remain confidential and constructive.
- When observing, you should always be able to learn something from the experience.
- Take opportunities, where appropriate, to become involved (e.g. when pupils are working in pairs or groups). Don't feel that all observation must be done at the back as if you were invisible but make sure the teacher is happy with this.
- Make sure you thank the teacher for the chance to observe the lesson.

Figure 4.1 Observation etiquette

2   those linked to target setting with the mentor;
3   those triggered by (subject) input (at the HEI).

The approach is systematic in that it is based on the completion of a generic proforma per lesson observed (see Figures 4.2 and A.1). Before the lesson, the observer decides on one or two foci (rubric: 'observation foci') and notes why she has done so (column: 'comments'). During the lesson, the observer completes the columns 'time' and 'description of action'.

This approach does not make use of fixed observation categories but, instead, allows the observer the freedom and flexibility to concentrate on changing foci. To some extent the lesson observation foci depend on particular lesson objectives. For instance, a Spanish lesson in the computer room, where pupils compose e-mail messages to their e-pals, invariably offers different opportunities for observation than a classroom-based lesson taught in collaboration with the foreign language assistant (FLA) focusing on the oral practice of transactional language relating, for example, to the topic 'clothes'. It is, therefore, important to find out from the teacher prior to the lesson what the objectives and the content of the lesson are.

Task 4.2 Identifying observation foci relating to departmental information

Compile a list of possible observation foci based on your study of the departmental information you looked at previously. What aspects of departmental practice described in the documentation would you like to find out more about through lesson observation? Then observe a number of lessons with these foci in mind.

Lesson observation sheet			
Class: *9L*	Time: *2.10–3.20*	Date: *08.10.*	Teacher: *M Beauchamp*
Observation foci:		**Comments:**	
target language use: teacher–pupil		*I wanted to see how a unit of work can be introduced and to collect ideas on how to give instructions and explanations, how to organise the classroom and how to conclude a lesson in the target language.*	

Time	Description of action	Reflection
2.10	*Pupils enter the room individually returning the teacher's greetings:* **T: 'Bonjour . . .' P: 'Bonjour, Monsieur. Comment ça va?' T: 'Ça va bien, Merci. Et toi??' P: 'Ça va +/~/-'**	*Pupils used to routine and responded automatically.*
2.15	*Oral introduction of topic 'school life'.* **'Aujourd'hui nous étudions le système d'enseignement, l'éducation en France. Qu'est-ce que c'est "l'enseignement" en Anglais? . . . Oui c'est ça.'**	*Used able pupil to translate to ensure comprehension.*
2.18	*Activity introduced by using able pupil to demonstrate how to brainstorm vocabulary relevant to school life.* **'Peter. Donne-moi du vocabulaire associé avec l'éducation. Tu parles et moi, j' écris.'** *Gestures and teacher writes answers on board.*	*Pupil followed instructions without hesitation.*
2.24	*Pupils put into groups of four:* **'Vous allez travailler en groupes de 4.'** *Teacher uses gestures and counts 1–4 to clarify. Teacher repeats the demonstration.* **'Peter, encore une fois. Tu parles et j'écris. Du vocabulaire associé avec l'éducation, s'il te plaît.'** *Number 'ones' in group asked to identify themselves. They are then told that they are scribes.* **'Numéro un . . . lève la main . . . numéro un, tu écris. Joanne, tu es numéro un, oui, alors tu écris. Voilà le stylo, tu écris. Marie . . . tu écris . . . OK? Numéro un . . . lève la main . . . Tout le monde comprend? . . . Vous écrivez.**	*Why were pupils put into groups after the demonstration? Giving pupils a number helped; by asking pupils to identify themselves there was no confusion.*

2.28	Ground rules of the brainstorm explained in English. Card clock used to ask time and to set a ten-minute time limit for group work. Teacher issues instructions and time scale using card clock. **'OK. Il est deux heures et demie. Regardez! Il est quelle heure? Oui, deux heures et demie. Vous avez dix minutes. Dix minutes. Combien de minutes Sharon? . . . Oui, dix minutes. Tracey, vous finissez à quelle heure? Tout le monde répète: "Nous finissons à deux heures quarante." '**	Why was the TL not used here? Process of setting a time limit seems a useful device. Pupils all on task. I guess they are used to brainstorming.
2.40	Brainstorm of known vocabulary brought to a close. **'OK. Il est deux heures quarante. Posez le stylo. C'est fini. Regardez moi. . . . Regardez moi. Wayne . . . c'est fini . . . regarde moi.'** Teacher asks each group: **'Vous avez combien de mots?'**	Would the element of competition have added motivation?
2.45	Teacher revises key words – les matières, le personnel, les bâtiments with the use of flashcards and graded questioning.	According to plan these words would serve as headings to allow pupils to put words into categories. Purpose of this activity not entirely clear.
2.47	Distracted pupil shuffles and talks to partner. **'Tais-toi, Wayne'** and gestures used.	Some pupils seemed unsettled. The fact that the teacher knew the pupil's name was very useful.
2.55	Teacher writes category headings on board. Asks for some words from the whole class. **'Voilà des catégories . . . les bâtiments, le personnel et les matières. Donne moi un exemple d'un bâtiment . . . l'école . . . très bien, le bureau, oui. Et le personnel? . . . le professeur, merci, le directeur, très bien. Et une matière? . . . l'anglais. OK. Voilà vous comprenez.'** As they shout out teacher asks which category to put the word in, repeats the words and writes them on the board. **'L'université, c'est une matière. Tout le monde, oui ou non? Non . . . et alors . . . Martin? Oui, c'est un bâtiment. Et le directeur . . . un bâtiment aussi, non? Excellent c'est une personne.'**	Did there need to be more examples? The teacher assured that all pupils understood what he was doing. Questions targeted: more able first then less able pupils.

(Continued)

Time	Description of action	Reflection
3.00	Pupils asked to work in groups to categorise words. **'Allez-y, continuez en groupes.'** Teacher walked around targeting groups which needed help. **'Vous comprenez? Les maths, c'est une matière? Oui, très bien. Donnez-moi d'autres matières. Regardez la liste. La géo? . . . oui la géographie. OK. Ecrivez la géographie ici. Bien. Une personne? Le surveillant, bien . . . ici. Très bien vous comprenez. Continuez. . . .'**	No one had to translate the instructions. Most pupils used English when deciding which categories words from brainstorm should go in. Could some sort of forfeit have been used to make pupils aware that use of English is not desirable?
3.10	Teacher interrupts pupils still in full flow, although some off-task. Teacher targets individuals with questions **'Donnez-moi trois exemples des matières, du personnel etc.'**	Teacher asked pupils who seemed to have been off-task.
3.15	Homework set: pupils have to copy the instructions into their homework diary. **'Les devoirs. Ecrivez trois phrases à sujet des matières à l'école . . . ça commence avec "J'étudie . . .". Ecrivez trois phrases pour les bâtiments: par exemple "Le college se trouve à une distance de . . .". "Il y a trois salles de français . . .". Et écrivez trois phrases au sujet du personnel: "Mon professeur de français s'appelle M. Beauchamp . . ." '** Able pupil translates.	Might it have been easier for all in the class and quicker to use English to set the homework?
3.20	Bell rings. Pupils dismissed in twos saying **'Au revoir'** to the teacher on exit.	Lesson running over. Do pupils think about what they are saying when they go through the routine?

Figure 4.2 Sample lesson evaluation

Observation can be a very effective learning experience for you, but it is up to you to make the most of it. With advance preparation and a concentrated focus it is very valuable time spent. However, where the observation is vague and unstructured, then potentially valuable insights into the teaching and learning process are lost. Table 4.1 lists a number of possible observation foci. Given their importance, particularly at the initial stages of initial teacher education (ITE), classroom organisation/management issues are listed not under teacher behaviour here but as a separate category.

It might be possible to use the *discussion* of observation notes as evidence of meeting certain QTS standards. Structured observation notes may not only be useful

Table 4.1 Possible MFL lesson observation foci

Category	Possible observation foci
pupil learning and response	contexts and type of TL use by pupils amount of productive language use by pupils per lesson amount of receptive language use by pupils per lesson nature of pupil participation in teacher-led activities nature of pupil involvement in pair and group work independent pupil learning, e.g. use of dictionaries and glossaries pupil time spent on-task types of off-task behaviour, e.g. talking, inattentiveness reasons for off-task behaviour, e.g. distraction by other pupils pupil achievement of lesson objectives
teacher strategies and behaviour	engagement of pupils: use of starter use of the TL for instructions and interaction use of body language, gesture, mime use of advance organisers development and revision of previous learning outcomes choice of activities in relation to objectives ways of communicating objectives to pupils ways of presenting new language amount and characteristics of teacher talk and pupil talk use of questioning techniques: question and answer exchanges; use of open-ended versus closed questions etc. use of differentiation (variation of) pace use of strategies to motivate pupils use of teacher-led activity, group work, pair work, individual work role of the teacher in group work, pair work and individual work teacher movement around the classroom strategies for teaching linguistic structures balance of teacher-centred and pupil-centred approaches strategies for continuous assessment and feedback to pupils administration of homework strategies for error correction use of plenaries (during and/or at the end of the lesson)
classroom management / organisation	settling pupils down arrangement of seating and classroom layout issuing books and equipment establishing a code of conduct strategies for reminding pupils of rules grouping arrangements for specific tasks use of the TL for classroom management/organisation use of praise and sanctions use of the TL for dealing with discipline matters strategies for dealing with disruptive behaviour

in facilitating the reflection process but can also be used as evidence of having addressed certain standards.

Lesson observation is, of course, also carried out by mentors of your work as the student teacher. The foci identified in Table 4.1 can equally be used by teachers observing (parts of) lessons taught by you. Dedicated lesson observation proformas are usually provided by the HEI for use when observing you.

Task 4.3 Carrying out lesson observations

Using the lesson observation in Figure 4.2 as an example, carry out a number of lesson observations of your own. A blank proforma (Figure A.1) is included in the Appendix. Choose one or two observation foci per lesson from those identified in Task 4.2 or those listed in Table 4.1.

After the lessons, complete the 'reflection' column. NB: Remember to keep your evaluative comments to yourself.

You might want to ask yourself reflective questions such as:

- What were the lesson's short-term objectives?
- What about the longer-term aims?
- How were the differing needs of pupils approached?
- How did the teacher deal with any issues that arose (behaviour, misunderstandings, etc.)?
- What learning took place exactly and how do you (and the teacher) know?
- What have you learnt? (ideas, activities, strategies – both positive and negative; changes to how you think you might plan your lessons).

The approach to lesson observation suggested above is suitable for a wide range of observation foci and does not require any specific preparation on the part of the observer such as the design of specific observation instruments.

On the basis of targets set, you might, however, want to design specific observation proformas or recording sheets for colleagues observing your lessons, such as, for example, a tally sheet to record how often you support TL instructions with gestures or how often you elicit answers from specific pupils.

In Figure 4.3 the lesson observation is not structured in a linear way according to the time of occurrences, but in columns, one column per learning objective identified for the lesson. The observer notes how individual learning activities relate to the various lesson objectives.

Task 4.4 Linking learning objectives to teaching activities

Following the example in Figure 4.3, carry out some lesson observations of your own linking lesson objectives and learning activities. Try to draw a 'shape' for the lesson, moving from the objectives, through the various stages/activities to help pupils make progress (Groups? Pairs? Whole class?) through to the plenary.

Ask the respective teacher before the lesson what the learning objectives are and note them in different columns. When observing the lesson, categorise the learning and teaching activities according to these columns. Do all the activities relate to one of the lesson objectives?

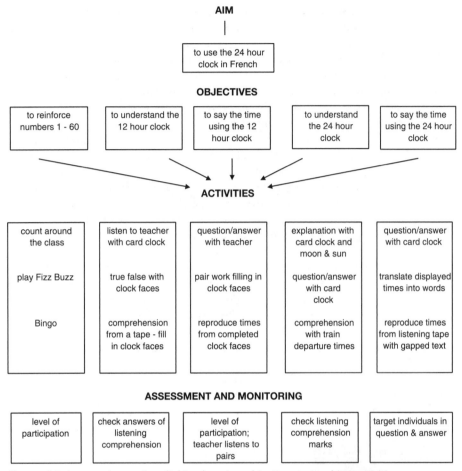

Figure 4.3 Lesson observation: linking learning objectives to teaching activities

Collaborative planning and teaching

The typical progression route for MFL student teachers is one from lesson observation via small-group and collaborative teaching to 'solo' whole-class teaching. It may also be the case that you may teach a section of a full lesson, e.g. a starter activity with one group while teaching a full lesson independently with another. What should be at the forefront is your training needs at that time: in which situations will you be able to develop your skills most effectively at this particular point? (see Fleming and Walls (1998) and Crozier *et al.* (2003)). During collaborative planning and teaching, student teachers gradually assume responsibility for planning and teaching (parts of) lessons with support from the class teacher (assessment should also play a part in these short teaching and learning episodes). By our definition collaborative teaching is different from team-teaching, which involves the co-operation of two experienced teachers.

Working with another adult in the class can be beneficial for learners as it significantly improves the pupil–teacher ratio and, therefore, the amount of attention individual pupils can receive.

Lesson observations carried out by you should, where possible, be preceded by, as well as followed up with, discussions with the class teacher. It is through these discussions that the class teacher becomes aware of your level of understanding regarding the processes necessary to plan and teach a lesson and enable you to maximise the benefits of lesson observations.

When you are working collaboratively with the class teacher you are in a unique position. You occupy the place of the learner, yet – at the same time – can increasingly empathise with the teacher. Being able to gradually assume responsibility for what goes on in the classroom allows you to develop an understanding of the skills required for 'solo' teaching. Moving from observation to collaborative planning and teaching involves discussions about, for example, how learning objectives are to be achieved, the teaching strategies and activities to be used and how these relate to the learning objectives identified.

In collaborative teaching the class teacher retains overall control and authority and allows the student teacher to participate in aspects of teaching which she is ready to develop. The level of student teacher involvement gradually increases. Invariably, careful planning features prominently in this process. Both you and the class teacher need to be clear at every stage of the lesson who is responsible for what. For a useful analysis of collaborative teaching with examples of effective practice, see Arthur *et al.* (1998: 123–5).

Figure 4.4 illustrates the gradual shift in responsibility from the class teacher to the student teacher. In order to make the graphical representation of this process easier it is divided it into six stages here.

Task 4.5 Collaborative teaching

With reference to Figure 4.4, assess which stage you are currently working at. Then discuss with your mentor and other members of the department you regularly work with what you need to do to consolidate and/or move on to the next stage.

Figure 4.5 is an example of a collaboratively planned lesson, which relates to Stage 3 of Figure 4.4. It uses a modified version of the lesson planning proforma suggested later in the chapter.

PLANNING AND EVALUATION

Lesson planning and you as the student teacher

Up to now in this chapter we have been referring to planning and planning collaboratively. Planning lessons is one hurdle many student teachers of MFL find challenging at the start of their course, and many find that it is tempting to spend hours trying to

stage	student teacher	class teacher	responsibility
1	observes	assists student teacher in choosing observation foci and evaluating observations	class teacher plans and carries out lesson
2	takes small group	shares lesson plan and provides diagnostic feedback, i.e. identifies strengths and weaknesses so that the student teacher can gain a better understanding and improve	class teacher plans lesson and discusses it with student teacher; class teacher is responsible for classroom organisation and management – student teacher is responsible for group only
3	takes class for parts of lesson	discusses with student teacher skills to be focused upon, discusses lesson plan, observes and provides diagnostic feedback	class teacher plans and carries out lesson except for parts, which it is agreed student teacher should take
4	collaborative teaching	increasingly less involved in the planning of lessons; observes and evaluates lesson and provides diagnostic feedback	student teacher gradually assumes responsibility for planning and teaches lesson with support from the class teacher
5	plans and teaches with class teacher support	advises on student teacher's lesson plan, observes and provides diagnostic feedback	student teacher plans and teaches lesson with support from the class teacher
6	plans and teaches 'solo'	advises on student teacher's lesson plan, observes and provides diagnostic feedback	student teacher plans and teaches the lesson; class teacher advises on planning, observes and provides diagnostic feedback

Figure 4.4 From observation via collaborative teaching to 'solo' teaching

produce the 'perfect' lesson plan. First, there is no such thing, second, too much time spent on planning takes away from the energy you need to teach and, third, planning is a skill in which you will develop confidence and effectiveness with practice and feedback. That is, however, *not* to suggest planning is unimportant; far from it, effective planning is essential.

Planning must start from a focus on the objectives:

- What do the pupils need to learn in this lesson/series of lessons?

Lesson plan			
Class: *8H*	Time: *9.20–10.30*	Date: *31.10*	Language: *French*

Lesson objectives	
Core	Extension
• *to familiarise pupils with the vocabulary and basic phrases related to places in a town* • *to introduce simple directions enabling pupils to recognise and give instructions to a stranger*	• *to understand and respond to questions when asking for directions* • *to ask the way to key places in town*

Previous learning outcomes
- *concept of masculine and feminine (with 'le' and 'la')*
- *'il y a' and 'il n'y a pas de' as lexical items*
- *'où est le/la . . .'*
- *'c'est un/une . . .'*

Resources required
flashcards of places – church, school, swimming pool, town hall, cinema, stadium, café, park, library
overhead transparency of a town plan showing these places
tape of 5 brief dialogues asking the way to places in town
worksheet for reinforcement

Time	Activities and strategies	Led by	Comments
9.20	*usher pupils in room, take register, check equipment in TL: Starter (grammatical le/la/l' odd one out) on all desks*	*student teacher*	*opportunity to build on previous experience*
9.23	*introduce objectives and state expectations in TL and English*	*class teacher*	*class teacher retains responsibility for the management of pupil behaviour throughout the lesson*
9.29	*flashcard work: listen, repeat; closed and open questions*	*class teacher*	*student teacher observes technique*
9.45	*cassette: listen for gist, detail, focus on language*	*student teacher*	*class teacher circulates to check all pupils are on task; student teacher practises working with a cassette player; focus is on giving clear instructions*

10.00	go through pupils' answers and rebuild dialogues	class teacher	student teacher assists less able pupils, gauges and monitors outcomes
10.10	use OHP to practise linguistic items; whole-class and pair work	class teacher	student teacher provides model answers and circulates to assist and monitor pupils
10.25	set homework in the TL and dismiss class	student teacher	class teacher circulates to check, pupils note instructions correctly

Homework
worksheet for reinforcement of places in town and directions

Action to be taken
<ul><li>prepare flashcard routine to build on what the teacher did in this lesson as a quick revision for next lesson</li><li>make up pair cards with the same symbols as on the flashcards</li><li>design linguistic support sheets for less able pupils to facilitate pair work in next lesson</li><li>define the roles of the class teacher and student teacher during the pair work activity</li></ul>

Figure 4.5 Lesson planning – collaborative teaching

This is closely followed by the supplementary question:

- How can this learning come about?

As background to both these questions is the third one:

- Where are the pupils now with their learning?

Atkinson (Atkinson and Claxton 2000: 81) has some ideas for activities which might help you learn how to plan and make progress in this area (not all of which are immediately applicable):

- Observational task, e.g. when observing a lesson look for all the signs that tell you something about learners, e.g. learning difficulties might be expressed by trying to copy from neighbours, furrowed brows, etc.
- Plan a routine for something, e.g. calling the register. Implement, review and modify.
- Timing – instead of planning how long an activity should take, plan to read the class reaction and stop the activity when appropriate.

- Plan a lesson which incorporates alternatives between which the teacher will select *in situ* according to the needs and mood of the pupils at the time.
- Practise visualising the lesson (what the learners are doing and what the student teacher is doing) as a movie *before* writing the lesson plan.

Lesson planning and series of lessons

Individual lesson plans need to be seen in the context of medium-term planning, the so-called units of work. These normally cover individual topics of study. Ultimately, lesson plans relate via units of work to the scheme of work, which outlines the work to be covered over a period of time such as an academic year or a period of study defined by examination specifications.

Lesson plans outline how a particular aspect of a unit of work is to be covered. Individual lessons need to be linked in terms of content as well as in the development of language skills. Chapters 3 and 6 provide guidance on how to ensure continuity and progression. Strategies such as recapping through 'question-and-answer' techniques, consistency in the use of visual aids, the use of homework to bridge the gap from one lesson to the next, the use of self- and peer-assessment, target setting and, of course, regular marking can all help to achieve a smooth transition from one lesson to the next.

Initially, MFL student teachers will be concerned with planning at micro-level, that is with (parts of) individual lessons, rather than at macro-level, the unit of work level. Nevertheless, these (parts of) lesson plans need to be firmly rooted in unit of work planning:

> In planning our lessons the all important question becomes not 'How can I occupy them in tomorrow's lesson?' but 'What is now the most pressing thing for them to learn in order to be able to perform the final activity satisfactorily?' 'What is the most effective and economical way of doing it?' and above all 'If they are to do that successfully, is there anything I must do first?' It is no longer a matter of generating activities that are sufficiently novel, stimulating or innocuous to be included but the more finite and easily manageable problem solving one of finding the most efficient means to ends.
>
> (Wringe 1994: 13)

When planning an MFL lesson you need to consider a number of important issues, which are discussed below. They are exemplified in Figure 4.6, a sample lesson plan.

It is very important to have *clear learning objectives* for individual lessons. It is considered to be good practice to spell out the objectives to pupils at the beginning of a lesson. There might, however, be some lessons, where an element of surprise or discovery might be preferable The objectives need to be identified and made explicit because they remind you of and indicate to pupils what should be achieved by the end of the lesson. They help pupils realise where they are going, what is asked of them

Lesson plan			
Class: *8E*	Time: *1.30–2.40*	Date: *25.11*	Language: *French*

Learning objectives

Core	Extension
• to ask the way to places in town using 'pour aller au, à la, à l'. . .' • grammar point: au, à la, à l' • to give directions using 'prenez la première/deuxième à gauche/à droite' etc.	• to follow directions on a grid/plan and to reproduce dialogues without verbal support • to use a wider range of phrases, such as 'passez . . ., continuez . . .' in further dialogues

Previous learning outcomes
Vocabulary for key places already introduced. Pupils have labelled a map. Pupils have learnt the song 'La première rue à droite'.

Resources required
flashcards of places, pair cards of places, CD of short questions and answers asking the way and giving directions, gapped text of transcript, grid/town plan

Time	Activities	PoS and ATs
1.30	*Starter: Flashcards game to remind pupils of key places: teacher-led repetition, graded questioning:* **'C'est . . .? C'est . . . ou c'est . . .? Qu'est-ce que c'est?'** **Objectives**	1.1a, 2.2c, 2.2d AT2 L1, 2
1.35	*Use same flashcards to introduce 'Pour aller . . .?';* *teacher-led:* *Place cards on wall; blindfold pupil; elicit 'Pour aller . . .?' from others; blindfolded pupil points to card from memory* **'Peter, où tu veux aller?'** *. . . le cinema . . .* **'OK. Pour aller . . . oui . . . au cinéma? Alors, Peter. Répète: Pour aller au cinéma?'**	1.1a 1.1b 1.3a AT2 L1, 2
1.50	*Pair work: pair cards, colour coded by gender, face down; one pupil asks 'Pour aller . . .?' other points out flashcard from memory; gender serves as a clue* **'OK. Travaillez avec un partenaire. Vous êtes "A" et "B". "A", tu poses la question: "Pour aller à la ou au". "B", tu reponds la-bas et tu indiques la carte. Vous avez beaucoup de cartes. Vous devez vous souvenir de la bonne carte.'**	2.1b, 2.1d 4.b AT2 L3, 4
2.05	*Group work: pupils devise a rule for au, à la, à l'. . .*	2.1a

(Continued)

Time	Activities	PoS and ATs
2.15	Teacher-led listening activity: asking the way to places; pupils use the pair cards to locate the places mentioned on a grid/ town plan **'Voici un texte à trous. Le texte sans mots importants. Ecrivez le texte, mais il faut remplir des trous. Utilisez les cartes pour vous aider.'**	1.1a, 2.2a, 4a, 4f, 3a, 3b AT1 L3
2.30	Individual work: gapped transcript to reproduce the listening text using the pair cards as guide; able pupils asked to reproduce text without the gapped transcript	1.1a, 1.1b, 2.1d, 3a, 3b, 3d (AT3, L3) AT4 L3, 4
2.36	**Plenary: What have we learnt today? How can you remember it most effectively?**	
2.38	**'Les devoirs. Sortez le journal de devoirs. Copiez les instructions.'** Write up homework in homework diary in English.	
2.40	Dismiss class **'Levez-vous la classe. Derrière les chaises. Ramassez des papiers. Silence. Au revoir la classe.'**	

ICT
Flashcards using clip-art

Homework	
Complete writing up the dialogue.	**AT4 L3,4**

Action to be taken for next lesson
OHT of the grid/town plan to check through homework.

Evaluation	
re. pupil learning Too many cheated in the pair work and used English. Was the pair work too demanding or badly explained? Written work showed poor spelling: do I need to expose pupils to reading comprehension before getting them to write?	re. own teaching I need to continue to work on my use of the target language to explain activities. I was too stilted and did not make objectives clear: pupils did not see the point of all activities. Slow change-over of activities: did I stick too rigidly to my lesson plan? Were my timings realistic?

Figure 4.6 Sample lesson plan

and what potential (future) application it may have. To articulate learning objectives in terms of 'By the end of the lesson, you will be able to . . .' statements can assist pupils in recognising the value of the work in hand beyond the immediate lesson context. Adopting this language and approach is likely to assist you in making the necessary links between lesson objectives and activities. The approach can be seen to make it easier for pupils to understand why they are working on certain activities, what they will be able to do when they have finished the activities, what knowledge, skills and/or understanding they will have gained and how the work in class helps them towards achieving the overall objectives.

The choice of objectives has to be firmly rooted in the context of the overall unit of work. 'One-off' lessons by and large represent a weakness and should be avoided (see also Wringe 1994: 13). At the beginning, it is difficult for a student teacher to see beyond the 'one-off', but it is important that even with your first plan, which may be only for one activity within a lesson otherwise taught by the class teacher, that you keep in mind as far as possible what the pupils have done previously and where they are heading, i.e. why *your* activity will help them make progress.

Importantly, lesson objectives should be multi-dimensional, embracing, among others, the following skills:

- lexical;
- structural/grammatical;
- functional (e.g. expressing likes and dislikes);
- 'communicative' (e.g. objectives concerning discourse and strategic competence);
- (socio-)cultural;
- transferable (e.g. use of reference material).

Objectives of a lesson should also be differentiated. The majority of pupils should achieve core objectives but some will be able to carry out extension work. Some pupils might, for instance, only be expected to remember five new items of vocabulary in a lesson whereas others can realistically be expected to remember eight as well as use them in conjunction with what they learnt in previous lessons such as expressing likes and dislikes. For a detailed discussion of differentiation, see Chapter 9.

When choosing lesson objectives, contextual factors, such as the day of the week and the time of day, also need to be borne in mind. When did pupils have their last MFL lesson? Do pupils come straight from PE? Is it the first or last lesson in the day? These and others questions need to be asked as pupils' concentration spans and physical and mental readiness for certain types of activity depend on such factors. Is it a 35-minute single or 75-minute double period? This has ramifications, for instance, for the choice and sequencing of activities, the variety of tasks or the amount of work to be covered. This is the sort of valuable information which can also be gleaned from effective lesson observation carried out by you as student teacher, as well as activities such as pupil tracking, likely to be organised by your school experience school.

Lesson objectives need to be defined on the basis of previous learning outcomes.

They need to build on what has come before by either consolidating it, extending it or applying it to different contexts. When planning a lesson you need to ask yourself questions such as: what can pupils realistically be expected to know already? Do certain words/phrases/concepts need to be revised or do they need to be introduced first? Are there any issues arising from previous lessons such as unfinished activities or homework to be collected in and marked? The sample lesson plan in Figure 4.6 includes a rubric on previous learning outcomes where MFL student teachers can note relevant points.

Once learning outcomes have been identified, suitable activities can be selected in order to achieve the objectives. Important questions at this stage include: are the activities chosen sufficiently challenging? Do they move learners on? Challenge applies to *all* pupils, whatever their attainment levels. Bland, easy activities are not going to stimulate pupils or move them on in any way. The description of activities to be carried out in a lesson is a prominent feature of a lesson plan. Activities can be described in terms of teacher action (Figure 4.6) and/or pupil action (see Figure A.2 in the Appendix).

The lesson plan proforma in Figure A.2 in the Appendix implies that all lessons should be started by making objectives explicit and be finished by summarising in a plenary what was learnt. We deem this to constitute good practice and it is adopted by most departments.

As part of the planning process you need to give some thought to what strategies you will use to set up and explain the various activities. For example, what TL instructions are appropriate or what type of interaction mode is best: teacher-led, group, pair and/or independent work? How will pupils best see the value in activities? You also need to try to anticipate potential problems/disruptions that may arise. For instance, do seating arrangements have to be changed between a teacher-led activity and the following group work activity? Such changes are best kept to a minimum. Where they are required, they need to be well managed: prediction and prevention of class management issues are key.

The sequencing of activities is very important. The paradigm of 'introduction – presentation – practice – exploitation – assessment' applies to lesson as well as unit of work planning (see Chapters 3 and 6 for details). Content should be broken down into manageable steps and, usually, input should come towards the beginning of the lesson when the receptiveness of pupils is highest (see Harris 1994: 34). Often, revision of work carried out in the previous lesson is necessary prior to new input.

The timing of activities is another essential consideration. Anticipating the length of a particular activity helps to make sure that a realistic amount of work has been prepared. Estimating how long activities will need can be initially very difficult for student teachers. Realistic use of lesson observation to time activities can help.

Pupil responses to classroom tasks vary, yet all types provide some feedback for you about pupils' readiness to move on. Pupils' facial expressions, the number of hands going up, the tone of voice and body language can all be signs of enthusiasm and confidence or boredom and inattentiveness. Pupils' willingness to engage in pupil–pupil and pupil–teacher TL activities gives you an opportunity to monitor the progress of individual pupils.

Timing activities precisely also helps to pace a lesson appropriately, that is to ensure that the change from one activity to the next happens at the right time. 'Pace' is often cited as a necessary improvement to a lesson, but what exactly is 'pace'? It certainly includes:

- a clear focus and purpose;
- making good use of the time available;
- keeping on track without being unduly distracted;
- ensuring administrative and organisational tasks are carried out efficiently;
- not creating an imbalance between 'teacher talk' and 'pupil learning/doing'
- reacting to pupils' responses (or lack of) to the learning activities in an appropriate manner.

As exact timing is not always possible it is advisable to have a number of end-of-lesson 'fillers' ready in case there are a few minutes left at the end of a lesson to reinforce what has been taught. These 'fillers' might be in the form of a quick game, which should be linked to the learning objectives of the lesson/unit of work providing opportunities for pupils to practise known vocabulary and/or linguistic structures, for instance, noughts and crosses, blockbusters, hangman or lotto, number drills or songs. For useful ideas, see Rumley and Sharpe (1993). It is a very good idea to collect some generic style games to use with any class. As your repertoire grows, you will become more confident in your adaptability in this area.

The availability of equipment, facilities and resources clearly also needs to be considered when planning and checked before teaching a lesson. Have I got the correct tape/CD?, What are the procedures for booking the TV and video recorder?, Is the ICT set up or do I have to book a laptop and projector?, How can I get the equipment into the classroom in time for the beginning of the lesson?, Is everything on my memory stick too and do I have back up? On the sample lesson plan proforma there is a rubric 'resources required'.

Lesson plans provide an opportunity to demonstrate how the programme of work meets the statutory framework. In England, this needs be done in terms of which statements of the programme of study and which attainment target and level description are covered, as well as links to the KS3 MFL framework as appropriate. For details, see the sample lesson plan in Figure 4.6.

Detailed planning and referencing help you become familiar with the statutory framework. It heightens awareness of the variety of tasks and skill areas covered by the lessons you plan over a period of time, whether or not work is pitched consistently and whether progression is built into consecutive lessons.

The sample lesson plan in Figure 4.6 also features a rubric for homework. Homework needs to be planned in advance in relation to the learning objectives identified for a particular lesson. Is a learning homework most suitable, followed by a short test at the beginning of the next lesson? Should a worksheet be administered asking pupils to match up the newly encountered words and phrases with pictures or symbols? Should pupils be asked to write a short dialogue using the new language? In Chapter 6, the rationale for homework is discussed in detail.

No.	Question	Examples of responses
1	Were my objectives for the lesson clear to me and did I achieve them?	*To me yes, but not to all the pupils. Pupils did not see the point of the listening activity.*
2	Did pupils know what they were trying to achieve at any given moment?	*Mostly, but pupils didn't value all of it. I should relate more to their expectations.*
3	Were my instructions clear?	*No, I thought so but did not always check if pupils understood; frequent pupil questions broke the flow of the lesson.*
4	Were the material and lesson content appropriate for the group?	*Yes, pupils seemed to enjoy the lesson.*
5	Did I cater for the range of abilities in the group? How?	*Yes, through differentiated objectives and activities.*
6	Do I need to rethink the order and structure of my lesson?	*No, but I need to think about the way I give instructions and how I record progress.*
7	Did I cope effectively with disruptions?	*Yes, there were no discipline problems but I did have to keep on at it.*
8	Did I use the target language appropriately?	*Partly. I did not always check comprehension and I should use more examples rather than launching pupils into the activities too quickly.*
9	Did everyone get the opportunity to participate?	*Yes. I targeted questions deliberately using names.*
10	Did I help the more reluctant and less able to join in?	*Yes. I worked with less able pupils during the pair work.*
11	Did I ensure that everyone was on task consistently and monitor their work?	*I tried, but often I heard English being spoken.*
12	Were pupils alert, confident, enthusiastic or apathetic, uncertain, obstructive?	*Pupils were mostly positive.*
13	Do I know what individual pupils' strengths and weaknesses are?	*I think so; better assessment and recording will help.*

14	Did I diagnose and assess pupils' difficulties? Did I respond to them?	*Assessment needs formalising; pupils might see more value in activities if they self- and peer-assess more.*
15	Did I comment on work, praising effort, achievement and accuracy and give encouragement?	*Yes. I tried to follow my mentor's advice on error correction.*
16	Do I know if the pupils learnt anything?	*Yes, but I have no 'hard' evidence of all the skills covered.*
17	Did I include pair/group work?	*Yes. I asked pupils to carry out a survey.*
18	Did I make good use of resources?	*Yes, I think so. The reading activity based on authentic brochures went well.*
19	Do I know all the pupils' names?	*Yes*
20	Did I cover cultural awareness adequately?	*Yes, I had brought in coins from different French-speaking countries.*
21	Did I and the pupils enjoy the lesson?	*Yes, pupils were on task most of the time and many put their hands up during the lesson.*

Figure 4.7 Sample lesson evaluation

Lesson evaluation

As a basis for planning subsequent lessons and in order to develop reflective skills, you need to evaluate how lessons went. As the sample lesson plan in Figure 4.6 shows, this can be done in terms of whether or not pupils have achieved the lesson objectives of, say, drafting and redrafting a short text and whether or not the activities and methods chosen were effective in bringing about pupil learning, for example, taking a class of 25 pupils to the computer room with two pupils working together on one computer. For a discussion of evaluation, see also Chapter 3.

Figure 4.7 provides a list of 21 questions, which can be used as a checklist to facilitate MFL lesson evaluation. Asking these questions about (parts of) individual lessons can also help foster links and continuity between a series of lessons.

As part of the evaluation process, you should also note whether any action needs to be taken before the next lesson (see the respective rubric in Figure 4.6). For instance, was there sufficient time to cover the whole lesson plan? Could certain activities not be finished? Have all objectives have been achieved? Do any aspects need to be revised in the next lesson?

Task 4.6 Lesson planning and evaluation

1   In consultation with (the) respective class teacher(s), prepare a number of lesson plans using the proforma in Figure A.2 in the Appendix for a specific class, which you have observed on a number of occasions already.
2   Discuss the lesson plans with the respective class teacher, teach the lessons and evaluate them against the quality of pupil learning and the quality of personal teaching. The 21 questions in Figure 4.7 and the proforma (Figure A.3 in the Appendix) are intended to help you with this.

Planning a sequence of lessons/unit of work

Planning a unit of work is more than simply ensuring the coverage of the content specified in examination specifications or a chapter of a coursebook. Medium-term plans ensure that learning is planned over a period of time and occurs step-by-step. Unit of work planning enables you to think carefully about the exact nature of learning intended to take place over time and can help ensure progression, which needs to be built in by teachers in a multi-faceted manner, from:

- pre-communicative → communicative activities
- simple →complex language
- short → longer spoken and written texts
- implicit → explicit knowledge of grammar
- scripted/didactically prepared (more salient) → authentic (less salient) language
- known/familiar (e.g. classroom, self) → unknown/unfamiliar (world knowledge, target country) words and topics
- teacher-led/aided (e.g. graded questions, examples) → independent (e.g. use of glossary, dictionary and other reference sources; pair-work, groupwork) interaction and working modes
- concrete → abstract ideas
- factual → non-factual/fictional spoken and written texts
- predictable → unpredictable situations
- less controversial → more controversial issues.

(Pachler 2000b: 511)

The process of planning a series of lessons raises a whole host of issues related to providing appropriate learning opportunities. Teachers need to ensure medium-term plans feature variety, breadth and balance. Implications for classroom organisation and management, resources, continuity and progression also warrant consideration (see Hurren 1992: 2).

> From (an initial overview of the forthcoming year's work) it may become apparent that some units are more interesting and have more potential than

others. Some may be more difficult and may contain more material and so need extra time or are best not begun near the end of term. Equally, one may become aware in good time of units of work that seem thin and may need supplementing and one may therefore be on the outlook for suitable additional materials or ideas for exploitation. . . . One becomes aware that certain pieces of language, certain skills, classroom activities and procedures will occur again and again throughout the year. They are therefore worth spending extra time and trouble on first time round to ensure that they are efficiently mastered from the start. Other, rather complicated activities or unduly time-consuming pieces of material may be isolated or marginal, and may therefore be either omitted or dealt with fairly perfunctorily.

(Wringe 1989: 26)

Importantly, learning opportunities must articulate with the statutory framework. If certain learning opportunities are not contained within one unit of work but required by the statutory framework, they need to be included in one of the following units. The level descriptions for each of the four skills of listening, speaking, reading and writing enable you to devise activities of differing levels of difficulty, thereby catering for the respective stage of learning of pupils and ensuring progression.

Illustrative, non-statutory schemes of work for Key Stage 3 are available in French, German and Spanish on the internet (see http://www.ncaction.org.uk/subjects/ MFL/). Among other things, they contain examples of grammar items, which should be included at different stages of the learning process. The non-statutory schemes of work also indicate topics, which might be selected to provide relevant contexts and content for MFL learning in the NC. The Key Stage 3 MFL Framework (see Chapter 1) is also very important here, as this provides a non-topic based approach to progression in language in Years 7–9 (see also Heilbronn 2004).

Task 4.7 Your department's use of the KS3 Framework for MFL

Using the departmental information you looked at previously, analyse how your department may have integrated the MFL KS3 Framework. Since it is non-statutory, the department may not have done this.

Talk to your mentor about the reasons why/why not and the advantages and drawbacks.

The coursebook can also offer support. Many coursebook writers suggest the level of performance demanded by particular tasks. You need to relate these notional levels of task difficulty to the pupils' levels of attainment. Discrepancy between the task difficulty and pupils' attainment levels signals the need to adapt the material. It is clearly not appropriate to set pupils certain tasks just because they are in the coursebook. Coursebooks do contain many suitable and appropriate tasks and much useful material. However, you need to evaluate all the tasks and material carefully in relation to the learning outcomes identified in the scheme of work. You also need to evaluate their appropriateness in terms of difficulty and in relation to the statutory framework and/or examination specifications.

The coursebook can provide a useful basis for planning. It often needs supplementing and the activities in it structuring and sequencing. Equally, frequently certain material has to be omitted. In our view, there is no such a thing as the ideal coursebook as certain skills and topics tend to be handled differently and more to the liking of the teacher by different coursebooks. Also, the amount of material provided by a coursebook does not necessarily coincide with the time available or the examination specifications followed.

Having a coursebook is a useful resource for learners as it visibly structures the teaching and learning material they encounter.

Some departments still pursue what could be described as a 'pick-and-mix' approach, writing their own worksheets, having sets of certain coursebooks, which they use for different topics. Such an approach can work very well but tends to be more demanding in terms of planning time.

For advantages and pitfalls associated with the use of coursebooks, see also Chapter 11.

Task 4.8 Exploring the relationship between individual lessons and the unit of work

Ask your mentor for a copy of the department's schemes of work. See how some of the lessons you have observed in Task 4.2 fit in with the department's unit of work planning: how do the lesson objectives relate to the unit of work objectives?

It is important to note that MFL student teachers should not plan units of work in isolation from colleagues. Schemes of work and departmental handbooks need to be seen as collaborative efforts. As Hurren (1992: 11) points out, the scheme of work acts as:

- a tool for developing coherent ideas on policy, methodology, priorities, subject matter, etc.;
- a basis for pooling expertise, sharing work-loads and apportioning responsibility;
- a means of ensuring a cohesion of approach, objectives, teaching methods and standards among colleagues;
- a device for monitoring the effectiveness of current practice;
- a means of expressing the department's work to other departments, to newly appointed colleagues, to head teachers and curriculum managers, parents, governors, advisers and inspectors;
- a device for interpreting into practice the guidelines of local policies, national criteria, National Curriculum, desirable methodology, etc.

A blank photocopiable proforma for scheme of work planning can be found in the Appendix, Figure A.4. The following section discusses how this proforma can be used. The issues discussed here are not dissimilar from those covered in the section on lesson planning.

Many MFL student teachers fear that they will fall behind more experienced colleagues by taking too long over particular aspects of units of work. Identification in advance of the number and length of lessons available for teaching a unit of work can help pace pupils' progress. This gives you, and of course pupils, a time-frame to work to.

The section on objectives in the unit of work plan in Figure A.4 indicates what pupils should achieve by the end of the unit. As in lesson plans, they should be multi-dimensional and differentiated into core and extension outcomes.

Main language items/structures refer to the vocabulary, phrases and structures to be covered. Although much is accounted for by examination specifications at Key Stage 4, important decisions for the teacher do remain even there. These include the identification of a core, which applies to all pupils in the group, and an extension for those who can carry out additional work. Also, you need to think about how individuals can be supported in acquiring the core. In addition, you need to consider which phrases need to be explained with reference to metalanguage and which can/should be taught as lexical items.

Methodology is as important as the content. By varying the types of learning activities, the teacher can make a judgement as to whether pupils of all learning styles and abilities have been catered for equally well. Periodical audits might be useful to monitor the extent to which teaching and learning are varied (see Task 4.9). The unit of work plan also features a rubric on 'main material and resources'.

Task 4.9 Auditing teaching and learning activities

How often do you employ the following teaching and learning methods in your teaching? Feel free to add to the list. 5 indicates 'very often' and 1 means 'never'.

investigation	5 4 3 2 1	Example
problem solving	5 4 3 2 1	Example
hypothesising	5 4 3 2 1	Example
trialling	5 4 3 2 1	Example
testing	5 4 3 2 1	Example
explaining	5 4 3 2 1	Example
exploring	5 4 3 2 1	Example
communicating	5 4 3 2 1	Example
memorising	5 4 3 2 1	Example
repetition	5 4 3 2 1	Example
drilling	5 4 3 2 1	Example
improvising	5 4 3 2 1	Example
inventing	5 4 3 2 1	Example
designing	5 4 3 2 1	Example
brainstorming	5 4 3 2 1	Example
role playing	5 4 3 2 1	Example
evaluating	5 4 3 2 1	Example

Does this information help you identify how MFL teaching may contribute to the fulfilment of the aims and objectives of a unit of work for all pupils in the class?

Source: Field *et al.* (2000).

Once the objectives are clear and the material and resources have been selected, core, reinforcement and extension activities can be identified. These activities should cover the language skills of listening, speaking, reading and writing and should be pitched at appropriate levels.

The main activities listed in a unit of work are likely to be those in which pupils can apply the newly acquired knowledge, skills and understanding.

The sections on core, reinforcement and extension activities do not require a condensed version of everything covered in the whole unit of work. The main activities should act as markers or benchmarks signalling a readiness to move on. It is, therefore, important that these activities are, where appropriate, cross-referenced to the statutory requirements or other relevant criteria. Careful monitoring of the activities through continuous and/or summative teacher assessment helps to ensure progression and continuity.

The section of the proforma entitled 'main homework' allows you to list the main homework tasks. Homework can, for instance, reinforce work covered in class, prepare pupils for future learning or involve them in creative activities. It is important that homework is carefully planned and contributes to the fulfilment of the stated objectives. For a detailed discussion of homework, see Chapter 6.

Importantly, unit of work plans also need to give an overview of the opportunities provided to assess and monitor pupils' progress.

As we have emphasised previously, activities need to be cross-referenced to the statutory framework in order for the MFL teacher to be able to monitor effectively whether pupils have achieved certain levels across the various skills and whether they progress in all aspects of their work. Core and non-core activities can serve to provide meaningful assessment information as can vocabulary tests, revision exercises etc. In addition, you should prepare summative assessment tasks, such as end of unit tests and end of unit goals, in line with the practices at the placement school.

Task 4.10 Unit of work planning

Observe a sequence of lessons with the same class taught by an experienced colleague:

1   Identify what you think the key objectives are and identify the activities planned to prepare the pupils to achieve these. For an example, see Figure 4.3.
2   How is the learning monitored and what action is taken by the teacher to compensate when successful learning has not taken place?

Unit plans require considerable thought and can be time-consuming to prepare. However, they facilitate the process of individual lesson planning and help to ensure progression and continuity and the inclusion of variety and differentiation.

Finally, unit planning should also take into account the need to provide pupils with the opportunity to become more independent in their approach to MFL learning. Rampillon (1994: 456–9) suggests that there is a need for activities which promote an enjoyment of the subject and enable pupils to become aware of factors potentially impeding their learning. Pupils should have opportunities to combine what they already know with new knowledge. This inevitably requires some guidance on the organisation of learning and the identification of individual needs. By presenting pupils with a range of learning strategies, Rampillon believes that pupils will develop a repertoire of learning techniques upon which they can draw in the future. Evaluation should include a review of whether such learning opportunities have, or have not, been provided. This information, should of course, be used to inform future planning. For a discussion of learning strategies, see Chapter 3.

SUMMARY

Lesson observation needs to be seen as an effective way to learn about MFL teaching and can represent an invaluable tool in the development and formation of a personal approach to MFL teaching.

Effective short- and medium-term planning are key characteristics of successful teaching. They help you in mediating and pupils in acquiring the necessary knowledge, understanding and skills in the course of their study of MFL.

Evaluation is an important integral part of an effective planning process.

FURTHER READING

Crozier, M., Gidley, R., Lertoria, T., Murphy, D., Slater, S. and Wardle, M. (2003) 'Starters and plenaries – a practical resource', *Deutsch: Lehren und Lernen 28*: 11–14.

A very clear introduction to the issues involved in planning for learning in MFL. Practical ideas to incorporate in plans for MFL teaching and learning.

Pachler, N. and Redondo, A. (2007) (eds) *Teaching Foreign Languages in the Secondary School: A Practical Guide*. London: Routledge.

This book offers practical advice concerning many aspects of MFL teaching incl. planning.

Wajnryb, R. (1992) *Classroom Observation Tasks: A Resource Book for Language Teachers and Trainers*. Cambridge: Cambridge University Press.

This text remains a very good guide to aspects to be considered when observing in foreign language classrooms.

5 Teaching in the target language

A critical appraisal (with Roswitha Guest)

INTRODUCTION

The use of the target language (TL) involves some key methodological issues for modern foreign languages (MFL) teachers. These include:

- how to ensure the TL is used best for instruction, interaction and communication and exactly how to structure the actual TL used;
- its effective use by pupils as well as teachers;
- whether, when and how the use of English may be appropriate in the learning and teaching process.

OBJECTIVES

By the end of this chapter you should:

- be able to consider the practice of teaching in the TL from the perspective of a basic understanding of theoretical issues and recent policy developments;
- be able to examine desirability and aims of teaching in the TL;
- be able to assess practicability of teaching in the TL in everyday MFL lessons;
- be able to identify the advantages of using the TL and how to exploit them;
- be able to assess the disadvantages of using the TL and how to overcome them;
- be able to understand strategies for effective TL use.

Rather than discussing the issues associated with TL use as a recurring theme in various places in the book, we cover them in one single chapter in order to provide a coherent overview of relevant issues. Therefore, the examples given need to be seen in the context of the respective chapters they are linked to, for instance examples of how to teach grammar in the TL need to be related to the overall approach to teaching and learning grammar outlined in detail in Chapter 7. In this chapter we briefly examine the theoretical arguments and discuss practical suggestions for effective TL use in the light of the most recent NC Orders. In addition, issues of TL teaching with particular relevance for you as a student teacher are included.

THE TARGET LANGUAGE IN THE MFL CLASSROOM: A SUMMARY OF RECENT DEVELOPMENTS

The various versions of the National Curriculum (NC) Orders in the 1990s established the expectation of TL use as the 'normal means of communication' (DES/Welsh Office 1990: 6) in the classroom and, indeed, a lesson conducted entirely in TL was generally regarded as successful and, indeed, still is (Ofsted 2004). This resulted in empirical research (see e.g. Dickson 1996; Macaro 1996, 1997; or Neil 1997) as well as a considerable body of pedagogical literature (see e.g. MacDonald 1993 or NCC 1992b) about whether this policy does in fact lead to the learning gains it promises *prima facie* and how TL use can best be implemented.

Issues relating to TL use are, of course, ostensibly twofold: on the one hand, they concern TL use by teachers, be it for basic routine or more complex procedural instructions, as was often the focus in the early to mid-1990s; on the other hand, they relate to TL use by pupils, be it with the teacher or peers. Its effective use by pupils became a focus after the MFL community had initially concentrated, published and debated on TL as 'teacher talk' for quite a period (see Neil 1996). More recently, the debate surrounding TL has opened up the discussion further as to the use (or not) of English in the MFL classroom. Is there a legitimate case for using English in certain circumstances? Can it further pupil learning in MFL? Does MFL learning and teaching in the UK need to rethink the status of TL in the classroom? (See Macaro 2001b; Meiring and Norman 2002; Butzkamm 2003; Barnes 2007). The debate has certainly moved a long way from clarity and progression of TL instructions to the development of a rationale for TL and English as to how best pupils can improve their foreign language skills. The current focus is on CLIL (content and language integrated learning) and other cross-curricular approaches.

Developments with the National Curriculum reflected to some extent this change in focus. While the NC Orders implemented in the early and mid-1990s promoted the so-called maximalist position on TL use, which assumes that 'there is probably no pedagogical value in learner use of L1 and almost certainly none in teacher use of L1' (Macaro 2000: 184), the publication of a revised NC at the end of the 1990s saw a shift towards the so-called optimal use position, which sees 'some value in teacher use of L1 and some value in learner use of L1' (ibid.: 184). Although the 1999 NC document contained no explicit references to the medium in which teachers should teach, expectations concerning pupil use of the TL were clear:

> The target language is the modern foreign language that pupils are learning. Pupils are expected to use and respond to the target language, and to use English only when necessary (for example, when discussing a grammar point or when comparing English and the target language).
>
> (DfEE/QCA 1999: 16)

In addition, in the 1999 National Curriculum Programme of Study, 3c states:

> Pupils should be taught to:
>
> Use their knowledge of English or another language when learning the target language.

The 2007 Programme of Study, however, makes a number of references to English (or another language) as being potentially helpful to learners when comparing languages, memorising or considering language patterns. This is made clear both in specific elements of the programme of study (PoS) and in the accompanying explanatory notes:

> 2.1c: c use their knowledge of English or another language when learning the target language
>
> 4d: make links with English at word, sentence and text level

The 2000 GCSE MFL criteria available at http://www.qca.org.uk/downloads/ 5708_modern_foreign_lang.pd(1).pdf (QCA 2000b: 3), which defined the subject-specific aspects of the GCSE, state that:

> A specification must require candidates to express themselves in the modern foreign language when speaking and writing. In listening and reading, where a response is spoken or written, it must be in the modern foreign language, except where a response in another language is a necessary part of the task (for example, in an interpreting exercise) or where a non-linguistic response is a natural and appropriate alternative to a response in the modern foreign language. A maximum of 10% of the total marks for the subject may be awarded for answers in English, Welsh or Irish. No more than half of this maximum allocation may be assigned to any particular assessment objective.

From this, clear inferences can be made about expected teacher use of the TL. The 2007 draft GCSE criteria, to be implemented from 2009, are less prescriptive, with no specific mention of the use of English. Recent Ofsted reports do refer to the limited use of English, but stress it should be planned (Ofsted 2004: 10).

There are, therefore, certain advantages of pupils' knowledge of their own and other languages acknowledged in policy documents.

ISSUES WITH THE TL

As far as teachers are concerned, TL use is an important issue for native speakers of English or other non-native TL speakers as well as native speakers of the TL. Native speakers of English face challenges such as developing the requisite subject knowledge and confidence of TL use for sustained periods of time. Native speakers of the TL need to take care to ensure their use of the TL is pitched correctly according to the linguistic proficiency of their pupils. Being a native speaker of the TL doesn't necessarily make TL use easier. For example, Macaro reports:

> In general, teachers saw exclusive or near-exclusive use of TL as being unattainable with all but the most motivated classes. Many felt that the task was certainly harder than the NC statements would lead one to believe. Some had felt guilty at first about lapsing into English but, because they were continually redoubling their efforts, had become reconciled to not being able to attain exclusive use.
>
> (1996: 6)

It is widely acknowledged that the artificiality of the classroom frequently militates against maximum TL use by pupils and teachers. Maximum TL use requires a suspension of disbelief both on the part of pupils and teachers, i.e. the willingness to pretend neither party speaks English and that the transactions and interactions of the classroom are 'authentic', which is often difficult and, one might argue, sometimes undesirable to sustain. The effort required both by pupils and by teachers to maintain maximum TL use can lead to reduced levels of 'performance' on the part of teachers and alienation from the learning process on the part of pupils, and, after all, the objectives of any series of lessons is for pupils' learning to progress rather than to maintain maximal (teacher) TL use. The development of good social relationships between teachers and pupils, it can be argued, requires non-curriculum specific TL, which learners do not have at their disposal. There are, in short, practical difficulties associated with maximum use of the TL.

The amount of TL used by teachers depends on many factors such as:

- ability and size of the group;
- motivation;
- group dynamics;
- receptiveness of the pupils;
- environmental factors;
- incidents during previous lesson or break;
- topic area;
- tasks to be attempted;
- discipline problems;
- interruptions from outside, etc.

These factors have an even greater influence on the amount of TL used by the pupils to respond to or initiate exchanges with the teacher and/or peers. Established classroom routines, adequate preparation and a feeling of confidence and security are vitally important in this respect.

While maximum exposure to the TL can be seen to be beneficial to the pupils' linguistic confidence and competence, in some respects, *teaching in* the TL does not automatically lead to *learning* the TL. Simulation of the goal, i.e. independent TL use by pupils in 'authentic', real-life situations, is not necessarily the best means. Clearly, in the acquisition-poor environment of the MFL classroom exposure to the TL by the teacher as well as the TL material can be seen to be vital in supporting the learning process. However, an important methodological question concerns the extent to which teachers should make the structure of a language explicit or how much they should try to mimic natural processes of language acquisition. Earlier NC requirements could be seen to be underpinned by a belief in the latter. Nevertheless, 'the case for learning the L2 "naturally", like babies acquire their L1, is not proven' (Macaro 2000: 178). Despite the fact that mother tongue use deprives learners of exposure to TL models, teaching in the TL needs to be systematic and planned in order to be effective. There are occasions when TL use can become a barrier to understanding and, therefore, to learning. There are certain circumstances when it is not appropriate and there are some when it is simply impossible. Importantly also, it needs to be remembered that teacher talk is different from native speaker talk (see Pachler 1999a or Macaro 2000) and that, therefore, classroom-based exposure to TL is different to that in the real world: the language is, of necessity, segmented, partial and carefully built up. In his review of research literature, Macaro (ibid.: 179) stresses that the mother tongue is the language of thought for all but the most advanced learners and that, therefore, it warrants careful consideration as a learning tool. Codeswitching (i.e. using both the TL and the L1) is described by Macaro as a natural and legitimate operation despite the possibility of interference from the mother tongue. He questions whether interference from the mother tongue is sufficient 'to counter-balance any beneficial cognitive processes that making links between L1 and L2 might bring about' (ibid.: 179). Macaro hypothesises that beginners use the mother tongue to help them decode texts and that beginners and more advanced learners use it to help them write texts. Also, he suggests that progression from formulaic expression to more 'creative'/independent use of the TL may well require some recourse to the mother tongue as the language of thought. In addition, learners need to feel clear about what they are doing and why.

In his own empirical work into TL use, Macaro (1996: 6) found that MFL teachers listed the following arguments for and against the use of the TL:

positive

- the amount of language that is acquired subconsciously by pupils;
- the improvement in listening skills;
- exploitation of the medium itself leads to new teaching and learning strategies;
- demonstrating to the pupils the importance of learning a foreign language;
- demonstrating to the pupils how the language can be used to do things.

negative

- TL for instructions can be time-consuming;
- reaching a point when remaining in the TL becomes counter-productive;
- teaching in the TL is tiring and an exhausted teacher stops to be effective.

The study also reports that challenging behaviour and/or poor motivation particularly influenced the judgement made by teachers about whether or not to use the TL.

TYPOLOGY OF TL USE

It seems unnatural to be against teaching in the TL, yet if it is such a natural thing to do, why does it cause such a debate among MFL teachers?

The National Curriculum Council non-statutory guidance, still valid despite its early publication date, offers the diagrammatical representation of TL use in Figure 5.1: the teacher and pupils interacting with each other inside the classroom as a preparation for TL use beyond the classroom.

The following three types of interaction can be differentiated:

- teacher–pupil
- pupil–teacher
- pupil–pupil.

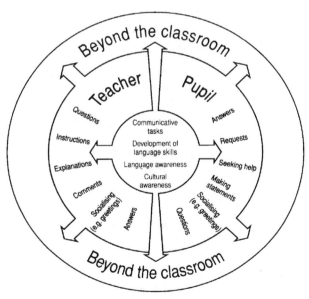

Figure 5.1 Using the TL

Source: NCC 1992.

Often departments identify key lexical items and phrases for each of these categories as *aide-mémoires* for members of the team in order to encourage appropriateness of TL use in relation to the level of proficiency of pupils as well as to foster standardisation across the department. For pupils, these lists become part of the passive and/or active vocabulary they are expected to know (see MacDonald 1993).

Experience and Ofsted inspection evidence suggest that, while a structured and well-planned approach can facilitate the coherent use of the TL by the teacher when interacting with pupils and – to a lesser extent – pupils responding to or even initiating interaction in the TL with the teacher, TL use between pupils is most difficult to achieve.

Task 5.1 Departmental policy on teaching in the TL

Obtain a copy of the departmental policy on the use of the TL by pupils and teachers. What approach do you feel it encourages: maximal or optimal, or is the message less clear? If possible, compare practice in your placement school with that experienced by student teachers in other schools.

Transactional language, i.e. the language of classroom objects, classroom interaction and classroom communication, needs to be taught just like other topic-related language. Possible strategies in this context are, for instance:

- the use of visuals, interactive whiteboard (IWB), PowerPoint, OHP or flashcards) depicting key words and phrases;
- classroom displays, which are regularly referred to in the course of teaching;
- building up a list of useful phrases and expressions in the back of pupils' exercise books;
- the encouragement of TL utterances by pupils when entering and leaving the classroom or when the register is called;
- the use of pupils as 'translators' to verify meaning in English;
- variation in voice and intonation as an incentive to pupils to repeat words or phrases many times, e.g. '*leise*', '*ganz leise*', '*schnell*', '*ganz schnell*'; or
- the so-called 'sandwich' method of 'wrapping' mother tongue instructions into two 'layers' of TL, e.g. '*Stellt euch leise hintereinander auf*' – 'Line up quietly' – '*Stellt euch leise hintereinander auf*'.

Task 5.2 Teaching transactional TL

Design some visuals in a format of your choice or other material for the teaching and practice of some specific transactional TL phrases for pupils in their first year of study of the foreign language. Test these out with your classes and revise them on the basis of pupil feedback and your reflection.

Task 5.3 Using the target language or English?

Below are some possible recommendations for using TL and English. Do you agree with them? How would you alter them to fit what you believe are more appropriate?

Use of the TL

Pupils need to be as familiar and secure in hearing, understanding and using the target language as possible. This will *not* happen if:

- You translate any TL immediately into English – pupils will just expect this.
- You resort to English at the first sign that they don't understand.

Some initial advice on using TL:

- You should plan it carefully, accurately and in an appropriate sequence.
- You should use all the strategies possible to avoid English where appropriate (e.g. visuals, gestures, etc. – this avoids having to say 'How do you say x in Fr/Sp/Ger?').
- You should use English only where it is pedagogically sensible and beneficial to do so.

When is English appropriate? When should TL always be used? This may depend on the following issues:

- Attitudes to TL in your school
- *Planned* use of TL/English
- *Spontaneous* use of TL/English
- TL in instructions
- TL in general classroom talk (e.g. praise, rewards, comments)
- *Your* use of TL – how accurate, fluent and spontaneous can you be?
- *Your* preparation of TL for lesson content: must be thorough, accurate and checked!
- TL for terminology, grammar.

THE DECONTEXTUALISED NATURE OF TL LEARNING IN THE CLASSROOM

As has been noted above, the case for TL use is loosely based on the assumption that pupils will acquire the foreign language by immersion in a similar way to how they acquire their own. However, the main conditions necessary for this process, that is, a 'real' need to communicate in the TL and the constant and varied exposure to (new) TL and the opportunity to try out and practise newly learnt words, phrases and structures, are invariably contrived and/or often absent in the MFL classroom. Mother tongue learning is highly *contextualised*, learning the TL in a classroom environment is highly *decontextualised*.

There is no doubt that pupils *acquire* many words, phrases and structures and can consequently use them passively and some even actively. These tend to be the most frequently used items of classroom language such as greetings, instructions, labelled items of furniture and equipment as well as the linguistic habits of the teacher. For real acquisition to take place, there needs to be the opportunity for constant reinforcement. This is one of the reasons why TL teaching tends to work well in the teaching of English as a Foreign Language (EFL) and of English for Speakers of Other Languages (ESOL): learners can often be sent out to practise what they have learnt in lessons and try it out in a variety of real situations when it is appropriate and they feel confident to do so. In MFL teaching and learning this is not really an option.

Other factors, such as class size, curriculum time and timetabling, make language acquisition unlikely, even if the teacher does use the TL throughout lessons. In a class of 25 or 30 pupils the opportunities for individual pupils to try out new words and phrases and to use the TL meaningfully are invariably limited and usually restricted to perfunctory standard responses. It is difficult for pupils to retain what they have learnt in a lesson without any further reinforcement until the next lesson, often some days away. There is, after all, little need and, therefore, little motivation to use the TL outside the classroom.

TRANSMITTING INFORMATION VERSUS REAL COMMUNICATION

According to one point of view the focus on active work with the TL by pupils rather than passive learning elevates TL use to communication. A closer examination of the communicative tasks of the classroom would suggest that very often pupils engage in little more than transactions devoid of an important criterion for communication, namely the desire to pass on personally meaningful and valued information: buying railway tickets, making dental appointments or giving directions to a cathedral in some foreign city do not normally fulfil this criterion. The fact that these tasks are conducted in the TL often makes very little difference to the pupils' perception of a 'real' conversation topic and rarely makes the topics more appealing. The issues pupils generally consider worth communicating are usually not suitable for lessons because they are personal and often not related to the task or topic in hand. Many of the situations pupils are expected to communicate in seem contrived as they are not commonly conducted by pupils in English, let alone in the TL.

In terms of classroom transactions and interactions there are, however, a number of opportunities for real communication such as '*Ich habe mein Heft vergessen*' ('I forgot my exercise book'), '*Kann ich einen Kuli haben?*' ('Can I borrow a pen?'), '*Kann ich aufs Klo gehen?*' ('Can I go to the toilet?'). In subsequent years this list needs to be expanded and built upon to ensure progression; whereas in Year 7 '*Entschuldigung, ich habe mein Heft vergessen*' ('Sorry, I have forgotten my exercise book') is acceptable, in Year 10 one might expect an explanation as well '*Entschuldigung, ich habe mein Heft vergessen, weil. . . .*' Not to encourage pupils to use the TL in these contexts is wasting valuable opportunities for TL use.

A great number of pupils can convey and transmit information, which is, indeed, a success criterion at GCSE. What most of them cannot do, however, is to communicate their own ideas, deeply felt emotions, strongly held opinions and all those abstract thoughts many pupils find challenging to communicate in their own language.

AUTHENTICITY OF TASKS

There is another problem with 'real' communication: the 'authenticity' of the tasks. How can 'real' communication take place in such an unreal setting? However hard we try to turn MFL classrooms into a 'foreign' environment, it is still, at best, only a simulation and perceived as such at most times by our pupils. It requires a great deal of good will and humour from the pupils to make it work. And even the use of 'authentic' material can work against the teacher. Authentic material for young native speakers, such as magazines and videos, are usually too ambitious for the MFL skills of pupils. The discrepancy between the chronological age and the linguistic age of pupils makes it very difficult if not frustrating to address their specific interests. Yet, material produced specifically for the young MFL learner (especially at Key Stage 4) are often perceived as boring, childish and patronising by pupils. This situation has improved a great deal, however, with access to a wealth of materials via the internet.

This problem is even greater, however, when it comes to communicating ideas and thoughts in a discussion. Pupils simply do not have the linguistic 'equipment' and sophistication to express themselves appropriately. Their level of language invariably stifles 'proper' and immediate expression often leading to frustration, embarrassment and, ultimately, opting out. It is very difficult in such situations to insist on 'TL only' rules: if we are interested in pupils' thoughts and opinions we need to allow them to express them. Exclusive use of the TL can make the building up of a good rapport with pupils a challenge, which is why the integration of high frequency words via the KS3 MFL Framework and the incorporation of a more appropriate level of challenge into the *content* of MFL lessons is so important.

SOME FACTORS LIMITING THE EFFECTIVENESS OF TL USE

There are certain limits to how much you can use the TL effectively in lessons. Teaching in the TL can be tiring for teacher and pupils. A lot of thought has to be given not only to the lesson plan but also to the wording of instructions and the level of the 'incidental' language, ensuring that pupils do not get left behind. It takes great concentration and perseverance not to do the 'natural thing', that is to answer the questions in the language they are asked. There is often the temptation to answer a pupil's question 'What page are we on?' with 'Top of page 48'. One possible strategy is to 'appoint' language guardians, who call the teacher to order in such circumstances, e.g. with '*Auf Deutsch bitte, Frau/Herr . . .!*' ('In German, please Ms/Mr . . .!').

Pupils' limited attention span can cause a considerable problem. A whole lesson is a long time for pupils to concentrate and few can do it. Indeed, research by Macaro (2000: 187) suggests that long lessons of more than 50 minutes had less average pupil use of the TL in teacher-centred activities than short lessons of approximately 35 minutes. And not only pupils. Members of staff (non-linguists) who support weaker groups have been heard expressing their discomfort at being exposed non-stop to the TL and experiencing considerable unease that they might be asked a question. It is easy to forget how challenging constant TL teaching can be. From time to time it can be hugely beneficial to remind oneself just how it feels to be in the learners' position. Often during Postgraduate Certificate in Education (PGCE) courses student teachers are taught a lesson in a foreign language they don't speak, where the teacher performs standard vocabulary presentation and practice activities, etc. Many student teachers dread being asked questions and realise how often they need to hear the phrases before they can repeat them. Teacher exposure to an unknown language can reinforce the awareness that pupils need plenty of individual/choral practice before being asked to produce new words, phrases or structures in context.

For those pupils who think that MFL are beyond them, unstructured teaching in the TL can confirm their feeling of inadequacy, potentially leading to demotivation and frustration and all the associated discipline problems. As MFL teachers, we need to guard against alienating pupils and try to avoid reinforcing their sense of failure to understand. This can be seen to be particularly important when teaching lower ability groups who need frequent reassurance in the form of repetition and comprehension checks, including in English. If such a lot of time is spent checking whether pupils understand TL instructions, when is the actual learning taking place?

This problem can be overcome by careful lesson planning: if the pace of the lesson is brisk, if the activities are varied, if all four skills are being practised and if there is a balance of 'stirrers' and 'settlers' (see Halliwell 1991b: 26), then unacceptably long spells of continuous TL should not normally occur.

Using the TL language should be a simulating challenge for you and your pupils, not a threat!

Task 5.4 Focused lesson observation

Observe some MFL lessons and focus on how the teacher:

- uses the TL to begin and end lessons;
- supports instructions and explanations with mimes and gestures to aid understanding;
- uses the classroom environment to support the use of the TL.

Also, what aspects of classroom management and discipline are dealt with in the TL?

TL USE FOR THE MANAGEMENT OF PUPIL BEHAVIOUR

The use of the TL for pupil management can be very effective. For instance, when pupils break a classroom or whole school rule, they are usually well aware of their misdemeanour. They are also familiar with the sanctions commonly used in their school and the expectations of their MFL teacher. The teacher can safely admonish the pupils in the TL. Even if the pupils do not understand the words, the situation has made the meaning quite clear.

Supported with gestures and near cognates such as '*Du sollst nicht auf deinem Stuhl schwingen!*' the message usually gets across, occasionally with the help of another pupil: 'She says you must not swing on your chair.' The tone of voice in which the reprimand is delivered, as well as the context, make comprehension possible. This approach does, however, assume that pupils know the rules of the MFL classroom. These should be made very clear in the first few weeks of Year 7 in English and subsequently reinforced and added to.

THE TEACHING OF GRAMMAR AND TL USE

Grammar is often perceived to be a difficult – if not the most difficult – part of the subject to be taught in the TL (see Dickson 1996; Macaro 1996; Neil 1997). However, quite a number of grammar points can be taught in the TL, particularly if there is an element of physical demonstration and visualisation. A playful approach as well as the continuous use of certain 'stock' types of activities, which can be used for a range of different topics, can help to minimise the need for complex instructions and explanations in English and make it easier to teach grammar in the TL. Demonstrations, illustrations and examples are worth many complicated explanations. The examples given in this chapter are to provide ideas and to be adapted appropriately to the relevant TL. You will need to plan the specific linguistic focus carefully.

Many pupils have difficulties with the German word order when a sentence starts with an adverbial of time. The following activity works well with Year 8. Having taught the activities, e.g. '*Ich gehe ins Kino*' ('I go to the cinema'), days of the week, e.g. '*am Montag*' ('on Monday') and the question word '*wann*' ('when'), the teacher writes the words *[ich] [gehe] [ins Kino]* and *[am Montag]* on individual A4 cards. A bigger sign is made for *[wann?]*. The class is divided into groups of five. The first three pupils go to the front and hold their words up in the correct sequence to form and speak the sentence. Pupil 4 holds up the *[wann?]* sign and asks the question. Pupil 5 – *[am Montag]* – joins them and four pupils re-form physically to make the correct sentence: *[Am Montag] [gehe] [ich] [ins Kino]*. Pupils then make their own sentences (on cards) and perform them.

Word order, in particular in the past tense, can be practised with cut-up sentences (auxiliary verb and past participle in different colours) mixed up in small envelopes. This task is almost always performed in the TL using familiar phrases such as '*Ist das richtig?*' ('Is that correct?'), '*Nein, das ist falsch!*' ('No, that is wrong'). It works particularly well if the same colours are used when introducing the past tense (on PowerPoint or an OHT, for example).

Pupils' speaking skills are often restricted by the number of verbs they know, which limits their communication. Verb endings are a frequent source of error. Pupils can revise and practise verbs and verb endings in the form of the following game (Figure 5.2).

Two hexagons are drawn on the board (side by side). Each corner of the hexagon represents a personal pronoun.

Elicit two verbs (regular verbs to begin with, then irregular and modal verbs much later) from the pupils and write them inside the hexagons (Figure 5.3). The class is

Figure 5.2 Hexagon 1

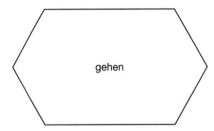

Figure 5.3 Hexagon 2

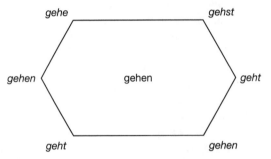

Figure 5.4 Hexagon 3

divided into two teams, the members of each team are numbered, the numbers written on pieces of paper and put in a box. A pupil picks a number and the two corresponding pupils from each team go up to the board. At the command '*Auf die Plätze, fertig, los!*' ('On your marks, get set, go!') pupils write the relevant verb forms at each corner of their hexagon (Figure 5.4). Conferring with their team is permitted. The first pupil to finish gets 10 points. One point is deducted for each mistake. The second pupil gets one point per correct verb form. This ensures that the fast and careless pupils do not always win.

Question forms are also difficult to learn for pupils. They can be learnt playing the battleship game. From a grid (Figures 5.5 and 5.6) each pupil has to select one square per row and per column without showing it to their partner. By asking relevant questions, e.g. '*Kommst du mit dem Auto zur Schule?*' (Figure 5.5) or '*Saugst du manchmal Staub?*' (Figure 5.6), they then try to find out what choices their partner has made. If they guess correctly, they can ask again; if not, their partner asks a question. The winner is the pupil who has found out all of her partner's answers first.

	ins Schwimmbad	in die Stadt	nach Amerika	nach London	zur Schule	zum Bahnhof	zum Golfplatz
mit dem Zug							
mit dem Bus							
mit dem Rad							
zu Fuß							
mit dem Flugzeug							
mit der U-Bahn							
mit dem Auto							

Figure 5.5 Wie kommst du . . .?

	Spülst du ab?	Mähst du den Rasen?	Wäschst du das Auto?	Führst du den Hund aus?	Räumst du dein Zimmer auf?	Kochst du?	Saugst du Staub?
oft							
manchmal							
nie							
ab und zu							
einmal in der Woche							
zweimal am Tag							
nur für Geld							

Figure 5.6 Hilfst du im Haushalt?

This works particularly well in the TL if the questions are quite cumbersome to translate into English. Provided the questions have been well practised before the game starts, most pupils tend to use the TL rather than switch back to English. Pupils would be familiar with the game from Year 7 where the language items used are much less complex.

Successful language games are usually said to:

- be based on known games;
- not be too long;
- not need lengthy explanations;
- have clear objectives;
- produce a winner.

Information gap exercises, such as finding out about somebody's timetable, work well if pupils are properly prepared: '*Was hast du montags in der ersten Stunde?*' is no more complicated than 'what subject do you have on Monday in the first period?'.

Kofferpacken (packing a suitcase) is another excellent activity for practising word order in the past tense as well as vocabulary; it also increases fluency.

In the *Kaufhaus* (department store) variation each pupil writes an item to be bought in a department store on a piece of paper. The class is then divided into groups (between 6 and 10 pupils). The first group lines up at the front of the class (getting them to pick a number from 1–6 out of a hat will prevent the scramble to avoid being the last in the line!) The first pupil starts the sentence: '*Ich war im Kaufhaus und habe . . .* (mentions his or her item or items) *gekauft*' ('I went to the department store and bought . . .') and puts the piece of paper into a(n authentic) shopping bag. The second pupil starts again: '*Ich war im Kaufhaus und habe ein . . .* (previous pupil's item) *und einen . . .* (own item) *gekauft*' – and so on to the last person in the line, who has, of course, the most difficult task of remembering all the items. Strangely enough, pupils tend to forget the '*gekauft*' (past participle), but remember all the shopping items. The *Kofferpacken* version (packing your suitcase) works very well with a real suitcase and real items.

CONVERSATIONS

One of the aims, if not the ultimate aim, of MFL teaching is to enable pupils to conduct conversations in the TL. They need to be well prepared for this and given the skills and confidence to use the TL in a carefully nurtured atmosphere.

Conversations in language learning usually grow from learnt phrases and role plays. For a discussion of how to develop speaking skills in pupils including the use of role plays, see Chapter 6. Role plays do have their limitations, though, as this example of a keen and very able pupil's frustration at the lack of conversational skills during an exchange visit demonstrates: 'I can ask for the butter at the breakfast table and what time we have to leave for school because we've done that. But I can't have a proper conversation and it makes me mad!' A purely transactional approach, therefore, seems too narrow. In order to go beyond the scripted, pupils need to be taught conversation strategies such as opening gambits, hesitating, agreeing, disagreeing, asking for help and support, expressing surprise and disbelief and many more. Much of this can be achieved by adding an element (albeit small) of drama, creativity or challenge.

Adding an element of unpredictability such as a lost granny, boiled eggs or their memory can make a routine role play such as *Im Fundbüro* (at the lost property office) much more interesting and entertaining for pupils. Introducing realia into role plays can liven things up considerably. Most pupils like bringing in unusual clothes, food (real or plastic) or toys – or pictures of these items, either cut out of magazines, drawn or obtained via information and communication technology (ICT).

For papers on the use on drama, see also the Special Issue of German as a Foreign Language 2004(1) available at http://www.gfl-journal.de/previous/index.html.

Apart from conversation strategies, there are other ways of organising role plays so as to encourage spontaneity. Instead of asking pupils to prepare a role play together with their partner, e.g. the shopkeeper together with the shopper, they can be grouped with peers in the same role, e.g. shopkeepers and shoppers in different groups. This way, when shopkeepers and shoppers come together, communication is more realistic and spontaneous because, while shopkeepers and shoppers do prepare possible answers in advance, they have to listen very carefully to each other in order to be able to respond meaningfully.

Another way you can help pupils make the transition from learnt response to genuine manipulation of the TL is to record the general conversations of groups and discuss with pupils how they can be improved to sound less like a GCSE oral examination and more like a real conversation.

Often, despite your best endeavours, pupils remain reluctant to 'spontaneously adopt the FL as their own language of self-expression in the FL classroom, even where the teachers have done so to a considerable extent' (Mitchell 1988: 164). In order to address the issue of spontaneous TL use, the 1999 NC Orders required pupils to be taught through 'using everyday classroom events as an opportunity for spontaneous speech' (DfEE/QCA 1999: 17). There was no guidance on how this best be done, however. Ofsted inspections clearly pointed to the fact the TL use by pupils remained a real challenge for MFL teachers (see e.g. Dobson 1998: 2) and subsequent Ofsted publications have continued the debate on pupils' independent use of the TL (Ofsted 2004). The 2007 Programme of Study has many more references to pupils comparing the TL with English (or another language) in order to help them learn and remember and 1.3b states that pupils should learn by 'using imagination to express thoughts, ideas, experiences and feelings'.

ASSESSMENT AND TESTING AND TL USE

Marking in the TL is a good way of increasing pupils' comprehension of the TL. Pupils are mostly interested in the teacher's comments and grades on their work.

Pupils can be given a TL mark scheme and comment list as part of the classroom vocabulary in Year 7. Once they are familiar with the scheme, peer-marking can be introduced. It is a popular activity with pupils, they love the instruction '*Hefte tauschen und korrigieren!*' ('Exchange exercise books and mark each other's work!'). They are usually very fair and try hard to find the appropriate comment. They often do this 'in role', i.e. playing the teacher using teacher language.

Also, pupils can be paired to count and tick off on a profile sheet how often their partner uses the TL.

The 2000 GCSE criteria stipulated that 'instructions to candidates (other than general instructions) should normally be in the language in which the candidate is expected to respond, except where the nature of the task would make the instructions too difficult to understand.' (QCA 2000b: 3). A policy of testing in the TL requires pupils to learn rubrics and instructions in the TL. This alone does not lead to increased spontaneous use of the TL by pupils as these rubrics are part of standard classroom vocabulary and pupils are expected to learn them like other transactional phrases. (For a detailed discussion of assessment issues, see Chapter 10.) In the 2007 draft GCSE criteria, the only stipulation is that boards list the TL rubrics to be used.

WORKING TOWARDS COMPETENCE IN TL USE

As can be seen in this chapter, you can use the TL meaningfully and effectively for a number of types of interaction in the MFL classroom.

Task 5.5 Useful *teacher* phrases

With reference to Figure 5.7, draw up lists of useful teacher phrases in your first and second foreign language for:

- everyday routines, classroom management and maintaining discipline
- giving instructions and explanations

for a class of your choice in Key Stage 3 and one for a class in Key Stage 4.
   How different are the lists for Key Stages 3 and 4? Is there an element of progression? If not, how could you build this in?

Task 5.6 Useful *pupil* phrases

With reference to Figure 5.7, draw up a list of lexical items pupils should – in your opinion – have mastered by the end of their first year study of the modern foreign language

- to interact with the teacher
- to communicate with peers.

Then consider how these lexical items could be taught and practised.

SOME POSSIBLE STRATEGIES FOR TL USE

1   Contextualisation increases comprehension. Always ensure pupils know what is going on. Pictures, demonstrations and examples must be carefully selected to avoid ambiguity.

Everyday routines, classroom management & maintaining discipline	Instructions and explanations by the teacher	Pupil interactions with the teacher	Pupil interactions with other pupils
taking the register	presenting new language	asking for clarification	asking for material/equipment
getting ready for the lesson	setting up activities	expressing problems and apologies	carrying out pair and group-work activities
tidying up at the end of the lesson	making oral comments	requesting explanations	initiating information exchange
dismissing the class	checking comprehension	giving excuses	playing games
offering praise and rewards	asking questions	asking for material/equipment	expressing agreement and disagreement
reprimanding and sanctioning pupils	making written comments in exercise books	making evaluative comments	assessing the work of peers
friendly asides, humorous remarks		asking for confirmation	using fillers
		requesting permission	
		answering questions	
		giving information	
		humorous remarks	
		linguistic experiments	

Figure 5.7 Using the TL for classroom instruction and interactions

2   Use of cognates or near cognates, particularly in German, not only increases the chances of comprehension, it makes pupils feel more confident and less apprehensive. (Over-reliance on cognates, however, should be avoided.)

3   Simplification of language, not only for teacher input but also for pupil production – a single well-chosen word can go a long way. A pupil's *'Entschuldigung, Amir'* ('Sorry, Amir') – he had interrupted Amir – can make the point quite adequately.

4   Pupil access to language – this can take the form of 'clouds' with the most

useful phrases and key words prominently displayed or lists in pupils' exercise books.

5   Teaching of key phrases – such as '*Wie heißt das auf Deutsch?*' ('What is the German word/phrase for . . .?') '*Wie sagt man . . . auf Deutsch?*' ('How do you say . . . in German?'), '*Darf ich bitte Englisch sprechen?*' ('May I please speak in English?'), '*Ich habe ein Problem, Herr / Frau . . .*' ('Sir/Miss, I have a problem'), '*Können Sie mir bitte helfen?*' ('Can you help me, please?'), '*Ich bin fertig.*' ('I have finished').

6   Rewarding pupils' spontaneous use of the TL – words and phrases remembered from previous lessons, an ambitious attempt (successful or not) at a new construction or a combination of words, etc. deserve to be praised by the teacher and their efforts recorded (in a separate column) in the mark book.

7   Screening out unwanted English contributions – this usually just means ignoring them.

8   TL-only sessions: during a designated (previously announced and cleared with parents) period of 15 minutes of a lesson only the TL may be spoken. Everyone who speaks English (including the teacher) suffers a forfeit. Initially these sessions tend to produce silent minutes. As pupils get used to them they get braver and more adventurous in their use of the TL.

9   Request box: pupils write phrases they need on a card and put them into the box. The TL phrases are compiled and presented and taught to the whole class.

10 Incorporation of 'real life' TL into speaking and writing: expressions of disbelief, how to pretend you're interested, how to compliment someone, etc.

Competence in TL use, as so many aspects of good practice, is difficult to achieve and requires a lot of practice. You can benefit from considering all aspects of TL use and should develop strategies to address them. Here are some targets a student teacher at the Institute of Education set herself for her induction year:

1   *Be supportive*: when a pupil wants to use the TL, I need to offer help and support. The nature of the support given may vary according to the age and the ability of the pupil.

2   *Be consistent*: I need to try hard to use the TL as often as possible to be a good role model. Sometimes it might mean claiming not to understand what they are saying just because they speak English.

3   *Be realistic*: I need to remember that the use of the TL is meant to enhance classroom teaching, and not to become an intolerable burden. It is sometimes a good idea to have a set period in the lesson when pupils know that they can speak to me in English and when problems can be dealt with.

4   *Be non-critical*: I must greet any attempt at using the TL positively or the pupil might not try again. The most important thing is communication, and any understanding of the message should be rewarded.

5   *Be challenging*: while asking for the impossible is demotivating, equally demotivating is asking for that which is banal and far below a pupil's

capabilities. I need to build progression into both my use of the TL and theirs, using, teaching and expecting more complex phrases with older and more able pupils.

6 *Be flexible*: if I want to encourage the use of the TL, I must be sufficiently flexible to respond to what happens in the classroom and to what pupils have to say.

7 *Make it worthwhile*: I must reward and acknowledge any efforts, be aware of what pupils are doing in the classroom and listen to two or three pupils each lesson so I can keep a record of their individual achievement as regards TL use.

8 *Involve the pupils*: pupils are much more likely to be motivated if they are involved. I can ask them to note and tick useful phrases or expressions in their exercise books each time they use them in the lesson.

9 *Promote a positive attitude*: the most important thing is that pupils do not feel threatened and it is up to me that they don't. I must present the TL as something I am going to do with them and in which all have a part to play and not as something that I am imposing upon them.

Task 5.7 Thoughts on TL use

How relevant are the above targets for your own practice? Draw up a list appropriate for the different groups of learners you work with.

SUMMARY

There is no doubt in our minds that optimum, i.e. sensitive and appropriate, use of the TL can make a beneficial contribution to the learning process of most pupils.

While for reasons such as time constraints and the lack of reinforcement outside the classroom it might seem unrealistic to expect any but the most able to be proficient and confident enough to chat spontaneously in the TL at the end of Key Stage 4, pupils can be expected to communicate meaning competently in a finite number of situations within the prevailing statutory framework. Optimum exposure to the TL has a clear contribution to make to achieving this aim.

Teaching in the TL alone is not enough to guarantee successful learning outcomes for *all* pupils. While the more enthusiastic and able pupils can be expected to respond consistently to the challenge given the right environment and levels of support, there will be pupils who will find it at best contrived and at worst alien.

FURTHER READING

Butzkamm, W. (2003) 'We only learn language once: the role of the mother tongue in FL classrooms: death of a dogma', *Language Learning Journal* 28: pp. 29–39.

This paper discusses the issues surrounding the use of target language and mother tongue for foreign language learners and clearly sets out the arguments in the debate.

Macaro, E. (1997) *Target Language, Collaborative Learning and Autonomy*. Clevedon: Multilingual Matters

A thorough examination of the use of target language and its effectiveness in language learning.

Meiring, L. and Norman, N. (2002) 'Back on target: repositioning the status of target language in MFL teaching and learning', *Language Learning Journal* 26: pp. 27–35.

This article presents the 'accepted' position on target language along with its interpretation in the MFL classroom and presents some convincing arguments for a reconceptualisation.

6 Teaching listening, speaking, reading and writing

INTRODUCTION

Until the mid-1980s, writing, for instance in the form of translations, dictations and essay writing, as well as reading, tended to predominate in modern foreign languages (MFL) teaching. Since then, however, the full value of speaking and listening has been recognised and generally the four language skills of reading, writing, listening and speaking have been equally weighted in the National Curriculum and in GCSE qualifications, although the 2007 draft GCSE criteria (QCA, 2007a) allow for slightly more flexibility, with 20–30 per cent possible for each of the four skills. Consequently, a multi-skill approach prevails, in which no one skill is usually taught discretely. The use of terminology such as 'respond', 'react', 'summarise' in the statutory framework encourages the integration of skills. Progression within each and across the four skills is an important issue.

In this chapter we start from the premise that an important aim of MFL teaching in the secondary school is the development of an ability in pupils to use and learn MFL independently from the teacher. To this end we suggest a structured learning process here based on clear objectives ranging from recognising, memorising and reproducing key linguistic items and structures to using them creatively as building blocks for personalised and meaningful MFL generation.

Because of its importance in helping pupils achieve this objective by extending and consolidating the work carried out in the classroom, homework is also discussed in this chapter.

OBJECTIVES

By the end of this chapter you should:

- appreciate how listening, speaking, reading and writing can be taught;
- be aware of the need for a gradual integration of these four skills;
- realise the importance of pupils taking control of input such as vocabulary, structures and functions and use them creatively, generating their own, personalised language;
- be aware of important criteria for selecting learning activities as well as the need for the sequencing of activities;
- recognise what constitutes meaningful homework in order to extend and consolidate work carried out in class;
- appreciate the importance of tailoring teaching to the needs of specific classes and the individual differences of the pupils within them.

THE IMPORTANCE OF SEQUENCING AND THE INTEGRATION OF MFL SKILLS

As noted in previous chapters, the development of communicative competence in pupils is an important aim of MFL teaching in secondary schools. Real communication consists of more than drawing on a bank of statements and questions suited to a given topic area. It requires language to be tailored to fulfil specific objectives by drawing on situational language and lexical phrases. It is, therefore, essential that pupils memorise, and learn how to memorise, vocabulary.

For Littlewood (1981) successful 'social interaction' is an important outcome of language use, which requires a certain level of linguistic and communicative competence and is reached via a number of phases of development. It can be very difficult to develop social interaction skills, particularly in a classroom setting. Therefore, we see it as one of the aims of MFL teaching to make pupils aware of the components which comprise successful communication.

One of the challenges for MFL teachers is to devise a programme of learning which progresses from a reliance of pupils on the teacher towards their independence, developing in pupils the ability to generate language of their own within a communicative framework. Both the teacher and pupils must be aware of the importance of the role of the teacher as an agent of learning throughout Key Stages 3 and 4.

Another challenge is the appropriate sequencing of teaching and learning activities. Individual MFL skills, we argue here, should not be taught independently of one another. Their development needs to be fitted within a coherent approach, which involves careful monitoring of learning and the selection of appropriate activities.

Although 'meaningfulness' of tasks and activities, e.g. 'authenticity' and the meeting of perceived needs, is important to further the development of language skills in pupils, the 'pre-communicative' phase is equally important in which 'context-reduced', i.e. less than communicative activities, occupy a valid place (see Barnes 2007).

In this chapter we identify various stages of development per skill area. These stages should not be viewed as a simple formula, which can be repeated lesson after lesson, unit of work after unit of work. The nature of the task or given learning objective(s) might not make it possible and/or desirable to cover all stages per skill. In particular, progression not only takes place within an isolated MFL skill but across a number of skill areas. Therefore, successful MFL lessons integrate a number of activities and exercises developing different (MFL) skills, which are carefully chosen to build on previous knowledge and understanding. The examples given in this chapter by no means represent an exhaustive list.

Essentially, the skills of listening and reading can be grouped together under the label of 'receptive MFL skills'. Similarly, speaking and writing can be categorised as 'productive MFL skills'. It is this categorisation, which we use in this chapter for the grouping of listening, speaking, reading and writing. However, it must also be remembered that both listening and reading can be *responded to* and that writing and speaking need *input* and *modelling* from reading and listening to inform their development.

MEMORISING, AND LEARNING HOW TO MEMORISE, VOCABULARY

Grauberg (1997: 5–33) presents a process for vocabulary acquisition, which is similar to the paradigm for language learning presented in Chapter 3 of this book. He distinguishes four stages – discrimination, understanding meaning, remembering and consolidation as well as extension – all of which require active intervention on the part of the teacher, yet which serve to guide the learner towards a greater degree of independent language use. These stages offer a medium-term and long-term perspective.

We feel it is important to present a range of vocabulary learning strategies in order that pupils can adopt strategies to suit their own learning styles.

Discrimination

Teachers are guided in their presentation of new vocabulary, in particular key lexical items, by the department's long-term plans. By using visual aids, information and communication technology (ICT), flashcards, the overhead projector (OHP), posters, (DV images), etc.), vocabulary can be placed in a broader (cultural) context. Teachers should place new vocabulary in a functional/communicative context. This can be achieved through the demonstration of potential use and/or by exposing pupils to spoken or written texts. Presentation by the teacher should not be purely a passive activity for pupils. Exposure to new lexical items and phrases can include the practice of pronunciation, the association with gestures and movement, the association with previously taught language and the answering of simple closed questions.

Understanding meaning

Teachers should present key vocabulary related to a new unit in a broader (cultural) context. GCSE specifications provide defined lists in relation to given topics, as do many coursebooks. For pupils to understand meaning in a multi-dimensional way, e.g. functional, grammatical, etc., there is a need for explanation by the teacher. Explanation is usually accompanied by pupils recording vocabulary for future learning. We would advise against a simple translation from the TL into English. Instead, we would encourage pupils to note down a meaningful example of use in context as well as the TL and mother tongue meanings of the new lexical item or phrase. In our experience, the rendering of new lexical items and phrases in semantic fields ensures better understanding and recall.

Grauberg (1997: 8) suggests that where inflected forms of words are contained in vocabulary lists, it may save time and effort to explain the infinitive form. Subsequently, pupils should be encouraged to note similarities and grammatical relationships with similar words encountered to assist with 'educated guessing' of meaning. The categorisation of vocabulary can be undertaken in several ways – grammatically, by topic, in the form of mind maps or in the context of stories, songs, rhymes and poems. A varied approach seems advisable.

Remembering and consolidation

A criticism of repeated classroom vocabulary testing is that pupils learn new lexical items for a specific, short-term and decontextualised purpose. However, this can be seen as a necessary prerequisite to consigning the vocabulary to the long-term memory. Field (1999b: 55) suggests a range of ways of learning vocabulary: alphabetical listing, listing according to grammatical concepts (verbs, nouns, adjectives, etc.), semantic field mind-mapping, repeated use in context, recital, colour coding or preference ranking. To these can be added, covering the English and testing oneself, covering the TL word and testing oneself, getting a friend or family member to test, matching synonyms, matching opposites, matching words to symbols, gapped texts and dictionary activities. Pupils should be encouraged to experiment with all these methods from early on in their learning process. By making vocabulary learning strategies explicit, teachers can help to ensure effective vocabulary learning takes place. Certainly teachers could draw on a range of strategies which mirror the different 'intelligences' identified by Gardner (1983) in his well-known work *Frames of Mind*, i.e. some learners may benefit from 'tactile' activities, where they have to move cards and match them up to learn vocabulary, others may feel recording the words and meanings on a cassette or as a podcast may be more beneficial for them. It is worth stressing at this point that the enthusiasm for the notion of multiple intelligences and their potential for pedagogy is not universally shared. For a critique of Gardner, see White (2004). If learners are being tested on vocabulary, then they need to be secure in what exactly they should be learning: spelling (including accents)?, meaning?, pronunciation?, gender/type of verb/category, etc.? All aspects? Graham (1997) notes that pupils feel vocabulary learning is more successful and enjoyable if it forms part of a game. Puzzles, word searches, quizzes and challenges can all be usefully deployed.

Extension

By extension we mean the stage at which learners transfer vocabulary from the short-term to the long-term memory. It involves active use for personal communicative reasons. You need to devise activities which require pupils to use key vocabulary for communicative purposes. This involves the use of the TL for speaking and writing, but may also involve listening and reading, the answering of focused comprehension questions, the completion of puzzles, the writing of short texts containing a set number of key words/phrases or word association activities. The use of synonyms and exercises demanding the use of opposites serve to extend the construct associated with the newly established meaning (see also Miller 2000).

Task 6.1 Matching vocabulary learning strategies to multiple intelligences

Some of Howard Gardner's different types of intelligence:

- logical intelligence
- linguistic intelligence
- bodily kinaesthetic intelligence
- spatial intelligence
- musical intelligence
- inter-personal intelligence
- intra-personal intelligence.

1   Can you categorise the vocabulary learning strategies below by the type of intelligence they may appeal to? (NB: any activity can fall into more than one category.)
2   Place the activities under each category into a sequence following the stages discussed above.

Where are there gaps? Consider additional activities, which can be placed into the model.
   Some vocabulary learning strategies:

Repetition, recital, categorising by grammar, categorising by topic, colour coding, testing oneself, being tested, placing in communicative context, matching to symbols, developing puzzles, completing puzzles, formal teacher-led tests, word searches, finding synonyms, finding opposites, dictionary work, rote learning, mnemonics, identifying key words in extended texts, etc.

RECEPTIVE MFL SKILLS (LISTENING AND READING)

Initially pupils have to recognise and identify key vocabulary, phrases and structures. Activities need to be devised in order to allow pupils to recognise both the spoken and written word and to apply meaning to new language forms. As can be seen in Figure 6.1, the pupil needs to proceed from the recognition of new forms via practice to using them in an individualised and personal way, rebuilding language within 'authentic' and realistic contexts.

Figure 6.1 Progression in receptive MFL skills

LISTENING (AND RESPONDING)

The continuum of examples in Figure 6.2 aims to show how MFL learning can be sequenced to encourage a development from identification and recognition of key linguistic items and structures to the use of selected language forms to express personal views. The approach outlined here, we feel, allows for continuity and progression over a period of time. For further practical ideas for listening, see Chambers (2007).

```
                    from
              pre-listening activities
          listening for gist/detail (content)
          focusing on linguistic structures
                    and forms
                    rebuilding
                      to
```

Figure 6.2 Listening (and responding) – an overview

PRE-LISTENING ACTIVITIES

Listening to a(n extended) passage without preparation can be an extremely difficult task. To understand the location and context of a text facilitates comprehension. This can be achieved/worked towards by way of pre-listening activities. The exact nature of a pre-listening activity is, of course, dependent upon the level of proficiency of the pupils.

Pupils can be set a number of lead-in tasks such as input and practice of key linguistic items through word associations or work with sentence cards taken from the text.

To analyse a listening text in terms of general features is a very worthy first step. Prior to the first listening, particularly when the task consists of fairly straightforward questions and answers, learners could predict what they might hear/what the answers might be and then the listening itself serves as a 'real' activity to check their predictions. (For a wide range of pre-listening and listening activities and discussion of some of the issues involved in listening, see Dahlhaus 1994; Turner 1995; Graham 2003; Fernández-Toro 2005.)

LISTENING FOR GIST/DETAIL WITH A FOCUS ON CONTENT

It is a particular skill to extract meaning from spoken stimulus material. To record details verbally and/or non-verbally while listening to a 'text' can be demanding. And to retain details as well as to respond to a 'text' after listening can also be a challenge to pupils.

Listening activities are best broken down into manageable chunks to suit the particular learning objectives of the lesson and/or the unit of work.

During the first listening pupils can, for instance, be asked to find out how many speakers are participating and guess the mood of speakers. They can count how many questions are asked. Also, they can tally how many known words are used or ascertain the location of a dialogue. Such activities help to contextualise the stimulus material. During the second listening pupils can be set activities to which they are asked to respond verbally and/or non-verbally. These responses can be used at a later stage as stimuli for follow-up work. Examples of non-verbal responses include the ticking of boxes within a grid, identifying statements as true or false, answering simple multiple choice questions, completing pictures and diagrams and matching simplified text to pictures and symbols as well as, e.g., raising a hand if they hear a certain word or phrase. Possible verbal responses are listed in Figure 6.5.

Pupils can also be asked to focus on specific details by having to answer 'closed questions' to which there is a specific answer, which can be found in the stimulus material such as prices, times, directions, ages, descriptions. For these activities to be successful pupils should be familiar with the key language the stimulus material contains.

A third playing of the recording might allow some of the pupils, who have not managed to do so already, to complete the activity.

FOCUSING ON LINGUISTIC STRUCTURES AND FORMS

In order to stretch pupils you can devise activities focusing on the linguistic structures and forms contained in the stimulus material. Pupils could, for instance, be asked to verbalise the non-verbal responses made initially.

One of the ultimate goals of listening activities is the ability of pupils to communicate and express themselves by transferring the language contained in the stimulus material from their passive to their active vocabulary.

Devising a gap-filling activity or providing a transcript out of order requiring pupils to find the correct sequence, asking them to match beginnings and ends of sentences can all be used to make them more familiar with the language forms, as can replacing key vocabulary with synonyms or correcting inaccurate sentences.

Consideration needs to be given to the extent of preparatory work on key vocabulary and essential linguistic structures. Box 6.1 Provides some practical hints.

Box 6.1 Some practical hints and considerations

Jo Bond

- Be aware of the level of the group – is it set or mixed ability? Only then select the listening material.
- Listen to the recording yourself first: a transcript does not indicate the speed at which language is spoken, nor the clarity of speech.
- The length of texts will depend on the ability level of the group. Bear in mind that more able pupils tend to have a longer concentration span. With mixed ability or lower ability groups it is advisable to do a series of short aural activities during the course of a lesson with other activities in between. This could be a long dialogue played in sections or several shorter exchanges broken down into clusters of two or three rather than all being played at once. This strategy also gives pupils the opportunity to improve on their last score within the same lesson, thus boosting their confidence in their listening ability.
- Play the recording at least twice but don't forget to explain *exactly* how you are going to do this. For instance, will you play the whole passage through with pauses for answers and then repeat it? Or will you play it in sections and repeat each section? Pupils find listening particularly difficult as it demands considerable concentration. Careful explanation at the outset can prevent unnecessary anxiety or constant interruptions during the exercise. If the quality of the recording is not so good, do not be afraid to repeat certain phrases or words yourself or to play it again. Those who could understand will have already completed the task by then, while those struggling will receive extra help discretely and not feel that they have failed.
- Do pupils need to be familiar with all the language in the text in advance? In most cases this is essential in order to build up their confidence in what can for many be a difficult and demanding exercise. However, in short extracts where many words are recognisable, e.g. hobbies, pupils will enjoy the fact that they can easily identify the new vocabulary with little effort.
- The use of answer forms: a quick table on the board or on a worksheet can be an effective way to elicit answers and useful for oral or written work afterwards. Gauge carefully the amount of information pupils have to give according to their ability. Also, stopping the recording and asking pupils to write down the last word they have heard can be fun and pupils will succeed provided that the speech is not too fast or indistinct.

REBUILDING

Once pupils have a very clear understanding of the content of the stimulus material and also of how these details have been expressed, the focus can shift towards rebuilding the text. Notes taken in previous activities can be used for this purpose. You can facilitate this process by providing a framework of targeted questions, moving from the expression of factual details to the expression of personal opinion.

READING (AND RESPONDING)

As a receptive skill the process of reading is not dissimilar to that of listening (Figure 6.3). Through reading pupils can be exposed to new language forms and structures. Activities are different in that the stimulus material is more varied and, crucially, visible to pupils. Access to source material is, therefore, more permanent. The notion of 'reading for pleasure' permeates the stages shown in Figure 6.3.

> **from**
> preparatory activities
> reading for gist/detail (content)
> focusing on linguistic structures
> and forms
> rebuilding
> **to**

Figure 6.3 Reading (and responding) – an overview

PREPARATORY ACTIVITIES

As with listening, pupils can benefit from being exposed to written texts after some prior preparation. At this early stage you can guide the pupil through the text: the content of the passage could be predicted with the help of visual clues or headlines. Also, word associations can be used to reactivate key lexical items.

It is important to encourage pupils to look out for clues. It may be that a particular text contains few clues or, indeed, an abundance of them. Newspaper articles contain headlines, subtitles and pictures. Cartoon strips tell the story in pictures supported by text. Texts containing 'direct speech' indicate the number of speakers. Advertisements consist of slogans and visual clues. All of these can be extrapolated from the main body of the text and serve as material in their own right. (For examples of the use of clues, see Brandi and Strauss 1985; Powell and Barnes 1996.)

READING FOR GIST/DETAIL WITH A FOCUS ON CONTENT

Once pupils have activated relevant linguistic items and structures and are familiar with the context of the text, they are ready to carry out a closer examination. The extraction of key facts and figures is an easier proposition once the context is clear. The teacher can provide tables, diagrams, true/false exercises, multiple choice activities to elicit non-verbal responses or single word/phrase answers, which serve to summarise the content of the text.

Both individual and pair work activities can encourage a closer examination of the text. Questions should be graded and structured, from closed to open, to maximise pupils' opportunities to answer correctly and gradually encourage longer verbal responses (for further ideas on reading, including on strategy instruction and types of task, see Hill 2004; Wright and Brown 2006).

FOCUSING ON LINGUISTIC STRUCTURES AND FORMS

Texts contain language forms relevant to particular contexts; referral to the language forms used in the text serves to reinforce those structures. You can devise activities requiring pupils to reproduce the specific structures introduced by a text. Gap-filling exercises focusing on particular grammatical forms, for instance, can serve this purpose. You could reproduce the text with verb/adjective endings missing, requiring pupils to complete certain sections from memory. Texts can be rewritten by substituting certain lexical items. Also, sections of the text can be reproduced in a jumbled form again requiring pupils to reconstruct the passage in a meaningful way. Clearly, work on activities of this nature also serves to develop pupils' writing skills (see Bramall 2002).

REBUILDING

By this stage pupils should be fairly familiar with the text. 'Open-ended' tasks allowing for a variety of different answers can stimulate original responses. Pupils can be asked to talk or write about their favourite character and what distinguishes her from others. They can be asked to continue a story, provide an explanation of the events portrayed or produce an alternative account. A response to a text of this nature is individual and personal. Reference material needs to be made accessible to facilitate the expression of opinions and interpretations.

READING FOR PLEASURE – EXAMPLES FROM AND REFLECTIONS ON CLASSROOM PRACTICE

It is difficult to build reading for pleasure into the weekly diet of MFL teaching. For a variety of reasons, pupils can be reluctant to carry out independent reading or it can be difficult to find appropriate material, particularly in less widely taught MFL. It would appear that quite a number of pupils do not read for relaxation or as a hobby – there are, after all, so many alternatives available in the form of TV, videos and computer games, etc. Without frequent practice the act of reading can appear more difficult and be perceived to take a lot of effort in relation to its 'competitors' and the 'pleasure factor' can disappear. And if the material to be read is in a foreign language . . .

Therefore, what is required, it seems, is to enable pupils to discover the pleasure in reading (see Swarbrick 1998). Material needs to be carefully selected for whole class work, or a wide range of types of text collected together. Pupils can select something which appeals to them from the collection, whether it is fiction, a sport report, a recipe, or an instruction booklet . . .

Table 6.1 Non-verbal response types

Response type	Ranking
completing diagrams	
drawing	
gap filling	
labelling	
mixing-and-matching	
multiple choice	
physical movement	.
ticking boxes	
true/false	

Table 6.2 Verbal response types

Response type	Ranking
agreeing/disagreeing	
answering in full sentences	
correcting	
gap filling	
interpreting	
mixing-and matching half sentences	
one-word answers	
paraphrasing	
rebuilding text	
sequencing	
summarising	
translating	
unjumbling text/scripts	

PRODUCTIVE MFL SKILLS (SPEAKING AND WRITING)

Imitation of 'foreign' sounds and the reproduction of accurate written forms comprise the earliest stages of developing productive language skills. Repetition and copying rely heavily on examples provided by the teacher. Eventually, the aim is the generation of personalised language by the pupil in order to satisfy a perceived communicative need (see Figure 6.4).

Figure 6.4 Progression in productive MFL skills

SPEAKING

The speaking activities discussed in this section (Figure 6.5) span the continuum from repetition to free expression. For further practical examples of speaking activities, see Graham (2007).

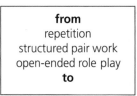

Figure 6.5 Speaking – an overview

REPETITION

Repetition exercises are a first step towards the development in pupils of speaking skills.

Use of visual aids

As can be seen in Chapters 3 and 11, the use of visual aids allows pupils to follow the process of labelling concepts, which can render the translation of words unnecessary. Many items of key vocabulary can be introduced and presented effectively in a visually recognisable form such as through ICT, flashcards, real objects, images on acetates or posters.

First of all, pupils should listen to the teacher. Once an item has been presented, pupils can be asked to repeat what they have heard. Often, teenagers prefer not to repeat in front of their peers because of being embarrassed or finding the task difficult. This can be overcome if you encourage the pupils to shout, whisper, sing and imitate. Longer words and phrases often cause problems. Chanting and clapping to a rhythm can be useful strategies.

You should not simply go through the list of lexical items, assuming that, once covered, learning has taken place. Images already shown need to be returned to and pupils asked to recall the relevant vocabulary. This can increase the pace of the lesson and keep the pupils attentive.

Pantomime competitions

Also, the class can be divided into smaller groups to carry out 'pantomime competitions' where pupils act out – through mime and gesture – what is depicted on individual visual aids. When pupils recognise what peers act out they say the word or phrase in question. All pupils should be encouraged to participate and the last rendition of a word or phrase should be pronounced correctly so that the correct pronunciation is reinforced.

Building up phrases backwards

Building up phrases backwards can also be of help, e.g. *'Je regrette, je n'en ai pas'* becomes *'pas, . . . n'en ai pas, . . . je n'en ai pas, . . . je regrette, je n'en ai pas'.*

Repeating a word or phrase if it is correct

In this activity you might present a visual image to the whole group and make either a correct or an incorrect utterance. Pupils are asked to repeat after you only if what you have said is correct. If what you have said is incorrect, pupils should remain silent. The activity works best if most of what you say is true (adapted from Buckby 1980: 7).

A more able pupil may be nominated to lead the activity or the class can be divided into smaller groups with more able pupils as group leaders.

Pupils are required to think, to demonstrate what they know and also to participate as group members. The skills of identifying and memorising language are beginning to be developed in this way. Support by the teacher is evident through providing choices.

Guessing

If you conceal the visual aids and ask pupils to shout out the corresponding word or phrase in the target language (TL), pupils are encouraged to use the TL even if they invariably make some mistakes. An element of competition can be introduced, for instance, by counting attempts.

In activities of this kind pupils are required to use their memory and to listen to peers. Correct articulation is rewarded and pupils practise the initial stages of communication.

Distributing visual aids

A natural progression towards communication is to use the same visual aids within a communicative context. There, you encourage pupils within a whole class situation to ask for the items represented on the visual aid in the TL. The 'reward' for an accurate request is for the pupil to receive the visual aid. The pupil hides it from the rest of the class. Once all the items have been distributed, the class is asked to find out from individual pupils what their particular visual aid depicts. If the request is correct, the visual aid is revealed; if the guess is wrong or the utterance is incorrect, an appropriate response should be made, e.g. '*Lo siento, no tengo . . .*' ('Sorry, I haven't got it.') or '*Lo siento, no es correcto.*' ('Sorry, that is not correct.'). The activity continues until all the items have been revealed. In this activity communication does take place, albeit within a supported environment.

STRUCTURED PAIR WORK

The next step towards the development of speaking skills in this framework is structured pair work. These structured pair work activities encourage repetition of set linguistic items and structures. Pupils neither respond nor communicate spontaneously, yet they do use functional language for a particular purpose.

Card games

A natural sequel to the activities above is, for instance, to provide cue cards for pairs to perform similar communicative acts in pairs. Reduced-size copies of the visual aids can be produced. Pupils work in pairs and successful communication is rewarded by the pupil making a correct utterance retaining the card. The game is over when one pupil has gathered all the available cards. This game can be played a number of times in succession.

Information gap activities

Information gap activities are another way of getting pupils to use the newly encountered linguistic items and structures in a communicative context.

Scripting and acting out role plays

On the basis of such preparatory speaking activities, but also listening and reading tasks, pupils can use the new language to script and act out role plays.

OPEN-ENDED ROLE PLAYS

From structured pair work pupils can move on to open-ended role plays. To make classroom communication of pupils more like 'real' communication, pupils need to be given opportunities to define and express their own needs. In open-ended role plays the language to be used for communication is not restricted to what has been introduced in a given unit of work, but pupils have an opportunity to transfer linguistic items and structures from previous units and/or use new ones found in glossaries, dictionaries or other resource material.

In one possible activity pupils write their own 'shopping list' and purchase these articles from an imaginary store. This store can be 'staffed' by pupils, who have a defined list of articles available. As a consequence pupils cannot predict what their peers will say. As dialogues progress, needs and requests will inevitably change, requiring original use of language. This might allow for a sense of ownership of the language used.

The introduction of an element of fun or unpredictability can help to make certain topics more immediately interesting to pupils. Rather than script a standard role play in a restaurant pupils can, for instance, be encouraged to invent a scene featuring a confused or reluctant waiter mixing up things and bringing the wrong orders.

Pupils can make recordings of their role plays under the supervision of the foreign language assistant (FLA). When all groups have had their turn, some of the recordings are played in class. This way, pupils can practise their pronunciation, improve their accent and intonation and use their imagination.

WRITING

While writing should be introduced after new lexical items and phrases have been heard and seen, the written word should not be withheld as there is the danger of pupils beginning to imagine their own spellings (see also Hornsey 1993).

The simplest form of writing is copying. At the other end of the continuum is the free expression of ideas within the constraints of the vocabulary and active knowledge of the grammatical forms available (Figure 6.6). For some very interesting ideas on combining reading and writing via stories, see Brandford (2007).

| **from** |
| copying |
| targeted practice |
| free expression through writing |
| **to** |

Figure 6.6 Writing – an overview

COPYING

Copying is not as simple a task as it might at first seem. Pupils need to copy accurately as a first step towards developing writing skills in the TL but also as a means of recording language forms for future use. Pupils cannot simply be expected to be able to copy without instruction and practice.

Many pupils find it difficult to concentrate and copy accurately. This difficulty can be overcome by providing activities requiring more focused attention than 'simply' copying. 'Mixing and matching' activities require pupils to select a meaning for a particular word. Pupils might be asked to complete a sentence by filling gaps, choosing words from a jumbled list or unjumble letters to make a meaningful word or phrase out of them, e.g. *locogie* = *'colegio'*. Computer programmes such as ordinary word processor packages or 'Fun with Texts' can be used effectively for this purpose, as can a wide range of websites allowing the teacher to input a list of vocabulary which is then used as the basis for a variety of web-based matching, copy writing, etc. activities. You clearly have a key role in identifying and/or correcting misspellings.

TARGETED PRACTICE

From copying, pupils can progress to targeted practice such as the following.

Substitution

The replacement of words by alternatives and the use of appropriate reference material is a valuable skill and possible next step. Similarly, unjumbling sentences can also be used to encourage accuracy. You should insist on accuracy and demonstrate the value of correct spelling. Redrafting is, for instance, one of the language skills specified in the Programme of Study of the National Curriculum. Pupils might occasionally be given the opportunity to design crossword puzzles and word searches containing key vocabulary as this requires them not only to know the vocabulary/ phrases in question but also to reproduce these accurately.

Repetition exercises

Writing is traditionally the form used to practise grammatical structures. Repetition exercises can reinforce correct forms of language. At the same time, work on grammatical exercises out of context can inhibit the aim of free expression. Grading activities in terms of difficulty can help to overcome this risk. You can provide alternative answers for, say, verb endings followed by pupils having to apply rules without such support. Such activities only tend to be perceived as meaningful by pupils if the teacher uses them in preparation for a communicative task such as, for instance, the writing of letters, emails, memos, faxes and messages requiring the use of information and linguistic structures in a meaningful way.

Responding through writing

Some activities outlined in the sections on listening and reading clearly require pupils to respond in writing in the TL. Support comes in the form of the text provided as a stimulus.

FREE EXPRESSION THROUGH WRITING

A common frustration in MFL learning is the inability to express oneself freely without resorting to translation. Pupils should be encouraged to 'experiment' with and exploit known language by prompting them to write short poems, jokes and slogans within most topic areas. Short stories and the production of texts based on 'my ideal . . .' allow pupils to use their imagination. You need to gauge the extent to which work of this nature is corrected: accurate language production needs to be reinforced, yet at the same time individual and personal use of the TL should not be discouraged.

Task 6.3 Productive language skills – speaking and writing

1   Observe a range of MFL teachers at your experience school. How do they encourage pupils to repeat new words and phrases? Use Table 6.3 to help you record your findings. Which strategy works with which learner types?

2   Pupils need a lot of confidence to speak to each other in the TL. With reference to Table 6.4, what forms of support are provided in pair and group work? Which work best with which learner types?

3   Figure 6.7 consists of three columns: learner types, activity types and support. Which activities are most suitable for which learner type and what support is required? Match up the items in the three columns. Base your choice on the classroom observations you have already carried out.

4   Follow up this task by including different activity types in your planning, then evaluate them.

5   For a range of classes, devise differentiated writing tasks and discuss them with your mentor or the respective class teacher.

Table 6.3   Strategies for repetition

Strategy	Year 7			Year 8			Year 9			Year 10			Year 11		
teacher initials															
whole group															
individuals															
small groups															
competition															
teacher changes voice															
teacher changes pace															
teacher changes pitch															
use of gestures															
use of visual aids															
others . . .															

Table 6.4 Support strategies for oral language production

Support	Comment
visual stimulus	
written stimulus (English)	
written stimulus (TL)	
props	
model examples	
'structure' tables	
scripts (complete or incomplete)	

learner types	activity types	support strategies
beginners	reporting facts	fishing lines*
weak intermediates	substitution	alternative answers
strong intermediates	selection of correct forms	model answers
advanced learners	joining halves of sentences	rules and structures
others – please list	gap filling	switchboards
	labelling	closed questions
	answering in sentences	open questions
	drill exercises	tables of facts and figures
	scripting	pictures
	free expression	symbols
	discursive writing	flow charts
	other – please list	others – please list

Figure 6.7 Matching learner types, activity types and support strategies

Note: * Fishing lines are drawn onto a sheet to join two ideas; these may be presented as a tangled web, forming a puzzle.

CREATIVITY AND IMAGINATION

Imagination and creativity can be seen to permeate all MFL work. Indeed, the National Curriculum Programme of Study (PoS) of the 1999 NC MFL Orders required that pupils should be taught through 'using the target language creatively and imaginatively' (DfEE/QCA 1999: 17), and this emphasis continues in the 2007 PoS. This notion hardly comes as a surprise as, in Miller's words: 'in the modern languages classroom . . . teachers are required, day after day, to involve their pupils in a collective suspension of disbelief' (Miller 1995: 1). And the National Curriculum Council non-statutory guidance notes that 'the interest and motivation of young learners can be stimulated by themes which relate to play and leisure – themes of fantasy, fiction and fun' (NCC 1992a: B9).

Traditionally teachers require verbal responses. However, you might also occasionally, and where appropriate, consider other communicative tools such as:

- drawing;
- modelling;
- composing music;
- dance;
- movement;
- poetry.

Allowing such a range of responses over a period of time enables the expression of new ideas to be generated in ways which mirror the human means of perception, i.e. through various senses.

Goleman (1996) stresses the need to assist pupils in the development of their emotional intelligence, which means that opportunities need to be built into the learning process to allow pupils to respond and therefore to understand, express and use feelings and intuition.

One of the challenges for MFL teachers lies in incorporating into lessons suitable material and activities at appropriate moments. By far not all language use is purely transactional and much is to be gained from the building of personalised patterns and structures. A multi-sensory approach allows for learning to be channelled in ways other than through verbal presentations. Songs, poems, puzzles, games, the creating of cartoons, artefacts and models can all enhance the learning process, appealing to pupils by adding variety and by catering for the diversity of their preferred learning styles.

The process of learning is not and should not be mechanistic. Language offers the opportunity for play, experimentation and even expression through means other than language. The stimulus for comprehension is often the context and the incentive for communication may be different from the need to communicate for transactional purposes. Poetry, for example, allows for the close analysis of language.

Some published recorded material such as *Un kilo de chansons* (Kay 1978) contains the continuous rhythmic repetition of simple phrases, set to music. Rap music can provide similar opportunities as can other material available via the internet. To allow pupils to record their own songs to a simple rhythm and to add basic musical accompaniment can be an effective way to link in with youth culture and pupils' interests.

It used to take a long time to produce puzzles in the form of word searches, crosswords or word snakes. Now, as mentioned above, many of these can be produced quickly and easily via one of the puzzle websites available. Pupils themselves can occasionally be asked to develop such activities and challenge peers to complete them. The production of personalised language forms, which actually serve a purpose, can lead to a feeling of ownership and achievement.

Television advertisements often make minimal use of language, yet communicate messages through imagery and symbolism. To develop advertisements of their own allows pupils to put limited language skills to good use within a sophisticated context.

Language is often the means by which instructions and explanations are communicated. Success can be measured in terms of how well such instructions have been understood and acted upon. To ask pupils to deliver instructions in the process of making a product such as a meal, model or artefact is a demanding exercise, yet it can be motivating in that TL use can be seen to have an impact on the listener as well as a concrete outcome.

For a detailed discussion of creativity in MFL and more examples of using creativity in MFL teaching and learning, see Jones (1992), Kavanagh and Upton (1994) or Miller (1995).

HOMEWORK

Homework can play a crucial role in the development of relevant (linguistic) skills in pupils. Given the fact that you, though vital in your role as agent in the learning process, cannot do the learning for your pupils, the extension of the limited exposure to the subject matter in lesson time through homework can be beneficial.

Homework can fulfil a number of different functions: it can supplement, extend and/or differentiate what happens in the MFL classroom; it can reinforce or con-solidate linguistic items and structures; it allows pupils to work at their own pace and make use of reference material such as dictionaries. On occasion, tasks partially completed in class can be finished off at home. Homework can also yield valuable evidence for assessment purposes.

It is very important to note that homework need not be confined to the skill of writing:

- listening can be fostered by pupils listening to relevant role plays or other texts on an appropriate medium for them (via the Web, as a recording, etc.);
- speaking can be encouraged by pupils recording pronunciation exercises, role plays or themselves reading aloud;
- reading skills can be developed through reading for pleasure outside the classroom;
- writing is often developed by way of completion of worksheets or exercises following on from oral or aural classroom work or scripting role plays. Drafting and redrafting with the help of ICT can also be meaningfully encouraged if pupils have access to a computer at home or at the school outside lesson time.

In addition to skill-specific tasks and activities, other areas such as cultural awareness, learning strategies and (inter)personal and research skills can be developed through homework. Prompted by some pictures with brief captions in the coursebook, pupils can be asked, individually or in small groups, to produce a leaflet on a region/country where the TL is spoken for a specific audience, e.g. a display for the school's open evening. You can either provide authentic resources such as leaflets for the task or pupils can be introduced to library resources including material on an electronic encyclopaedia. Pupils can be asked to extract relevant information from source material in English or the TL, simplify and, where necessary, translate it.

From time to time the learning or revision of key linguistic items or structures might be an appropriate homework task. In order to enable pupils to gain most of such homework, they need to be taught some strategies how to learn new linguistic items and structures as well as revision techniques. Regular revision of some ten minutes or so a day can, for instance, be more effective than isolated longer revision sessions; simply reading words or texts again and again might be less effective than saying words aloud or using underlining or highlighting techniques; revision plans can help to prioritise and avoid omitting important information; mixing topics that are more appealing with ones that are (perceived to be) more challenging might avoid reluctance to revise; making revision notes may help as may making up mnemonics, acronyms such as 'UE': *Unión Europea* or word associations such as *tiempo: hacer calor, hacer frío, mal tiempo . . . .* For a range of useful homework ideas, see Buckland and Short (1993).

As can be seen in Chapter 4, in order to maximise its benefits, homework needs to be planned into units of work and lessons, i.e. thought about carefully in advance. Care needs to be taken that the departmental and school policies on homework are adhered to, for instance in terms of homework days. Appropriateness and manageability are other important considerations when deciding on the quantity and nature of homework.

Instructions need to be clear and unambiguous and the use of the TL for setting homework needs to be thought of carefully. It is important to feed back to pupils regularly and preferably in the following lesson how well they have done and in class to go over some of the areas which caused problems to them. In providing feedback you need to adhere to the departmental and school marking policies, which will often specify a system of grades as well as the nature of TL to be used for feedback. The policy could, for instance, specify that pupils are given a list of grades in English and the TL on a handout, which they stick into their exercise books for reference and which are used consistently across the department and/or school. For assessment, recording and reporting, see also Chapter 10.

Task 6.4 Giving written feedback to pupils

1   Draw up two lists of comments in the TL you think are appropriate in giving written feedback to pupils about their homework, one list for each Key Stage. What sort of content might be included in these comments?

2   Next, ask your mentor or the class teacher for permission to collect in a set of books for each Key Stage and note the comments your colleagues have made about pupils' work.

3   Then, compare your lists with the comments found in the exercise book and study the departmental marking policy.

4   Finally, discuss the findings with the teacher in question.

Task 6.5 Designing a guide for parents

Devise a guide for parents with suggestions how they can support their child's independent study and homework. Activities might include vocabulary testing, providing opportunities for listening to and reading the TL, researching holiday destinations.

SUMMARY

Both MFL student teachers and pupils should recognise the importance of sequencing activities and integrating MFL skills within a communicative framework. Each MFL skill must be developed equally in order to allow pupils to generate language in 'authentic' situations and in an independent way.

Creativity is an important and integral part of MFL work.

Homework can be used meaningfully to extend and consolidate work carried out in class.

FURTHER READING

Grauberg, W. (1997) *The Elements of Foreign Language Teaching*. Clevedon: Multilingual Matters.

This book explores a wide range of fundamental issues in the teaching and learning of MFL and provides excellent insights into aspects such as phonology, vocabulary and the four language skills.

Pachler, N. and Redondo, A. (2007) *Teaching Foreign Languages in the Secondary School: A Practical Guide*. London: Routledge.

This book provides a good source of further thoughts concerning the issues introduced in this chapter as well as for most of the other chapters in this publication.

Swarbrick, A. (2002) *Aspects of Teaching Secondary Modern Foreign Languages: Perspectives on Practice*. London: Open University/RoutledgeFalmer.

A wide-ranging book concerned with a variety of important topics in teaching and learning MFL, including approaches to the four language skills.

7 Teaching and learning grammar

INTRODUCTION

The ability to use language grammatically correctly is a key component and an integral part of effective communication in the target language (TL). This chapter is based upon the premise that the development of communicative competence is a key goal for modern foreign languages (MFL) teaching and learning in the secondary school. Importantly, however, communicative competence is used here to encompass grammatical competence, socio-cultural competence, discourse competence and strategic competence (see Pachler 2000a). In particular, this chapter deals with grammatical competence as a subset of communicative competence.

OBJECTIVES

By the end of this chapter you should:

* understand some of the important issues concerning the teaching and learning of grammar in the secondary MFL curriculum;
* appreciate the need for a structured approach to the teaching and learning of grammar;
* be aware of one possible framework for and be able to make informed choices about the teaching and learning of grammar in support of the development of communicative competence.

MFL methodology is characterised by considerable changes in the importance afforded to grammar over time. Until the late 1970s and early 1980s, the so-called grammar translation method prevailed, which came about in the wake of MFL teachers' eagerness to assert equality of status with classical languages. In the grammar translation method, TL structures are typically arranged according to perceived usefulness and in increasing order of supposed complexity with new grammar rules being introduced and explained in the mother tongue, exemplified in the TL and practised through translation out of and into the TL (see Allford 1999: 232). The grammar-translation method can be seen as an expression of MFL teachers' perceived need to justify the position of their subject on the curriculum by stressing the potential for analytical thinking and the training of the mind MFL learning affords. Focus on language forms in grammar-translation often came at the expense of learners' ability to communicate effectively in speaking.

Examinations and their syllabuses/specifications, i.e. the General Certificate in Education O-level and the Certificate in Secondary Education, reflected the emphasis on grammar and accuracy.

The nature of this approach and of the examination system accompanying it is widely judged to have contributed to a lack of pupil motivation to study MFL at secondary level.

In the mid-1980s the General Certificate of Secondary Education (GCSE) was introduced. It emphasised communication in a narrowly defined number of topics with clearly specified linguistic items/phrases, functions and structures at the expense of accuracy. The pendulum swing from great emphasis on form to great emphasis on meaning led to the publication of two consecutive National Curriculum documents in the 1990s, which put little emphasis on grammar.

In recent years, grammar has seen something of a renaissance. Pressure from the grass roots has led to changes in the Subject Criteria, the national criteria published by the Qualifications and Curriculum Authority (QCA), which govern the General Certificate of Secondary Education (see QCA 2000a, 2007a). While the national criteria continue to consider structural aspects of the TL in the main as a means to an end, they now do feature explicit reference to grammar. For example, all GCSE specifications must, among other things, require candidates to 'understand and apply the grammar of the language, as detailed in the specification (grammar lists are provided for French, German and Spanish)'; and specifications must specify grammar and linguistic structures; and '[allocate] for each of AO2 and AO4, at least 10% of the total marks to knowledge and accurate application of the grammar and structures of the language prescribed in the specification'.

Similarly, the GCSE consultation Criteria (QCA 2007a) state the following: 'For each of AO2 (*speaking*) and AO4 (*writing*), at least 10% of the total marks for the subject must be allocated to knowledge and accurate application of the grammar and structures of the language prescribed in the specification.'

This trend must be seen also as a consequence of developments earlier at advanced level and as an attempt to avoid a further increase in the gap between GCSE and A level. The most recent GCE/AS/A level Subject Criteria published by the QCA (see http://www.qca.org.uk/13516_14816.html) feature a detailed and differentiated list of structures to be covered at Advanced Subsidiary (AS) and at Advanced (A) level for French, German, Spanish and Urdu. Of course it must also be seen as an attempt to build on the National Literacy Strategy (NLS) at primary level (see DfEE 1998a and Chapter 1) and the introduction of the KS3 MFL Framework.

The refocusing on grammar follows a heated debate in the recent past about whether the requirements of examination specifications and associated approaches to MFL teaching pre-higher education were appropriate in their demands regarding awareness, knowledge and understanding of grammar and whether they furthered the development of transferable and independently expandable MFL learning skills.

As of late the question is no longer whether or not grammar should be taught, but instead how, why and when (see also Jones 2000: 146; Meiring and Norman 2001, 2007). Learning how to teach grammar effectively is a crucial aspect of your development as a successful teacher of MFL (see Macrory 2000).

In private, many MFL teachers have always held the view that 'there comes a time when pupils must learn some grammar of the TL' (Rivers 1975: 105) irrespective of prevailing methodological trends. Halliwell (1993: 17), for example, points out the value of learning grammar as opposed to acquiring the language. She sees learning as a conscious process and she considers it to be quicker than acquisition through immersion. While not conclusive, there is increasingly research evidence pointing to the importance of form-focused instruction, i.e. explicit grammar teaching (see Ellis 1997; Han and Ellis 1998). However, building language forms around grammatical rules independently of communicative needs can be argued to serve no real purpose. Bertrand Russell put forward the view that:

> The purpose of words, though philosophers seem to forget this simple fact, is to deal with matters other than words. If I go to a restaurant and order my dinner, I do not want my words to fit into a system of other words, but to bring about the presence of food.
>
> (in Page and Hewett 1987: 6)

Clearly, the communicative context determines the form of the message conveyed by a speaker or writer. Grammatical accuracy can be argued to be secondary if the message is understood. Nevertheless, pupils need a grammatical base in order to be able to generate language of their own as opposed to merely reproduce set phrases of others. Communicative competence and linguistic competence should, therefore, not be seen as separate entities (see Miller 2002). Learners should not be inhibited in terms of communicative competence due to an adherence to a strictly linear approach to learning grammar, i.e. from simple to complex. Lightbown and Spada (1993: 114) note that 'it is neither necessary nor desirable to restrict learners' exposure to certain linguistic structures which are perceived as being "simple"'. As Grauberg (1997: 99) rightly points out, even the simplest exchanges require complex language (see DeKeyser 2005, for some insights into what makes learning grammar difficult). To empower learners to operate in the present tense only, for example, can 'strand them linguistically' (see Jones 2000: 149). Sequencing of grammar learning can enable learners to build up patterns and structures incrementally.

To teach learners certain grammatical features as set phrases can be legitimate in so far as it can stand pupils in good stead, for example, in preparation for their public examinations, which feature transactional exchanges in narrowly defined contexts. However, this should not be done at the expense of the development in pupils of an understanding of language and of an ability to generate language of their own. A more beneficial long-term strategy seems to us to be to pay specific attention to language with transferable value, such as the key verbs, lexical items, pronouns, adjectives, adverbs or gender markers.

This chapter focuses on the need to address the development of grammatical awareness, knowledge and understanding in pupils in a well-planned and structured way within the context of communicative processes. We suggest that grammar should not be presented in isolation but in a coherent framework and that it should not be left to pupils to absorb grammar by osmosis.

Task 7.1 Key issues in grammar learning and teaching

The following are what may be considered key issues involving grammar in language learning and teaching:

- Terminology – use of it at all? In TL? In English? In both?
- Explicit instruction/implicit learning/both?
- Systematic introduction of structures/more ad hoc (when the need arises)/a balanced approach?
- Practice with drills/exercises?
- 'Rules' – if, how and when? In what format? In which language?
- Grammar for recognition? Grammar for production?

Reflect on the issues listed. What are your initial thoughts on them *before* you read the rest of the chapter?

PEDAGOGICAL GRAMMAR

Definitions of the word 'grammar' are manifold: they range from a 'theory of language' to a description of 'the (syntactic) structure of a particular language'. Of these grammars, work by applied linguists on what they call 'pedagogical grammar', which focuses on language teaching, syllabus design and the production of teaching material, is of particular interest to MFL teachers (see Mitchell, 2000).

At ages 11–16 it is particularly difficult for the MFL teacher to strike the right balance between accuracy and meaning. To what extent should MFL teachers tolerate errors when encouraging communication? Page (1990: 103–4) is unequivocal about the role of grammar: 'Correct grammar, like pronunciation, serves a social function. It tells the world something about what sort of person we are in the same way as our clothes, our lifestyle, and the newspaper we read.'

While perfect grammatical accuracy is not necessary for communication to take place, it can be argued that to operate effectively as a TL speaker or writer, we have to understand – to some extent – the possibilities that grammar affords us. The ability to recognise linguistic patterns and to make use of and apply grammatical rules aids communication rather than inhibits it. This is recognised by the 2007 NC PoS, which states:

> The study of languages should include:
>
> c the grammar of the target language and how to apply it.

This was also present in the 1999 Orders, and constituted a marked departure from previous versions, in which there was no explicit and little implicit mention of grammar. Knowledge of and application of grammar also feature frequently in the level descriptions accompanying the 2007 PoS.

Success at GCSE increasingly requires awareness, knowledge and understanding of grammatical features. Careful preparation of pupils in examination techniques and familiarisation with past examination papers as well as standard 'grammatical' paradigms and standard role plays and letters to be adapted by pupils according to context continue to be useful strategies for gaining good examination results. However, there is a growing need for applied grammatical knowledge, which is reflected in the 2000 GCSE Grade descriptions (see QCA 2000b: 3–4, http://www.qca.org.uk/downloads/5708_modern_foreign_lang.pd(1).pdf and Figure 7.1).

	Speaking	Writing
Grade F	Candidates take part in simple conversations showing some ability to substitute words and phrases. Their pronunciation is generally accurate, and although there may be grammatical inaccuracies, the main points are communicated.	Candidates write short sentences, and respond to written texts by substituting words and set phrases. Although there may be mistakes in spelling and grammar the main points are communicated.
Grade C	Candidates develop conversation and simple discussions which include past, present and future events, involving the use of different tenses.	Candidates express personal opinions and write about a variety of topics, both factually and imaginatively, including past, present and future events and involving the use of different tenses..
Grade A	Candidates express and justify points of view, and produce longer sequences of speech using a variety of vocabulary, structures and verb tenses.	Candidates produce longer sequences using a range of vocabulary, structure and verb tenses. Their spelling and grammar are generally accurate.

Figure 7.1 Extracts from the GCSE Grade descriptions

Grammar is no longer merely implicit. You must make yourself aware of these specifications in relation to your teaching language(s). The lists provide examples and also indicate elements where only receptive knowledge is required.

To some extent, grammatical understanding can be seen to provide foreign language learners in classroom-based settings with a short cut. The limited curriculum time available, usually not more than 10–12.5 per cent, and the acquisition-poor nature of classroom-based learning do not tend to allow for natural acquisition. Grammar can be seen as a tool enabling TL use and the use of specific and technical terminology, i.e. metalanguage, offers learners access to reference material. The teaching and learning of grammar at 11–16 is neither undesirable nor inappropriate. In order to be beneficial, it does, however, need to be structured carefully and a range of issues need to be taken on board during the planning process as, for example, Jones (2000b: 151–3) notes (see Figure 7.2). Both under- and over-emphasis on grammatical structures can lead to frustration and can militate against free expression. The exact nature of the teacher's methods will depend on, among other factors, her personal teaching style, pupils' individual needs and differences, the coursebook followed or the general approach adopted by the whole school in terms of language work (see Everett 2005, for some ideas for making grammar more permanently a part of pupils' language production).

FOUR STAGES OF DEVELOPING GRAMMATICAL AWARENESS

The four stages of developing grammatical awareness delineated below (see Figure 7.3) are intended to link the teaching of grammar to the 'presentation-practice-production' paradigm introduced in Chapter 3. Stages 1–4 are not meant to promote curriculum planning based on grammar-orientated objectives alone. Instead, a structured and graded approach of developing linguistic understanding is advanced, which is closely linked to other objectives, such as semantic knowledge across different contexts or functions (e.g. expressing likes and dislikes, asking for, refusing, etc.):

> Research findings . . . challenged the traditional grammar-based course by suggesting that learners acquired particular structures in an order which was psychologically determined but not susceptible to explicit instruction. Acquisition took place in stages and the notion that a learner had fully acquired a structure after a period of instruction was naive. Learning did not occur in linear and progressive fashion but was an organic process characterised by backsliding, leaps in competence, interaction between grammatical elements, etc.
>
> (Heafford 1995: 10)

This notion of an 'organic' nature of language development has implications for teaching and learning. Turner advances the view that a purely thematic, topic-based approach to planning and syllabus design with an unsystematic and disorganised presentation of the grammatical system (e.g. categories of words, the notion of tense, syntactical considerations including cases, the gender of nouns and the notion

1 Selection:
Within the overall schematic picture of a typical five-year learning programme, the teacher needs to select structures that will be useful in terms of transfer value as regards other structures and other contexts in order to maximise their generative capacity for the learners. In other words, it is useful to teach structures, which can be used elsewhere, in different combinations, in conjunction with other structures and as springboards for independent language use. . . .

2 Sequencing:
. . . It is the role of the teacher to help the learners to make the connections through a mixture of inductive and deductive approaches, with extensive exposure and opportunities to practise making the link. . . .

3 Recycling:
While the constraints and needs of classroom learning necessitate some drilling of discrete items as an aid to internalisation, it is helpful to the learners to be shown how a structure learnt in one context may be recycled in another one. . . .

4 Moving from 'form' to function:
. . . This involves a shift from 'skill-getting' to 'skill-using' and envisages the learner moving from a stage of very conscious attention to the language form to a more unconscious use for real communication purposes. . . .

5 Grading of input:
It is sometimes useful to restate a very obvious principle such as this assertion that, as well as a sufficient quantity of examples, teachers need to present appropriately graded examples to the pupils. In this way, the first examples will be easier, straightforward and contradiction-free and thus susceptible to helping the learners to infer the pattern(s) and thus to be able to test their hypotheses. . . .

6 Use of terminology:
Unfortunately, the issue of grammatical terminology has become . . . something considered so abstract as to be beyond pupils' comprehension. This (can be seen as) a little condescending. It is the quality and timing of a presentation and explanation of a grammatical structure that is important and not the terminology *per se*. As Carter cogently argues: 'It is not taught for its own sake but to provide an economic and precise way of discussing particular functions and purposes' (Carter 1997: 24).

Figure 7.2 Some issues associated with teaching and learning grammar

No.	Stage
1	input
2	explanation
3	habit-forming
4	communicative application

Figure 7.3 Four stages of grammar teaching and learning

of agreement, the mood of verbs, etc.) is unhelpful to pupils. Based on the late Christopher Brumfit, she proposes a graded, spiralling approach based on grammatical aspects of a language in conjunction with semantic aspects (the meaning of words and sentences) underpinned by the criterion of 'usefulness to the pupil' (e.g. What does the pupil need to do well in the standardised examination?) with a view to providing a 'tool for learning' (e.g. What helps the pupil in becoming an effective language learner?) (see Turner 1996: 17–18). 'Organising the grammatical core in conjunction with the topic areas means that structures are always contextualised and related to language use.' (ibid.: 18) For example, the topic of 'directions' could be seen to lend itself well to the teaching of imperatives (the command form).

The role of grammar in foreign language teaching and learning is complex. Teachers' decisions need to take into account what is known about the foreign language learning process. Pachler (see 1999a: 97) identifies four broad stages of learning grammar:

1 *Noticing*
   The identification that language forms patterns and the labelling, in the learners' own words, of these patterns. (This is where the teacher's carefully planned presentation of the grammar can play a key role, e.g. by intelligent use of ICT to enable more 'noticing' of the forms and changes).

2 *Integrating*
   The process of identifying and labelling through personal rule formation needs to be related to existing grammatical knowledge.

3 *Internalising*
   Learners need to apply their own rules in order to manipulate language forms for their own purposes. This completes the process of committing the form to the long-term memory.

4 *Proceduralising*
   Use of the structure becomes 'automatic' through regular usage in a range of contexts.

From this follow important pedagogic questions, such as: to what extent should these processes be made explicit to pupils? And, how can they be taught?

The input stage

Two main approaches to providing input can be distinguished: an *inductive* approach, where linguistic structures are introduced through examples from which to develop (personal) rules, and a *deductive* approach, where the pupil is provided with a grammatical rule or pattern followed by examples before putting it to use.

Both methods have a legitimate place in MFL teaching and learning. Grammar is highly conceptual, which appeals to some pupils more than others. Certain aspects of language are difficult to explain. Why, for instance, is the word 'table' feminine in French and masculine in German and why has it no grammatical gender in English? To accept certain concepts as given and to apply some rules in a mechanical way without trying to understand them seems on occasion to be a sensible way forward. Nevertheless, having understood a grammatical concept, for instance gender, many pupils are able to work out a rule, such as for adjectival agreement, from a set of carefully constructed examples.

Some pupils can get a sense of security from understanding language patterns and rules. Forth and Naysmith (1995: 78) distinguish:

- *'external' rules*: 'the kind of statements, diagrams, tables, etc., which we can find in coursebooks, grammar reference books or which we as teachers provide';
- *'internal' rules*: 'the learner's own intuitive, informal hunches of how elements of the language might work'.

While they stress that there is 'no one, single approach to the presentation and use of grammar rules in the classroom' (ibid.: 80), they posit that learners should be encouraged to reflect on how they themselves use rules and what works for them. Teachers should encourage learners to challenge grammar rules, for instance, by:

- asking pupils to change or modify rules presented in their coursebooks so that they are clearer and more accessible;
- asking pupils to add their own examples;
- asking pupils to re-present rules in the form of classroom poster-displays perhaps with the addition of pictures or diagrams.

(ibid.)

Input is concerned with the selection of material and of a suitable approach. One possible consideration is for items, which can be seen to be of future use and are, therefore, 'transferable', to be explicitly taught, especially in the early stages of learning. Such items need to be readily understood by all learners and the teacher needs to be sure that they are relatively simple to understand. Ellis (1994: 91), referring to research by Green and Hecht (1992) on what constitutes easy-to-learn rules, lists the following features:

- those that refer to easily recognisable categories;
- those which can be applied mechanically;
- those that are not dependent on large contexts.

Task 7.2 Grammar rules

Write a rule for the English use of 'yet' and 'still' as in 'I've not been to London yet' and 'I've still not been to London'.

- How did you go about approaching this task?
- When is it useful to resort to a rule and when does it help to refer to examples?

The selection of grammatical items to be covered within units of work is not simple. Some topics lend themselves more easily to new grammatical input than others (e.g. the topic 'Around town' for the teaching of the imperative). However, the selection of grammar points to be covered requires the consideration of more complex questions, such as:

- Which items need to be 'recycled' from previous units covered?
- Which items meaningfully build on existing knowledge?
- Which items should not be explained in full at this stage, but will require revisiting at a later date?
- Which items can be treated as lexical items at this stage?

The schemes of work produced by QCA (QCA 2000a; also available at http://www.ncaction.org.uk/subjects/MFL/) and coursebooks tend to include suggestions concerning grammar items to be covered. Where possible, account needs to be taken of prior learning and how certain grammatical concepts link with what has come before. Also, extension activities for more able learners are important in so far as the decision to treat certain grammatical structures as lexical items/phrases at a particular stage of learning may not be appropriate for all learners.

Task 7.3 Examining the grammar content of the GCSE Criteria

Consider the grammatical items listed within the GCSE Criteria (QCA 2007a: http://www.qca.org.uk/qca_11999.aspx) for your teaching language(s). Which items do you consider to be essential? How can the underpinning concepts be taught to MFL learners in the early stages of their learning experience?

Task 7.4 Grammar input

Figure 7.4 shows an outline of a unit of work used by one MFL department. The section on grammar has been left blank. In light of the language functions as well as the core and extension language listed, consider:

- What should be included in the grammar section?
- Which of these grammatical points should not be explained but presented as lexical items?

Compare your answers with the way the coursebook(s) used by your placement school approach(es) the topics of personal detail and daily routine and, where possible, discuss them with a colleague.

Pupils need to be prepared for the demands of new language features. Also, they need to be trained to identify patterns, structures, exceptions to rules, etc. and be able

Year 8	Personal details and daily routine	
Language functions		ATL
Be able to: 1 exchange details about the family 2. introduce people 3. describe and understand appearance 4 describe places and buildings 5. talk about chores 6. describe daily routine at home		AT1 L3 & 4 AT2 L2,3 & 4 AT3 L3 & 4 AT4 L3 & 4
Core language		Extension
names of members of immediate family description: hair, eyes, height, weight name of rooms household chores routines		other relatives description of personality other accommodation more complex routines and chores
Grammar		
Key activities		
letter to penfriend design ideal home identikit pictures		

Figure 7.4 Grammar and the unit of work

to learn from the teacher's corrections. You need to be aware of possible misconceptions and difficulties pupils might have, which might impact upon their motivation.

Grauberg (1997: 104) stresses the importance of the text on which introductory work is based. In his opinion it should:

- deal with a topic of interest to the learners;
- build on lexical and grammatical knowledge acquired earlier;
- at the same time have the attraction of novelty;
- feature a context, which lends itself to varied and interesting practice where form and function are brought out clearly without distortion to normal use.

In our reading of Grauberg, we interpret 'text' very broadly as any type of stimulus material, be it written or spoken.

Rutherford (1987) advocates a process of 'consciousness raising' focusing the learner's attention on features of the TL, which are deemed by the teacher to be significant at a given stage of learning. This might well involve a degree of comparison with the mother tongue, the breaking down of larger items into component parts, etc. in order to sensitise the learner to the structure of the TL.

Hawkins (1984) conceives of grammar learning as a voyage of discovery and argues against a prescriptive model. The recognition that different learners will respond to different approaches requires teachers to understand a wide range of techniques and to develop strategies to suit specific learner characteristics.

The discussion of the inductive and deductive methods below is intended to provide a framework within which a range of strategies for grammar teaching can be categories and consequently better understood.

The inductive approach – an example

Pupils need to be made aware of the concept of gender early on. In German, for instance, the awareness of this concept should precede the introduction of the case system. The teaching of the accusative case can be done meaningfully in the context of the topic of 'family and pets'. The assumption in this example is that the new vocabulary has already been introduced (see Chapter 3 for presenting new language and question–and–answer techniques) and that the teacher follows a policy of discussing new grammar items within the context of familiar vocabulary.

Pupils could be presented with a number of sentences such as those in Figure 7.5.

Ich habe *einen* Bruder.	Ich habe *ein* Kaninchen.
Ich habe *eine* Schwester.	Ich habe *eine* Katze.
Ich habe *ein* Meerschweinchen.	Ich habe *einen* Wellensittich.

Figure 7.5 The accusative case in German

The pupils are then asked to sort these sentences according to categories of their own choice. Some pupils will choose the categories according to whether the object is a person or an animal. Clearly from the examples given, pupils would not be wrong to apply such categories. The purpose of the inductive approach is for pupils to make up and apply rules of their own, which fit the examples provided. As the examples given in Figure 7.5 are ambiguous and allow for different interpretation, the MFL teacher needs to provide further examples in a structured way, which lead the pupils to the intended focus. Eventually the majority of pupils should choose the categories: '*einen*', '*ein*' or '*eine*'.

In groups, pupils are then asked to discuss (in English) the ways in which they have categorised the sentences and why and to attempt to generate a rule, which is subsequently discussed in a plenary. An example of one such rule could be: 'If you have something masculine you add "-en" to "*ein*". If it's feminine stick with the normal "*eine*" and for neuter stick with "*ein*".'

At this stage it is sufficient for the MFL teacher to say that the inflections occur after '*haben*'. Once the concept is familiar a more formal explanation of the accusative case can be attempted. In this approach new metalanguage is not introduced until the pupil has demonstrated understanding of the concept through use of language familiar to her at the point of input.

In another example, the inductive approach can be used to teach the perfect tense in Spanish. Pupils are asked to read the penfriend letter in Figure 7.6 and underline or highlight any linguistic patterns they seem to notice. In this example it is the auxiliary '*haber*' in the present tense plus the respective past participle. The teacher then elicits pupil observations in the TL and collects them on the board/OHP. The grammatical rule that infinitives ending in '-ar' form the past participle in '-ado', those ending in '-er' and '-ir' in '-ido' is subsequently explained in the TL by drawing parallels to the similarities and differences in the English language. In this way, appropriate use is made of English for comparing and contrasting with the mother tongue.

Albacete 7 de septiembre

Querida Alison:

¿cómo estás? He vuelto al colegio hace una semana y he empezado mis clases. Lo he pasado muy guay este verano ¿ y tú? He viajado a la costa de Valencia con mi familia y he ido a la playa todos los días por las mañanas donde me he bañado y donde antes del almuerzo hemos jugado mucho al balónvolea con amigos nuevos que he conocido allí.

Me he puesto muy morena. Mi hermana y yo hemos ido a la discoteca por las noches y hemos disfrutado mucho. Mis padres han ido al restaurante todas las noches y han comido comida típica de la región. También hemos visitado pueblos famosos como Elche y sus museos.

He recogido mis fotografias del laboratorio esta mañana y estoy muy contenta con el resultado. He seleccionado cuatro fotos para madarte para que puedas ver lo bonito que es la costa del este de España.

De momento nada más.

En tu carta háblame de tu verano, por ejemplo: ¿has estado de vacaciones? ¿has visitado a tus amigos? ¿has viajado?

Recuerdos a tu familia y espero recibir tu carta pronto.

Con cariño, tu amiga
Sonia

Figure 7.6 Introducing the Spanish perfect tense

Task 7.5 The inductive approach

Try to think of another example for the inductive approach appropriate for your first foreign language and discuss it with your mentor or another teacher you regularly work with.

The deductive approach – an example

For many pupils the concept of grammatical gender is difficult to conceptualise. One possible way of introducing the definite article to pupils is by providing them with a table such as the one in Figure 7.7.

THE					
le	=	**m**asculine	**le** chat	=	**the** cat
la	=	**f**eminine	**la** souris	=	**the** mouse
les	=	**p**lural	**les** chiens	=	**the** dogs
l'	=	before a vowel (**a, e, i, o, u**) or '**h**'	**l'**araignée	=	**the** spider
			l'hôtel	=	**the** hotel

Figure 7.7 The definite article in French

Pupils are then asked to complete the exercise in Figure 7.8 by referring to the table in Figure 7.7.

1. .... cheval (m)	2. .... cahier. . . (pl)	3. .... torture (f)
4. .... lapin. . . (pl)	5. .... prénom (m)	6. .... sœur (f)
7. .... hôpital (m)	8. .... stylo. . . (pl)	9. .... jour. . . (pl)
10. .... anniversaire (m)	11. .... poubelle (f)	12. .... animal (m)
13. .... frère. . . (pl)	14. .... éléphant (m)	15. .... femme (f)
16. .... homme (m)	17. .... serpent. . . (pl)	18. .... table (f)

Figure 7.8 Practising the definite article in French

The deductive approach to grammar teaching can, for instance, also be used in the context of the perfect tense in French. This can be a stumbling block for pupils and for them to devise a comprehensive rule can be too difficult. Pupils should be able to produce a series of rules, which the teacher might want to pull together. The flow chart in Figure 7.9 gives an example of such a structure, which can help pupils to generate many sentences. Such an approach may be suitable for more able pupils preparing for their GCSE examination.

Although this chart is not all-encompassing – it does not take account of reflexive verbs with indirect reflexive pronouns, which require no agreement – it does provide a useful point of reference assisting pupils in generating TL utterances and can be taught in stages. The columns allow coverage of '*avoir*' verbs in isolation from the *être* and reflexive verbs. The need for past participle agreement can be added to the column as learners progress.

One way to help pupils remember which verbs take *être* in the perfect tense is to present a mnemonic. The first letters of the following verbs spell out MRS TRAVENDAMP RDR: *monter, rester, sortir, tomber, revenir, arriver, venir, entrer, nâitre, descendre, aller, mourir, partir, rentrer, devenir, retourner.*

Pour formuler le **passé composé** vous avez besoin de:				
un sujet	**un verbe auxiliare**		**un participe passé**	
je tu il/elle nous vous ils/elles	*avoir* ai as a avons avez ont	*être* suis es est sommes *êtes* sont	é stem + i u	irregular

Alors, choisissez le verbe.

Est-ce que c'est un verbe réfléchi?

oui	non
• utilisez être comme auxiliare • n'oubliez pas le 'me/te/se/nous/vous' entre le sujet et le verbe	C'est un verbe MRS TRAVENDAMP RDR?

		oui	non
		utilisez 'être' comme auxiliare	utilisez 'avoir' comme auxiliare

ajoutez l'accord au participe passé:
  f.   sg.:   -e
  m. sg.:   -
  f.   pl.:   -es
  m. pl.   -s
			n'ajoutez pas d'accord au participe passé

Figure 7.9 The perfect tense in French

Task 7.6 Inductive or deductive approach?

1   Focusing on the scheme of work for one particular year group, make a list of three or five grammar points for each approach. You might find it useful to look at the grammar summary of the coursebook.
2   In your opinion, which grammar points lend themselves to an inductive approach and which to a deductive one?

The explanation stage

The high level of complexity of language can tempt MFL teachers to provide quite detailed explanations of grammatical concepts. The exploration of concepts might on occasion seem easier to achieve through the medium of English than that of the TL as the process of learning might be accelerated in this way by focusing pupils' attention on linguistic structures in a conscious manner. However:

> central to the language learning process must remain 'exposure, exposure and more exposure', that only through the constant engagement of receptive skills can learners begin to get a feel for a language, to sense nuances of meaning, to produce spontaneously.
>
> (Heafford 1995: 12)

Heafford also suggests (ibid.) that 'we need to experiment with various forms of formal grammar teaching to see which approaches least compromise exposure to the TL and which most help accuracy'. Careful selection of TL forms used by you as part of general classroom talk serves to reinforce rules and patterns taught in an explicit manner, although there may be some carefully selected use of English. Pachler (1999a: 102) notes that it is, therefore, incumbent upon teachers to provide rich and varied but carefully considered input, which can be exploited by:

- focusing pupils' attention on noticing new structures;
- providing activities to use new and old structures to formulate personal meaning;
- assisting learners to reflect on learning and their own use of language.

For strategies for teaching grammar in the TL, see Chapter 5. As discussed in Chapter 5, where there are pedagogically sound reasons for using planned English, this should be considered, where it moves pupils' learning on. There may be, for example, a perfect opportunity to hold a productive plenary, where the new grammar point is discussed and any misconceptions dispelled.

Use of metalanguage

The choice of whether or not to use metalanguage such as 'verb', 'noun', 'adjective' remains a question of professional judgement of individual teachers within a coherent departmental approach. You have to decide in line with the approach taken by your placement school to what extent to use metalanguage. The National Literacy Strategy, which features a number of grammatical concepts to be developed during Key Stages 1 and 2, might provide some guidance (see Figure 7.10 based on DfEE 1998a: 68).

Syntax	Superlative
Adjectives	Passive voice
Nouns	Adverb
Pronouns	Clauses
Verbs	Imperatives
Tenses	Prepositions
Comparative	Active voice

Figure 7.10 Grammatical concepts covered in the National Literacy Strategy

The non-statutory schemes of work for Key Stage 3 (see QCA 2000b) and the GCSE Criteria for Modern Foreign Languages (QCA 2000a) also provide expectations for learners' exposure to and understanding of grammatical terminology. Cornell (1996: 28) suggests that by the time they study MFL as a subsidiary part of their degree programme, students should understand and use the following terms and concepts:

- the 'word classes' or 'parts of speech' (noun, verb, adjective, etc.);
- the main sentence constituents (subject, direct object, indirect object; clause);
- the concept of tense;
- for German, the nomenclature of the case system;
- miscellaneous terms which would include, for example, relative pronoun, reflexive;
- pronoun/verb, subjunctive, imperative, modal verb, auxiliary verb, past participle, active/passive, but not that many more.

Task 7.7 Explicit knowledge of grammatical terms

With reference to the list of terms and concepts drawn up by the National Literacy Strategy (Figure 7.10), the recommended schemes of work, the GCSE Criteria and KS3 Framework for Modern Foreign Languages and Cornell's list, consider which grammatical terms pupils should be able to explain (know explicitly):

- by the end of Key Stage 3
- by the end of Key Stage 4.

By introducing new linguistic structures through unfamiliar terminology MFL teachers run the risk of their pupils struggling with concepts at a level one step removed from the linguistic phenomenon itself. On the other hand, using 'pupil-friendly' terms may deny pupils maximum use of reference material in support of their learning. The use of terminology like 'doing words' and 'describing words' arguably has a place in the learning process and pupils should not necessarily be discouraged from using their own terms. Making some selective, carefully planned and well targeted use of the mother tongue when discussing and reflecting on grammar can help pupils develop personal terms and rules. Metalanguage can be introduced once a concept is understood by pupils.

Task 7.8 Grammatical concepts

Table 7.1 shows some grammatical concepts in alphabetical order.

1   In what order do you think they should be first introduced?
2   Ask your mentor or another colleague you work with frequently to place them in an order. Do you both agree?

Table 7.1 Sequencing grammatical concepts

Concept	Ranking
adjectival agreement	
definite and indefinite articles	
expressions of quantity	
gender and number	
imperative	
negatives	
perfect tense	
present tense	
transitive and intransitive verbs	

The habit-forming stage

The role of the teacher does not end with the explanation of concepts contained in Table 7.1. Explanation is useful if learners are to proceed to using structures and to developing good language habits. Accurate use of the TL by pupils should be one of the aims of MFL teachers with the ultimate goal of pupils reaching a point when language forms 'sound' or 'feel' right or wrong. A first notion of an intuitive 'feel' can be worked towards by habitual use of the TL.

The process of developing a 'feel' for correct language forms requires a lot of practice and MFL activities need to serve a purpose beyond the generation of accurate language as an end in itself.

In a further example, the introduction of the perfect tense in Spanish in Figure 7.11 is followed up by the habit-forming activity in Figure 7.12. Pupils are given a combination table based on the language used in the penfriend letter. Their task is to generate as many grammatically correct sentences in the perfect tense as possible. Pupils have to use the correct form of the past participle. At the same time they have

he has ha hemos habéis han	comer disfrutar empezar estar ir jugar (lo) pasar seleccionar viajar visitar	al baloncesto a la playa/a la montaña a Málaga/Francia/América de vacaciones el museo/la discoteca estupendo/guay/muy bien fotografias las clases pueblos famosos comida típica	a las ....y media antes antes del almuerzo dos semanas durante las vacaciones en el verano esta mañana por las mañanas por las noches

Figure 7.11 Practising the Spanish perfect tense

ich	bin	mit Klara in die Stadt	**gegangen**
wir	sind	um 16 Uhr	**angekommen**
sie	hat	eine rote Hose	**getragen**
du	hast	Pommes Frites	**gegessen**
Sie	haben	eine Tasse Tee	**getrunken**
ihr	habt	einen tollen Film	**gesehen**
er	ist	mit dem Bus	**zurückgefahren**
es	hat	zwanzig Fenster	**gehabt**

Figure 7.12 German word order

to find the correct complement to the verb. The use of an adverb(ial) of time can be made optional. Differentiation can, therefore, be built into this activity by outcome, i.e. the number of sentences pupils generate, or by task, i.e. the number of variables pupils are asked to combine. For a fuller discussion of differentiation, see Chapter 9.

Another example of a habit-forming activity is given in Figure 7.12. German word order in the context of the perfect tense can be practised by writing a number of sentences on card, mixing the cards up and asking pupils (in pairs or groups) to reconstruct correct sentences.

As an extension to this activity, adverb(ial)s of time can be added such as: *gestern, vor zwei Tagen, am Abend, um 10 Uhr, letzte Woche, zu Mittag* or *am Vormittag*. This allows pupils to practise the positioning of adverb(ial)s of time including the inversion of subject and auxiliary verb. To differentiate the activity further, the sentences could add up to a story for pupils to recreate.

The application of rules is easier for some pupils than for others. There is a need to grade activities to cater for the different needs of pupils. In this way should one level prove too difficult, pupils can attempt the preceding one or pupils can quickly move on to the next level if they find one too easy. The levels can be set in a variety of different ways. An example of this is given in Figure 7.13, which shows one way of practising present tense verb endings in German in the context of 'hobbies, pastimes and weather' by referring to a 'rule' or paradigm, in this case a conjugated verb in the present tense.

The assumption is that pupils have been informed that the exercises are designed to enable them to conduct a survey of who does what and in which weather conditions. First, pupils select the correct ending from a given list. Second, they apply the 'rule' in given examples and, third, they use the rule to generate language of their own.

Activities of this type bridge the use of grammatical 'rules' or paradigms and their communicative application by preparing pupils for a survey, e.g. of what pastimes pupils pursue in different weather conditions.

It is crucial that you consider the length of time required for pupils to master particular grammatical concepts. This will, of course, vary from pupil to pupil. Input and explanation stages may occur on several occasions as understanding develops. Opportunities for practice must be introduced on a regular basis and the revisiting of grammatical features needs to be well planned.

Die Regel			
ich spiel *e*	wir	spiel *en*	
du spiel *st*	ihr	spiel *t*	
er/sie/es spiel *t*	sie/Sie	spiel *en*	
Teil 1			
Schreibe den richtigen Satz!			
1. Meine Schwester spiel *e* *t* *en* gern Fußball.			
2. Mein Freund schwimm *st* *t* *e* im Hallenbad.			
3. Mein Bruder und ich tanz *e* *t* *en* in der Disco.			
4. Ich geh *st* *en* *e* oft in die Stadt.			
5. Sie schreib *e* *st* *t* viele Briefe.			
Teil 2			
Schreibe einen ganzen Satz!			
6. Mein Vater *(kochen)* das Abendessen.			
7. Wir *(wollen)* etwas trinken.			
8. Ich *(suchen)* meine Kleidung.			
9. Sie *(spielen)* gern Volleyball.			
10. Ja natürlich, ich *(schwimmen)* besonders gern.			
Teil 3			
Was macht man, wenn . . .? Erfinde eine Antwort.			
11. Was macht sie, wenn die Sonne scheint?	*Sie geht ins Schwimmbad, wenn die Sonne scheint.*		
12. Was machst du, wenn es regnet?	. . .		
13. Was machen wir, wenn es schneit?	. . .		
14. Was macht er, wenn das Wetter schlecht ist?	. . .		
15. Was macht ihr, wenn es sehr schön ist?	. . .		

Figure 7.13 Practising present tense verb endings in German

Task 7.9 The development of grammatical concepts

We suggested above that some topics lend themselves better to the introduction and practice of certain grammatical concepts than others. Consider which topics lend themselves particularly well to the teaching of certain grammatical concepts.

1   Choose three to five grammatical concepts from Figure 7.10 and consider through which topic they might meaningfully be introduced.
2   Reflect on how long it will take learners to master the concepts and their application, and consider Miller's (2002: 141–55) principles of grammar teaching (Box 7.1).
3   Identify other topics in which practice of the structures could be included.

Box 7.1 Miller's principles of grammar teaching

- Learners cannot learn (or 'acquire') a grammatical structure unless they are exposed to *multiple examples* of it.
- Each of those examples must occur in the *context of a plausible speech act*. Knowledge of rules in isolation from any context will promote the use of anglicisms since the only links that learners will be able to create between abstract syntactic system and speech act will be the ones that operate in their own language.
- Learners must understand how *grammatical choices* can correspond to the expression of *social and interpersonal relationships*. The most obvious example of this is the choice between familiar and polite forms, but these correspondences operate across much wider areas of the language.

Communicative application stage

A key feature of communicative language teaching is the emphasis on the message as opposed to the linguistic form, on conveying meaning rather than demonstrating knowledge about language. While we deem the conveying of meaning to be central to MFL teaching at secondary level, we recognise the need for systematic coverage of the grammatical system linked to thematic progression. From pre-communicative language practice, including implicit and explicit manipulation of linguistic patterns and structures pupils need to be moved on to communicative application.

Marking and error correction are important in the language learning process. Constructive feedback on pupils' TL production can reinforce accurate use and is an important tool in moving pupils from pre-communicative to communicative language use. Beaton (1990: 42–3), suggests that '[when] errors are corrected, it goes without saying that revision of the correction is essential. . . . there needs to be an incubation period in which the learner acquires a feel'. Work featuring a considerable number of mistakes and errors is a clear sign that the pupil is not ready to progress to the stage of using language in 'authentic', communicative situations. Pupils' readiness to progress to communicative situations, therefore, needs to be carefully monitored. You need to consider the nature of her feedback carefully. It is important to strike the right balance between providing constructive support and demotivating pupils through over-correction. For a more detailed discussion of marking and error correction, see Chapter 10.

Once comfortable with certain structures, pupils should be given opportunities to apply these language forms meaningfully. The use of the TL for a perceived purpose and with success can lead to a sense of achievement. One example is the information-gap activity in Figure 7.14 focusing on the German perfect tense.

Another example of the communicative application stage is, for instance, an activity known as the 'alibi game', which is useful when reinforcing the perfect and imperfect tenses as well as question forms in any foreign language. (For other examples of the 'alibi game', see Langran and Purcell 1994: 24 or Miller 1995: 7.)

The teacher sets the scene in the respective TL: 'The crown jewels have been stolen

A	am Morgen	am Nachmittag	am Abend
Freitag	zur Schule gehen mit dem Bus fahren Erdkunde haben		Hausaufgabe machen Kassetten hören mit dem Computer spielen
Samstag		in die Stadt fahren einkaufen gehen neue Schuhe kaufen	
Sonntag	zur Kirche gehen Großmutter besuchen Kaffee trinken und Kekse essen	zum Park gehen Fußball spielen angeln gehen	

B	am Morgen	am Nachmittag	am Abend
Freitag		in der Kantine essen mit Freunden plaudern Deutsch haben	
Samstag	im Bett bleiben um 11 Uhr Frühstück essen die Zeitung lesen		zu Hause bleiben fernsehen um 10 Uhr ins Bett gehen
Sonntag			Hausaufgaben machen ein Buch lesen Briefe schreiben

Figure 7.14 Was hast du am Wochenende gemacht?

from the Tower of London over the weekend. Two suspects have been arrested when they were seen in the vicinity around the time the theft has occurred.'

Two pupils are asked to play the role of the 'suspects'. Any number of paired pupils can act as 'suspects'. The 'suspects' have to prepare a story between them, which will serve as their alibi. The rest of the pupils are tasked with formulating questions, which they will ask the two 'suspects' in turn. The aim is to extract information, which shows that the two 'suspects' are making inconsistent statements. Once familiar with the format of activity, pupils can be asked to work in groups supported by the teacher and the foreign language assistant, who circulate from group to group so that pupils get a number of opportunities for language production.

Once an alibi has been thought of and questions have been devised, the first pupil is 'questioned' and peers note the responses. Afterwards the second pupil is 'questioned' and the questioners note the information provided. The questioners are required to use the information extracted to compile a report and a recommendation for 'prosecution'.

The activity requires pupils to extract and use information through the medium of the TL and allows for repetitive practice of a particular linguistic form. At the same time pupils are generating their own forms of language.

Task 7.10 Task 7.1 revisited: Key issues in grammar learning and teaching

Having read the chapter, how do you now view the following issues in the teaching and learning of grammar?

Terminology – use of it at all? In TL? In English? In both?

Explicit instruction/implicit learning/both?

Systematic introduction of structures /more ad hoc (when the need arises)/a balanced approach?

Practice with drills/exercises?

'Rules' – if, how and when? In what format? In which language?

Grammar for recognition? Grammar for production?

SUMMARY

Grammar is an important aspect of the foreign language learning process and you need to use your professional judgement and take on board theoretical considerations when deciding on your personal approach to grammar teaching.

Teachers and learners need to be aware that grammar is not assimilated instantly, nor can it be presented in an oversimplified, linear fashion. Learners need time to become accustomed to what they notice about the TL and transform it to personal use.

Grammar can be taught and learnt explicitly and implicitly. Either way, successful learning is, at least in part, dependent on the teacher's skill in planning, presenting and enabling practice as well as opportunity for personalisation of language forms. There are no hard and fast rules governing the teaching and learning of grammar, but a carefully structured and thought through approach can be seen to be helpful. In this chapter we presented a possible framework aimed at helping you develop a coherent approach to the teaching of grammar.

It is important to remember that, in the context of MFL teaching and learning in the secondary school, grammar should not be taught in isolation from communicative objectives. At the same time, pupils should not be left to assimilate and absorb information without the support and guidance of the MFL teacher.

FURTHER READING

Macrory, G. (2000) 'Learning to teach grammar in the Modern Foreign Languages Classroom', *Research in Education* 1: 1–11.

A particularly useful article for beginning teachers of MFL, exploring the development of approaches to teaching grammar.

Meiring, L. and Norman, N. (2001) 'Grammar in MFL teaching revisited', *Language Learning Journal* 23: 58–66.

This article summarises the grammar debate in MFL teaching and learning and provides some interesting suggestions.

Pachler, N. (1999) 'Teaching and learning grammar', in N. Pachler (ed.) *Teaching Modern Foreign Languages at Advanced Level*. London: Routledge, pp. 93–115.

This chapter, despite appearing in a book focusing on advanced level foreign language teaching, provides a useful introduction to, and overview of the teaching and learning of grammar.

8 Developing cultural awareness inside and outside the modern foreign languages classroom

INTRODUCTION

The ability to understand the cultural context of foreign language use is a key aspect of effective communication in the target language (TL). Unsurprisingly, therefore, the development of cultural awareness is an important and integral part of the National Curriculum (NC) modern foreign languages (MFL) Orders. Cultural awareness is more than simply the identification of different cultural characteristics or knowledge about the countries where the TL is spoken. It involves the understanding and appreciation of different ways of life. The programme of study (PoS) of the NC suggests a particular approach to the teaching of cultural awareness, which is based around ethnographic methods, i.e. the use of 'authentic' materials and contact with native speakers. It aims to enable pupils to identify with, recognise and draw comparisons between the cultures of their own country and the countries where the TL is spoken. While a lot can be achieved in the MFL classroom, cultural awareness is often more meaningfully developed outside. Importantly, the pupil's point of view and her experiences should be taken as a starting point and not necessarily specific aspects of the target culture (see Pachler 1999b: 84; Jones 2000).

In this chapter we discuss possible approaches to cultural awareness at 11 to 16 and describe activities which require and enable pupils to use the TL inside (including internet and e-mail projects and working with a Foreign Language Assistant) and outside (educational visits, exchanges and work experience abroad) the classroom (for practical ideas, see Pachler 1999a, 1999b, 2007b).

In order to enhance their value, activities involving TL use and the development of cultural awareness outside the MFL classroom should relate to, build on and extend work carried out in MFL lessons. Importantly, they need to be planned carefully and pupils need to be prepared well for them.

While you will not necessarily always have the opportunity to be involved in activities such as visits abroad, you should, wherever possible, try to become involved in preparing any pupils at your placement schools engaging in such activities. The ability to provide opportunities for pupils to develop the use of the TL and their awareness of the target culture(s) beyond the MFL classroom is often considered a distinct advantage by schools when looking for new members of staff.

OBJECTIVES

By the end of this chapter you should:

- understand the rationale for and some important issues of the development of cultural awareness in MFL teaching;
- be aware of possible approaches to and strategies of developing cultural awareness in pupils through MFL teaching including internet and e-mail projects;
- recognise the value of educational activities outside the MFL classroom;
- understand what is involved in organising a range of learning opportunities outside the MFL classroom.

DEVELOPING CULTURAL AWARENESS: WHY?

The target culture can be seen as inextricably linked to the TL (see McBride and Seaga 2000). In order to understand language and its use fully, an awareness and knowledge of culture are important (see Pachler 1999b: 78). While it is possible to teach the culture(s) of a country in a way which is divorced from its language(s) – and in the past coursebooks have tended to provide English accounts of aspects of the way of life of the target culture(s) such as cultural facts, figures and habits – we do not believe this is necessarily appropriate in the context of the NC because:

- it ignores the inter-relationship of 'language-and-culture' (Byram *et al.* 1994);
- it adds a level of abstraction;
- it requires pupils to imagine the potential rather than experiencing real use of the TL.

To place language learning within a cultural context is to make both the TL and the target culture(s) more accessible and understandable. The task for the teacher is to some extent to recreate and simulate the cultural environment and to create a purpose for realistic language use within that environment while ensuring that learning activities are not contrived.

A further important reason for developing pupils' cultural awareness is to learn to empathise with speakers of other languages, to understand that there are other ways of life and to tackle (negative) stereotypes. Stereotypes are not necessarily a bad thing; they can be seen as a strategy to simplify perceptions of other peoples (see Byram 1989: 70). There is, however, a danger that, by exaggerating the typical in the target culture(s), the perception pupils have of the ways of living and communicating in the target culture(s) become distorted (see ibid.: 16; Byram and Risager 2002). You, therefore, need to guard against negative stereotypes as well as engage in awareness raising about the use of (negative) stereotypes (see also Pachler with Reimann 1999).

Task 8.1 Pupil questionnaire

Devise a questionnaire for Year 7 and Year 11 pupils to elicit their views on typical characteristics of native TL speakers.

- Is the tendency to stereotype linked to pupils' existing level of general knowledge?
- Where do pupils get their ideas from?

What can/should you do to take pupils forward in their cultural understanding and break down possible (negative) stereotypes?

Coursebooks can vary enormously in the representation of the cultures of the countries where the TL is spoken. Many coursebooks provide a multicultural picture. However, coursebooks tend to date quickly. This ephemeral nature of presenting culture in print requires you to use supplementary, up-to-date authentic materials, such as articles and pictures from magazines and newspapers or audio and video recordings of programmes concerned with current issues including up-to-date material available via the internet (see also Chapter 12).

Among many other criteria (for details, see Chapter 11), coursebooks can be evaluated against a number of culture-related criteria (see Meijer 1998); they include:

- functionality, e.g. does the coursebook concentrate on facts and knowledge about the target culture?
- target audience, e.g. are materials selected in accordance with the likely interests of the target audience?
- diversity, e.g. does the coursebook take account of intracultural differences;
- realism, e.g. is the representation of culture in the coursebook authentic? Are (negative) stereotypes in evidence?
- intercultural approach, e.g. are attempts made to make comparisons between home and target countries?
- choice, e.g. do learners have the possibility to choose culture-related topics they are particularly interested in?

Task 8.2 Evaluating the culture content of a coursebook

Evaluate one of the coursebooks in use in your partnership school against some of the above criteria. How well is the target culture presented?

Then, carry out an internet search for relevant materials to supplement an aspect the coursebook in your opinion doesn't cover very well.

For guidance on internet use in teaching and learning, see Pachler (1999c).

DEVELOPING CULTURAL AWARENESS: HOW? BROWN'S FOUR STAGES OF ACCULTURATION

Brown's four broad stages of acculturation (see Brown 1986: 36) are used here are as one possible way of conceptualising the development of cultural awareness (Figure 8.1). Each of these stages cannot be separated from the natural process of maturation and not all need necessarily occur. In all of them you can play an important role in guiding and encouraging pupils. The four stages do not imply a linear progression. Slipping back and leaping forward are characteristics of the development not only of linguistic but also of cultural awareness.

For a range of other possible approaches to the teaching about the target culture(s), see Pachler (1999b: 83–90).

No.	Stage
1	excitement
2	alienation
3	recovery
4	acceptance

Figure 8.1 Four broad stages of developing cultural awareness

Excitement

For many young pupils, the learning of MFL is exciting. Year 7 will sometimes offer pupils their first encounter with MFL, some will have been introduced to MFL earlier, and, as a result of recent government policy as outlined in Chapter 1, this number is set to increase rapidly. An introduction to a new culture offers a range of interesting learning opportunities. After all, Continental Europe is not completely alien. The study of the target culture(s) from the security of the classroom offers some shelter from the challenge of 'the foreign' or 'the other'. The behaviour and the way of life of others from an outsider's perspective can be stimulating and fun.

The challenge facing you, therefore, is to provide ample opportunities for pupils to engage in activities related to the target culture(s). This can be done in a number of ways.

The use of anecdotes involving your personal experiences, supported by realia and photographs, can provide a personal context for the presentation of the target culture(s). A story by the MFL teacher about participation in a '*Faschingszug*', for example, can demonstrate that experiencing a foreign culture can be very enjoyable.

The internet provides an effective way of accessing relevant authentic material and to carry out research into the target cultures. For example, the Goethe-Institut offers some interesting projects such as *Das Bild der anderen*, an international e-mail project for young beginners available at http://www.goethe.de/ins/pl/lp/prj/bld/deindex.htm, or Odyssee, an intercultural e-mail game available at http://www.goethe.de/lhr/pro/odyssee/index.htm. The Institut Français also has some interesting material and links, see http://www.institut-francais.org.uk/, including a link to 'culturesfrance' (http://www.culturesfrance.com/). Some excellent links are available from the Instituto Cervantes at http://londres.cervantes.es/, including one on 'hispanism' (http://hispanismo.cervantes.es/). A great amount of cultural information and awareness can be gained by accessing the online versions of national and regional TL newspapers and magazines.

A fundamental methodological consideration is whether to stress cultural similarities or differences at an early stage. Research suggests that attention should initially be given to similarities as 'doing so can undermine the human tendency to exaggerate and generalise differences' (Pachler 1999b: 85).

Similarities between the pupils' own way of life and that prevailing in the countries where the TL is spoken can be accentuated, for example, at a very early stage by a display of 'foreign' foods available in the local supermarket.

Task 8.3 Stressing cultural similarities

What ways of stressing the similarities, rather than the differences, between home and target cultures at an early stage of MFL teaching and learning can you think of?

The simulation of cultural practices in the classroom allows pupils to demonstrate their knowledge. Setting up a French café or organising a meal are very popular activities. To provide such culinary delights in a restaurant situation for 'customers' other than fellow pupils is even more rewarding. Parents, colleagues, even adult MFL learners can act as customers for the pupils.

You should explore the cross-curricular dimension of cultural awareness. Aspects of the target culture(s) might be taught in other subject areas such as Geography, usually but by not necessarily always in English, which can be built on in the MFL classroom. In Geography, for instance, pupils often study a European country other than the UK with a focus on geographical questions such as 'What/where is it?', 'What is it like?', 'How did it get like this?', 'How and why is it changing?', 'What are the implications?' The study of a European country other than the UK provides opportunities for you to feed into other subject areas.

Task 8.4 Cross-curricular links

Examine the statutory requirements, e.g. for Geography. These can be accessed on the internet at http://www.nc.uk.net/.

1 Find out what aspects of the target culture(s) can be found and where links are possible.
2 Through discussion with teachers of Geography find out more about when and how these aspects are taught.
3 Make up a quiz drawing on knowledge of the target culture(s) incorporating details from the NC Geography Orders. Use the results of the quiz as a basis for cross-curricular and cultural discussion. You may want to invite colleagues from other subjects to one of your lessons to demonstrate the full value of cultural awareness.

The project 'Science across Europe', part of 'Science across the World' organised by the Association for Science Education, available online at http://www.scienceacross.org, allows pupils to compare their work on scientific topics with peers across Europe and the wider world. There are a range of resource units in a wide range of languages providing stimulus material on topics such as acid rain, using energy at home, renewable energy, drinking water, food, global warming or domestic waste. Databases of participating schools are also available. Work on these units can meaningfully combine learning objectives relating to Science as well as MFL. Box 8.1 shows an adapted sample activity from the pack 'What did you eat . . . ?'.

Box 8.1 Eating habits – a comparison

Compare the information from a school in a country where the TL is spoken with that from your class.

1. Compare:

    (a) the pattern of daily life: when other pupils get up, start school, etc.;
    (b) who chooses and prepares the food;
    (c) what is eaten for breakfast;
    (d) snacks and sweets eaten;
    (e) arrangements for meals during the school day.

2. Do pupils in the target country think that eating a good breakfast is important?
3. What do you think is responsible for the similarities and differences in the foods eaten by pupils in the target country?
4. Did you learn about any traditional beliefs about foods? Can they be explained by science?
5. Are eating habits in both countries changing? If so, how?
6. Do you think that most pupils eat a balanced diet?
7. Are pupils concerned about the links between diet and disease? If so, do their concerns differ in the two countries?

8. Compare food labels from the two countries. How is the nutritional value of food shown? Do the same foods contain the same ingredients?
9. What suggestions can you make for improving the diet of your class?

Task 8.5 Eating habits – a comparison

1 Consider how these tasks could be linked to your MFL department's unit(s) of work on food and drink and illness.
2 By talking to your mentor or an interested class teacher as well as a teacher from the Science department, explore which of these activities could be carried out in MFL lessons and which in the Science lesson.
3 How could they be translated into the TL and how can the contents be covered in the TL?

Alienation

The greater the personal involvement with another culture, the more differences become apparent. Dealing with alternative ways of life can be threatening and challenging. Goal-oriented and purposeful personal contact with TL speakers as well as appropriate activities, such as educational visits to the target culture(s), can help pupils to understand certain differences in context and reduce the potential threat by engaging pupils in reflecting on and discussing perceived differences between cultures.

Task 8.6 Personal awareness raising

This task provides you with an opportunity for self-reflection:

1 In Figure 8.2 list 10 items you would choose to represent the culture of your home country and 10 items you would choose as representative of the culture of a country where the TL is spoken. What influenced your choice?
2 What differences are there between your two lists and what do they tell you about the cultural differences between the two countries or your own perceptions about these differences?
3 In Figure 8.3 list how each of these differences could be addressed in the MFL curriculum: by display work, classroom activities, project/enquiry work or visits abroad?

Many schools organise day visits abroad, which can be used to encourage pupils to investigate familiarities and differences of their own and the target culture. The relationship between language learnt and its potential use should be highlighted by the provision of structured activities when abroad.

	'home' country	'target' country
1		
2		
3		
4		
5		
6		
7		
8		
9		
10		

Figure 8.2 Choosing items representing culture

display work	classroom activities	project/enquiry work	visits abroad

Figure 8.3 Accounting for cultural differences in MFL teaching

Figure 8.4 illustrates how pupils might be given an opportunity to reflect on cultural differences around the topic of 'bullfighting'. Work on this activity can be meaningfully extended through letters or e-mail messages with partner schools or display work as described above.

LAS CORRIDAS DE TOROS

Torear es considerado como un arte y no un deporte. La tradición de las corridas de toros se remonta a más de trescientos años. La crianza de toros salvajes adecuados para llevar a las plazas de toros es normalmente llevada por ciertas familias que viven del mundo del toro y de las corridas. Torear y criar toros salvajes se pasa de padre a hijo.

Hay toreros que desde que son niños estan en las plazas y torean a vaquillas (toros pequeños). Ellos ven y viven el mundo de los toros desde muy pequeños en casa y así, cuando pueden, ellos van a torear también.

No sólo hombres pero también mujeres y niños torean en las plazas.

Hay **corridas de toros** y **novilladas:** las corridas de toros consisten en torear seis grandes toros de entre seiscientos y setecientos kilos de peso. En las novilladas se torean a toros pequeños de trescientos a cuatrocientos kilos de peso. Toreros jóvenes empiezan con novilladas y luego pasan a torear toros grandes.

Otro tipo de toreo es el **Rejoneo** que es torear y matar al toro montado a caballo; estos se llaman *rejoneadores* y son magníficos jinetes.

Los toreros visten el **traje de luces** que es muy especial y de un color favorito del torero. Lleva una **montera** sobre la cabeza y una **coleta** de pelo detrás. Cuando el torero se jubila, se corta la **coleta** y así pues esto es una expresión española. Por ejemplo cuando una deportista abandona el deporte se puede decir: ella *'se corta la coleta'*!

Los toreros son muy religiosos y antes de cada corrida se toman unos minutos para meditar y rezar.

También son muy supersticiosos y llevan algún detalle para tener buena suerte.

Todas las personas conectadas con los toros como toreros, rejoneadores, criaderos y otros hablan de su respeto y amor a los toros. Ellos admiran a un animal tan bravo y valiente. En las corridas, los toreros se enfrentan al toro para arriesgar su vida y jugar con la idea de la muerte. El toro va a morir y el torero puede morir también!

Si un toro es muy valiente, el torero puede perdonar su vida reconociendo así su valor.

El torear es una tradición muy española y es un espectáculo muy popular con españoles y extranjeros.

En Portugal, sur de Francia y en algunos países de Sudamérica también hay corridas de toros pero no matan al toro. En España matan a los seis toros de cada corrida todas las tardes de la temporada taurina.

Vocabulario

la crianza de toros	the breeding bulls	montado a caballo	on horseback
se remonta	it has existed since	matar al toro	to kill the bull
las plazas de toros	bullrings	Jinetes	horse riders
toros salvajes	wild bulls	traje de luces	bullfighter's costume
Vaquillas	young bulls	montera	bullfighter's hat
Novilladas	bullfights with young bulls	Coleta	bullfighter's hair worn as a pony tail
Morir	to die	'se corta la coleta'	s/he retires
Rejoneo	bullfighting on horse back	temporada taurina	bullfighting season

(Continued)

Tareas

Ejercicio 1: ¿verdad? o ¿mentira?		
	¿verdad?	¿mentira?
1. Torear es un deporte.		
2. Todos los toreros son hombres.		
3. 'Se corta la coleta' significa empezar una profesión.		
4. Rejoneo es torear montado a caballo.		
5. Las corridas de toros son un espectáculo reciente.		
6. Los toreros son muy religiosos y superticiosos.		

Ejercicio 2: Encuesta

Pregúntale a cinco compañeros de clase:	1	2	3	4	5
1. ¿Crees que la tradición es importante?					
2. ¿Crees que las corridas son un espectáculo emocionante?					
3. ¿Te gustaría ver una corrida de toros?					
4. ¿Opinas que las corridas son crueles para el toro?					
5. ¿Te parece que las corridas se deben abolir?					
6. ¿Crees que las corridas sin matar al toro son acceptables?					

Ejercicio 3: ¿a favor? o ¿en contra?

Cuántas personas están a favor?   ....% está a favor de las corridas
Cuántas personas están en contra?   ....% está en contra de las corridas

Figure 8.4 Las corridas de toros

Recovery

A positive response to discussions about perceived differences can be a sign of recovery. First-hand experience of the target culture(s), the productive use of personal knowledge, skills and understanding through displays or presentations for the benefit of others can lead to a familiarisation with the target culture(s). Recovery can be worked towards, for instance, by engaging pupils in 'experimentation' with the target culture(s) and comparison with their own culture. At this stage of developing cultural awareness cultural similarities might once again be accentuated.

Similar to a task in this chapter for you as a student teacher, a useful activity (adapted from Jones 1995: 27–34) comparing two cultures is to ask pupils to put into a shoe box 10 items they feel represent their own culture. The scenario is that this will be buried for future generations to find. A brief written or taped explanation should accompany the artefacts. A similar exercise is then undertaken only this time the 'time capsule' should contain 10 articles representing the culture of a country where the TL is spoken. The selection of artefacts should stimulate meaningful discussion about the TL culture in question, particularly in relation to the perceived 'home' culture.

Neuner and Hunfeld suggest the use of what they call 'universal experiences of life' as a basis for intercultural comparison. They list a number of such experiences, loosely translated from German here (see Neuner and Hunfeld 1993: 112–13):

- fundamental experiences, e.g. birth, death, living;
- personal identity, e.g. personal characteristics;
- social identity, e.g. private self, family; neighbourhood, local community, nation;
- partnership, e.g. friendship, love;
- environment, e.g. house and home; local area, nature, civilisation;
- work, e.g. making a living;
- education;
- subsistence, e.g. food, clothing;
- mobility, e.g. traffic;
- leisure and art;
- communication, e.g. media;
- health care, e.g. health, illness, hygiene;
- ethics, e.g. morals, values, religion;
- events, e.g. past, present, future;
- spirituality, creativity, imagination, emotions, memory, etc.

Task 8.7 Cultural comparison

1   Examine the scheme of work at your school experience school and try to match the 'universal experiences of life' listed above to particular topics.
2   Then, devise a number of activities comparing pupils' own culture with the target culture(s) for a particular class you teach for one of these areas. For guidance you might want to have a look at how available coursebooks approach the topic of 'education' and how they compare 'school life' in England to the target culture(s).

Acceptance

Acceptance is more than tolerance. Some, particularly more advanced, learners can be seen to embrace certain aspects of the new culture. Participation in and interaction with the target culture(s) through communication in the TL can help to develop the ability to analyse and critically appraise 'otherness'.

For pupils of appropriate maturity taking part in an exchange can present an invaluable experience. Preparation for and follow-up to an exchange are important. Pupils could present an account of their stay – individually or collaboratively – for the benefit of parents and other interested parties. The identification of positive experiences and the public appreciation of the specific TL culture can not only be a motivating factor for the pupils themselves, but also a source of reassurance for other pupils less advanced in the process of acculturation.

Task 8.8 Encouraging acceptance of the target culture(s)

Look through the departmental scheme of work and note classroom activities requiring use of the TL to collect information, for instance, surveys:

1   Consider how such activities could be extended to include communication with a parallel class in the partner school abroad.
2   Through discussion with your mentor or another interested class teacher, investigate the possibility of setting up such a project.

INTERNET AND E-MAIL PROJECTS

Most schools have links, sometimes even established partnerships with educational institutions abroad and many encourage penfriend and e-mail links. Useful resources in this context are http://www.etwinning.net, http://www.epals.com and http://www.globalgateway.org.uk/ (see Pachler (2007b) for details on the use of the internet for project work; see also http://www.goethe.de/ins/ie/prj/scl/enindex.htm, a Goethe-Institut online resource in English for school projects; a UK-based case study and guidelines on how to find e-mail partners can be found in Chapter 12). E-mail projects can provide useful opportunities for realistic and meaningful communication. For example, survey work carried out in the classroom or the local community can be extended through an e-mail project to which a series of lessons is dedicated. Pupils can share, compare and analyse their findings with (those of) pupils in a partner school.

When considering the use of e-mail or the internet in MFL teaching it is important to ensure they are properly embedded in the scheme of work. Experience suggests that personal contact with a colleague tends to be an important factor in ensuring the success of work involving partner schools abroad. Successful projects tend to have very clear aims and objectives and a clearly defined thematic structure and time-frame. It is advisable to divide classes into smaller groups who in turn communicate with small groups in a partner school. This way, the teacher can ensure all pupils can get actively involved and flexibility in the development of topics is allowed for.

Project work might comprise the following phases:

Preparation: co-ordination between teachers in both schools
Phase 1:   pupils introduce themselves, their schools, their environment in writing and pictures
Phase 2:   questions and answers, exchange of information

Phase 3:   exchange of detailed answers based on research; follow-up questions

Phase 4:   analysis and comparison of results

Phase 5:   (joint) presentation of results (e.g. compilation of a display, brochure, newspaper, video/audio recording or webpages), summary of learning outcomes, project evaluation, goodbye letters

Each group should be required to keep a log or learner diary in which they reflect on their work, note new vocabulary and structures, etc. From time to time, group work needs to be supplemented by plenaries during which the teacher provides necessary input – for example, on strategies for working independently – revises previous learning outcomes relevant to the project and during which pupils are required to report on the progress they have made. This way the teacher can ensure that pupils stay on task. The teacher also needs to be available throughout to clarify any difficulties, questions and misconceptions pupils might have. Decisions will need to be taken, for instance, whether pupils' messages have to be checked by the teacher before they are sent and to what extent redrafting by the teacher is required. Alternatively, pupils in the partner school could be asked to provide diagnostic feedback for each other. A further important consideration concerns the use of the TL. Where possible, pupils should be encouraged to use the TL during group work to communicate with each other and with peers in the partner school. Experience suggests, though, that the mixing of languages might at times be required and necessary to ensure maximum outcomes (see Butler and Kelly 1999).

Projects can meaningfully be linked to controversial topics, about which pupils have an opinion which they are keen to communicate, as well as to real life experiences of pupils, such as their reading, listening and viewing habits, school life, hobbies and pastimes, family life etc.

Task 8.9 Planning an internet or e-mail project

Drawing on the guidance given above and in Chapter 12 (see also Pachler 2007b), develop an internet/e-mail project in conjunction with your mentor or an interested class teacher, which relates to a relevant topic in your placement school's scheme of work. You might want to use the following framework when planning your project:

- preparation required;
- age-range;
- objectives (linguistic and cultural);
- activities and time-scale;
- useful links and resources;
- methodological considerations.

To share your ideas and experience with others, post them on the Lingu@Net Forum at http://www.mailtalk.ac.uk/lists/linguanet-forum.html or on the FLTeach Forum at http://www.cortland.edu/flteach/ and invite comments from colleagues.

EDUCATIONAL VISITS, EXCHANGES AND WORK EXPERIENCE ABROAD

Curiosity about the culture(s) of the countries where the TL is spoken can be a form of intrinsic motivation for some pupils. Many MFL departments are eager to provide opportunities for pupils to visit countries where the TL is spoken. Pupils who have (had) such an opportunity can have an increased interest in the subject and the TL as a means of finding out more about the respective countries and cultures. In some cases first-hand experience of the target culture(s) can lead to acculturation in later life. Some pupils, however, can get frustrated and demotivated as the result of a 'culture shock'. Negative experience might lead to estrangement, anger and hostility (see Brown 1986: 35). Teachers involved in visits and exchanges should, therefore, not take anything for granted. Some pupils will have experience of travelling, others may never have stayed away from their own homes. Some pupils will have a good general knowledge base, whereas others may even be unaware of the geographical location of the country in question. School visits should be accompanied by meaningful linguistic and cultural awareness tasks, which can be of a cross-curricular nature.

MFL departments in many secondary schools offer their pupils visits to a country where the TL is spoken. Three main types of activities can be distinguished: visits, exchanges and work experience placements. The type of visit undertaken by pupils tends to reflect their linguistic, social and cultural development. While on visits the exposure to the target culture and the TL tends to be tightly structured and controlled and the pupils tend to remain in close contact with their English-speaking peer group throughout their stay abroad, the number of opportunities to interact with native speakers and their way of life increases on exchanges. These are in the main organised around the pupils' stay with exchange partners, whom they may know already from previous visits, letters and/or e-mail links and whose families tend to act as an inter-face between the 'otherness' of life in the foreign culture and the 'universal' features of life at home. Work experience placements abroad often present the greatest challenge to pupils and tend to depend on adequately developed personal, social and linguistic skills in pupils who need to cope, frequently independently, with the vocational and occupational demands made by TL interactions in the 'world of work'.

If the opportunity arises, you should try to observe the various tasks involved in preparing and planning visits and exchanges at their placement schools. Many valuable lessons can be learnt from teachers with relevant experience.

We would strongly recommend newly qualified teachers (NQTs) work in tandem with experienced MFL teachers on planning visits and exchanges and take on responsibility for some of the tasks involved only gradually.

Visits and exchanges can help to make both the TL as well as the target culture(s) more accessible to pupils and can be motivating. They provide valuable opportunities to find out more about the target culture(s) and can help to illustrate that the TL can be used effectively for communication. Also, visits and exchanges can enrich pupils' general knowledge base by giving them an opportunity to experience first-hand the excitement of travelling, meeting new people and finding out about their way of life.

One key element of successful visits and exchanges is having *clearly delineated aims and objectives*. Both staff and pupils need to be aware what the benefits and reasons for carrying out such an activity are.

When organising exchanges, finding a suitable partner is another essential pre-requisite. Often, personal contacts with teachers abroad are most effective. To establish good channels of communication is equally important. Preparatory visits can provide useful information. The British Council offers a useful online service for schools called Global Gateway available at http://www.globalgateway.org.uk/. This is an international website enabling users to engage in creative partnerships. The site describes itself as 'a one-stop shop, providing quick access to comprehensive information on how to develop an international dimension to education'.

Fisher and Evans (2000) make the following practical suggestions based on their research study into the effects of school exchange visits on attitudes and proficiency in language learning:

- Prepare pupils for the kind of language they will need when staying in the family, for example, including a range of expressions of social convention in the scheme of work and continuing to focus on the sometimes neglected area of pronunciation.
- Offer guidance to parents about the value of linguistic support for the exchange pupil staying with their family and offer suggestions as to the amount and nature of the correction and encouragement they give.
- Offer guidance to parents on ways of helping pupils settle in, for example, using photographs as a prompt.
- Consider arranging the exchange schedule to include a weekend with the family straightaway.
- Seek to develop pupils' cultural awareness before visiting the country, with an emphasis on 'the acquisition of ways of investigating and observing' (Snow and Byram 1997: 31) to prepare pupils better for their stay.
- Discuss 'language gathering' strategies, encouraging pupils, for example, to keep diaries or log-books of all new language they use.
- Be encouraged to look for evidence of linguistic progress in the pupils on their return and to build on this in their subsequent teaching.
- Encourage pupils to maintain contact with their partner through correspondence and e-mail.
- Use the exchange experience to contribute to an overall ethos within the department of promoting language learning as part of a real communicative experience.

Task 8.10 Aims and objectives of visits and exchanges

Where possible, find out what the aims and objectives of the visits and exchanges organised by your school experience school are, for instance, by asking appropriate members of the MFL department or by having a look at some documentation used in a recent visit.

It is important to fully understand, cover and comply with all *legal responsibilities and requirements* and abide by school, Local Authority (LA) and/or any other regulations and guidelines. These cannot be covered in this chapter. They must be considered fully in the planning of any such activity in conjunction with senior colleagues in school. Activities beyond the classroom should not be taken on lightly. Useful guidance is *inter alia* available from the government (originally published in 1998 by the DfEE) entitled *Health and Safety of Pupils on Educational Visits*. See http://www.teachernet.gov.uk/wholeschool/healthandsafety/visits/. A three-part supplement to the good practice guide was produced in 2002:

- *Standards for LEAs in Overseeing Educational Visits* (http://www.teacher net.gov.uk/docbank/index.cfm?id=2576) sets out the functions of the educational visits co-ordinator in schools and the levels of risk management that LAs and schools could use;
- *Standards for Adventure* (http://www.teachernet.gov.uk/docbank/index.cfm?id=2577) is aimed at the teacher or youth worker who leads young people on adventure activities;
- *A Handbook for Group Leaders* (http://www.teachernet.gov.uk/docbank/index.cfm?id=2578) is aimed at anyone who leads groups of young people on any kind of educational visit. It sets out good practice in supervision, ongoing risk assessment and emergency procedures.

There are many issues to consider when organising, or accompanying, a trip or visit. To be sure of the latest information, it is best to check the websites listed above.

Task 8.11 Issues to consider when accompanying/organising trips

Look up the website http://www.teachernet.gov.uk/wholeschool/healthandsafety/visits/ and the associated guidelines. Find out what you can on the following issues:

- insurance implications
- parental/guardian consent
- ground rules
- being 'in loco parentis'
- supervision ratios
- necessary travel and medical/emergency documentation
- transport/drivers
- financial issues – pre and during the trip (charging for the trip and spending money on it)
- emergency procedures
- other.

HOSTING EXCHANGE PARTNERS

The hosting of exchange partners is also not as simple as it may at first appear. Before the visitors arrive the teacher in charge of the exchange has to ensure that visitors and hosts are appropriately matched. For this purpose a proforma could be devised. The following information, provided by parents and the pupils themselves, might be useful: name, sex, age, a passport photograph, number of brothers and sisters and their ages, pets, personality, hobbies, whether they would prefer a boy or girl with similar or different characteristics to themselves.

Task 8.12 Matching pupils

You have been asked by your head of department to match up the Spanish and English participants on the annual Spanish exchange:

1   Design a checklist including all the relevant details and information you will need to know about individual pupils to enable you to match them.
2   How does your list compare with the criteria used by your placement school?

The teacher with responsibility for exchange visits might want to try to help the visiting members of staff, for instance, by organising excursions to local places of interest. Planned excursions for visitors and hosts can provide useful opportunities for the TL to be used in authentic situations. Many schools insist that during such journeys pupils have to sit next to their own exchange partners. This can avoid divisions by nationality and create opportunities for interaction. It is well worth considering visits to places familiar to the British pupils and to provide activities, which necessitate – through collaboration – communication and explanations between the visitors and the hosts. See Turner (2001) for some useful ideas and advice on working with exchanges.

In order to give the exchange a suitable profile, it is important to involve the senior management of the host school. A formal welcome in an assembly serves at least two purposes: first, it demonstrates courtesy and, second, it introduces the exchange partners to the unique experience of school assemblies and the ethos of the school as a whole. A reception or welcome party is often an integral part of a successful exchange visit. At such an occasion host families could be introduced to visiting pupils and visitors and hosts can get to know each other in an informal atmosphere.

There are also arrangements to be made for when the foreign pupils visit and take part in life at the British school. There, visiting pupils can shadow host pupils and accompany them to lessons. Clearly, colleagues have to be asked if they are happy to have in some of their lessons visiting pupils who could, for instance, be used for cross-curricular work.

Parents might wish to become involved in the exchange by providing 'family' days where they put on further excursions on free days at weekends. It might be useful to provide a list of possible venues and activities to support parents in arranging days out for their visitors. Often parents are happy to organise social events during the exchange at their own homes. It is quite common that host institutions put on a farewell disco.

There is always the risk of some pupils feeling homesick. Providing a list of telephone numbers of all participating families can allay some concerns and allow visiting pupils and their hosts to network among each other if necessary. Approval to distribute telephone numbers in such a way needs to be sought from all concerned.

It might be appropriate to remind parents that while visiting pupils are in their homes they are responsible for them which includes, for instance, determining meal and bed times.

PUPILS AS ETHNOGRAPHERS

While on a trip or exchange, pupils require a focus for their learning, both linguistically and culturally. This is usually provided in the form of a quiz, or a set of tasks/ activities for pupils to complete while in the TL country, often preceded by a preparatory task or series of activities where the pupils are familiarised with their destination, etc. and prepared linguistically as appropriate. These are very useful approaches and can perhaps be the starting point for something a little more ambitious, where pupils take on the role of 'researcher' and thereby not only assume more responsibility and independence for what they investigate, but also do so in a way more personal to them and their reactions/priorities, as well as those of their TL country environment and experience. Tasks intended for the whole group, the type referred to at the beginning of this section and in frequent use, are of necessity generic and can sometimes result in 'facts and figures' approaches (for example, 'How high is the church spire? When was it built?, etc.).

Roberts and her co-authors (see Roberts *et al.* 2000) outline how (initially) university students (although they do also refer to upper secondary pupils) can become 'ethnographers' in their work during stays in a TL county. Ethnography is a methodological approach in research where the researcher lives (or spends substantial time) with the subjects of his or her research and learns as much as possible about that particular way of life; this research approach was used extensively by anthropologists for example to study the lives of tribal people and has been extended by sociologists to research in to particular social groups (including teachers!).

Roberts *et al.* argue that learners who have an opportunity to stay in the TL country can be trained to do an ethnographic project while abroad. This would involve them in studying the local people as they interact with their environment and culture. This is obviously on a much larger scale when the 'ethnographer' is a university student spending a year abroad to that of a KS3 or KS4 pupil on a trip or exchange. But many of the ideas are still applicable: learners could be asked to do the following:

- Keep a diary (in L1 and TL where possible and appropriate) of what they do and their reactions/responses. Some key language/examples could be provided or a framework.
- Using digital photographs (or video), certain events (within the home, at school, in town, etc.) could be recorded and annotated (how different/similar is this to my life?, What is different exactly?, What do I think of this?).
- Using audio technology (MP3, iPod, etc.) music examples could be brought back and a similar 'review' conducted.

- Realia (posters, tickets, etc.) could be collected and commented on.
- Each learner could be encouraged to investigate something which particularly interests them, e.g. cooking/eating out, sport (of a particular type), facilities for young people, dance, music, theatre, education, family life, media (newspapers, TV, internet).
- Learners could then 'package' their research into an output of their choice and 'disseminate' it (to the class, to staff, to parents, to the exchange school).

In our opinion, this is an approach worth investigating. The issue of target language and mother tongue is obviously a challenging one, but, we would argue, the purposes of a TL experience (whether at home or abroad) are not only linguistic. Many linguistic advantages will occur alongside investigations in to other (cultural) issues and, from a learner's perspective, an approach involving L1 as well as the TL enables them to work at a far more sophisticated level on content than otherwise. Learners should, nevertheless, be encouraged to work subsequently in the TL where possible on the comments they have already made in L1.

THE FOREIGN LANGUAGE ASSISTANT (FLA) AS A CULTURAL RESOURCE

Working with FLAs can present a very valuable opportunity to enhance MFL work across all stages of cultural awareness. Therefore, if the support of an FLA is available, this should be maximised. Useful guidance on how to work with the FLA is, for instance, available from the National Association for Language Advisers (NALA) and the British Council (see http://www.britishcouncil.org/languageassistant/ Channel 4 1995; NALA/Central Bureau 1992; Page 1997; Rowles *et al.* 1998). There might be occasions when you have the opportunity to work with FLAs during your initial teacher education and some student teachers may have worked as FLA themselves. In any event, you need to be aware of the potential of working with FLAs and how to maximise this resource in preparation for your work as qualified MFL teachers.

FLAs are, in the main, used by departments to allow pupils to come into contact with native speakers of the modern foreign language(s) they study, to provide a direct link to the culture(s) associated with the TL as well as more specifically to provide opportunities for pupils to speak and to prepare them for their oral examinations.

One of the advantages of FLAs is the fact that they tend not to be that much older than the pupils themselves and potentially, therefore, constitute a resource regarding the particular areas of their interests.

The NALA/Central Bureau guide on working with FLAs (1992: 11–12) provided a range of valuable ideas and suggests a number of different ways in which the cultural dimension can be portrayed with the help of the FLA which still apply:

- straightforward – and probably simple and concise – presentations by the FLA on an aspect of their background, followed or preceded by questions from the pupils;

- role play, whereby the FLA portrays national figures, professions, members of society within their country;
- establishing differences and similarities by questioning pupils closely about their own culture and encouraging them to articulate their views on what they understand to be characteristic of other countries;
- data collection and project preparation with the FLA working with particular groups on specific cultural dimensions, e.g. music, sport, leisure, the media;
- working on European awareness projects with other departments within the school;
- collecting newspapers and magazines throughout the year and keeping an ongoing survey of, for example, sport results, major events, local incidents, political happenings, leisure and arts activities;
- joint FLA/pupil compilation of 'A day in the life of a pupil/commuter/ shopkeeper/lorry driver, etc.' as perceived in both countries;
- using maps and historical viewpoints from the FLA's own country to obtain comparative viewpoints;
- using magazines and the press for cultural update but also for predictability exercises where issues are ongoing;
- discussing not only habits and customs but also attitudes (e.g. towards racism, class, religion, poverty, leisure).

Morgan and Neil (2001: 80–2) suggest the following advantages of working with and team teaching with an FLA:

Main advantages:

- a genuine communicative partner and native speaker model;
- an additional source of the target culture often allowing for stereotypes to be challenged;
- an extra 'teacher'.

Considerable advantages to team teaching with the FLA:

- the teacher–pupil ratio is improved;
- the TL can be modelled in an authentic way (role plays, for example);
- pupils, particularly for GCE A level topics, can have the benefit of different cultural inputs and viewpoints from two sources of instruction;
- the 'team' can in itself act as a good model for pupils in terms of how to operate collaboratively.

Task 8.13 Working with the FLA

1	Through observation, note what classroom activities have been made possible by the presence of an FLA.
2	Scrutinise a number of lesson plans of your own and identify opportunities, which would enhance pupils' learning if an FLA were available.

SUMMARY

Pupils need to develop cultural awareness as an integral part of their MFL learning, for example, for linguistic and educational reasons. You, as the teacher, play an important part in facilitating the development of cultural awareness as relevant activities require in-depth knowledge and understanding of the target culture(s) as well as very careful planning and structuring.

In this chapter we presented a possible framework for developing cultural awareness making use of a range of learning opportunities inside and outside the MFL classroom, including first-hand experience of the target culture, for example, by way of contact with FLAs, internet/e-mail projects or visits, exchanges and work experience abroad.

In developing cultural awareness, particularly outside the MFL classroom, thorough preparation is vital in order to safeguard the welfare of pupils and to ensure success. It is imperative that teachers give due consideration to relevant legislation, regulations and guidelines.

FURTHER READING

Byram, M. (1997) *Teaching and Assessing Intercultural Communicative Competence*. Clevedon: Multilingual Matters.

A very thorough and detailed book investigating the areas covered in this chapter clearly and presenting the surrounding research evidence.

Byram, M. and Feng, A. (2004) 'Culture and language learning: teaching, research and scholarship', *Language Teaching* 37: 149–68.

This paper provides an excellent overview and discussion of the fundamental issues involved in this topic.

Jones, B. (2000) 'Developing cultural awareness', in K. Field (ed.) *Issues in Modern Foreign Languages Teaching*. London: Routledge, pp. 158–70.

An interesting chapter which explores ways in which the teacher can further pupils' cultural awareness in the MFL classroom.

9 Pupil differences and differentiation in modern foreign languages teaching and learning

INTRODUCTION

It is fundamentally important for you to recognise that pupils are individuals with different needs. No group of pupils is ever homogenous. Differences in areas such as gender, interest, self-concept, self-esteem, social class, ethnic background, first language, previous attainment/experience or creativity can, for instance, determine pupils' degree of progress, achievement or participation in modern foreign language (MFL) work.

In any given class there is normally a combination of factors pertaining to individual differences, which is one of the reasons why teaching is a highly complex process. In order to minimise differences in classes, some schools operate a setting policy, where some departments – usually including MFL – group pupils according to certain criteria but particularly their attainment. In a school where setting takes place pupils can be in different sets in certain subjects like MFL, English and mathematics. Other schools adopt a streaming policy. On entry they place pupils into (attainment) groupings across the whole curriculum with pupils being taught in the same group in all or most subjects of the curriculum. This happens often on the basis of test scores in English and mathematics and/or information passed on from the pupils' primary schools. Nevertheless, MFL classes, be they setted, streamed or mixed-ability, invariably contain pupils, for example, with different ability levels, interests and backgrounds. For a discussion of mixed-ability grouping (in MFL teaching), see Redondo (2000); Ainslie and Purcell (2000); Hallam and Deathe (2002).

You need to ensure that all pupils can participate, become involved in lessons and have learning experiences of equal worth. Individual differences should be catered for by building classroom practice on the notion of equality of opportunities in education: that is helping all pupils to realise their full potential or to maximise their aspirations. To achieve this, three issues are of particular importance: setting suitable learning challenges, responding to pupils' diverse learning needs and overcoming

potential barriers to learning and assessment for individuals and groups of pupils
(see DfEE/QCA 1999: 20–3). The notion that pupils respond consciously or
unconsciously to the expectations of the teacher, be they explicitly stated or implied,
is generally accepted. From this follows that high expectations by you in terms of
achievement and behaviour of pupils can help pupils fulfil their potential. Differentiation, which is discussed in detail in this chapter, aims at maximising pupils' potential
by building on their prior learning and taking into account their individual
differences.

Catering for the full range of differences in and individual needs of pupils and
helping all pupils maximise their potential is very challenging. It requires the
recognition of pupils' individual differences and needs, familiarisation with their
backgrounds and the identification of appropriate teaching strategies and activities
(see also Turner 2000: 134–50).

The 1999 National Curriculum (NC) documentation includes a section on
inclusion for all subjects. Inclusion is defined implicitly as 'providing effective
learning opportunities for all pupils' (DfEE/QCA 1999: 20, http://www.nc.uk.net/
nc_resources/html/inclusion.shtml). It sets out three principles that are essential to
developing a more inclusive curriculum:

- setting suitable learning challenges;
- responding to pupils' diverse learning needs;
- overcoming potential barriers to learning and assessment for individuals and
  groups of pupils.

It was in the spirit of the original NC for all pupils to study an MFL from the ages of
11–16, but, as was outlined in Chapter 1, this was altered in 2004 to ages 11–14.

Booth *et al.* (2000) provide explicit guidance at all levels of provision (see in
particular Section C1 entitled 'Orchestrating learning', pp. 75–88). They encourage
teachers to audit their own practices in terms of whether:

- lessons are responsive to pupil ability;
- lessons are made accessible to all pupils;
- lessons develop an understanding of difference;
- pupils are actively involved in their learning;
- pupils learn collaboratively;
- assessment encourages the achievements of all pupils;
- classroom discipline is based on mutual respect;
- teachers plan, teach and review in partnership;
- teachers are concerned to support the learning and participation of all
  pupils;
- learning support assistants are concerned to support the learning and
  participation of all pupils;
- homework contributes to the learning of all.

We believe in the entitlement of all pupils to study an MFL in some form and this
chapter is intended to provide guidance for you on how to make available support to

pupils who experience possible barriers to foreign language learning. See Pachler and Redondo (2005) for a collection of papers on inclusion in MFL.

OBJECTIVES

By the end of this chapter you should:

- appreciate the importance of getting to know your pupils as individuals with a view to catering for their different needs;
- consider strategies for addressing these needs.

ENTITLEMENT

You need to ensure that you make the full programme of work defined by the statutory framework accessible to all pupils, as 'the right to share the curriculum . . . does not automatically ensure access to it, nor progress within it' (NCC 1989: 1). In order to achieve this, individual pupil differences need to be identified and pupils' individual needs assessed. Only then can the process of *addressing* pupils' individual needs begin in order to maximise the rate of progress and to enhance the degree of participation.

The 1999 National Curriculum Orders also have subject specific inclusion information at http://www.nc.uk.net/webdav/harmonise?Page/@id=6010&&Subject/@id=3959. This is outlined as follows:

> To overcome any potential barriers to learning in MFLs, some pupils may require:
>
> - support in learning to understand, read and write a MFL, including the use of ICT, particularly when they are unable to express themselves orally
> - alternative communication systems, such as signing or symbols, to develop language skills and understanding
> - help in learning to distinguish between the sounds of a particular language to compensate for difficulties in hearing
> - support to compensate for difficulties in seeing visual cues or gestures when developing conversational language.

Four important principles of equality of opportunity in making the full programme of work available to pupils are *entitlement, accessibility, integration* and *integrity* (see DES/Welsh Office 1991: 56–7). According to these principles:

- all pupils have a right to participate in the study of MFL;
- as a MFL student teacher you need to ensure that activities are planned and delivered in a way that allows all pupils to become involved in the MFL learning experience and that the individual needs of pupils are catered for;
- pupils with special educational needs (SEN) should participate in MFL activities alongside pupils without SEN, where possible without substantial alteration of the programme of work or where necessary with modifications to it;
- activities need to be of equal worth and not patronising or tokenistic to the pupils concerned.

Such general aspects of policy statements need be of concern to you, particularly if you view MFL learning as an entitlement for all pupils and believe that it is an essential element of a broad and balanced curriculum. These general aspects of education policy can be particularly helpful when the need arises to argue the case for MFL which, sadly, is often necessary, particularly at KS4.

Task 9.1 MFL for all?

Do you believe that MFL should be taught to all pupils, particularly in Key Stage 4? If so, list arguments in support of MFL for all in the curriculum. If not, outline your reasons against.

In your opinion, what would be the implications of 'languages for all' again at 11–16 for MFL teachers?

How do you see the proposed MFL for all KS2 learners affecting MFL at 11–16, both positively and negatively?

DIFFERENTIATION

Important background information and ideas for any discussion of differentiation are provided by two current UK government agendas:

- Every Child Matters and its associated implications (for example, it underpins the Standards for Qualified Teacher Status);
- Personalised learning, a goal which has been put forward for a number of years as aspirational in education in England and Wales.

Every Child Matters (http://www.everychildmatters.gov.uk) clearly informs the introduction to the 2007 programme of study (PoS):

Learning and undertaking activities in languages contribute to achievement of the curriculum aims for all young people to become:

- successful learners who enjoy learning, make progress and achieve
- confident individuals who are able to live safe, healthy and fulfilling lives
- responsible citizens who make a positive contribution to society.

Personalised learning is a term which has proved difficult to define precisely. The following definition was provided by the DfES (now DCFS, Department for Children Families and Schools, again reflecting the widened agenda of Every Child Matters). Personalised learning is defined as having five components:

- assessment for learning (see Chapter 10);
- effective teaching and learning;
- curriculum entitlement and choice for pupils;
- changes to the organisation of a school, such as workforce remodelling;
- and going 'beyond' the classroom into the community through initiatives such as extended schools.

(*TES* 2007)

In the above definition, differentiation forms part of 'effective teaching and learning', and is crucial to every pupil achieving her potential as far as possible.

The notion of 'differentiation' is a key strategy in catering for differences in a group of learners. It is based on the principle of helping individual pupils achieve to the best of their ability by planning learning experiences that take into account their individual characteristics, particularly in terms of ability and interest, as well as their prior learning.

Differentiation requires careful and thoughtful planning. You need to adapt the way in which the subject matter is presented at the input/presentation stage, for instance by using a range of visual aids and by varying the presentation of new lexical items and structures. At the practice and exploitation/production stages you need to offer pupils opportunities to interact with the subject matter at different levels and in different ways. Allowing pupils to talk/write about themselves in the course of MFL work and enabling them to relate their own experiences to the way of life of people in the target culture(s) can make the study of MFL relevant to pupils and the TL a vehicle for self-expression. In this way, pupils can draw on their different experiences for the purposes of MFL learning.

The 2007 Programme of Study (QCA 2007b; http://www.qca.org.uk/library-Assets/media/MFL_KS3_PoS.pdf), for example, states that the curriculum should provide opportunities for pupils to:

4f listen to, read or view a range of materials, including authentic materials in the target language, both to support learning and for personal interest and enjoyment

Apart from an awareness of pupils' individual differences, you need to anticipate what difficulties might arise from the subject matter and skills to be taught, for instance whether the pronunciation, orthographic conventions, linguistic structures or semiotic boundaries are different to those in the mother tongue(s) of pupils and, therefore, need particular attention or whether the types of activities, material or interaction modes might pose certain difficulties. In preparing a lesson or unit of work, you need to consider strategies to provide reinforcing support for some pupils while stretching others.

Task 9.2 Pupil perceptions of a unit of work
Following the completion of a unit of work, or a short series of lessons, depending on the stage of your school experience, issue the pupils with a brief questionnaire asking them to identify what they found easy, difficult and/or enjoyable within the unit. You will need to remind pupils of the tasks and activities undertaken in the unit of work. How can this information be used to inform future planning and the differentiation of work? Discuss the findings with your tutor or a class teacher you work with closely.

In its non-statutory guidance to MFL teachers, the National Curriculum Council (NCC) suggested the differentiation of MFL work according to three categories (see NCC 1992a: E3). Despite its early publication date, this model is still applied widely:

- *core*: language items and structures as well as tasks, which all pupils are expected to master;
- *reinforcement*: tasks for those pupils who need more practice in order to achieve the planned core outcomes;
- *extension*: language items and structures as well as tasks for those pupils capable of carrying out more advanced and complex work than their peers.

Similarly, learning outcomes are often categorised as those elements which *all* pupils can cope with, those which *most* can manage and those which only *some* may achieve.

Figure 9.1 shows an example of how the first three categories can be applied to the planning of a unit of work in order to cater for the needs of all pupils in the class. It follows the approach to planning suggested in Chapter 4. On the basis of

Im Restaurant	
Year: 9	Number and length of lessons: 5 × 70mins
Learning objectives	
Core - to be able to read and understand a menu - to be able to order food from a menu in a restaurant - to be able to understand the waiter/waitress - to be able to pay the bill	*Extension* - to be able to ask for clarification of what items on a menu are - to be able to complain about the quality of food provided - to be able to question the bill - to be able to ask to pay by cash or card

(Continued)

Main language items/structures		

Core	Extension
common items of food and meals common restaurant phrases and structures	Kann ich mit . . . bezahlen? Es gibt ein Problem. Mein Essen ist kalt/nicht gut etc.

Main materials and resources
visual aids (ICT, flashcards, OHTs), authentic menus, recordings of short dialogues, transcripts of recordings

Main activities	PoS	ATL
Core:		
• visual aids to present items of food	1.1a 1.1b	AT2L1
• categorise food into starters, main courses and desserts	2.2a 4a 4b	AT3L3
• listening activity extracting details of food ordered	4g 2.2e,f,l,j	AT1L3
• structured pair work: ordering food	2.2b, c	AT2L3
• open-ended role play in a restaurant	2.1d	AT2L4
• reading exercise from menus with unfamiliar foods, matching with descriptions	2.2g, i	AT3L4
• writing descriptions of types of food/meals	1.1a. b	AT4L4
Reinforcement:		
• compile vocabulary list of basic foods		AT4L1
• categorise dishes contained on samples of menus		AT4L1
• decipher recorded dialogues from jumbled transcripts	2.1b(e) 3d 2.1d 2.2a,	AT3L2
• use gapped text of recorded conversations as a prompt for pair work	c 2.2i 4b 2.1e 2.2b	AT1L2 AT2L2
• prepare open-ended role play in pairs/groups		AT2L3
• use reference material and drill exercises to practise		AT3L3
• match items of unfamiliar foods with descriptions		AT4L2
Extension:		
• provide additional vocabulary to learn	1.1 a, b	AT2L1
• devise own menu to cater for full range	2.1e 3d	AT3L4
• rework recorded dialogues from details extracted from tape	2.2i, k	AT1L4
• conduct pair work without scripts but with visual prompts; insist that 'extension' vocabulary and phrases are incorporated	2.2e, f 2.2j	AT2L4
• prepare open-ended role play but in groups which perform together; ask all the waiters and all the customers to prepare together; pupils do not know exactly what peers will say	1.3a, b	AT2L5
• research and describe traditional English dishes in the TL	1.4b	AT3L5 AT4L4

Homework:		
• note and learn vocabulary • complete drill exercises reinforcing common vocabulary and phrases • write the scripts of dialogues • produce a full menu in German • prepare for end of unit goal	as above	as above
Assessment opportunities		
Continuous: • peer assessment of pair work • take in marks for listening • mark drill exercises, menu, transcripts • one-to-one assessment of role plays	as above	as above
Summative: • in mixed ability groups write and act out a short play to be videotaped: a family is celebrating exam success, but all goes wrong in the restaurant • end-of-unit test covering listening, reading and writing	as above	as above

Figure 9.1 Sample unit of work plan

differentiated learning objectives the unit of work 'In the restaurant' identifies a range of activities building on what pupils already know and covers a number of learning opportunities at various levels in order for the full attainment range to be challenged.

Task 9.3 Challenge in MFL teaching and learning

What does 'challenge' look like in MFL lessons? What can help increase the challenge?
  Below are some ideas where the challenge may be increased. Can you think of similar ways of helping increase the challenge?

- Requiring learners to introduce other elements to the work they are producing, e.g. sometimes/often/never/etc.
- Taking away support, e.g. book or overhead transparency (OHT) when pupils practise a role play.
- Adding a challenging element: cognitively (getting them to think), emotionally (adding an extra dimension to the task), linguistically, (un)predictability, spontaneity.
- Using opportunities for pupils to think and be independent *or* providing more support where required.

In a unit of work the various activities are normally cross-referenced to the specific coursebook, worksheets or other resources available to, or used by, the department to

Differentiation type	Description
Text	level of difficulty/type of stimulus material
Task	level of difficulty of what learners are asked to do with the stimulus material; number of tasks
Outcome	quantity and quality of performance/attainment expected from pupils
Support	amount of teacher time/access to reference material, etc. available to pupils
Interest	opportunity for pupils to choose tasks, stimulus material, medium, etc.

Figure 9.2 Some types of differentiation

make individual lesson planning easier. This is not possible here but needs to be done in any planning you carry out.

In this unit of work, as in the model outlined above, all pupils are expected to complete the core activities. At appropriate times in the unit some pupils are set reinforcement activities consolidating core learning objectives while others work on extension activities in order to gain a deeper knowledge and understanding and develop additional skills. As Figure 9.2, adapted from Convery and Coyle (1993: 3–5), illustrates, this can be done in a number of ways.

Below are some examples of how the types of differentiation identified in Figure 9.1 relate to the unit of work 'In the restaurant'. Those pupils who complete the core tasks more quickly can be set additional extension activities, allowing pupils who need it more time to complete the task. For instance, the core task of writing descriptions of types of food/meals can be followed by the extension task of researching and describing traditional English dishes in the TL.

Pupils can be given the same task(s) but different stimulus material, for instance, to extract meaning (categorise food into starters, main courses and desserts) from authentic texts (from different menus). This is an example of differentiation by text.

Alternatively, pupils can be given the same stimulus material but differentiated tasks to complete. Pupils can, for instance, be asked to listen to a dialogue in a restaurant. Some pupils can focus on word recognition by choosing items of food/dishes they have heard from a list while others also write down additional items they hear, which are not included in the list.

Differentiation can also come via open-ended tasks, for instance, producing a menu. This is differentiation by outcome. It allows for differences in quantity as well as linguistic difficulty of work produced such as the use of core vocabulary by some pupils and extension vocabulary by others. It also allows pupils to bring their own interest to the task, for instance by including their favourite dishes.

Different levels of support constitute another possibility. The amount of time the you spend with individual, pairs or groups of pupils or the access to reference material can vary. Pupils can be asked to perform a role play in a restaurant by producing a script with the help of a gapped text, from visual clues, by working simply from a scenario or by making use of help from the foreign language assistant (FLA).

When differentiating by interest, you might allow pupils to choose from a range of stimulus material or activities, for instance, pupils could choose one of a number of menus or select from a range of scenarios for pair or group work. They might assume different roles in pair or group work, for instance, play the waiter or the client, or invent things that may go wrong to add spontaneity to dialogues, such as the waiter bringing the wrong order or there being a hair in the soup, which necessitates the inclusion of language associated with complaints.

When differentiating programmes of work, you need to ensure that reinforcement and extension activities are of equal worth and that pupils who are working on reinforcement activities do not feel belittled in their capability.

Task 9.4 Differentiated lesson planning

Following the guidelines for lesson planning given in Chapter 4, plan a number of differentiated lessons for a Key Stage 3 class you have already worked with/observed and, therefore, know the range of individuals within the class. You may wish to use the unit of work in Figure 9.1 as a point of reference:

1   For every key activity consider what form of support you can provide for pupils. How can you cater for pupils' different needs? And, how can support be phased out gradually?
2   Consider means by which a task can be presented to pupils of different abilities. Will the inclusion of illustrations help? How many examples will you provide? What size print will you use on materials?
3   Devise follow-on activities, which enable pupils who finish sooner than others to extend their knowledge, skills and understanding within the given topic area. How will you reward the completion of this supplementary work without it feeling like 'just more work'?
4   Also devise suitable reinforcement activities for those pupils who are not (yet) ready to carry out extension work, but where challenge is still present.
5   Discuss these lesson plans with your tutor or the respective class teacher.
6   Ask if you can teach the lessons you have planned with the respective teacher observing and providing feedback on what worked well, what did not work so well and how you could improve (in) these areas.

In the remainder of this chapter we discuss a number of pupil differences and identify a range of different teaching strategies to cater for them. The differences discussed are:

- gender differences;
- pupils with English as an additional language (EAL);
- pupils with SEN;
- exceptionally able pupils;
- pupils with motivational difficulties.

The various teaching strategies identified in this chapter need to be seen in the context of differentiation.

GENDER DIFFERENCES

It is important for you to be aware of gender differences. There has recently been an upsurge in investigations into these differences in the MFL classroom. These investigations include both wider ranging research and more localised descriptions of practical approaches (see Taylor 2000; Barton 2002b; Davies 2004; Chambers 2005). Inspection reports by the Office for Standards in Education (Ofsted), and statistics reported by the government, for example, have frequently drawn attention to the fact that girls tend to do better than boys in a range of school subjects, including in MFL. Table 9.1 confirms this. Many schools and MFL departments are looking at what they can do to tackle this issue.

Table 9.1 Percentage of pupils entered gaining GCSE A*–C

	Boys	*Girls*	*Gender gap*
French	58	69	11
German	63	74	11
Spanish	62	71	9

Note: DCSF figures cited in *TES*, 6 July 2007.

The realisation that there are certain differences between boys and girls is clearly important. Clark and Trafford (1996) report a range of research findings on the basis of which you might be able to take pre-emptive or remedial action. These remain valid now and are shown in Table 9.2.

It is important for you to consider and use effective strategies to address these research findings and thereby cater for gender differences in MFL. Field (2000) warns against a simplistic approach to gender differences and suggests that you need to bear in mind gender-related matters, which include maturational rates, motivational factors, teaching and learning styles, parental support and attitudes, concentration spans and behavioural matters. You should guard against adopting 'boy friendly' and 'girl friendly' approaches to redress any perceived imbalances, but instead draw on a broad understanding of gender-related issues to inform planning and delivery methods (see Barton 2002a and Harris 2002, for some interesting perspectives on these issues).

Task 9.5 Gender differences

Observe a number of MFL lessons focusing on the participation rate of boys and girls, both during whole-class activities and pair/group work.

Devise a tally sheet, which helps you in recording, for instance, how often boys and girls put up their hands or make a contribution to a lesson. Also note which strategies the teacher uses to encourage equal participation by boys and girls, such as targeting questions to specific pupils.

Then discuss with your tutor or a relevant class teacher possible strategies for ensuring equal participation of girls and boys, referring to Box 9.1 as appropriate.

Table 9.2 Gender differences

Research findings	Pre-emptive/remedial action
Differences in the perception of usefulness, enjoyment and difficulty of MFL between girls and boys	When planning programmes of work, are the perceived interests of boys and girls taken into account, e.g. in the choice of types of sports to be taught in the context of the topic 'hobbies'?
Boys tend to have a less conscientious approach towards their work and mature later than girls	Are accuracy and communication being encouraged equally?
Boys tend to do better than girls at problem-solving whereas girls tend to be better at verbal reasoning	When planning programmes of work, are different learning styles being catered for, e.g. are various types of activities being used?
Boys tend to be more demanding of time and attention from the teacher than girls	Are boys and girls given the same amount of teacher attention? Is there a gender balance in who is asked to answer questions in class?
The presentation of girls' work can be 'seductively' better than that of boys	Is presentation but one of a number of assessment criteria such as effort and accuracy?
Girls tend to be less obviously disruptive than boys, less confident about speaking than boys but more concerned about 'getting it right'	Are boys and girls equally encouraged to carry out oral work and perform role plays in front of the whole class?
Boys tend to give less attention to lesson and course work and more to revision and examination work	Are both formative/continuous and summative assessments used? Are learning and revision strategies being taught explicitly?

Box 9.1 Boys' attitudes to learning MFL

- Boys see MFL as different from other curriculum subjects and as making distinct demands. Differences relate in particular to:

    - the central position of the teacher in language classrooms (as a model for language and culture, enthusiast, manager and teacher);
    - classroom interaction being predominantly dependent on understanding and using another language;
    - the volume of learning in MFL that is based on language, rather than content;
    - the emphasis on accuracy in MFL learning and the relative absence of opportunities to explore 'ideas';
    - the complex and cumulative nature of MFL competencies, of having to persevere and the consequent difficulties of 'catching up' for those who fall behind;

- the importance of particular working practices on which successful performance depends; and
- the elusive nature of MFL as a subject and the lack of 'reality'/ 'relevance' that it has for some boys.

- Having a teacher whom boys would judge to be 'good' is an important dimension of engagement, especially in a subject where classroom work tends to be strongly teacher-centred.
- Boys respect and want teachers who can make learning in MFL exciting and engaging and who can also maintain an orderly and purposeful classroom. 'A good teacher', in boys' eyes, is one who respects individuals, who can engage pupils over the span of the lesson and across lessons, vary pace, find ways of involving them actively in their learning, find opportunities for some degree of choice, sustain an orderly and purposeful atmosphere, and have fun. 'Having a laugh' is not inconsistent with orderliness; what boys dislike are lessons where 'a bit of fun' escalates and the teacher is unable to get the class back on track.
- Neither boys nor girls see MFL as strongly gendered (earlier research showed a stronger link between the subject and its gendered image).
- Boys seem less concerned about whether a teacher is male or female than about the quality of the teacher.
- 'A good MFL lesson' is one in which there is a clear and explicit reason for all the activities which a teacher organises; this includes answers to why choral repetition, why pair work, why listening tasks, why writing and how these activities help learners learn and make progress in MFL.
- Boys recognise their own underperformance and can suggest reasons for it. Some believe that their individual performance can be improved if, for example, they have more ownership of content, task and strategy. A few see trying to improve as futile. For some, the potential for underperformance may have its seeds early on in their MFL learning in school.
- Because the pedagogy of MFL is so teacher-centred, boys who are underperforming tend to see the teacher as responsible for the difficulties they have in their learning.
- Where boys fall behind in MFL and feel lost or disoriented, 'messing about' is a way of responding; given the distinctive nature of MFL, the subject appears to be particularly vulnerable to such a situation.
- Because of the cumulative nature of learning in MFL, underachievement, once established, is difficult to correct. Boys become caught in a downward spiral and can feel excluded; strategies for helping them to catch up and keep up seem to be particularly important for MFL classrooms.
- Learning MFL is, for some boys, an 'unreal' experience; the reality factor increases when pupils meet and can communicate with native speakers within school or on visits to other countries or cultural centres.
- Learning MFL is seen as 'hard' by many boys. The task of learning a second MFL in school is not necessarily experienced as easier since the second language's structure and conventions are usually perceived as different.

Note: This information is amended slightly from Barry Jones and Gwenneth Jones (2000: 46–7) and summarises the key findings from their research into boys and MFL

PUPILS WITH ENGLISH AS AN ADDITIONAL LANGUAGE

This is a very interesting debate for you as MFL student teachers, where the majority of the lesson is normally conducted in the TL. Clearly, a pupil's own language competence is important when learning a new language, and competence in a range of languages may be very advantageous if links are encouraged. Learners of EAL have another language as their L1 – this could prove fruitful in your MFL classroom.

Task 9.6 Learners with EAL

From your observations, discussions and readings, consider the following questions:

- How might pupils with EAL be *disadvantaged* in MFL classes?
- Conversely, how might they be *advantaged*?
- What steps can you as the teacher take to *maximise their learning*?

Obtain some written MFL work completed by a learner with EAL:

- What feedback would you give this pupil?
- What characteristics do you notice?
- Are these different because the pupil has EAL?

EAL is defined on the Multiverse website (http://www.multiverse.ac.uk/index.aspx?menuId=583) as:

> English as an Additional Language (EAL) is the expression used in the UK to refer to the teaching of English to speakers of other languages. Current statistics indicate that almost 10 per cent of pupils in maintained schools are learning English as a second, third, or indeed fourth, language, in addition to the language spoken in their families and over 300 languages are spoken by pupils in UK schools. The term is now preferred to English as a Second Language (ESL) as it indicates that pupils may use two or more languages other than English in their every day lives; it also suggests that learning English should be viewed as adding to a pupil's language repertoire, rather than displacing languages acquired earlier. The term 'bilingual' is also commonly used to describe children learning EAL; this is sometimes used to focus less specifically on the learning of English and more on the wider issues that concern children brought up in more than one language.

The National Association for Language Development in the Curriculum (NALDIC), the professional association of teachers specialising in EAL, states:

> Pupils learning EAL share many common characteristics with pupils whose first language is English, and many of their learning needs are similar to those of other children and young people learning in our schools. However, these pupils also have distinct and different needs from other pupils by virtue of the

fact that they are learning in and through another language, and that they come from cultural backgrounds and communities with different understandings and expectations of education, language and learning.

(www.naldic.org.uk/ITTSEAL2)

The challenge for you as student teachers is to take into account, and build on the linguistic and cultural understanding, skills and knowledge pupils bring to the classroom.

In the MFL classroom with the TL as the main means of instruction, interaction and assessment, weaknesses some pupils may experience in their command of English need not necessarily be a disadvantage. Linguistic skills in languages other than English can offer a basis for comparative and contrastive language work for the whole class.

Some schools run language awareness programmes with aims such as '(to bridge) the "space between" the different aspects of language education (English/foreign language/ethnic minority mother tongues/English as a second language/Latin)' (Hawkins 1987: 4). Such programmes might, for instance, include an examination of which languages are spoken in (particular parts of) the world, what families of languages there are and how languages are 'related' to one another. This might help pupils in the application of language learning strategies such as the use of cognates. Also, work might be carried out on an awareness of the diachronistic dimension of language development through the comparison of, say, the TL and English on the basis of a few words or phrases. Pupils could be shown how particular words have changed in form or meaning over a period of time. This might help them appreciate that form and function of language are determined by their use and that language evolves over time. From this pupils might gain an appreciation that certain features of the TL, such as different grammatical genders, which they might perceive as 'idio-syncratic', were at one time also characteristic of the English language. An invaluable resource in developing such programmes is Crystal's (2003) encyclopaedia of language. Another important point of reference is, of course, the National Literacy Strategy (NLS; DfEE 1998). For a brief discussion of the NLS, see Chapter 1. Language awareness programmes should build on the understanding pupils are developing during their time in primary school, in particular work on metalinguistic understanding and writing frames.

MFL departments should have a key role to play in the development of a whole school language policy. Mother tongue and MFL teachers might work collaboratively and follow a clear and consistent policy to assist pupils in their language development. (see e.g. Kingman 1988: 69)

MFL learning can be beneficial for pupils in terms of developing general language skills including summarising, redrafting and varying language to suit context, audience and purpose. Beyond functional aspects of foreign language teaching and learning there is also the need to become familiar with the structure of the TL. All these activities can be seen to reinforce work carried out in English and be beneficial in terms of the development of pupils' understanding of and ability to use language. The skills of paying attention to detail and of producing accurate spoken or written utterances are transferable from one language to another. In the TL sounds or patterns can normally not be taken for granted because they are, in the main, unfamiliar. Pupils have to pay attention to every letter and sound, which can be easier in the TL because the amount of input tends to be finite/limited. This attention to detail can be a valuable skill for pupils with difficulties in writing and listening to their mother tongue/English.

> **Task 9.7 Literacy and foreign language work**
>
> Familiarise yourself with the National Literacy Strategy and the National Curriculum Orders for English.
> Drawing on your reading as well as your observations of English lessons and teaching in a primary school, what specific examples of literacy-related foreign language work can you think of?

PUPILS WITH SEN

Many classes include pupils who have 'learning difficulties significantly greater than those of the majority of children of the same age'. They are referred to as pupils with SEN. The Warnock Report (1978) came to the conclusion 'that services should be planned on the basis of one child in five requiring some form of special educational provision at some stage'. This led to the recognition by the 1981 Education Act of the value of the integration of pupils with SEN into mainstream schools where possible.

The following categories of learning difficulties have been identified by the DfE/Welsh Office (1994: 6):

- a physical disability
- a problem with sight, hearing or speech
- a mental disability
- emotional or behavioural problems
- a medical or health problem
- difficulties with reading, writing, speaking or mathematics work.

The revised SEN Code of Practice was published in 2001 (DfES 2001). For details about the Code of Practice and other SEN-related resources, see the Teachernet available at http://www.teachernet.gov.uk/wholeschool/sen/. This has important implications for the work of all teachers, including modern linguists. Subject teachers have an important role to play in the identification and support of pupils with SEN. Where an individual education plan (IEP) is drawn up, you need to familiarise yourself with its content. IEPs aim to set out the following (http://www.teachernet.gov.uk/management/atoz/i/individualeducationplan/):

- the short-term targets set for or by the child;
- the teaching strategies to be used;

- the provision to be put in place;
- when the plan is to be reviewed;
- success and/or exit criteria;
- outcomes (to be recorded when the IEP is reviewed).

The IEP should focus on three to four targets, which relate to the areas of communication, literacy, numeracy and behaviour and social skill. It should be discussed with the pupil and parents and reviewed at least twice a year. Subject specialists need to liaise closely with the school's special educational needs co-ordinator (SENCO) as well as, on the basis of knowledge of the nature of a pupil's learning difficulties, help to achieve the specified targets or learning objectives in class.

Task 9.8 Identifying pupils with SEN	During your work at your first school experience school, enquire about the procedures in place in the MFL department concerning the identification of pupils with SEN. Compare them with those of the MFL department at your second school experience school or discuss similarities and differences with the procedures identified by a fellow student teacher placed in a different school.

A report from CILT and the NCC (NCC 1993: 1) notes that pupils with SEN can benefit in three main aspects of MFL work, i.e. in terms of:

- linguistic development;
- social development;
- cultural awareness.

The findings of this project clearly underline the principle of entitlement to the study of an MFL for all (see also McKeown 2004).

For more information and advice about working with pupils with SEN, see also the website of the National Association for Special Educational Needs available at http://www.nasen.org.uk/.

Some teaching strategies

You need to use a wide range of strategies in order to cater for pupils' individual differences. There is no specific methodology for teaching pupils with SEN. The strategies described here tend to be considered to constitute good practice in MFL teaching and learning generally. They do not only pertain to pupils with SEN. Since we feel that they can be particularly useful when teaching pupils with SEN, they are discussed at this point.

Consistency in approach

As an MFL student teacher you aim for consistency in approach in your teaching because familiarity with the format of material, types of tasks used and with classroom routines can increase the accessibility of the content of work for pupils.

As was noted in Chapter 5, using certain 'stock' types of activities can be reassuring to pupils. It can help minimise the amount of TL instruction needed and allows pupils to carry out their language work without apprehension about not knowing what to do.

Greeting pupils in the TL on entry to the classroom and expecting pupils to make a TL utterance in response or when calling the register can serve to reinforce a sense of purpose of TL use for pupils. It also provides a regular opportunity to reinforce key linguistic items and structures.

Planning in terms of small, achievable steps

In the tradition of the graded objectives movement reducing the content of work to a manageable size and breaking it down into small, achievable steps are also often used. Memorising new words and phrases is an important skill in MFL learning. Manageability of the number of new lexical items you introduce at any one time or the number of items pupils have to remember in order to complete a task successfully can be particularly useful for pupils with SEN. This can help them gain a sense of security and achievement as well as break down possible affective barriers towards the TL. In their final report in 2007, Lord Dearing and Lid King emphasised that a one menu suits all approach is not working for many of our children (2007: 38).

Using praise

Praise for effort and/or achievement is one form of feedback as are constructive comments when marking pupils' work. For marking, error correction and feedback, see Chapter 10.

Many teachers have adopted systems of praise and encouragement, which are attractive to pupils and make them want to achieve. 'Small' steps of progress made by pupils with SEN deserve equal praise as the 'bigger' steps of progress made by pupils without SEN. As Black and Jones (2006: 4) explain, this necessitates knowing exactly where the pupils are in their learning:

> Effective learning demands an alternation of feedback, pupil to teacher and from teacher to pupil. Thus the starting point for a classroom activity may be a question formulated by the teacher to ascertain the pupils' existing understanding of a topic. This implements a first principle of learning, which is to start where the learner is, rather than to present strange new ideas to overlay the old and cause confusion.

Task 9.9 Praise and encouragement

1   Find out what system of reward and praise are used by the MFL department at your school experience school.
2   Talk to a student teacher placed in a different school and find out what reward and praise system she uses.
3   Compare the two systems for pupils with SEN in particular.

Planning in terms of multi-dimensional progression

The NCC non-statutory guidance for England and Wales (1992) suggested that progression should be built into MFL work in a number of ways (see Figure 9.3).

from		**to**
concrete	ideas	abstract
simple	aspects	complex
specific	themes	general
factual	topics	non-factual
classroom	experiences	wider
familiar	contexts	unfamiliar
less	controversial aspects	more

Figure 9.3 Multi-dimensional progression
Source: Adapted from NCC (1992: D2).

Figure 9.3 has clear implications for unit of work and lesson planning, which can be explored in Tasks 9.10 and 9.11. For multi-dimensional learning objectives, see also Chapter 4.

Task 9.10 Planning for progression in MFL teaching I

Look at the scheme of work for Key Stages 3 and 4 of the MFL department at your school experience school.

1   Make a note of how many times certain topics, for instance, free time or holidays, are taught across Key Stages 3 and 4.
2   Discuss with your tutor or a class teacher with whom you work closely what is taken for granted when a given unit of work, e.g. free time or holidays, is revisited at Key Stage 4 and how much revision of material covered at Key Stage 3 is necessary.
3   Now try to relate the different approaches in how topics are covered in Key Stages 3 and 4 to the continuum in Figure 9.3. How is progression from concrete to abstract, from simple to complex, from specific to general, from the classroom to the wider world or from the familiar to the unfamiliar etc. built in?

Task 9.11 Planning for progression in MFL teaching II

Look at a scheme of work for any year group of the MFL department at your school experience school:

1 Note how two consecutive units of work build on existing knowledge and skills.
2 Discuss with your tutor or a class teacher with whom you work closely what is taken for granted at the beginning of the new unit of work and how much revision of linguistic items and/or structures covered in previous units is necessary.

Your findings for this task are likely to vary considerably according to which units of work you choose and at what stage of the linguistic development of pupils they come. Therefore, carry out this task with a number of different units across different stages of the learning process.

Creating a non-threatening learning environment

For pupils who are not as confident in speaking, opportunities should be created to practise in pairs or small groups with you or the foreign language assistant rather than in front of the whole class. This can avoid feelings of insecurity about perceived incorrect TL production. Extended periods of practice of a small amount of TL can also help pupils in this respect, as can short bursts of pair work (paired practice of a few new words) or a timed period (e.g. a strict 30-second slot with a countdown perhaps on the projection screen/interactive whiteboard) where all the class practise individually to themselves the one new phrase or question.

Clarity of presentation and using clear instructions

For pupils with difficulties with reading, worksheets and other writing, e.g. on the board or PowerPoint, need to be clearly legible and sufficiently big. Visual support as well as uncluttered presentation of material are also important. The board and screen should be visible from all angles of the classroom. All of this can be particularly important of course for pupils with visual difficulties.

Pupils with difficulties with hearing should, of course, be encouraged to sit in a position that allows them to lip-read if necessary.

Instructions in the TL should be clear and precise and, where possible, be accompanied by visual support, e.g. the word 'listen' in the TL can be used together with a symbol of a tape or a mime, i.e. the teacher pointing to her ear. Symbols and instructions used by the coursebook should be the same as those used on worksheets as well as assessment material in order to avoid confusion. Familiarity with 'stock' types of tasks can also help to keep instructions manageable. (See also Chapter 5.)

Presenting new language with the help of visual support

As can be seen in Chapter 6, new language forms can be presented through reading and listening activities. Pupils with SEN are more likely to have difficulties with the highly conceptual nature of MFL learning. Visual support in the form of pictures and flashcards as well as real objects such as, for instance, fruit can make non–abstract language more immediate and accessible. Subsequently you can use the visual support material effectively as stimulus material for language practice and production.

Creating opportunities for non-verbal responses

Equally, the opportunity for pupils to respond physically to stimuli, that is for instance by miming, making gestures, ticking boxes, can help them overcome difficulties in speaking and writing. By agreeing physical responses with a class, for instance what mime to use for *'juego al tenis'* ('I play tennis'), pupils are given an opportunity to contribute to the lesson content. Pupils could be asked to stand up, put up their hand or hold up a word card when they identify a specific word or phrase in a listening text.

Planning in terms of tangible and practical outcomes

Tangible and practical outcomes and 'products' of the learning process, such as a project booklet produced with the help of ICT building on drafting and redrafting, a collage for display purposes or the focus on the process of learning, such as carrying out simulation tasks, can help pupils in breaking down real and perceived difficulties with the linguistic content. The NCC non-statutory guidance for England and Wales offered many suggestions concerning 'concrete goals' and considers them as essential elements in the planning of units of work (see NCC 1992a: G1–13).

Recycling small amounts of language

Because of the importance of the ability to memorise linguistic items and recall them, with which pupils with SEN are more likely to have difficulties, the key to successful MFL learning for pupils would appear to lie in presenting new language in different guises, 'recycling' small amounts of language in many different ways, yet in familiar types of tasks, to engage pupils in the process of carrying out activities without being aware that they are repeatedly practising the same language content.

Task 9.12 Production of a study guide for a unit of work

In a collaborative teaching situation, work alongside pupils who have difficulties with MFL.

1   Make a note of the particular difficulties experienced by them. These may include bringing the right equipment, using reference material, maintaining concentration, recalling key vocabulary, understanding instructions and other aspects identified in this chapter.

2   As a result of your findings produce a short 'study guide' for a future unit of work. This guide may include an equipment check, activities such as puzzles and games to reinforce key vocabulary, guidance on how and where to find reference material, a 'skills' profile ('can-do' checklist) and help on what to do if objectives prove too difficult. Assume that the pupils will be able to work with a support teacher. To assist you with this task, refer to the unit of work plan. The guide might also include guidance on established TL routines.

3   On completion, discuss the guide with your tutor or a class teacher with whom you work closely.

EXCEPTIONALLY ABLE/GIFTED AND TALENTED PUPILS

There are some pupils whose individual differences relate to their exceptional ability and who have the potential for exceptional achievement, often in a range of subjects. Another widely used term for these pupils is 'gifted children'. For a discussion of working with very able pupils, see also J. Jones (2000a) and the various publications from NAGTY, the National Academy for Gifted and Talented Youth (http://www.nagty.ac.uk).

Clearly a key consideration in working with pupils of exceptional ability is their identification in order to avoid underachievement and to be able to take remedial action. Early identification of exceptionally able pupils is particularly important as they may display symptoms similar to those shown by pupils with motivational difficulties: they may appear inattentive or exhibit attention-seeking behaviour and underachieve. George (1993: 3) distinguished three types of behaviour characteristic of gifted underachievers:

- low self-esteem;
- academic avoidance behaviour;
- poor study skills, poor peer acceptance and lack of concentration.

NAGTY stress that identification of gifted pupils is not a straightforward process.

George lists a number of ways of identifying exceptionally able pupils, among them teacher observation, checklists, intelligence tests and achievement test batteries.

Denton and Postlethwaite (1985: 31–2) suggest a non-subject-specific checklist as a possible means of identification of very able children. Gifted pupils have the following characteristics:

1   Possess superior powers of reasoning, of dealing with abstractions, of generalising from specific facts, of understanding meaning, and of seeing into relationships.
2   Have great intellectual curiosity.
3   Learn easily and readily.
4   Have a wide range of interests.
5   Have a broad attention-span that enables them to concentrate on and persevere in solving problems and pursuing interests.
6   Are superior in the quantity and quality of vocabulary as compared with children their own age.
7   Have ability to do effective work independently.
8   Have learned to read early (often well before school age).
9   Exhibit keen powers of observation.
10 Show initiative and originality in intellectual work.
11 Show alertness and quick response to new ideas.
12 Are able to memorise quickly.
13 Have great interest in the nature of man and the universe (problems of origins and destiny, etc.).
14 Possess unusual imagination.

15   Follow complex directions easily.
16   Are rapid readers.
17   Have several hobbies.
18   Have reading interests which cover a wide range of subjects.
19   Make frequent and effective use of the library.
20   Are superior in mathematics, particularly in problem solving.

A number of checklists of this nature can be found in specialist literature. These can serve as *aide-mémoires* in identifying exceptionally able pupils.

The particular challenge for you working with exceptionally able pupils is always to provide work that stretches them and to have high expectations (see HMI 1992: vii).

This is, of course, also an aim for all learners: to provide sufficient challenge to enable them to make progress. For some excellent ideas on getting pupils to think, see Lin and Mackay (2003).

There are also a number of helpful websites, which offer advice on effective teaching of more able MFL learners, such as the QCA's *Guidance on Teaching the Gifted & Talented in MFLs* available at http://www.nc.uk.net/gt/languages/index.htm.

Task 9.13 Identifying exceptionally able pupils

What MFL specific knowledge, skills and understanding characterise exceptionally able pupils? Draw up a list of indicators which in your opinion signal exceptional ability in MFL learning and discuss them with your tutor or a class teacher you work with closely.

Some teaching strategies

When working with exceptionally able pupils you need to look out for the characteristics described above. Tasks, activities and exercises need to be challenging and stimulating for all pupils, including pupils with exceptional ability (see McLachlan 2002). There is, once again, no distinctive methodology for working with very able pupils or pupils with exceptional ability. The inclusion of extension work into a programme of study building on differentiated learning objectives is a strategy used by MFL departments to cater for more able and exceptionally able learners in a class. Often it is not so much the quantity of work set than its nature that is important. Below are some suggestions, which represent good practice in MFL teaching generally but which may appeal to more able and exceptionally able learners in particular.

Using creativity and problem solving

The language prescribed in GCSE examination specifications tends to be functional and can be perceived as narrow. Therefore, you need to ensure, through careful planning, that there is room for 'risk taking' and 'experimenting' with language as this can benefit more able pupils in particular. Working with language can take the form of manipulation. Pupils capable of higher level work in particular can gain a lot from exploring and articulating thoughts and ideas.

Conundrums and puzzles allow for the use of language by appealing to pupils' imagination. Also, open-ended tasks in the respective TL can present pupils with a challenge allowing them to use their imagination and to solve a problem in a creative way. One example is known as *'Le jeu des poubelles'*. A collection of authentic materials and realia are placed in a bag. These might include menus, bus tickets, food wrappers, receipts, magazines, newspaper articles, personal letters or audio recordings. The aim of the activity is for pupils to adopt the role of a detective. This involves scrutinising the materials and (re)creating a story featuring an imaginary or real person, who has (supposedly) collected the materials during a period of time in the target country. Outcomes can range from creative prose writing to role plays. Activities like this allow for the use of pupils' imagination. They draw on lexis from various topics and require pupils to make use of reference material.

The development of learning activities for peers on their own or in pairs or groups can also offer a challenge to more able pupils in particular.

Going beyond understanding detail

GCSE specifications tend not to go much beyond the identification of details within TL texts. Responding to texts by adapting the meaning of poems and songs or drawing out themes and images portrayed in texts are all higher level skills. To 'experiment' with language extends beyond the manipulation of grammatical forms and can include the expression of meaning through a range of literary techniques.

Fostering independence

Learner independence is important. More able and exceptionally able pupils are often effective independent learners. You can try to build on this by encouraging more able and exceptionally able pupils to reflect on how they learn, practise and exploit new language. They can then devise activities and provide some input for peers, for instance, from time to time become involved in 'teaching' other pupils. Keeping a 'learning diary' is one way to encourage reflection. Work by Dam (1990, 1995) demonstrates the value of self-evaluation in the TL, both in terms of the ability to manipulate the language learnt and in motivating pupils. Striving towards independent language learning and language use is also a feature of teaching and learning MFL at GCE A and A/S level. For a detailed discussion, see Pachler and Field (1999).

Focusing on accuracy and nuances of language use

To help them improve accuracy, pupils can be encouraged to carry out language analysis tasks such as the comparison of different language styles and registers. To contrast the language forms used in two newspaper articles covering the same story can, for instance, be a very productive way of addressing how language is used beyond conveying essential facts. Again, some strategies recommended for pupils of GCE A and A/S level may be appropriate for other 'able' pupils (see Powell 1999; Field 1999a).

Conceptualising

In Chapter 7 we argue that grammar requires conceptual thinking. Invariably, this challenge appeals to some pupils more than others. To provide pupils with texts and examples and ask them to draw conclusions about the structure of the TL can be a demanding task. Given the opportunity, some pupils might be able to produce explanations, which can be used by you for teaching certain grammar points to the whole class.

Developing extended cultural awareness

To research particular cultural issues with the help, for instance, of articles from the press, reference material or the internet can appeal to pupils. The focus is on learner independence and the extension of pupils' general knowledge. It can also help pupils to place MFL learning into a wider cultural context. For a discussion of authentic material, see Chapters 3 and 11, for the use of the internet, see Chapter 12.

To provide texts such as short stories, poetry and prose to complement topics covered in a unit of work with extended reading/reading for pleasure is a possible strategy. You need to carefully monitor work carried out by pupils on such supplementary material and make time available for feedback and discussion. The outcomes can be rewarding for both you and the learner. Monitoring of progress might be achieved by the pupil recording her efforts in a learner diary. You can build into lesson plans and/or your non-contact time, for instance, at break or lunchtime, opportunities to discuss progress with pupils. This way a record of the work carried out is kept and the pupils themselves are involved in building up a profile of their achievements.

Task 9.14 Working with exceptionally able pupils

1   Examine activities in an existing unit of work. Consider which of the following, or any other challenging activity types could be added to stretch exceptionally able pupils:

- research skills;
- creative writing;
- extended reading;
- translation;
- conundrums;
- grammar exercises;
- preparing a presentation.

2   Develop relevant materials and, in collaboration with your tutor or a relevant class teacher, plan how to work with an exceptionally able pupil on extension tasks throughout the unit of work.

3   When evaluating the project, consider the impact of your work on the attainment and motivation of the pupil.

4   Consider how various of these activities might provide suitable challenge for a wider range of pupils.

PUPILS WITH MOTIVATIONAL DIFFICULTIES

One particular challenge for you are pupils who display behaviour patterns that are disruptive to the delivery of lessons or those who are indifferent to the tasks planned. Pupils in these categories tend to be insufficiently motivated towards their study of MFL. For a detailed discussion of motivation, see Chambers (1999); see Bartrum (2006) for a study on peer group influences.

Internal as well as external motivation facilitate learning (see Child 1993: 47–51). Internal or intrinsic reasons for wanting to learn could, for instance, be the wish of pupils to tell a penfriend about themselves, the desire to complete a challenging task or to win in a competitive situation. External or extrinsic reasons for wanting to learn could be the need to pass an examination at the end of compulsory schooling as a means of entry into post-16 education. Research would suggest that the more immediate the reasons for wanting to learn and the more they can be determined by the learner, the more influential they are. There are some excellent studies on what it is that learners of MFL see as their reasons for their perceived success or failure in the subject (see Williams *et al.* 2002; Williams *et al.* 2004; Graham 2004).

Cajkler and Addelman (2000: 2) list some elements to increase motivation. (See also the Special Edition of *Language Learning*, Vol. 53(1).)

Fun is obtained from:

- smiles
- language games
- competitions which anyone can win
- competitions which the 'best' can win
- friendly jokes and quips
- puzzles
- problems to solve
- making things
- moving about
- the unexpected
- the unpredictable
- the privilege of relaxing now and then
- success in learning.

Motivators include:

- some kind of reward (time out, a fun activity, a comic to read, etc.)
- praise by peers
- genuine, warm praise by the teacher
- a special visitor
- an attempt to show that tasks are relevant
- a clear understanding of what the task ahead is (notes, target sheets, verbal explanation, work schedules)
- success in learning.

To make lesson objectives explicit and occasionally to negotiate them with pupils can be motivating. Making objectives explicit is considered to be good, and widespread practice as it enables the learners to set targets. Many coursebooks feature unit objectives in the form of a preamble or as a 'can-do' self-check list. The differentiation of objectives and the avoidance of unrealistic objectives are particularly important when working with pupils with motivational difficulties. This is effectively demonstrated by Deane's (1992) diagram (see Figure 9.4), which illustrates that to have unrealistic objectives can lead to a 'downward spiral'.

Task 9.15 The use of explicit objectives

1   Examine the coursebook used by your school experience school for one particular year group from the point of view of whether and how unit objectives are made explicit. Also, observe how the MFL teachers, whose lessons you observe, communicate lesson objectives.

2   Devise an end-of-unit goal for a specific unit of work. Engage pupils in a discussion about what is required to achieve this goal. Make a note of the pupils' comments and then translate these into meaningful learning objectives. This allows you to measure the value of each planned learning activity by relating it to the agreed objectives.

Some teaching strategies

Below are some additional teaching strategies, which – as with the ones already introduced earlier in this chapter – apply to MFL teaching generally but might prove to be particularly useful in the context of working with learners with motivational difficulties.

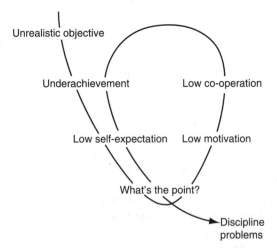

Figure 9.4 Michèle Deane's downward spiral

Source: © Deane (1992: 44)

Target setting

One of the challenges you face teaching MFL in secondary schools is the fact that the (externally) accredited assessment of pupils' proficiency tends to take place in the main, particularly in non-modular specifications, only at the very end of pupils' period of study. Because many learners find it difficult to derive motivation from this long-term objective, the content required by the examination specification needs to be broken down into achievable steps and pupils' progress monitored through effective assessment for learning (see Chapter 10). This way pupils can aim at achieving short-term targets.

Personalised language and purposeful activities

In her book on working with reluctant learners, Alison points out the importance of ensuring that the language pupils are exposed to is '*their own language* and that they see a *valid purpose* in learning it' (Alison 1993: 20). This is a notion frequently echoed by MFL teachers. For the presentation stage, Alison identifies the strategies of letting pupils find out for themselves what they need to learn and to give them opportunities to show what they already know while for the practice stage she lists strategies/ activities involving speculation, remembering, timing, guessing, the manipulation of objects, competition and the inclusion of pupils' ideas in the lesson.

Emphasis on enjoyment and creativity

Shaw (1994) makes a similar suggestion in an account of his experience with reluctant learners, that pupils should be involved in the production of language where the emphasis is on enjoyment and creativity. He describes a task, which is based on the use of stimulus material from authentic sources, for instance pictures, short texts or adverts from newspapers or magazines, in English or the TL, as a basis for language production. Pupils are allowed to mix the TL with English. As examples of pupils' work Shaw quotes, for instance: 'uno, dos, tres – I know Shaw's address', 'A man in a dress? Is he inglés?' or 'Monumental cities: Vivo en Birkenhead' (Shaw 1994: 39).

The pacing of lessons and the use of a variety of tasks and material

The pacing of lessons and the use of a variety of tasks and material, which is an important consideration in planning MFL lessons in general, are particularly important for pupils with motivational difficulties.

Halliwell (1991b) suggests that there needs to be a balance of 'peace and quiet' as well as 'stimulation and excitement'. In support of this she proposes an important concept in planning of interactive MFL lessons, namely the balance of 'settling' and 'stirring' activities (see ibid.: 25–6). MFL teachers, she argues, should and do carefully consider whether an activity is 'stirring' – such as oral work, competitions or games – increasing pupils' engagement or whether it is 'settling' – such as copying, labelling or listening – helping to calm pupils and, as a consequence, lessons down (see ibid.: 3–4).

Variety in the use of teaching strategies, whole-class work, group work, pair work, independent study, as well as the use of a range of teaching aids such as recordings to the whole class, carousel activities, listening stations, the overhead projector, language games and software or CD-Rom packages, individual ICT work, drama and songs, can help to motivate pupils.

Use of competition

Often, the introduction of a competitive element, which focuses on pooling the strengths of individual pupils in a team or allows pupils to compete against their previous performance or their own targets – rather than on identifying their individual weaknesses for the benefit of a small number of 'winners' for whom the competition serves as motivation – also works well.

The use of vocational contexts

Vocational settings can provide useful contexts for MFL learning. Combining work related activities with language learning can provide useful contexts for MFL work and can have a beneficial motivational impact. Pupils working through scenarios taken from the world of work, such as those suggested in the context of the optional Language Units available within the advanced vocational certificate of education (AVCE), are considered to be of motivational value because they are perceived to be relevant to pupils. Both at KS3 and KS4, you can build in more vocational contexts to the work undertaken in the classroom, whether this aspect is an element of the official external assessment or not. For information and resources about vocational contexts in MFL, see the *Vocational Languages Resource Bank* at http://www.vlrb.org.uk/.

Task 9.16 The use of teaching strategies

With reference to Table 9.3, observe a number of MFL lessons focusing on what strategies MFL teachers in your school experience school use in working with pupils in order to overcome some difficulties commonly experienced by them. Following your observations discuss with your tutor how you can include these and other suitable strategies in your own teaching.

WORKING WITH SUPPORT TEACHERS AND TEACHING ASSISTANTS

An important aspect in catering for the different needs of pupils in the MFL classroom is working with support teachers (see also Chapter 2). These might be (peripatetic) SEN specialists, staff specialising in EAL assigned to individual or groups of pupils, teaching assistants or colleagues from within the MFL department providing support with specific groups.

Working in tandem with other adults in the classroom is not always easy as it raises a number of important issues such as who is responsible for which aspect of the

Table 9.3 Catering for individual needs of pupils

Pupil difficulty	Strategies observed	Additional strategies identified in discussion with colleagues
short concentration span		
poor organisational skills		
lack of confidence		
untidy writing		
weak first language skills		
isolation from other pupils		
difficulties with spelling		
physical/sensory impairments		
difficulties with memory skills		
lack of interest generally		
poor general knowledge and cultural awareness		

lesson. Of particular relevance for MFL contexts is the question of what MFL skills a support teacher has. In order to maximise the impact of 'another pair of hands' in the classroom on pupil learning, it is essential that you carefully plan lessons together with the support teacher.

As support teachers work very closely with particular pupils they can be intimately familiar with pupils' needs. This expertise can be invaluable, for example, when designing worksheets and other teaching material. Support teachers are often willing to act as a 'model learner' to demonstrate role plays, pair work, games and puzzles. Organising 'carousel' lessons and group work can become easier with help from a support teacher, who can supervise a particularly demanding activity and/or circulate around the classroom.

For a detailed discussion of working with other adults in the classroom, see Redondo (2007).

Task 9.17 Working with support teachers I

During your work at the school experience school, enquire about the nature of support MFL teachers receive by talking to MFL staff as well as some support teachers. What do they consider to be best practice in collaborative work?

Task 9.18 Working with support teachers II

When working with a support teacher, where possible:

1   Design a list of key TL phrases. This allows the support teacher to help pupils with their productive MFL skills if she is not an MFL specialist.
2   Discuss the presentation of material in advance of lessons and adapt existing worksheets. What are the key features and underpinning principles of the changes?
3   Consider which support activities the support teacher could use with pupils when a given activity designed for the whole class proves too difficult. A set of very basic activities on numbers, days, dates, personal details, gender rules and other core linguistic items can support her work on the reinforcement of pupils' key linguistic skills.

Task 9.19 Planning a lesson taught with a support teacher

Refer to the sample lesson plan in Chapter 4, Figure 4.7. Modify this lesson plan by building in the use of a support teacher.

SUMMARY

It is very important to recognise that pupils are individuals with different needs, for instance, due to their ability, gender, interests, motivation, social class, self-concept, self-esteem, ethnic background or creativity and that, therefore, no teaching group is homogenous.

A big challenge for you is to identify individual differences and needs in pupils and to devise strategies to cater for the needs of all pupils in a class.

FURTHER READING

Barton, A. (2002) 'Learning styles: the gender effect', in A. Swarbrick (ed.) *Teaching Modern Foreign Languages in Secondary Schools: A Reader*. Buckingham: Open University Press, pp. 272–85.

This chapter is a good introduction to the debate on gender and MFL teaching and learning.

Lee, J., Buckland, D. and Shaw, G. (1998) *The Invisible Child: The Responses and Attitudes to the Learning of MFL Shown by Year 9 Pupils of Average Ability*. London, CILT.

A useful book which explores factors surrounding the motivations of secondary pupils when learning a foreign language.

Redondo, A. (2000) 'Mixed ability grouping in modern foreign languages teaching', in K. Field (ed.) *Issues in Modern Foreign Languages Teaching*. London: Routledge, pp. 122–33.

A key chapter outlining the ongoing discussion as to how to manage different levels of attainment in the MFL classroom.

Support for Learning: Special Issue, edited by N. Pachler and A. Redondo (2005) 'Inclusive approaches to teaching foreign languages', *British Journal of Learning Support*, 20(3).

An issue which provides MFL teachers with a range of views, research and advice on teaching learners with special educational needs.

10 Assessment, marking, recording and reporting

INTRODUCTION

Rendall (2003) asks, in the context of the use of ICT in MFL, 'What makes the average learner feel like a "loser" '? and lists the following points:

- not being able to understand or follow during a lesson;
- making no visible progress;
- continuing to make errors;
- repeating the same errors without improvement.

These can be seen to apply more generally in (language) learning of course, and effective assessment can go some way to address the issues: 'Successful learning occurs when learners have ownership of their learning; when they understand the goals they are aiming for; when, crucially, they are motivated and have the skills to achieve success' (ARG, 1999: 2). The overarching question here is: how can learners learn better/more effectively and what role does assessment play in this process?

Assessment is integral to modern foreign languages teaching and learning. It plays a prominent role in the statutory framework and it has been subject to a lively educational and public debate in recent years. There has also been a substantial amount of significant research into assessment; research which has – and continues to be – directly informed and influenced practice. The main outcomes of this research have included a distinct focus in schools on assessment *for* learning, i.e. assessment practices and techniques which actively move the learner on to make progress and improve their understanding of how and why they are learning in the way they are. Assessment *for* learning has evolved from the term 'formative assessment' and, similarly, this is contrasted with assessment *of* learning, the broad equivalent of 'summative assessment' (see Wiliam and Black 1996). Work on assessment for learning, particularly by Black and Wiliam, has been very influential in the UK educational context (see Black *et al.*

2002; Wiliam and Black 2002; Black and Wiliam 2003). This work on assessment more generally has led to a linked specific research focus on MFL (see Black and Jones 2006) as well as practical application of assessment for learning techniques and approaches (see Barnes and Hunt 2003; Mutton 2007).

In this chapter we do the following:

- discuss general principles and purposes of assessment;
- outline the assessment process;
- discuss the main types of MFL assessment in the secondary school;
- give examples of MFL assessment activities, tasks and exercises.

Our discussion of assessment of MFL needs to be seen in the wider context of the developments touched upon above, i.e. a move towards assessment for learning and a readjustment of perspectives in what assessment involves.

While we contextualise our discussion in this chapter by way of the statutory requirements for England, i.e. the National Curriculum (NC) and the GCSE criteria, much of what is said about assessment issues is generic and, therefore, equally relevant to student teachers learning to teach in Wales, Scotland, Northern Ireland and beyond. Additionally, we refer to the Common European Framework (CEF), setting assessment of MFL in its broader European context.

OBJECTIVES

By the end of this chapter you should:

- understand the key principles and some important purposes of assessing MFL learners, including assessment *of* and *for* learning;
- be familiar with key assessment terminology;
- understand the various stages of the assessment process;
- be aware of important issues of and a range of activities for MFL assessment;
- have an appreciation of internal and external assessment, including teacher assessment, pupil peer- or self-assessment and the GCSE examination.

STRANDS OF ASSESSMENT

Assessment consists of two separate but interlinking strands. The first, and one that tends initially to be more prominent for you, comprises the legislation, policy and documentation (often issued on a national level, but which frequently also has regional and local/school-based elements/dimensions). The results of this type of assessment often culminate in local, regional and national performance tables, comparing schools, pupils, local authorities, etc.

The second strand, arguably the more important in the context of this book and your development as a teacher, is made up of the ways in which pupils' knowledge, skills, understanding, work, learning are improved, or aimed to be improved, and monitored on a class/individual basis. The successful implementation of this second strand is essential for the results of the first to improve, i.e. without what happens in the classroom being carried out effectively, pupils' attainment will not be improved. These two strands could be seen as the *macro* and *micro* dimensions of assessment. As a student teacher, you are concerned with *both*. Figure 10.1 presents details of the macro and micro strands of assessment at KS2–5.

Key documents for macro strand:

- Key Stage 2 non-statutory guidelines for MFL (http://www.nc.uk.net/nc_resources/html/MFL_k2.shtml)
- Key Stage 2 framework for MFL (http://www.standards.dfes.gov.uk/primary/publications/languages/framework)
- Key Stage 2 QCA schemes of work (http://www.qca.org.uk/qca_11752.aspx)
- Local (school/LA) schemes of work, recommendations, etc.

Key issues for micro strand:

- Assessment issues and practices at this age range
- Pupils' individual achievements, progress and targets
- Assessment of all four language skills, plus e.g. language learning skills, knowledge about language, cultural awareness etc.
- Transfer of assessment and progress information during KS2 and particularly from KS2 to KS3

Key Stage 3:

Key documents for macro strand

- Key Stage 3 framework for MFL (http://www.standards.dfes.gov.uk/secondary/keystage3/respub/mflframework/about/ks3_mfl_framework/)
- National Curriculum for MFL: statutory requirements (http://www.qca.org.uk/qca_12218.aspx)
- Key Stage 3 QCA Schemes of Work (http://www.standards.dfes.gov.uk/schemes2/)
- Local (school/LA) schemes of work, recommendations, etc.
- ASSET languages/languages ladder (http://www.assetlanguages.org.uk/)

Key issues for micro strand

- Use of any assessment information transferred from KS2 (including MFL, literacy, etc.)
- Pupils' individual achievements, progress and targets
- Assessment of all four language skills, plus e.g. language learning skills, etc.

- How individual pupils can assess themselves honestly and accurately and know how to move their learning on
- The introduction and effective use of peer assessment and benchmarking
- Raising aspirations in MFL to encourage learners to continue in to KS4

Key Stage 4:

Key documents for macro strand

- Specifications and criteria for GCSE or other accredited programmes (http://www.qca.org.uk/libraryAssets/media/qca-07–3158_MFL_draft_GCSE_crit.pdf)
- Statutory *entitlement* for MFL (http://www.qca.org.uk/qca_7000.aspx)
- Alternative approved qualifications (http://www.ndaq.org.uk/; http://www.qca.org.uk/14–19/qualifications/approved_quals_mfl.pdf)
- Local (school/LA) schemes of work, recommendations, etc.
- ASSET languages/languages ladder (http://www.assetlanguages.org.uk/)
- Coursework: different rules for comments, etc., going to be far less important for MFL

Key issues for micro strand

- Pupils' individual achievements, progress and targets
- Continued and progressive use of self and peer assessment against assessment criteria and other benchmarking possibilities
- Assessment of all four language skills, plus language learning skills etc.
- Different options, different choices – taking GCSE earlier (what do they then do in Year 11?)
- ASSET languages instead of GCSE?
- Alternatives to GCSE? (e.g. CBLC)

POST 16:

Key documents for macro strand

- Specifications for AS/A2 or other accredited programmes (http://www.qca.org.uk/qca_7005.aspx)
- AVCE optional language units (http://www.qca.org.uk/qca_7009.aspx)
- Local (school/LA) schemes of work, recommendations, etc.
- ASSET languages/languages ladder (http://www.assetlanguages.org.uk/)

Key issues for micro strand

- Pupils' individual achievements, progress and targets
- Sustained use of self- and peer assessment and emphasis on independent learning and improvement
- Assessment of all four language skills, plus language learning skills, content knowledge, etc.

Figure 10.1 The 'macro' and 'micro' strands of assessment at Key Stages 2–5

You need, therefore, to develop expertise in the two strands outlined in Figure 10.1, and mesh them together successfully. For example, at KS4, your knowledge of KS4 external examination requirements and specifications is crucial in providing effective assessment for learning advice for your learners, enabling them, for example, to self-assess their written and oral work, know what is expected of them in listening and reading etc. The macro strand in each Key Stage feeds into the micro strand of application in the classroom. The *external* assessment criteria, however, should never take over from the key question of 'how can this learner improve what they are doing and feel more confident about their learning?'

DEFINITION OF TERMS

By way of an introduction to the theory and practice of MFL assessment, Figure 10.2 provides a glossary, defining and explaining some important terminology.

Term	Definition
Achievement	Progress made by pupils in relation to past performance
Attainment	Progress made by pupils in relation to the statutory framework
Assessment *for* learning	Assessment which focuses on the next steps to improve learning. This involves both feedback and feed forward
Assessment *of* learning	assessment which describes/summarises what a learner has achieved/attained. A snapshot of achievement. It also informs teachers how much of and how well a group of learners has progressed against the intended learning outcomes
Assessment criteria	The criteria by which a piece of work of whatever type is assessed. These criteria need to be clear both to teachers and learners
Criterion-referenced	Assessment which is judged according to the fulfilment of a description of a task, or a set of agreed criteria. If everyone fulfils the criteria, then everyone passes
Diagnostic	Assessment opportunities aimed at identifying strengths and weaknesses in current performance and providing pointers for future work
Evaluative	To ascertain how well individual teachers or schools are performing
External assessment	Assessment opportunities designed by outside agencies such as Awarding Bodies; the standardised GCSE
Fitness for purpose	The extent to which an assessment opportunity reflects the reasons for carrying out the assessment
Formative/continuous assessment	Assessment opportunities, which are ongoing and an integral part of teaching. An ongoing process of gathering information on the processes of learning, the extent of learning, and on strengths and weaknesses, which provides learners and teachers with information for future planning to meet an individual pupil's needs; takes place during the course of teaching and is essentially used to feed back into the teaching/learning process

Internal assessment	Assessment opportunities carried out by the teacher (teacher assessment) or pupils (self- and/or peer assessment); designed by the teacher or coursebook writers
Norm-referenced	Assessment which measures all learners against each other and can place learners in rank order in relation to their peers. Marks are sometimes altered up or down if too many candidates succeed or fail, irrespective of the difficulty of the test or the ability of the candidates
Peer assessment	Judgements made by one's peer(s) about one's own proficiency or achievement
Predictive assessment	Using a range of data of prior attainment to provide indicators of future potential attainment and minimum target levels
Proficiency	Level of linguistic skill and knowledge in relation to external criteria
Reliability	The accuracy with which an assessment opportunity measures progress, attainment, achievement, proficiency, etc.
Self-assessment	Judgements made by the learner about his/her own proficiency or achievement
Standardised assessment	Assessment opportunities devised by outside agencies, such as Awarding Bodies or the National Foundation for Educational Research (NFER)
Summative assessment	Assessment opportunities coming at the end of a unit of work, term, year or course. These opportunities may be used to select learners for movement between classes, sets, streams or institutions. They are also used for certification purposes. Assessment which takes place at the end of a course of study or part of it and which measures learners' performance over that course or part of it; it provides information about how much learners have progressed and how well a course has worked
Validity	The extent to which an assessment opportunity measures what has been taught and what pupils should have learnt

Figure 10.2 Glossary of MFL assessment terminology

The assessment process requires you to ask yourself three important questions: why, what and how to assess? The purposes of assessment, i.e. the reasons why you assess, are manifold. For instance, assessment is a tool:

- to generate information for pupils about their learning;
- to ensure that learning objectives have been reached;
- to motivate pupils;
- to gather data for reporting what pupils know, understand and/or can do;
- to select pupils (e.g. for groupings in school or for opportunities in later life);
- to identify strengths and weaknesses in pupils;
- to provide certification;
- to fulfil statutory requirements;
- to measure standards and hold teachers accountable.

This list of reasons why you assess pupils clearly shows that assessment is inextricably linked to teaching and learning. Assessment opportunities need to reflect learning objectives, which in turn reflect the statutory framework and examination specifications and not be a 'bolt-on'. The answer to the question what to assess is, therefore, to be found in lesson, unit of work and scheme of work plans, as well as learners' needs from your (and their) assessment of their progress. Your planning needs to take place with assessment in mind.

When considering how to assess MFL learning, a number of general principles can be identified; assessment should:

- be an integral part of teaching and learning and follow from curricular objectives;
- inform future teaching and learning;
- provide useful information about the progress, achievement and attainment of pupils to relevant parties;
- involve the learner in the process;
- come at regular intervals to provide a critical mass of data to validate judgements and to motivate the learner;
- consist of a variety of methods to make data more reliable;
- be manageable.

> **Task 10.1 Personal assessment experience**
>
> 1   Think about a number of different ways in which your MFL learning has been assessed in the past. What were the purpose and the nature of the assessments?
> 2   Then, consider if the assessments were fit for purpose. List the strengths and weaknesses of the various assessments you undertook.

You need to plan the assessment of and for pupils' learning on the basis of the principles identified above as well as in recognition of its purposes. Figure 10.3 offers a summary of what assessment of pupils' learning means in the context of your work in schools.

WHAT IS ASSESSMENT *FOR* LEARNING IN MFL?

First, it is necessary to establish the basic elements you are assessing in MFL learning. These might consist of all four skills:

- listening (and responding);
- speaking;
- reading (and responding);
- writing.

No.	Stage
1	Decide on what learning objectives are to be assessed, *e.g. for pupils to show that they are able to order a meal in a restaurant or for pupils to have an understanding of how to formulate and when to use the imperfect tense*
2	Decide on the type of assessment, *e.g. whether to use continuous or summative teacher assessment or pupil self- or peer assessment*
3	Define the criteria to be used in relation to the planned learning outcomes/ objectives
4	Select tasks from the teaching material suitable for assessment purposes and/or design tasks reflecting the types of teaching material used
5	Collect evidence, *i.e. carry out the assessment*
6	Pass judgement, *i.e. mark pupils' work, and/or use self- and peer assessment in the process*
7	Record the data, *e.g. note results in the mark book*
8	Report the data, *i.e. feed back the results to relevant parties as verbal comments (in writing or orally), grades, percentages, levels etc.*
9	Review and evaluate the assessment process and outcomes: *was the assessment valid and reliable? What diagnostic information did it yield to inform future teaching and learning? What, if anything, needs to be retaught or reexplained on the basis of the evidence gathered? Might a different approach yield better results?*

Figure 10.3 Nine stages of the assessment process

Plus:

- cultural awareness;
- grammatical knowledge/understanding;
- knowledge of language;
- language awareness;
- learning/communication strategies used.

All these areas form part of what learners need to progress in their language learning. Effective assessment for learning, i.e. ways of helping pupils move on and make progress, is beneficial in all these areas, not just the purely 'language' based ones.

Assessment for learning has been defined, according to Weeden *et al.*, (2002: 24–5) as doing the following:

- Is integral to teaching.
- Involves sharing learning goals with pupils.
- Aims to help pupils know and recognise the standards they are aiming for.
- Requires adjusting teaching to take account of the results of assessment.
- Is underpinned by a confidence that every pupil can improve.
- Requires a recognition of the profound influence assessment has on the motivation and self-esteem of pupils.

- Needs the provision of effective feedback to pupils so they can recognise their next steps and how to take them.
- Involves pupils in self-assessment.
- Encourages the active involvement of pupils in their own learning.
- Involves both teacher and pupils reviewing and reflecting on assessment data.

For advice and practical ideas on assessment for learning in MFL, see Mutton (2007), Barnes and Hunt (2003), and the QCA sites at http://www.qca.org.uk/qca_4334.aspx, and http://www.qca.org.uk/qca_4369.aspx where you will find case studies, etc. There are also useful definitions and discussions of terms at a site presented by Jones at http://www.ittmfl.org.uk/modules/teaching/1e/janejones.htm).

THE COMMON EUROPEAN FRAMEWORK OF REFERENCE FOR LANGUAGES AND ASSET LANGUAGES

The Common European Framework http://www.coe.int/t/dg4/linguistic/CADRE_ EN.asp, introduced before 2000, is now published in over 30 languages and has gradually been adopted or at least consulted more by the MFL community in the UK. The framework outlines what learners of foreign languages 'can do' at a range of stages in their progress while learning. After the Nuffield Languages Enquiry and the resulting National Languages Strategy (see Chapter 1) recommended a new accreditation system, the Languages Ladder (http://www.dfes.gov.uk/languages/DSP_languagesladder.cfm) launched in May 2005, the CEF is seen as a background framework to the progression built into the system at the time of writing administered as ASSET Languages http://www.assetlanguages.org.uk, albeit that the steps in between stages for ASSET languages have been created to be much smaller. Both the CEF and ASSET Languages 'can do' statements cover all four skills. The government's Languages Ladder site (above) outlines how the various levels of attainment 'map' on to one another, including the National Curriculum.

NC LEVELS AND ASSESSMENT

Making use of the National Curriculum levels for assessing pupils and setting targets has been the cause of a lot of debate among the MFL community. Officially, levels 1–8 plus exceptional performance are to be used at the end of KS3 to describe a pupil's general level of attainment in each of the four skills. However, many departments have 'levelled' individual pieces of work, divided levels up in to smaller steps (calling them perhaps 3a and 3b), presented the descriptions in 'pupil-friendly' language, and other practices to attempt to use the material available as effectively as possible. Departments of course can use the levels exactly as they wish as long as they report using them at the end of the Key Stage. It is worthwhile, however, to look at some of the key issues and, perhaps, key controversies, surrounding the NC levels. The descriptors were amended for the new National Curriculum Orders applicable from September 2008:

- NC levels should be assessed *across a period of time*, they are not ideally designed for individual pieces of work;
- pupils need the 'glue' of the language too, i.e. the high frequency words focused on in the KS3 MFL framework;
- learners must keep revisiting vocabulary/topic language and see how it can be revised and adopted in different contexts;
- there has been substantial disagreement about the way the levels deal with accuracy, progression, breadth, depth, etc;
- tasks have to be designed to enable pupils to reach certain levels, i.e. to provide opportunities to use the different tenses, etc;
- pupils need to be aware of how much vocabulary they know too – not just linguistic/grammatical factors which help them progress upwards through the levels. This is particularly important for those pupils who may not be able to progress very far from level to level, but who nevertheless are increasing their breadth of vocabulary;
- optional tests and tasks are available to help teachers see particularly how the levels work;
- pupils need to be helped and set targets to move up the levels – without knowing where you're aiming, how can you get there? The teacher needs to build language up with them, show, demonstrate, share, etc.

ASSESSMENT TASKS

When designing assessment tasks, it is crucial to ensure that assessment criteria are clear to all parties. What is needed to succeed at this task? What elements should be included? How will these elements be 'marked'? Is there a model or a benchmark that would help pupils make progress towards the criteria? Knowing the final destination, that is, the type of work required in order to achieve a certain level or grade is helpful both for teachers and pupils. Teachers mark more fairly; pupils see what they need to do in order to improve. The key question arising out of effective use of criteria, benchmarks and successful plenaries is one which is often very difficult to answer: if I were a pupil in their class, would I be able to describe how I could improve my learning?

In covering the statutory requirements, pupils need to be given chances to experience a range of learning opportunities. The choice of assessment tasks needs to reflect this variety. Therefore, you need to use different types of assessment activities, which accurately measure what you have taught and should have been learnt (validity) and which can easily be replicated and are dependable, i.e. yield similar results if carried out at a different time or by a different teacher (reliability). Assessment tasks should be chosen on the basis of their usefulness as learning tasks. Activities, which allow pupils to show what they *can* do, understand and/or know rather than focus on their weaknesses, are potentially motivating. There are many different learning activities which can yield useful evidence, be they oral, written, graphic or even product-based. Examples of useful evidence are: role plays, simulations, questioning, interviews, poems, descriptions, short written answers to questions, notes, printouts, games or flyers/leaflets.

PREPARING FOR EXTERNAL ASSESSMENT

In order to prepare pupils well for external examinations, you need to consider a change in pattern. Throughout your teaching at Key Stages 3 and 4 you need to use types of tasks that prepare pupils for what external examinations require. For example, you have to ensure that the rubrics and visual clues/symbols you use for/to support target language (TL) instructions and scene setting on your worksheets and continuous assessment tasks coincide with those included in the examination papers. The inception of assessment and testing in the TL was accompanied by a redefinition of types of activities to be used for external, standardised assessment. These activities increasingly appear to be chosen with a view to accommodating assessment and testing in the TL and do not necessarily cover the full range of tasks traditionally used by MFL teachers and coursebook writers. The draft GCSE criteria (QCA 2007a) specify that awarding bodies must list the TL rubrics that may be used in assessment tasks.

ASSESSMENT ACTIVITIES

In Figures 10.4–10.6 a range of assessment activities, which do not involve the use of English, are discussed and evaluated in terms of their advantages and disadvantages as well as the resulting implications for you. The categories 'features' and 'implications for teachers' overlap to some extent. We feel, nevertheless, that this distinction makes the description of some features of assessment tasks more transparent. This description of types of activities is intended to familiarise you with commonly used types of activities. It is also intended to guide your choice of assessment activities and to clarify which type lends itself best to which aspect of MFL learning.

The description of these activities is guided by the work of Neather *et al.* (1995) and Powell *et al.* (1996) on TL testing. Neither the lists of tasks nor their descriptions purport to be exhaustive. This typology aims to serve as a starting point for designing formative and/or summative teacher assessment opportunities.

Task 10.2 Analysing end-of-unit assessment tasks

Choose a unit of work devised by the MFL department at your school experience school:

1   Make a list of the types of activities featured in the unit of *work*. Compare this list with the types of activities of the unit *assessment*. What other types of activities listed in Figures 10.4–10.6 could you use?
2   List the purposes, strengths and weaknesses of the individual assessment tasks.
3   With reference to Figure 10.3, consider how similar or different these assessment activities are to the way in which your own MFL work has been assessed in the past.
4   Discuss the findings with your tutor or a class teacher with whom you work closely. Also, discuss the reasons for using particular assessment tasks for particular purposes.

No.	Activity	Features	Implications for teachers
1	multiple choice, e.g. true/false, ticking correct answers	a carefully designed test focusing on specific aspects can distinguish between pupils who understand, know and/or can do and those who cannot/ do not; analysis of results can identify areas of weakness; the system does not allow for an understanding of why pupils fail; reliability is high but validity is low; there is the danger of pupils guessing	in order to allow for remedial action need to analyse on an individual basis
2	gap filling	there is a danger that pupils know/understand what is required but are unable to show it due to deficiencies in productive language skills; the method is easily manageable and marking allows for simple indication of right or wrong	the activity lends itself well to end-of-unit tests; the integrative nature of the task makes it difficult to identify and act upon problems
3	labelling in the TL	easy to administer but little more than a vocabulary test; content rather than application of knowledge is tested	you need to select appropriate moments to use such tests; use early in a unit of work allows you to address shortages in knowledge
4	selecting the correct answer from a range	allows pupils to demonstrate their receptive skills (listening, reading) without having to rely on their productive ones (speaking, writing); allows for guessing	you need to analyse results to identify the reasons for the answers given; you should ensure that pupils, apart from demonstrating the final outcome, are able to reason the process so that you can give purposeful feedback
5	matching language to symbols/images	the method is reliable if all the symbols are recognisable; it is manageable but does allow for guessing; it provides little useful information for future teaching	the activity is mainly suited to end-of-unit tests; marking, on the basis of the identification of right and wrong, is simple; self- and peer marking can be used

(continued)

6	note taking	integrative nature; careful categorisation is required in order to identify pupils' strengths and weaknesses	grading needs be based on broad and comprehensive indicators in order to take full account of the evidence generated
7	recognising false statements relating to a passage	the understanding of gist can be identified through simply marking right/wrong; there is a risk of alternative interpretations of the text by pupils	pupils can mark their contributions themselves although a detailed teacher-led feedback session can be useful
8	answering comprehension questions in the TL	pupils must be aware of the need to answer in the TL; it needs to be clear whether comprehension or the ability to respond accurately in the TL is being assessed	you need to mark the work yourself to ensure consistency; qualitative feedback (written comments), as opposed to grades, should reward accurate expression
9	sequencing and reassembling texts	the reasons for pupils' choices should be more important than the final product; the process is not reliable, but it is valid and manageable	you should provide opportunities to discuss the process rather than simply grades awarded; you could give feedback through peer discussion
10	summaries	pupils' development can be monitored if the focus is on the process; the risk is that productive skills are assessed instead of comprehension; validity is high, despite the low level of reliability	you should assess pupils' plans, application and knowledge separately and attach qualitative comments to any grades; allocate grades to the different skills displayed

Figure 10.4 Receptive language skills – listening and reading

---

Task 10.3 Identifying assessment criteria

The activities in Figures 10.4–10.6 are presented outside the context of the unit of work they would have been designed for.

Hypothesise about the learning objectives which might be associated with these activities, and draw up a list of criteria against which you could assess pupils when carrying out work related to these activities.

No.	Activity	Features	Implications for teachers
1	whole class question and answer	pupils may lack the confidence to contribute despite being able to do so; the general tone and enthusiasm of the class are subjective indicators for achievement	you need to structure and target questions carefully in order to acquire a general picture of the entire group's achievement
2	structured role play	the amount of time needed constrains manageability; assessment criteria are particularly important and the content needs to be defined; there is a need to distinguish between memory skills and the ability to build language independently	you need to focus marking on particular criteria; instructions must be very clear; the focus should be communicative competence
3	open-ended role play	allows pupils to produce language independently; future learning needs can be identified; it can be difficult to relate criteria to individuals' competence	as marking can be subjective, you need to identify clear criteria; one outcome could be the identification of personal objectives and targets for future development
4	information gap in pairs/ groups	the ability to communicate the message is important; reliability is low as the reaction of the partner is unpredictable; the direct experience is authentic but lacking in objectivity	you are the observer; pupil self-assessment is a feature of this activity
5	oral presentation	explicit criteria are particularly important and the content needs to be clearly defined	you need to brief pupils in advance of the presentation; there is potential for peer assessment to support your judgements
6	oral essay responding to stimuli	pupils need to be familiar with the task type and the content; there might be tensions between the open-ended nature of the task and the invariably limited linguistic means of pupils	performance requires rehearsals; peer assessment is possible if all are aware of the criteria; grading should be based on broad indicators
7	conversation/ interview	realistic conversations require an integration of speaking and listening skills; the authenticity of such a direct assessment reduces validity and reliability	you should allow pupils to lead the conversation and react to the unexpected; qualitative comments should be reflected in the grades awarded

Figure 10.5 Productive language skills – speaking

No.	Activity	Features	Implications for teachers
1	labelling, listing and vocabulary tests	these 'low level' activities reflect knowledge of the TL but demonstrate no application skills	useful as interim assessments; self-assessment is possible
2	writing messages	the ability to communicate the message is important; tasks can be differentiated	you need to reward successful communication; over-correction can be inhibiting
3	repetitive drill exercises	tasks are not authentic but have diagnostic value	such exercises serve as useful interim assessments; their content should not be divorced from the communicative context
4	essays and free expression	the integrative nature of the task means that poor knowledge can hide an ability to write and vice versa; successful application of process skills can be shown through clarity of expression; essay writing is not authentic but pupils tend to consider it to be a valid assessment task	you should separate grades for knowledge and process skills

Figure 10.6 Productive language skills – writing

GENERAL TYPES OF MFL ASSESSMENT USED IN SECONDARY SCHOOLS

This section discusses three general types of internal and external assessment associated with MFL teaching and learning in secondary school:

1   teacher assessment (formative and/or summative);
2   pupil self- and/or peer assessment;
3   national tests and/or tasks.

We have already noted that MFL assessment needs to be related to the specific statutory requirements as well as to the learning objectives of units of work and particular lessons.

Teacher assessment

Teachers' professional judgement is essential in the assessment process. Assessment and testing need to arise naturally out of the teaching and learning context. In the course of initial teacher education (ITE), you need to learn to make valid and reliable judgements about pupils' progress in terms of the statutory requirements and/or the examination specifications as well as in relation to lesson and unit of work objectives. MFL teachers in England are currently required to report on pupils' attainment in terms of NC levels across the four skills of listening, speaking, reading and writing. Familiarity with the MFL department's and school experience school's assessment policies is another prerequisite for developing competence in assessing pupils' achievement and attainment. A typical departmental policy on assessment might cover, for instance:

- agreement trialling, that is, marking and grading pupils' work and matching it to the statutory framework and/or grade descriptions as a team;
- target setting with and for pupils;
- the use of self- and peer assessment;
- marks/comments and feedback;
- the nature of a departmental portfolio including samples of annotated pupils' work (pieces of pupils' work, which are cross-referenced to the statutory requirements and have teacher comments attached explaining, for instance, how the work was completed) in order to reach a shared understanding and interpretation of the statutory requirements;
- the overt use of assessment criteria clearly linked to teaching and learning objectives;
- a mixture of both continuous and summative assessment activities covering all four attainment targets (ATs) across a range of different contexts/topics including a range of different task types;
- the use of effective, multi-skill language activities for assessment;
- the use of the TL for instructions and feedback on assessment tasks;
- the systems to be used for marking/grading pupils' work;
- the use of dictionaries.

Task 10.4 Agreement trialling

Listen to various examples of recordings of pupils' oral language production and look at some examples of pupils' written work. Try to match the pupils' work to the statutory framework or other relevant assessment criteria. For instance, what statements of the programme of study (PoS) or levels do the pieces of work cover?

You can reach your judgement on pupils' level of attainment/achievement through continuous/formative assessment, using normal teaching activities to yield assessment evidence, or through specifically designed summative assessment, for instance, end-of-unit tests. For details, see Mutton (2007).

> **Task 10.5 Devising summative teacher assessment**
>
> 1 Devise an end-of-unit test for a class you are currently teaching. Clearly relate it to the unit objectives, base it on the principle of TL use, cover all four skill areas and match individual tasks to the statutory framework.
> 2 Discuss your test with your tutor or the relevant class teacher and ask if you can administer the test to pupils. Then, mark the scripts. Note any queries, problems, insecurities, observations, etc. you have as a basis for a follow-up discussion with your tutor or the class teacher.
> 3 Also, speak to a couple of pupils immediately after they have taken the test. Ask them if they feel that the test allowed them to demonstrate what they think they *can do, understand* and *know*. Find out what they *liked* and *disliked* about the unit and the end-of-unit test.

Marking, recording and reporting

An integral part of teacher assessment is the marking and correction of errors in pupils' oral language production and written work, such as homework, exercise books or coursework. Marking and error correction are means of providing diagnostic feedback to learners about their progress, achievement, attainment and/or performance.

For you as an MFL student teacher the departmental handbook is a useful point of reference as it usually features a policy statement on marking. Marking policies should be in line with the overall school policy ensuring consistency across members of a department but also across school subjects for the benefit of the various 'audiences' of assessment such as pupils, parents, inspectors and the wider public. The departmental policy on marking might, for instance, give guidance on how criteria for assessment or the terminology of the statutory framework can be made available in a language that is readily understood by pupils. It might include guidance on when and how to use grades, ticks and/or verbal comments. There might be reference to the use of the TL, that is, when to use the TL and when to comment in English. If the departmental policy contains a list of phrases or a bank of comments in the TL to provide feedback on pupils' written work, you should use it.

There are a range of different types of errors such as (see Beaton 1990: 42–4):

- *grammatical errors*, for instance, in the formation and structure of words (morphological), in the meaning of words (semantic), in the building of sentences (syntactic) or in spelling (orthographic) and punctuation;
- *failures in 'sociolinguistic competence'*: the inappropriate use of language in relation to the social context, e.g. use of the informal '*du*' form in a formal situation;
- *failures in 'strategic competence'*: e.g. lack of 'repair' strategies in the case of a breakdown in communication and lack of availability of alternative means of expression;
- *errors in the instrumental function of language*: lack of success in transactional terms for a variety of reasons such as bad pronunciation.

The following three hypothetical pupil questions posed by Page (1990: i–ii) are very important when discussing marking and error correction. They might be addressed in the departmental documentation and you should seek advice on departmental practices in these respects:

1   What do you mean, it's wrong?
2   What do I have to do to make it better?
3   Why should I get it right anyway?

The first question requires the teacher to define what a defective performance is and the second what action is to be taken in order to improve it. . . .

If communicative competence is the objective, why do the adjectives have to agree anyway since, in the main, mistakes in agreement do not affect communication?

It is important to recognise that there are no definite answers to the questions identified by Page above. Answers vary (see Beaton 1990: 40–1) according to:

- *the level of the pupils*: for instance, insecurities in the formulation of the future tense are approached differently when made by a Year 8 pupil who has just been introduced to the concept as opposed to a Year 11 pupil preparing for public examination;
- *the objectives associated with the task*: for instance, in a gap-filling exercise designed to assess how well pupils have understood the concept of difference in gender, respective mistakes are less likely to be tolerated than in a piece of creative writing;
- *the interaction mode between teacher and pupil*: for instance, whether mistakes occur in a written or oral utterance, in whole-class or pair or group work situations.

You need to be clear what constitutes mistakes or unacceptable deviations from the expected norm and feed back to the pupil what can be done to remedy mistakes.

Research into assessment for learning has focused a great deal on comments and marks. Comments, particularly where they are specific (both linguistically and regarding content, structure, etc.), and where the advice can be implemented by the pupil to improve her learning are felt to be most useful, whereas simply giving marks or grades 'can have a *negative* effect as pupils will not read comments aimed at improving work as they will automatically look at the grade first' (Black *et al.* 2002: 9).

If assessment/marking criteria are clear, a short checklist on what has been done/not done can give more time/opportunity for constructive comments or make comments relevant to the stage the learners at (NC, GCSE, GCE AS, etc.). Targets can be set by the teacher and by the pupil and almost a dialogue can arise where teacher and pupil are genuinely discussing ways to improve learning. This arises more naturally if a question is asked in the comments e.g. 'Can you add more varied adjectives?'. In order to help pupils learn from their mistakes and for them to build on diagnostic feedback, pupils should be encouraged to re-examine marked pieces of work and correct certain mistakes, as well as implement advice. This should involve a two-way process. You may have written some excellent and helpful comments which, if followed, should help the learner make progress. This only happens if the learner engages with these comments. It could be an expectation in your class that learners write a response to your comments, perhaps immediately (e.g. setting themselves what they see as an appropriate target arising from the comments) or on their next piece of work, indicating how the comments have been acted upon. A difficult area to find definitive answers is whether all mistakes need to be corrected all the time, which could be very demotivating, or whether 'marking' should focus on learning objectives paramount at that particular point. There are also issues with regard to assessing tasks where content and language are both focused upon, such as in content and language integrated learning (CLIL) work (see Morgan 2006).

Task 10.6 Departmental marking policy

1 Study the marking policy of the MFL department at your school experience school.
2 Ask your school-based tutor or a class teacher with whom you work closely if you can have a look at a set of books/some pieces of work she has marked to help you with the implementation of the departmental policy. Some MFL departments have statement banks with relevant comments, which help you in marking.
3 Ask your tutor or the class teacher for an opportunity to mark a set of books following the recommended procedures. Make a note of any queries, problems, insecurities or observations you have. Then, discuss your queries with your tutor or the class teacher and ask for her advice.

Once assessment evidence has been generated, you have to record it systematically with a view to reporting it to relevant parties, such as pupils or parents. Currently, parents in England are entitled to one written report on their child's progress per academic year and a report in terms of NC levels per AT at the end of Key Stage 3.

In order to be able to identify pupils' progress in terms of individual skills, many MFL teachers subdivide their mark books into sections. See Figure 10.7 for an example of how this might be done.

The section on the TL allows you to record, for example, spontaneous use of the TL in role play situations or pupils making a particular effort in using the TL in pupil–teacher and pupil–pupil interactions. In assessing pupils' spoken language, you should offer encouragement to pupils who make contributions to lessons. To record these in the mark book might provide an incentive to some pupils. Also, to accept approximations might be a useful strategy to encourage oral TL production by pupils. In another section, the individual term targets set for and by pupils could be recorded in the markbook, as well as more formal targets and other data, e.g. schools now expect all pupils to have a target grade for GCSE which is recorded and monitored.

Name	TL use	Listening		Speaking		Reading		Writing		Homework	
		level / mark incl. bench-mark	. . .								
Date											
1.											
2.											
. . .											
Nature of activity											

Figure 10.7 Sample mark book page

The grading systems used to record MFL marks varies from school to school with some departments, for instance, awarding numbers out of 10, others using a system based on letters. Whichever system is used, there should be consistency between teachers.

Task 10.7 Recording assessments in the mark book

1   Discuss with your tutor the departmental approach to recording marks in the markbook. Agree with her how you should record marks of assessments you are undertaking.

2   Then, record assessments you have carried out on the basis of the guidelines given to you. Discuss your progress and any difficulties with your tutor.

Task 10.8 Writing a report

1   Find out about the school's policy for report writing and ask your tutor for some specimen report proformas and sample reports. On the basis of your own records, your 'professional' opinion and the sample reports, write a report on a number of pupils of different abilities of a class you teach. Choose pupils your tutor also knows well.

2   Discuss the reports you have written with your tutor. Do they reflect what she thinks of the pupils? Did you have enough evidence to formulate objective judgements?

Pupil self- and/or peer assessment

The importance of the involvement of pupils in the assessment process is widely recognised:

> Learners need to know:
>
> - Where they are in their learning
> - Where they are going
> - How to get there
> - Peer and self-assessment help learners to understand this.
>
> (Black 2005)

Self- and peer assessment (see also Stobart and Gipps 1997: 17; Morley and Truscott 2006) are part of the assessment for learning process, and can be built in to MFL teaching and learning. It should be part of your planning process to integrate this type of assessment in to the series of lessons, so that pupils benefit as much as possible from the input. A possible order for how your learners might engage in assessment of their learning could be as follows:

1 Self-assessment of work (using personalised checklist and specific criteria for task).
2 Peer assessment (using criteria).
3 More self-assessment.
4 Teacher assessment.

To be most profitable, this process should ideally focus on key pieces of work, although the principles above could apply to any task. Ideas and criteria need to be shared with the class via overhead projector (OHP), copies or interactive whiteboard (IWB). Plenaries also have a vital role to play: how well have they, as individuals, met the lesson objectives? What needs to be done now? Many schools now have target sheets at the end of a week's work: what I've learned, what I need to do now, targets in all four skills. End-of-unit profiles or 'can-do' checklists allow pupils to evaluate themselves and set targets. These are increasingly included in coursebooks as 'Lernzielkontrollen' or 'bilans'. The use of the TL by pupils and teachers needs to be given particular attention when carrying out such activities. Individual or small group support from the foreign language assistant (FLA) is one strategy you can use to maximise the use of the TL when working with 'can-do' checklists. In order to be able to assess themselves effectively, learners need:

1 to be aware of the specific objectives of a task/lesson/unit;
2 to be able to make meaningful comments on their own/their peers' performance in these areas.

These might include a wide range of elements, each of which needs to be clear to learners and each requires practice for them to be able to make comments which are useful and constructive. Such practice should also include examples of good responses, so they have a benchmark for what they are looking for. Individual items may include:

- pronunciation of new items;
- overall pronunciation (how French/German/Spanish did I/you sound?);
- inclusion of all required 'bits' (i.e. did I/you make sure all elements of the task were complete?);
- accuracy of tenses, adjectives, possessives, etc.;
- range of language used (did you/I include different tenses, different sentence structures, etc?).

To enable learners to be able to make real learning sense of assessment activities such as these and to keep a record, many departments and MFL teachers use simple checklists with certain key activities on which pupils can record their assessment of themselves and their peer's assessment of their work (the list may require a score or a comment or both). For many shorter tasks, some element of self- and peer assessment may be appropriate, but this is often best achieved through a generic style set of questions/prompts which can apply to most oral/written tasks for example. This type of assessment for learning may be particularly appropriate in a plenary, when the real process of learning is being discussed. In order to do this in the TL, you need to offer possible comments and/or collate some with the class.

How can pupils self-assess?

- self-checking activities;
- routinely testing themselves on vocabulary;
- carefully scrutinising their work/assignments before submitting them to the assessment of others (personal 'First Aid Kit', see Barnes and Hunt 2003);
- checking achievement against 'can do' lists;
- developing ability to identify own weaknesses and difficulties (traffic light system);
- using benchmarks as a model for own work.

How can pupils peer assess? (based on Black 2005):

- criteria need to be understood;
- modelling exercises are needed where task requirements are abstract;
- need for justifying WHY something is better/correct, etc. – encourage learners to discuss their own examples;
- need to learn to collaborate and listen to each other;
- in groups, give group members roles – one can be the 'challenger': whenever anyone comes up with something, the challenger says 'why'?, etc.;
- teach learners to assess their progress keeping the aims and criteria in mind, to become independent;
- get pupils to look at tests and invent the mark scheme, get them to set questions for tests, so they can decide what makes a good question, why set it, etc.

Assessing speaking: an example of possibilities

First, self-assessment and/or peer assessment could take place using criteria you have supplied at the start of the task (e.g. simple tick sheets listing elements to be included such as hobby, day of the week, with whom, where, opinion, as well as broader issues such as accuracy of pronunciation). The class could then work out what would be an excellent response, given the criteria. Alternatively, an excellent response could be presented *first* as a model to be adapted. The approach should vary according to the stage of the learning:

- how much support do the pupils need?
- do certain pupil groups need support while others can work in a more open manner?

A plenary to this activity could consist of a discussion on what *exactly* makes an excellent response to this task and what now needs to be done to improve. Pupils can decide then on their own individual targets arising out of the activity. An additional element to activities such as this on some occasions could link the activity and responses to NC levels, with pupils looking at the level descriptions and deciding whether their response matches the criteria.

In the example in Figure 10.8, the level descriptions of the NC are broadly applied to 'holidays and leisure activities'. Pupils assess their attainment by marking the relevant boxes with a diagonal line when a task is attempted, followed by a second diagonal line forming a cross when the task is successfully completed. When you have assessed the task the box can be coloured in. Cross-referencing learning outcomes occasionally against the statutory framework and/or examination specifications allows pupils to become aware of what is required to improve and progress as well as of the different levels of difficulty of certain tasks and activities. While evidence from such pupil self-assessment tasks serves a real purpose in that it helps to diagnose learning needs and to describe progress, it cannot be equated with formal attainment at the given level. However, this approach allows pupils to become involved in the assessment process and take responsibility for part of it. With advanced/higher ability learners this approach might even be attempted in the TL with guidance from the FLA.

Assessment at KS4 and the General Certificate of Secondary Education (GCSE)

There is a range of different assessment opportunities at Key Stage 4:

- GCSE Full or Short Courses;
- Other approved qualifications, some of which are for pupils attaining below NC level 3.

Care needs to be taken that the qualifications chosen by a school at the end of Key Stage 4 are approved (see http://www.accreditedqualifications.org.uk/).

Level	AT1 Listening	AT2 Speaking	AT3 Reading	AT4 Writing
5	To be able to understand when someone explains about a possible date, e.g. cinema, disco, etc. ☐	To be able to respond to a suggested date, making suggestions and negotiating a meeting place and time. ☐	To be able to extract details of tourist amenities from authentic brochures. To be able to revise an itinerary from details available with a set budget and constraints. ☐	To be able to seek details from a tourist information office in preparation for a future holiday; friends recommended the area and you would like more details. ☐
6	To be able to understand details of tourist spots when described by the attendant at the tourist office. To be able to recognise recommendations as well as details of prices, times, costs, etc. ☐	To be able to give an oral account of activities when on holiday abroad. To be able to ask a friend about details of his/her holiday. ☐	From a range of texts, to be able to comment upon the events related to someone's holiday. To be able to plan a holiday in a different location for particular people from details of previous holidays. ☐	To be able to complete a diary for a holiday at a given location; write postcards to friends to provide more detail of the events portrayed in the diary. ☐
7	To be able to follow and understand advertisements about holiday locations from TV or audio broadcast. ☐	To be able to provide a critical narrative of local amenities for tourists from notes – but not from a script. ☐	To be able to understand relevant details from an official proposal for a holiday theme park planned for the locality. ☐	To be able to produce a leaflet supporting / protesting against the proposed holiday theme park planned for the locality. ☐

Figure 10.8 Pupil self-assessment sheet 'Holidays and leisure activities'

The GCSE examination is externally set and administered by Awarding Bodies. Specifications must adhere to the GCSE criteria laid down by the Qualifications and Curriculum Authority (see http://www.qca.gov.uk). At the time of writing, schools can choose from the following Awarding Bodies: the Assessment and Qualifications Alliance (AQA, available at http://www.aqa.org.uk/), the Edexcel Foundation (available at http://www.edexcel.org.uk/) and Oxford, Cambridge and RSA Examinations (OCR, available at http://www.ocr.org.uk/).

The distinctive features of GCSE examinations are expressed in the aims of the GCSE draft criteria for MFLs (QCA 2007a), which state that GCSE specifications in modern foreign languages should encourage pupils:

- to derive enjoyment and benefit from language learning by following a coherent, satisfying and worthwhile course of study;
- to develop understanding of the language in a variety of contexts;
- to develop knowledge of the language and language learning skills;
- to develop the ability to communicate effectively in the language;
- to develop awareness and understanding of countries and communities where the language is spoken;
- to recognise that their linguistic knowledge, understanding and skills help them to take their place in a multilingual global society and also provide them with a suitable basis for further study and practical use of the language.

At the time of writing, the GCSE comprises separate assessment components for all four ATs. The Assessment Objectives (AO) in the criteria are listed below (QCA 2007a), and can vary in individual specifications from 20–30 per cent of the total assessment:

- AO1 Understand spoken language
- AO2 Communicate in speech
- AO3 Understand written language
- AO4 Communicate in writing.

Short courses cover two of the four assessment objectives.

Continuous or periodic assessment, such as coursework, has the advantage of spreading assessment over a period of time rather than grouping it all at the end. The GCSE coursework option tended to be used by many schools for the assessment of pupils' written work under the criteria pre-2007. Coursework is, however, likely to be less prominent in many subjects including MFL in the next few years after announcements made by the QCA in 2006 http://www.qca.org.uk/2586_17443.html. According to their review, there should no longer be teacher-set and assessed coursework in MFL. It should be replaced by controlled assessments. In the latest GCSE criteria, it is stated that at least 75 per cent of the assessment must be externally marked, leaving a maximum of 25 per cent for controlled assessment. The draft criteria (QCA 2007a) outline what is expected of controlled assessments.

The use of dictionaries is not permitted in any external assessment in the GCSE criteria (ibid.). While there clearly are problems associated with incorrect use, including overuse, of dictionaries in examinations, the ban on dictionaries in examinations can be seen to be questionable as far as the development in pupils of desirable foreign language learning skills is concerned. Also, it sits uneasily with requirement 2.1e of the 2007 PoS NC, which states that pupils should be able to 'use reference materials such as dictionaries appropriately and effectively'.

Task 10.9 GCSE specifications

Ask your tutor or the relevant colleague at your school experience school for a copy of the GCSE specification used in the school and familiarise yourself with its specific requirements. What do you perceive to be the strengths and weaknesses? What implications can you discern for your work with Key Stage 4 classes?

The GCSE criteria specify that for AO2 and AO4 (speaking and writing) 'at least 10% of the total marks for the subject must be allocated to knowledge and accurate application of the grammar and structures of the language'. In addition, lists of specified grammatical structures for French, German and Spanish are included.

The GCSE is not without problems and critics. Lack of space does not allow for a detailed analysis here but a few points can, nevertheless, be enumerated:

- Despite the 25 per cent controlled assessment option, the GCSE is ostensibly a terminal examination, testing the outcomes of five years of study, rather than an assessment of the learning process; it thereby militates against 'assessment motivation' (see Adams 2000: 207) and places a lot of emphasis on memorisation.

- The fitness for purpose of the examination is questionable: to what extent does it test what pupils should be taught in the context of the NC? For example, how well are pupils' cultural awareness or their ability to use reference material examined?

- The examination appears to have a considerable backwash effect on teaching and learning at Key Stage 4, often leading to the PoS of the NC being relegated in favour of 'teaching to the test'. This can result in a narrow rote-learning approach and has led to considerable emphasis being placed by many departments on the teaching of examination techniques and examination practice, for example in the form of so-called mock exams. See also Barnes (1999).

- The policy of testing in the TL (i.e. the requirement for test questions and answers to be in the TL) together with a skills-based approach (i.e. separate papers for listening, speaking, reading and writing) raises certain questions about the reliability and validity of the examination: how authentic are the tasks pupils are asked to perform, i.e. to what extent do they mirror real-life TL use? For example, to what extent are spontaneity and unpredictability of real-time language use reflected in the examination?

Pachler (2000a: 30) posits that the methodology underpinning the GCSE is characterised by:

> a narrow transactional-functional orientation in which pupils are prepared for the linguistic (and non-linguistic) needs of tourists, such as making travel arrangements, going to bars, restaurants, museums, booking into hotels,

buying petrol for the car etc, with the emphasis on 'getting by'. On the one hand this approach is characterised by a heavy emphasis on recall of often random lexical items and phrases derived from narrowly defined, idealised interactions and exchanges at the cost of transfer of knowledge and skills across topics. On the other hand, it tends to ignore the teenage learner's communicative needs and does not allow her to engage in meaningful and realistic interaction, both supposedly central tenets of communicative methodology.

This view is supported by research into examination performance by cognitive psychologists, who found that IQ had no impact on GCSE examination performance. Instead, general memory ability was found to account for up to 20 per cent of variance in examination results, which suggests that the GCSE relies more on memory than on understanding. According to the report:

> [for] all candidates above a basic intelligence threshold, GCSE favoured those who could reproduce memorised material rather than those who were capable of devising original solutions (Cassidy 1999).

The report also suggests that factors such as motivation, application, study methods and home background were significant factors of GCSE performance.

At the time of writing it remains to be seen whether recent changes to the NC, as well as the draft GCSE criteria (QCA 2007a), such as the increased emphasis on language understanding, and the introduction of more choice, both in the specifications and possibly for individual schools to make their own suggestions, are sufficient to address the weaknesses identified above:

> We still appear to be operating in an environment where the link between assessment and learning is that assessment determines the curriculum – decisions of how a subject is to be tested are made before content and teaching methods are decided.
>
> (Adams 2000: 208)

SUMMARY

Assessment should be integral to MFL teaching and learning and not 'bolt-on'. It is multifaceted and serves many purposes.

Teacher assessment, aimed at providing constructive guidance and information on the teaching and learning process, is governed by your professional judgement based on knowledge of specific groups of pupils.

Pupil peer and self-assessment should be used in order to allow pupils to feel ownership of and take responsibility for their learning.

You are required to work within the respective national statutory assessment framework. It is one of your responsibilities to prepare pupils for external assessment at the end of secondary schooling. Familiarity with the statutory requirements for internal and external assessment is, therefore, imperative.

FURTHER READING

Barnes, A. and Hunt, M. (2003) *Effective Assessment in MFL*. London: CILT.

This book looks at all the main aspects of assessment in MFL and has a number of practical activities and reflective tasks to enable you to develop a deeper understanding of the issues.

Jones, J. and William, D. (2007) *Modern Foreign Languages inside the black box. Assessment for learning in the Modern Foreign Languages classroom*. London: GL Assessment.

This booklet suggests a range of ideas on how to develop formative assessment and on how to promote pupils' learning.

Black, P. and Jones, J. (2006) 'Formative assessment and the learning and teaching of MFL: sharing the language learning road map with the learners', *Language Learning Journal*, 34: 4–9.

An article jointly written by an MFL teacher educator and an assessment researcher which brings together the generic aspects of assessment for learning with the subject specific requirements of MFL.

11 Managing resources and learners in the MFL classroom

INTRODUCTION

As a modern foreign languages (MFL) student teacher you should have a whole range of material and resources at your disposal. The nature of the subject requires a variety of methods and material and a regular change of focus. The restricted range of linguistic means available to pupils to express themselves and the need to cover the language skills of listening, speaking, reading and writing equally are determining factors. Some resources are used with great regularity, others are deployed from time to time to enhance and enrich learning experiences. This chapter covers the most commonly used resources, namely those, which find application in almost every lesson.

The use of material and resources in the classroom is inevitably related to teaching and learning activities discussed in Chapter 6 and elsewhere in this book. Engaging pupils in a wide range of activity types demands highly developed classroom management skills. Pupils need to be guided and instructed how to use learning material effectively. For internet-based approaches, see Pachler (2007b).

The effective management of learning processes is integral to good teaching. There are generic issues and strategies, which are discussed in many useful publications, e.g. Neill (1993) or Watkins (1999). In this chapter we discuss the issue, which is of considerable concern to you embarking upon your first experience of classroom teaching, in the context of foreign language teaching and learning and in relation to the use of specific resources and material.

The effective use of resources and material is an essential component of effective teaching and learning. Pupils need to know the purpose of activities and the value of resources in relation to lesson objectives. Establishing positive attitudes to activities aids transition and makes the relevance of learning activities understood. To stimulate the use of the target language (TL) in the classroom requires careful planning and the encouragement of pupil involvement. Pupil participation depends upon pupils being interested, motivated, challenged and capable of full engagement. None of these can be taken for granted.

You should not be a slave to the resources available. As seen in Chapter 4, learning objectives in units of work and lesson plans should determine the process of learning. Course and supplementary material should be selected in line with the learning objectives and the coursebook.

The development of linguistic skills and cultural awareness is best achieved through a variety of means. The writers and publishers of course material tend to be acutely aware of this. For many years now course materials have included audio material, visual aids, worksheets and, more recently, DV material and computer software and associated websites. But it is very difficult for one single coursebook and its ancillary material to cover all aspects at the same depth and with the same quality.

The various versions of the National Curriculum (NC) stimulated the publication of much new course material. Due to the confines of this book, let alone this chapter, as well as rapid changes in this field, a detailed evaluation of available resources for different MFL is not feasible. There are, however, professional organisations and bodies such as the National Centre for Languages (CILT; available at http://www.cilt.org.uk) and the Association for Language Learning (ALL; available at http://www.all-languages.org.uk/) that offer strong support networks and publish useful MFL-specific publications and resources.

Learners must take part in different types of activities ranging from whole class work, small group work, pair work to individual/independent work – all covering the skills of listening, speaking, reading and writing. This 'four by four' approach generates a multitude of variables, all of which you must bear in mind when selecting and using resources and material. You need to plan and organise activities which maximise learning opportunities. In this way, effective lesson management can be seen as an outcome of careful planning and positive teacher–pupil relationships. This is something you should always remember: a well-planned, correctly 'pitched' and 'paced' lesson is more likely to succeed as far as class management is concerned. Learners are more likely to be engaged in their learning and to see the activities as worthwhile. It is crucial that you are seen by learners to be in a position of authority, to command respect and attention and to convey high standards. Hargreaves and Evans (1997) point out that from the outset, teachers must establish a certain presence to prevent pupils from turning the classroom into a 'circus without a ringmaster'.

This chapter also provides a framework enabling you to undertake a personal evaluation of course material and indicates effective and potential uses of the range of resources and material available. You invariably have to select, adapt and generate material irrespective of whether or not a coursebook and its ancillary material are used. This requires a level of competence and confidence in the handling of resources and the recognition of the relevance and appropriateness of the material.

Many student teachers tend to be very anxious about pupil misbehaviour. By conveying high standards you can establish positive attitudes to teaching and learning activities. It would be naïve to suggest that all misbehaviour can be pre-empted, but awareness of what characterises successful lessons is a useful starting point. The Elton Report (DES 1989), among other things, identifies the following features of successful lessons: good planning, rewards for pupil effort, variety and interest, availability of resources and alertness on the part of the teacher. This advice is still valid. Adherence to clear whole-school policies and procedures and a willingness to share responsibility for the management of learners also helps to foster an atmosphere of stability and security.

Nevertheless, an awareness of the types of misbehaviour likely to occur assist you when considering pre-emptive measures. The Elton Report acknowledges that most forms of misbehaviour are, in fact, minor misdemeanours. An alert teacher can plan to pre-empt, even be aware of impending opportunities for misbehaviour – too much classroom talk, excessive noise, pupils not getting on with work set, interfering with other pupils and excessive movement. When starting your school experiences, you will soon realise that some resources and activity types can more easily lead to pupil misbehaviour than others. Focused lesson observation of experienced colleagues, careful planning, clear guidance and instructions, organisation and monitoring are necessary skills to ensure that learning rather than work avoidance takes place (see Bromfield 2006).

OBJECTIVES

By the end of this chapter you should:

- be familiar with a framework intended to guide you in evaluating the use of material and resources;
- have developed an understanding of the classroom management issues associated with different material, resources and learning activities;
- be aware of the range of resources and material available for day-to-day use in the classroom;
- recognise the potential and pitfalls associated with different resources and material;
- be aware of the role of the different resources and material in developing the language skills of listening, speaking, reading and writing.

CLASSROOM MANAGEMENT

Although use of particular types of material and resources is determined to some extent by methodological considerations, you must ensure their effective use. In our view, good practice in MFL teaching in the secondary school is characterised by a balanced and purposeful use of and the avoidance of over-concentration on particular types of material and resources. Each of the various types of material and resources has the potential to enhance, support and structure learning. Variety can help you to appeal to pupils' wide range of learning styles and interests.

In order to deploy a range of material and resources to provide the variety of activities required to maintain pupils' interests, you need to establish an agreed code of conduct. This must not be at variance with any school code of conduct and procedures. You must ensure any classroom rules you implement reflect whole school/departmental policy as appropriate.

Use of the TL for classroom management purposes demands careful consideration. Wragg (1984: 67) listed the 11 most common rules used by teachers (see Task 11.1) and you should consider how they can be operationalised in the TL.

Task 11.1 Types of classroom rules

To what extent are the following types of rules listed by Wragg relevant to the MFL classroom?

- no talking when the teacher is talking;
- no disruptive noises;
- rules for entering, leaving and moving around the classroom;
- no interference in the work of others;
- work must be completed in a specified way;
- pupils must raise hand – not shout out;
- pupils must make a positive effort in their work;
- pupils must not challenge the authority of the teacher;
- pupils must show respect for property and equipment;
- rules to do with safety;
- pupils must ask if they do not understand.

Consider how these classroom rules might be adapted and presented to pupils through use of the TL. This may include displays with symbols and pictures, role plays and teacher-led presentations. How can these be reinforced through regular use? What rewards and sanctions could be linked to the code?

Establishing and maintaining a code of conduct through rules, routines and procedures demand that you draw on a wide range of presentation and communication skills. All pupils must understand the code and recognise its value as well as the need for sanctions when it is breached. At times, classroom management will require you to use non-verbal communication as pupils may find a TL explanation difficult to follow and may feign non-comprehension as a work avoidance strategy. You must take care to be aware of gestures and postures, which signal different messages in different cultures. Not only do you need to develop and use these skills, you also need to be able to read the body language of pupils to gauge levels of interest, motivation and involvement. Robertson (1989) identifies some aspects of body language that facilitate communication and contribute to the development of positive relationships:

- *body orientation:* Your position in relation to pupils helps to determine role definition. While face-to-face on a one-to-one basis can be perceived to be confrontational, sitting side-by-side can lead to higher levels of co-operation. This is relevant for teacher–pupil (helping individuals) and pupil–pupil (e.g. pair work) interaction.
- *bodily posture:* Standing straight with the chin held high tends to indicate a wish to dominate (whole class work). Leaning towards someone with a warm smile can indicate encouragement (question and answer activities).
- *head movements:* Nodding is important as it signals permission to speak as well as agreement. Reticent speakers can be encouraged in this way (question and answer work).
- *eye contact:* Eye contact can be seen as a sign of mutual respect. The higher the interest level in a person/topic, the greater the amount of eye contact tends to be (whole class teaching).
- *use of voice:* Volume, pitch, tone, speed, expressiveness and articulation can convey messages associated with mood, e.g. anger, calm, frustration, control, interest or boredom. It is essential to exaggerate features like these to accentuate the precise meaning of what is being said (as well as to ensure that greater attention is maintained rather than the 'switching off' which may occur with a monotonous voice).
- *hands and feet:* Open postures (hands and feet pointing slightly outwards) convey a sense of welcome and calm. 'Inward pointing' represents insecurity.
- *facial expressions:* Exaggerated expressions, e.g. smiles, frowns, inquisitive looks, agreement, pleasure, should all be part of your repertoire.

Task 11.2 Giving basic instructions

Conduct a brief microteaching session with other student teachers on the theme of giving classroom instructions. As the teacher, mime all instructions (coats off, bags on the floor, pens out, books on the table, listen, repeat, copy, etc.). Once your peers have mastered the messages you are conveying, list each instruction and add the simplest form of the TL to the mimes.

Effective lesson management should be more concerned with the promotion of good behaviour and attitudes than the use of sanctions in response to misbehaviour. Rewards, praise and encouragement must be placed in the context of the TL. Many MFL departments will have developed standardised approaches through the use of agreed phrases. For a detailed discussion of TL use, see Chapter 5.

Selection and use of material and resources need to be determined by the intended learning outcomes. Effective use of certain material and resources requires particular types of activities and pupil response and the use of certain material and resources in turn affects classroom layout and seating arrangements. The characteristics of each classroom and each group, established practice, the age of pupils and the types of planned activities all affect your decisions about room layout. The use of particular resources requires focused individual work, the use of reference material, interaction with others through group and pair work or movement around the classroom to support communication (e.g. surveys). You need to consider carefully the seating arrangements which best facilitate different activity types. You should experiment with different classroom layouts. However, you should not do so without consultation with and agreement of the respective class teacher.

Essentially, four types of classroom layout can be distinguished:

- *rows:* One advantage of seating pupils in rows is that they are less able to copy and disrupt through inappropriate talk. Sitting in a row assists with concentration and disruptive pupils can be isolated from others in the class. One disadvantage is that the arrangement hinders collaborative and co-operative work. Pupils are unable to see each other's faces to assist them in the communicative process. Also, the sharing of resources and material can be problematic.
- *the horseshoe:* The teacher can stand or sit in the centre and thereby have ready access to all pupils. Pupils are able to see each other and pair work is relatively simple to organise. However, movement to the corners of the classroom can be difficult. The teacher is almost always face-to-face with pupils, even when assisting individuals with independent work.
- *groups of desks:* Not all pupils are facing the teacher for whole class work. Due to the proximity to each other, pupils might be tempted to interfere with each other's equipment. However, this greatly facilitates interaction between pupils for both, group and pair work. Movement around the classroom can be eased by careful placement of desks.
- *desks placed around the edge of the room:* Many computer rooms, for example, require pupils to face the wall, which can prevent distraction by other pupils. Often this provides a large space in the middle of a room, where teachers can work with groups of pupils who require support or extension. This arrangement can also be useful for carousel lessons. However, pupil collaboration for pupils seated around the edge of the room can be difficult, particularly where there is insufficient space between work stations or where there are no swivel chairs. Whole class explanations require pupils to move their positions.

Different teaching styles, different activities and different groups require different layouts. You need to remain flexible and be prepared to adapt according to the particular demands and needs.

This discussion of classroom management cannot provide hard and fast rules. It merely raises some issues, which warrant consideration at the planning stage. The examination of different types of resources also contains guidance on classroom management issues specific to each resource and is not intended to relate simply to the use of one particular resource.

THE COURSEBOOK

Potential and purpose

For many pupils the coursebook is their first point of contact with the TL and its culture. It can offer a form of security in that it organises the language content and conveys messages about the values, attitudes and culture of TL speakers, albeit from the point of view of its writer; the user needs to beware of this:

> One of the functions of coursebooks is to present the language in such a way that it is learned as effectively and quickly as possible. This implies that the coursebook writers have a view on how language is learned and how it is best taught. Although the coursebook may not seek to impose a rigid methodology on learners and teachers, nevertheless the way it organises its material and the kind of activities it promotes can have a profound influence on what happens in the classroom.
>
> (Cunningsworth 1995: 97)

Recent coursebooks tend to be structured and tailored to suit GCSE examination specifications and the statutory requirements such as the use of the TL for instructions and explanations. Many coursebooks and teachers books cross-reference activities and tasks to the NC and KS3 MFL framework in order to help you in your planning. Frequently, colourful photographs are used and (quasi-) authentic texts provide cultural detail in an attempt to open up pupils' minds. It could be argued that coursebooks are a quasi-authentic window to the life and culture of native speakers.

Coursebooks can contain brief summaries of the content in terms of vocabulary, structures and grammatical rules linked to particular exercises. Some provide examination practice. The coursebook can help you in sequencing activities to bridge the gap between the known and the new and provide graded exercises allowing for steady progression and lead towards independent study. It can function as a resource for presenting new language, contain reference sections on grammar and vocabulary, stimuli for classroom activities and self-directed study as well as support for student teachers (see Cunningsworth 1995: 7; Barnes, 1997).

The coursebook is primarily a resource and learning tool for pupils. It is a resource which enables pupils to work independently from the teacher. This, in turn, allows you to work with individual pupils. When using a coursebook, you need to bear in mind common causes of misbehaviour identified by Davison (2000: 122): 'boredom; an inability to do the work a teacher has set; and effort demanded for too long a period without a break'. You, therefore, need to ensure that instructions are clear and understood by all pupils. Comprehension checks are essential and they can take different forms. First, TL instructions can be translated by a pupil for the whole class. You can use question and answer techniques to ensure comprehension. Visual displays of instructions, particularly when there is more than one exercise to be completed, and demonstrations of the activity by way of an example prior to pupils commencing are very useful. Second, you should not set independent work until whole class work has enabled the practice of specific language skills and has established a confidence in pupils to undertake the task. Finally, you should set clear time limits for activities, enabling learners to pace themselves. This should, of course, be done as appropriate in the TL. Such an approach helps to establish a routine as well as a secure working environment.

Davison (2000: 126) also points out that a teacher should be 'on hand to give academic help'. Once again, it is crucial to establish routines: raising their hand before talking or using reference material before asking you are widely used strategies. Pupils should be made aware of the need to wait their turn, to ask courteously, where possible in the TL, and not to waste time waiting for assistance while you attend to other pupils but to attempt another aspect of the activity in the meantime.

It would be erroneous to assume that careful plans never go wrong. In particular, during pair, group and/or independent work it is difficult for you to be sure that all pupils are on task and fully engaged all the time. Sometimes you may need to reprimand some pupils. Kyriacou (1991: 92–6) advises that reprimands should be targeted correctly and that teachers should avoid expressing anger (see also http://www.behaviour4learning.ac.uk/). The behaviour, not the pupil, should be criticised and 'quiet words' are often more helpful than whole class reprimands. Very often positioning yourself near to potential miscreants, stares, using body language and gestures can refocus pupils without creating a hostile and confrontational atmosphere. More serious misbehaviour may require more serious action. Kyriacou (1986: 161) points out that teachers must not respond without consideration:

> What must be borne in mind is that when taking action, the teacher needs to take account of its effect on the individual pupil, its effect on the class, its relationship to school policy, and its short term and long term consequences.

During individual work you need to circulate to assist pupils with difficulties and also to monitor the activity. Research carried out in the USA (see Taylor 1994: 162) indicates that quick teacher feedback and the close monitoring of individual performance increase the quality of pupils' work. While pupils are working individually using the coursebook, you should monitor the class by looking and walking around the room. When assisting individuals, it is sensible to place yourself so that you can see the majority of the rest of the class. Turning your back to the majority of the class can be an invitation to pupils to display off-task behaviour.

Kyriacou (1991: 53) calls qualities like those described above 'withitness' and suggests that these skills improve with experience. Task 11.3 sets out a step-by-step approach to developing 'withitness'.

Task 11.3 Withitness

1   Observe an experienced teacher engaging pupils in independent and individual work. Try to identify signs of misbehaviour.
2   Relate the signs of misbehaviour to possible causes.
3   Identify strategies deployed by experienced teachers, which create the belief that they have eyes in the back of their heads.

Pitfalls and possible problems

No coursebook is perfect. In some, the presentation of new language and structures can appear cluttered. Because of a focus on the introduction and practice of new language in a wide range of topics, there are rarely extended passages. The cultural aspect of a coursebook can date quickly, which can lead to a false impression of the culture of the countries where the TL is spoken. To introduce cartoons and fictional characters in a bid to achieve greater durability by being less susceptible to changes in fashions and trends runs the risk of presenting a stereotyped or even non-TL culture-specific view of life in the target countries. Language is underpinned by the cultural and social context of its use. For commercial reasons, coursebooks tend to be designed for as large an audience as possible. They are, therefore, invariably impersonal and pupils may associate them more with life in the classroom than life in the countries where the TL is spoken. The extent to which coursebooks allow for the 'personalisation' of language through the solving of realistic problems through authentic communication tends to be limited.

Understandably, coursebooks reflect the writers' own preferred methodology. Grammar, for example, can be presented inductively or deductively but there often tends not to be much of a choice of methods within one coursebook. When using the coursebook as a guide to unit of work and lesson planning, you need to exercise professional judgement according to the learning needs of pupils and make deliberate choices and select material best suited to achieving the learning objectives identified for a particular class.

Obviously, too, the coursebook is limited in its coverage of the examination specification. According to Cunningsworth (1995: 55), syllabuses tend to contain the following:

- forms: structures and grammar;
- functions: communicative purpose;
- situations: context of language use;
- topics.

A coursebook contains a finite set of activities and exercises to cover these four aspects, which can be adequate but may also be either insufficient or ample in number. This means you need to be either selective or to supplement according to the needs of pupils and the time available. Often and importantly, you also need to grade and sequence the activities in a coursebook to take account of the needs of a particular class.

Unlike in some Continental European education systems, coursebooks do not have to be vetted by the respective government ministries for suitability. MFL departments in UK secondary schools are free to choose coursebooks from competing publishers (or not to choose one at all and to create a tailored set of resources for the department). MFL teachers need to judge the suitability of coursebooks for themselves. Many questions need to be asked about a coursebook:

- Does the coursebook lend itself to extending an active knowledge of vocabulary and does it stimulate oral work in a variety of contexts?

- Is the accompanying listening material appropriate?
- Does the coursebook develop reading strategies through a variety of types of text encouraging the use of a range of reading skills and providing information of real interest?
- Does it serve as a model of accurate writing in appropriate styles?
- Is grammar presented as well as recycled in an attractive and meaningful way?
- Is an accurate cultural impression presented, free of negative stereotyping in terms of class, gender, race, ethnicity, social relationships and personal feelings?

The coursebook is a teaching and learning tool and should be used and adapted to fit a specific learning context rather than simply be followed. Cunningsworth (1995: 137) suggests a useful method to decide whether to adapt an exercise or change it altogether. This method is shown in a slightly modified form in Figure 11.1.

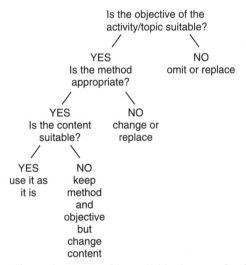

Figure 11.1 Flow-chart for evaluating teaching activities in coursebooks

---

Task 11.4 Evaluating a coursebook

The following task is meant to help you to evaluate a coursebook (adapted from Cunningsworth 1995: 3–4):

1   Select a coursebook used by a class you have observed or teach and use the criteria in Figure 11.2 to evaluate it.
2   Where any responses to these questions are negative, consider in what ways the course material could be supplemented and/or adapted.

No.	Criteria	Evaluation
A	**Aims and objectives**	
1	Do the aims of the coursebook correspond to aims and objectives expressed in units of work?	
2	Does the coursebook allow for different teaching and learning styles?	
3	Is the coursebook comprehensive in its coverage of topics?	
B	**Design and organisation**	
1	What components make up the total course?	
2	How is the content organised? (structures, functions, topics, skills)	
3	Are the grading of exercises and progression suitable for all learners?	
4	Is there adequate recycling and revision?	
5	Are there reference sections? (grammar, vocabulary, etc.).	
C	**Language content**	
1	Does the coursebook provide material and activities to allow for vocabulary and grammar learning?	
2	Does the material include opportunities for pronunciation work?	
3	Are style and appropriacy accounted for?	
4	Are there examples of language use in a range of contexts?	
D	**Skills**	
1	Is equal emphasis placed on the development of all four skills?	
2	Are there opportunities for the integration of skills?	
3	Is the content of extended reading passages suitable for learners' interests and the level of the majority?	
4	Are listening materials authentic and accompanied by background information? Are exercises graded?	
5	Are speaking activities designed to equip learners for real life interactions?	
6	Do writing activities allow for a suitable range of styles?	
E	**Topics**	
1	Is there enough variety and range of topics?	
2	Will the topics help to expand learners' cultural awareness?	
3	Are women portrayed and represented equally to men?	

4	Are people represented with reference to ethnic origin, occupation, disability, etc.?	
F	**Methodology**	
1	Is the methodology underpinning the coursebook suitable for the learning environment?	
2	What level of learner involvement is expected?	
3	How broad is the range of activities for presenting new language?	
4	Is communicative competence developed?	
5	Does the coursebook contain advice to learners on study skills and learning strategies?	
G	**Teacher's book**	
1	Is there adequate guidance for teachers on the use of the coursebook and accompanying materials?	
2	Do accompanying materials adequately cover teaching techniques for language items such as grammar and culturally specific information?	
H	**Practical considerations**	
1	What is the total cost of the coursebook and associated material?	
2	Are the books strong and long-lasting?	
3	Are the materials attractive?	
4	Do any of the materials require particular equipment and if so are these available in the department?	
5	Can the course be used without particular materials?	
6	What can and cannot be copied?	

Figure 11.2 Criteria for choosing a coursebook

Task 11.5 The coursebook and the statutory framework

Analyse one unit of work of your choice for Key Stage 3 and one for Key Stage 4 in a coursebook used by your school experience school and describe to what extent the programme of study (PoS) statements of the National Curriculum are met. Figure 11.3 shows a sample recording sheet for the PoS for England.

Discuss the findings with your tutor or a class teacher you work with frequently.

No.	Statement	Comment
1.1 a	Developing the skills of listening, speaking, reading and writing in a range of situations and contexts	
1.2 b	Recognising that languages differ but may share common grammatical, syntactical or lexical features	
1.3 b	Using imagination to express thoughts, ideas, experiences and feelings	
1.4 a	Appreciating the richness and diversity of other cultures	
2.1 e	Use reference materials such as dictionaries appropriately and effectively	
2.2 k	Deal with unfamiliar language, unexpected responses and unpredictable situations	
3 b	The interrelationship between sounds and writing in the target language	
3 d	A range of vocabulary and structures	

Figure 11.3 Matching NC PoS statements to MFL coursebook activities

VISUAL AIDS

Most coursebooks now provide a wealth of visual aids in the form of overhead transparencies, flashcards, cue cards, information and communications technology (ICT) and video material. You often supplement these with similar aids designed by you and also with posters, diagrams and display work. All have their place in the learning process and provide useful foci for pupils' work.

Potential and purpose

Visual aids are often used to present new language forms and to promote the practice of the language skills of listening, speaking, reading and writing. They provide a non-verbal link between the actual language used and the idea or concept expressed. David Nunan notes that the use of realia and/or symbolic representation is close to the 'natural approach' (see Nunan 1989: 195). As the link between words and concepts represented by visual aids is in the main arbitrary – with possibly the exception of onomatopoetic words – they can be used to avoid translation. Translation could be considered an obstacle at this early stage of learning as it can slow down and lengthen the process of skill development. An overemphasis on word-for-word translation can be considered as a hindrance.

In order to facilitate the learning process, visual aids should be clear and instantly recognisable. You need to help the learner progress beyond simple one-word utterances. Visual aids should, therefore, also represent a series of words and phrases rather than just single items. It should be recognisable by all pupils, irrespective, for instance, of their ethnic or social background, but at the same time it should represent the cultural context of the TL where possible. The use of bold colours and simple pictorial representations tend to ensure easy recognition by pupils.

The use of flashcards is usually associated with whole class work. It requires high levels of pupil concentration and participation. Ground rules need to be clear. Chapter 6 provides suggestions for activities, some of which require pupils to put hands up, others to shout out. You need to make the conditions clear and to establish routines for different activity types. Pupils are required to speak publicly, which demands a non-threatening and supportive atmosphere. Kyriacou (1991: 66) asserts the need for the teacher to appear calm and controlled. Placing flashcards in order, not dropping them on the floor, effectively targeting and sequencing of questions all contribute to this aura. You may well wish to script questions on the reverse side of flashcards to ensure pace and flow.

Flashcards should be made visible to all pupils. The layout of the classroom is important. A horseshoe layout lends itself well to flashcard work, enabling equal access for all pupils and allowing you to approach individuals as a means of securing their attention and targeting questions.

You need to make it a priority to get to know and use pupils' names to be able to target questions. Individual pupils should be asked questions they can answer, to encourage participation. For some this will involve simple repetition and for others the answering of open questions. You should use praise and encouragement freely. Pupils failing to respond should be asked similar questions again at a later stage to demonstrate care and concern for their progress. This helps you to demonstrate that you make good use of pupil responses and that learning outcomes are ensured for all pupils in the class (see Kyriacou 1986: 105).

A further teaching skill identified by Kyriacou in whole class teaching activities is the maintenance of pace and flow. Chapter 6 illustrates several activities, which can be undertaken with presentation software, flashcards or overhead transparencies. Maintaining pace means adjusting activities as pupils seem ready, not necessarily changing resources. Very often activities to follow the use of flashcards and other visuals are slower in pace and calming. Susan Halliwell (1991b: 3–4) suggests the notion of 'stirrers' and 'settlers', which can help to maximise pupil participation and prevents the risk of over-excitement.

Whole class activities such as the use of flashcards and other visual aids require you to deploy effective strategies to maintain good class control. These include use of gestures, eye contact, movement around the room and effectively targeted questions. Such activities are meant to engage the whole class. Interruptions and disruption on the part on individual pupils are, therefore, very undesirable. Breaches of the code of conduct can be dealt with by referring to assertive discipline techniques (see e.g. Rogers 1982 and http://www.behaviour4learning.ac.uk/). Rather than breaking the flow of a lesson, miscreants' names can be noted on the board and appropriate action taken later. This avoids disruption of the activity in hand, prevents the potential for confrontation and enables private rather than public admonishment.

An important purpose of using visual aids is to illustrate the meaning of new lexical items and to enable the learner to discriminate between key sounds and peripheral detail. Visual aids can motivate pupils to speak by providing non-verbal clues and by creating a context for communication. They can also be used to encourage inter-action through pupil involvement. Once pupils are able to discriminate sounds, words and phrases, flashcards can be distributed among pupils and games played. Learners can give instructions for the movement of objects and overlays on the overhead projector, or a picture or story can be built up step-by-step on the interactive whiteboard as images appear in or out of sequence on the screen. You need not direct activities yourself but pupils can be asked to come to the screen or handle the flashcards. Information introduced in this way can offer a recognisable, colourful and attractive context for writing. Pictorial representations can be used to decorate texts and provide clues for gist comprehension as well as the extraction of detail in reading exercises. Similarly, cue cards can be used to focus pupils' attention when carrying out listening comprehension work.

In his discussion of the use of images and pictures in foreign language teaching and learning, Allford (2000) usefully distinguishes 'convergent' and 'divergent' exploitation tasks. He posits that divergent, i.e. open-ended tasks should be used where possible to maximise opportunities for spontaneous and meaningful productive language use. Allford stresses that convergent, i.e. closed and often inauthentic tasks can limit the potential value of images and pictures in the foreign language learning process. In the use of pictorial images the distinction between learning new language, which may entail a focus on form, and language use, which is suited to essential practice of already familiar language, should not be overlooked.

Pitfalls and possible problems

The use of visual aids can be exciting and stimulating. Visual aids can be very effective tools to encourage repetition and the reproduction of language forms. Therefore, you need to develop the necessary skills for using them effectively.

However, you need to bear in mind the need for pupils to make real progress in their learning. Audio-visual course material used in the late 1960s and 1970s followed a set format: learners listened to 'texts' and watched film strips. For each and every unit they listened, repeated and responded to simple questions. The film strip prompted reactions from the learner. The content of each unit of work remained distinct and separate from the previous units. Consequently, learners found it difficult to transfer known language to, and use it in, this new context. You need to be aware that they run the same risk when using visual aids. This is not to belittle the value of visual aids in the language learning process, however.

Overuse of one set of visual aids can be stultifying. Given the limited range within any particular topic, activities need to be changed regularly to maintain pupils' inter-est. You need to provide ample opportunity for practice, reusing the same language forms within different contexts.

One phrase should be represented by one visual symbol. Consistency is important:

to introduce new images for familiar language can be seen to be as ineffective as to introduce new language with known images.

Visual aids tend to be used by MFL teachers as a strategy to achieve a number of different purposes such as to increase comprehension, facilitate interaction, avoid translation or increase cultural awareness.

Once able to respond comfortably to visual aids in a teacher-centred activity, pupils can be asked to use small cards depicting similar images for a variety of activities. For instance, a game of 'pairs' can be played providing pupils with opportunities to practise new language. Pupils put the cards upside down on the desk and have to remember where matching pairs can be found.

'Happy families' requires pupils to communicate information to each other. Accurate communication is rewarded by obtaining a card from a peer. Pupils need to complete a set of four to win. For instance, cards depicting four goods which can be bought from four different shops can be made into playing cards. The entire pack of 16 is shuffled and distributed to four players. Player 1 turns to her left and asks player 2 in the TL for a particular item: '¿*Tienes el queso?*' ('Have you got the cheese?') or the name of the shop where they can purchase certain types of goods *¿Tienes algo de la carnicería?* ('Have you got anything from the butcher's?'). If player 2 has the card depicting the item in question or a relevant card she must pass it to player 1. Player 1 will give player 2 a card of her choice (which she does not feel she needs) in return. If player 2 does not have a relevant card she will reply: *'Lo siento, no tengo'* ('I'm sorry I haven't got it'). Player 2 then turns to player 3 and requests a card. The conversations continue around in this way until one player has a full set and wins the game.

In this example, visual aids in the form of cue cards clearly stimulate real communication. Yet, the range of language is restricted to suit the language abilities of the players.

Task 11.6 Visual aids

Which visual aids are used by MFL teachers at your school experience school?

1   With reference to Table 11.1 and through discussions with MFL teachers, find out the purposes for using the aids. Which visual aids fulfil which of the stated purposes?
2   Does the use of visual aids require specific classroom management strategies?
3   Use visual aids in a collaborative teaching situation for a particular purpose, which you should agree on with the relevant class teacher.

Table 11.1 Purposes of the use of visual aids

Purpose	Presentation software	Flashcards	Cue cards	OHP	Realia	Displays
to encourage oral presentation						
to aid comprehension						
to present new language						
to increase cultural awareness						
to provide a context for language use						
to enable communication and interaction						
to avoid translation						
other – specify						

PAIR WORK

Pair work needs very careful management. Kagan (1988, quoted in Bennett and Dunne 1994: 166) points out that co-operative learning must be accompanied by effective classroom management, which includes paying attention to pupil behaviour and the structure and sequence of activities in a lesson. Bennett and Dunne (1994: 171) also quote the findings of the National Oracy Project, suggesting that pair work is a helpful preparation for group work and that younger pupils respond more positively to the smaller grouping.

Deciding on pairs is important. Quick practice (and this, of course, can be limited to *very* quick practice, e.g. 15 seconds to practise three new vocabulary items) is often best undertaken by friendship pairs or two pupils positioned side by side. This reduces unnecessary movement. Instructions need to be clear and noise is an important issue. Denscombe (1980, quoted in Kyriacou 1991: 62) suggests that loudness does not necessarily equate to a loss of control. We concur with this assertion; if interaction is purposeful, you should allow acceptable levels of noise.

The sequence and structure of a lesson are crucial. Pair work requires careful preparation and demonstration. The length of an activity needs to be spelt out clearly. During pair work you should circulate around the class, listening to pupils' oral work, making informal and formative assessments. This way, pupils know that an activity is important. To avoid the indignity of trying to shout louder than a classroom full of pupils speaking at once, you can circulate giving advance warning that a pair work activity is due to end imminently. Pupils also need time to quieten down. Once warned that an activity is coming to an end, an effective strategy to achieve silence is to count backwards from ten to zero in the TL, encouraging pupils to join in the 'countdown' or have a distinctive timer or piece of music loaded up via ICT. Such a routine, once established, can be very effective. Another is to write 'silence' on the board slowly in the TL until all pupils fall quiet. Following pair work activities, you can reward good work by asking some pairs to demonstrate to the class. Transitions from one activity to another are always problematic and need to be planned for. Pair work, which can be hectic and exciting, is a relatively high-risk activity in this respect. You need to develop a bank of strategies to end 'stirrers' effectively and to continue with 'settlers'.

Task 11.7 Ending lively activities

Observe experienced teachers, including those in other subject areas such as music and drama, and note:

- the ways lively activities are brought to a close;
- the types of activities which follow lively activities.

GROUP WORK

In principle, managing group work is not so different to pair work. Group work, however, often takes longer and pupils perform different roles within the small group. Group work rarely requires only a single instruction. Projects demand discussion, negotiation, planning, redrafting and presentation. Pupils can be allocated tasks to fit these demands – scribe, researcher, presenter, actor, editor, etc. Clear instructions and briefing sheets in the TL are helpful. Pupils need to be aware of the need for teamwork and how they can interact with peers to inform their own contributions. This involves careful consideration of groupings – mixed ability, gender mix, ability groups, friendships, learning needs etc. As Bennett and Dunne (1994: 167) note, the structure of lessons, where co-operative work takes place, is complex and pupils must be prepared to assume different roles from traditional teacher-led situations.

Research into the optimum size of groups (see Kagan 1988) has come to no firm conclusions, but you should, nevertheless, be aware of some of the findings. Teams of four are suggested as the ideal, teams of three often result in two teaming up together and excluding the third. Teams of five can lead to cliques. On the other hand, the larger the number of pupils in a group, the greater the possible lines of communication. A final issue is the number of roles required by the task set. You should bear these issues in mind when planning for group work.

Pupils can be prepared for group tasks from the start of a lesson. As they enter the classroom, you should determine seating arrangements. You can place coloured or numbered cards on tables. On entering the classroom each pupil is given coloured or numbered slips of paper indicating which table to sit at. This prevents unnecessary movement during the lesson and also signals that you are in control. The mechanics of grouping pupils are relatively simple. However, the reasons for placing pupils in defined groups are often complex and require your professional judgement.

AUTHENTIC MATERIAL

When asked at interview how to make the learning of MFL interesting, many prospective MFL student teachers reply that they would appeal to pupils' interests. Authentic materials offer you the opportunity to expose pupils to material produced for 'real', out-of-classroom contexts and for specific purposes. With the arrival of the internet, this task has become much easier for you.

Potential and purpose

Authentic materials can be one very effective resource. If used sensibly and sensitively they can motivate pupils, particularly if they are up-to-date and reflect the current context and culture(s) of the TL. Their use fits well within the aims and objectives underpinning communicative language teaching.

Authentic texts, either for listening, reading or viewing, are produced not with didactic-pedagogical objectives in mind but with the general intention of conveying information and/or ideas to speakers of the TL. The focus is on the message and tools other than language are used to help to communicate this message. The format and design, the style and, indeed, the content are moulded to suit a particular audience or readership. As a consequence, authentic material contains cultural information and overt clues to meaning. The level of language need, therefore, not be the sole determining factor for suitability. Learners can draw on their existing general knowledge to predict meaning.

In their book on learning MFL from authentic texts, Little *et al.* (1989: 29–67) discuss a number of exercise types for working with authentic texts such as the use of comprehension questions, information extraction techniques, predictive activities, vocabulary organisation, productive exercise chains, rewriting texts or letter writing.

Use of authentic material serves several purposes. Simple props such as labels, packets, menus, timetables and advertisements can provide the bridge between the classroom and the real world. This bridge can reinforce your aim of demonstrating that what is taught and learnt in the classroom is actually of real use. The very fact that the material is recognisably designed to fulfil a social function can be motivating.

Undoubtedly, material must be selected with care. Pupils need to be able to understand and interact with the content and this is clearly not through word-for-word translation. Apart from drawing on existing skills and knowledge, pupils can develop particular strategies for comprehension. Focusing on headlines and titles, relating pictures to key phrases and understanding captions all contribute to gist understanding, which pupils need to develop.

Qui?	Quoi?	Où?	Quand?	Comment?
Wer?	Was?	Wo?	Wann?	Wie?
¿Quién?	¿Qué?	¿Dónde?	¿Cuándo?	¿Cómo?

Figure 11.4 Working with authentic texts

Little *et al.* also suggest a widely used technique for reading comprehension, which is based on the use of question words for content categorisation as a basis for language production (see Figure 11.4 adapted from Little *et al.* 1989: 99–101).

Many authentic materials lend themselves to particular topics and you can be very creative in their use. Prices on posters and publicity sheets for supermarkets can support the reinforcement of numbers. Even the use of telephone directories can achieve this. The benefits in terms of developing pupils' cultural awareness are obvious. Menus, town plans, tourist guides contain language relevant to examination specifications but also to the realistic needs of pupils when visiting countries where the TL is spoken.

Authentic materials also provide excellent models for language production by pupils. Advertisements in particular can stimulate creative language use and can provide an appropriate context.

When used sensitively, authentic materials offer a great deal (see Fawkes 2001). Kavanagh and Upton draw attention to four important considerations, which are adapted here (see Kavanagh and Upton 1994: 12):

- the material must be interesting for pupils; the same text will probably not be of interest to all pupils in a class;
- the content must be accessible and objectives clearly defined and understood; this can guard against pupils feeling that they have to understand the meaning and grammatical function of every word;
- the task itself must appeal and *authentic material* should involve *authentic tasks*;
- the nature of the task should be varied and relevant to the original purpose of the text.

Pitfalls and possible problems

Above we considered it to be an advantage that authentic materials are not designed for use in the classroom. This can, however, also be a pitfall. No allowance is made for the learners' lack of knowledge of vocabulary nor is the grammar used designed to support a particular stage of learning. Passages need to be placed in context. To expose a learner to authentic texts without prior preparation can be demotivating. Consequently, efforts should be made to introduce the topic, present key phrases and even ideas expressed in the text in advance. The length of many passages is daunting.

Pupils need to feel comfortable with a text before embarking on reading or listening to it. Tasks designed for particular texts can be graded. Activities involving the high-lighting of key vocabulary, such as times, dates, addresses and prices do not require a detailed understanding. The identification of particular details can be achieved through non-verbal responses.

Mitchell and Swarbrick (1994: 2) stress the need to 'exploit pre-knowledge' to pre-empt learner alienation when faced with a lengthy authentic text. In Chapter 6 examples of such preparatory activities, such as identifying known vocabulary or inferring meaning on the basis of headlines, are discussed.

Another benefit of using authentic material can also lead to problems: the materials are *not* designed for the reader to focus on the *language* used *but* more to understand the *message*. The tasks designed for a text need to match this aim.

Working in groups with authentic material can be problematic. Often pupils may be distracted by the material being used by other groups. Access to reference material inevitably involves movement to other areas of the classroom. Pupils do not always work at the required pace and pupil absence can inhibit the work of others in a group.

Kyriacou (1991: 61) advises that teachers establish ground rules in advance:

- pupils should move from their seats for specified reasons only;
- only a pre-specified number of pupils should be out of their seats at any given time;
- pupils should be presented with tasks in stages, with time limits on each stage;
- pupils should demonstrate completion of a stage to the teacher.

EXEMPLIFICATION

The range of material available varies enormously. The activity described here is designed to familiarise pupils with the format and content of newspapers without requiring an in-depth knowledge of the vocabulary of and background to particular articles.

Pupils are issued with newspapers, or given the opportunity to access newspapers online. They are asked to cut out five articles, which depict a happy event and five which depict a sad event. They then separate the headlines and pictures from each story. From the text they extract five key sentences, which serve as a summary of the events. The headlines, pictures and summary are exchanged with another group, whose task it is to reproduce the story. For support, a pupil from each group may read the entire story in private but she is only allowed to report back to her group without reference to the text.

In order to relate the content of lessons to pupils' 'real' needs and interests, the material selected could relate to a planned visit abroad. Pupils can be presented with brochures of all the places they are likely to visit. In groups they are asked to extract from the brochures details of opening times, cost of entries or accessibility and to draw up an itinerary. Again, this activity can be done online. In the event of the visit being to a partner school abroad, pupils from the partner institution could be approached to provide details of possible excursions. Recorded interviews and written surveys are useful this context. This way authentic material can be used to develop effective communication for real purposes.

Task 11.8 Authentic material

1   Examine whether the use of authentic material is built into a unit of work currently in use in your school experience school.
2   Devise an exercise appropriate for a Year 9 class you are currently teaching or observing around some authentic material. Then, with the same material, devise an activity for a Year 11 class you are currently teaching or observing. Do any principles for the use of authentic material with pupils of different levels of linguistic skill emerge?
3   Seek out some authentic material and devise activities, which support the learning objectives of a unit of work of a specific class. Discuss the material and tasks with your tutor or a relevant class teacher; then adapt them as necessary. Ask your tutor or the class teacher if you can teach the activity.

RECORDED MATERIAL (ANALOGUE AND DIGITAL)

Potential and purpose

Apart from representing a welcome change from the sound of the teacher's voice, the use of recorded material provides faithful reproduction of authentic speech and examples of relevant vocabulary and grammatical items in quasi-authentic situations. Listening to recorded texts can obviously improve comprehension but it can also stimulate language production. In terms of comprehension it is important to exploit the fact that recordings can be replayed. The recordings are 'faithful' in that each time a passage is replayed it remains the same. The speakers' intonation, pronunciation and accent as well as the accompanying background noise are constant. This allows for the development of comprehension in stages (see Dakin 1976: 167–8). Learners need to have the opportunity to decipher the sound system independently of the information processing required, to orientate themselves, to pick out relevant detail and then to confirm that they have constructed correct forms of meaning when listening.

Recordings allow you to structure language production and use repetition. Using recordings allows learners to note that different speakers share a phonology despite varying local accents. Indeed, learners need to be aware of the range of regional accents in order to be prepared for future language use.

Recorded material is also a valuable resource as a stimulus for more independent language use. Activities requiring non-verbal responses to record details expressed in passages allow pupils to rebuild 'texts'. Coursebooks nearly always provide transcripts for the passages contained on the accompanying audio material. These allow for the skills of reading and writing to be integrated with listening and for work to focus on the particular language forms used. Activities can be devised using transcripts of recordings: this sort of activity can help reinforce the sound/spelling links so important for language development.

Digital audio recordings can be made available to pupils for use on portable devices such as MP3 players and computers and handheld digital recording devices allow for easy recording of oral language production. Useful free software packages in this context are Audacity, a free, open source software for recording and editing sounds available at http://audacity.sourceforge.net/, or PocketVoice, a freeware sound recorder at http://www.xemico.com/pvr/ (see also Chapter 12).

The ubiquity of digital video recording devices, such as digital video (DV) cameras and even mobile phones, allows for easy production of DV material and resources. And websites such as YouTube, as well as streaming of video content by TV stations over the internet, allow for easy access to digital video material. However, in view of the use of audio rather than video recordings in examinations, there remains a need to work with audio recordings as well.

For a detailed discussion of DV production, see Burn (2005). For details on the use of speech technologies in foreign language teaching and learning, see Pachler (2002).

Pitfalls and possible problems

Audio recordings lack the glamour of video recordings and comprehension of the spoken word can be very demanding without access to the accompanying para-linguistic support of gestures, expressions and visual background/contextualisation. Dakin comments on the dangers of using recorded material purely for drill purposes. The benefits are limited when learners use language as if there is 'an absence of meaning' (Dakin 1976: 57). In order to be realistic, listening must take place in a context, so that the listener can place the language heard into a perceived situation, helping understanding of what the speaker means. The placing of a passage into a communicative context may well be a preliminary task, yet it is essential to do so in order to convey relevance and meaning of a passage. For a detailed discussion of the teaching of listening skills, see Chapter 6.

Audio material can be an effective tool in developing good linguistic habits. There is a place for repetition and drill exercises, for instance, through listening to songs and rhymes. Pronunciation can be focused on without necessarily fully comprehending the words. To attempt to place such an activity in a communicative context is worthy but may well lead to frustration. Pupils may opt out and resort to the 'tum te tum' effect described by Dakin, when pupils imitate the sounds without distinguishing the words (see Dakin 1976: 55).

It is difficult to separate listening comprehension skills from memorising. Many pupils may need to hear a passage several times.

Many teachers view listening activities as 'settlers'. Use of recordings in whole class situations requires silence, which you need to ensure before the listening activity commences. Frequently pupils disrupt listening activities with questions, which could have been answered in advance. Clear instructions often include a statement on how many times a passage will be heard, that pupils need to sit quietly throughout, that answers required are verbal or non-verbal, that answers are expected in the TL/English or in note form/full sentences and that questions do/don't follow the structure of the text.

As a whole class activity, recorded material should be able to be heard by all and there should be no loose trailing wires that represent a health and safety hazard. Standing centre stage and needing to respond to pupils appearing to lose concentration, without making a noise is demanding. It is during such activities that body language, gestures, eye contact, classroom scanning are essential. Pupils should be aware that any form of misbehaviour impinges on the quality of learning of others and that misdemeanours will be noticed and dealt with afterwards. You should avoid disturbing the whole class for the sake of one miscreant, but must not allow this to prevent action being taken. An essential part of Kyriacou's concept of 'withitness' (see above) is the readiness on the part of the teacher to take action.

It is clear that the use of audio recordings is invaluable. However, you need to be confident in using them and selective in your choice of listening material. An awareness of what makes a passage difficult beyond the actual content facilitates the selection of 'texts'. Length of passage, speed of speech, local accents, background noise, number of speakers all contribute to the difficulty of a text. Activities need to be carefully structured to suit the learning process and the level of difficulty of tasks needs to be increased gradually. Support for less able listeners, for instance in the form of differentiated listening tasks, is crucial. Visual aids in the form of clues and prompts can be used to provide such support. Pupils need to know the purpose of listening activities and, in order to prevent constant interruption, pupils should be informed in advance of how many times they will hear the passage.

Task 11.9 Using recorded material

Listen to a range of recorded material from a variety of courses.

1   What do you notice about the different approaches?
2   Which type of passage lends itself to repetition, gist understanding, extraction of detail, rebuilding of language or stimulates language production?

KEY WEB-BASED SOURCES OF SUPPORT, INFORMATION AND IDEAS

- www.ttrb.ac.uk (Teacher Training Resource Bank): This is a good starting point for you as student teachers. It is regularly updated, has links to sites relevant to initial teacher education issues of all types. The site also offers access to a range of reading, research and other source material, useful for your own practice and professional development and also for assignments and small-scale research projects. We would recommend visiting this site. If you carry out a search, you will find that often linked articles are listed, along with qualified teacher status (QTS) Standards and other related sites. This site has links to two related sites which are equally useful for student teachers. The first is Behaviour4Learning http://www.behaviour4learning.ac.uk

which has links and resources related to class management and behaviour issues, and the second is Multiverse, at http://www.multiverse.ac.uk. The latter focuses on learner diversity and once again has related links and back-up material on a wide range of associated issues.

- http://www.teachers.tv (Teachers TV): Teachers TV is a digital TV channel for educators and is available on Freeview but programmes can also be viewed through and downloaded from the channel's website. The website can be can searched by curriculum subject, key stage, topic, type of pro-gramme etc. Programmes are generally accompanied by a range of sup-plementary resources, e.g. lesson plans, commentaries from the teachers involved etc. as well as a brief synopsis of the programme before you watch. It is a good resource for all sorts of occasions, e.g. to see some real examples of teachers implementing assessment for learning in their classrooms, to observe how a 'behaviour expert' helps solve a teacher's class management issues with a particular class, and so on.

- http://www.teachernet.gov.uk (Teachernet): Teachernet provides easy access to all sorts of relevant material and resources for educators with a particular emphasis on information about government initiatives, guidelines and requirements. It also includes some useful advice on professional development. In addition, the site offers some practical teaching material, for example in relation to assemblies.

- http://www.tes.co.uk (*Times Educational Supplement*): Again, this is a very good starting point, and 'a window' on the wider educational context (e.g. the comments and ideas posted by experienced teachers). As well as being a very good way of looking for teaching posts, it offers a wide range of resource ideas and materials, many of which are ready to be used, e.g. on the interactive whiteboard (although, as you will have realised from this chapter, however good a resource might be, it still needs your personal, contextualised input in light of knowledge of that particular group of learners and their needs). As with the other sites, you can search using a number of filters.

SUMMARY

Some resources and material are used very regularly by MFL teachers.

Each resource serves a particular purpose in the MFL teaching and learning process and it is important to devise appropriate activities to maximise the effectiveness of individual resources.

In order to ensure maximum effectiveness of teaching and use of resources, good classroom management skills are important.

There is a temptation to 'follow the book', yet you should recognise that course-books are only one of many 'tools of the trade'. Learning is enhanced by a variety of approaches and certain resources appear to be more suited to particular situations than others. Good MFL teaching is based on the identification of desirable learning outcomes followed by the selection of appropriate methods and strategies to achieve these.

In using the material and resources it is important to remember that lesson plans and units of work should contain variety as well as progression. The range of activities should not be narrow even if certain activity types appear to be more favoured than others by particular groups of pupils.

Within any class there will be a range of abilities as well as preferred learning styles. You need to be able to vary teaching styles and use of resources to suit pupils' needs.

FURTHER READING

Barnes, A. (1997) 'Buyer beware – evaluating MFL materials', *German Teaching* 16: 2–4.

This article looks at factors to consider when choosing resources for MFL teaching and learning.

Chambers, G. and Norman, N. (2003) 'Take six books', *Language Learning Journal*, 28: 40–8.

This article compares and contrasts textbooks and advises on their use in the MFL classroom.

Halliwell, S. (1991) *Yes – but Will They Behave? Managing the Interactive Classroom*. London: CILT.

This book remains a very useful source of ideas for developing classroom management skills with a subject specific dimension.

12 The use of ICT in modern foreign languages teaching and learning

INTRODUCTION

For many years now, the use of technologies has had a meaningful role to play in modern foreign languages (MFL) classrooms. Where traditionally it tended to be mainly tape recorders, overhead projectors (OHPs) and TV and video recorders, there is now a plethora of digital (computer-based) technologies which can make a useful contribution to MFL teaching and learning inside and outside your classroom.

In recent years there has been a significant growth in foreign language learning online and by distance. Due to lack of space, this chapter focuses mainly on ICT use that supports face-to-face teaching. If you are interested in foreign language (FL) learning online and by distance, you can keep abreast of developments by, for example, reading the online journal *Language Learning and Teaching* (http://llt.msu.edu/), in particular, the regular column by Robert Godwin-Jones on emerging technologies.

OBJECTIVES

By the end of this chapter you should:

- understand the rationale behind the use of new technologies in MFL teaching and learning and how they can contribute to achieving MFL learning objectives;
- understand the potential and some of the characteristics of new technologies and how to exploit them;
- be able to make decisions about when, when not and how to use them in your MFL teaching;
- be able to evaluate some key applications and their contribution to MFL teaching and learning.

If you are keen on keeping up with new developments, which are frequent in this area, and as book publications are invariably only as up to date as their publication date – this book being no exception – you are encouraged to visit the webpages of the EDUCAUSE Learning Initiative (http://www.educause.edu/eli), in particular the '7 Things You Should Know About' series of briefing sheets (http://www.educause.edu/7ThingsYouShouldKnowAboutSeries/7495) which feature new and emerging technologies and are regularly updated.

The distinction of 'traditional' and 'digital' technologies is, of course, in many ways artificial and flawed. For example, TV and video are increasingly available digitally, the OHP is being replaced by visualisers in many MFL classrooms and computer-assisted language learning applications (CALL) have been in use in MFL classrooms for many years. Therefore, the field is characterised as much by 'evolution' as it is by 'revolution'.

Technological aids that have found their way into FL classrooms more recently are interactive whiteboards, virtual learning environments (VLEs) and content/learning management systems (C/LMSs) and social networking tools. Figure 12.1, created in the mind-mapping package Inspiration® 8, attempts to provide a rough conceptual overview of ICT and MFL in classroom contexts without specific reference to any statutory requirements.

Roughly speaking, technology can be seen to support teaching as well as learning by virtue of its characteristics and potential operationalised through the application and tools designed and programmed to exploit them. Rather than adopting a skill-based approach, this chapter focuses on the dimension of applications and tools and examines some in terms of their relative merits for teaching and learning in general and for MFL teaching and learning in particular.

Technologies have been used to enrich pupils' language learning experience and have allowed learners to practise language skills independently according to need. Early applications tended to follow a behaviourist, drill-practice paradigm. Simple text manipulation programs and exercise generators remain popular (see e.g. 'Fun with Texts' (http://www.camsoftpartners.co.uk/fwt.htm) or the WIDA Authoring Suite (http://www.wida.co.uk) and Exercise Generator Plus (http://www.clarity.com.hk/program/exercisegenerator.htm), Hot Potatoes (http://hotpot.uvic.ca/) and MaxAuthor (http://cali.arizona.edu/docs/wmaxa/); in addition, web-based applications such Quia (http://www.quia.com/) and SMILE (http://clear.msu.edu/teaching/online/mimea/smile/v2/) are widely used). Jim Dubner's Cutting Edge CALL (computer-assisted language learning applications) demos (http://www.writing.berkeley.edu/chorus/call/cuttingedge.html) offer an example of what is possible in terms of web-based language learning.

Text manipulation software allows pupils to make changes to previously written text. Sue Hewer (1997: 2) distinguishes the following types of activities:

- sequencing words, sentences and/or paragraphs;
- replacing existing words;
- inserting additional words;
- gap filling, including cloze tests;
- unscrambling words or chunks of text;
- reconstructing a text in part or in its entirety.

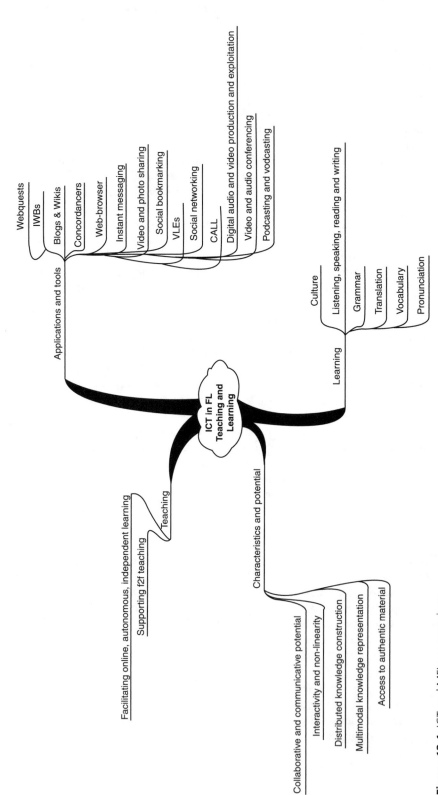

Figure 12.1 ICT and MFL: an overview

She deems text manipulation to have the potential to produce tasks that:

- improve (pupils') knowledge of structure;
- improve their knowledge of form;
- apply and improve their knowledge of collocation;
- consolidate and improve their vocabulary;
- consolidate and improve their spelling and punctuation.

(ibid.: 12)

However, developments in standard applications such as word processors and presentation software as well as multimedia technology (see Mediator; http://www.matchware.com/en/products/mediator/) now allow for the combination of authentic spoken and written texts as well as culturally rich visual stimuli supporting the constructivist learning paradigm, which is based on the premise that learning is a process of discovery, information processing and expression. The drag-and-drop principle on which many of these programs are based enables even very young pupils to generate and produce meaningful FL content of their own.

The same applies to developments in digital audio and video. Programs such as 'Audacity' (http://audacity.sourceforge.net/) or 'Pocket Voice Recorder' (http://www.xemico.com/pvr/) as well as various digital video editing packages such as 'Movie Maker' or 'Final Cut' allow for the straightforward production of digital video artefacts by teachers and/or learners (see Burn, 2005) and online photo- and video-sharing services such as Flickr (http://www.flickr.com/) and YouTube (http://www.youtube.com/) allow users to post and access a huge range of visual material that can be exploited for language and culture learning in creative ways. Clearly, the use of such tools, particularly supplemental to in-class activities, brings into focus a number of issues, including how to ensure appropriacy and suitability of material and pupil use and avoid potential risks discussed widely in the media etc. It is important to take these issues seriously and to take the necessary precautions, among others adherence to relevant school and departmental policies and guidance.

Technologies give learners access to a range of resources in the target language (TL) and enable them to find out about how people of TL communities speak and live. Proponents of the social-interactionist view of foreign language learning (that is, through social interaction in the TL with others) stress the importance of technology as a tool for communication. In an interesting review of research on networked language learning, Kern *et al.* (2004) discuss what is currently known in the field with particular reference to linguistic interaction and development, intercultural awareness and learning and the development of multiliteracies and identity. They point out that online communication does not necessarily lead to more complex FL production, that cross-cultural and intercultural understanding does not automatically result from online communication and that connectivity does not necessarily translate into learning. Among other things, the role of pedagogical mediation (that is, managing the complex interrelationship of variables impacting on and influencing learning) is important. They also report research by Kramsch and Thorne (2002) who argued that it was not linguistic misunderstanding but a clash in cultural frames and communicative genres that impeded learners and that demands on communicative competence and negotiation may be different on the internet. Furthermore, they refer to Thorne (2003) who points out that communicative practices are 'tightly bound to the materiality of the medium' through so-called 'cultures of use', i.e. differences in the norms, attributes and use of applications, programs and tools across generations, social groups, interest groups, national groups, professional groups, etc. With reference to various pieces of work by Warschauer and Lam, Kern *et al.* (2004: 254) draw several conclusions for language pedagogy and research from their literature review:

> First, because language learners do not just speak a language (a standard singularity) but speak from particular social positions (a plurality), teachers and researchers should be less concerned with learners' conformity to standard language norms in their online language use and more concerned with how well learners can use all their available linguistic, cognitive, and social resources to negotiate the linguistic, interactional, and cultural demands of online discourse. Second, what is important about language and literacy development on the Internet is not just the ability to read and write in comprehensible language, but also the ability to negotiate new roles and identities.
>
> Socialization and identity construction can have either a facilitating or restrictive effect on language and literacy development, depending in part on whether instructors encourage learners to participate as creative producers of new media and as agents of purposeful communication and action.

In short, they posit that FL learning and teaching online is less about teaching 'old things in new ways' but instead about '(helping) students enter into a new realm of collaborative inquiry and construction of knowledge, viewing their expanding repertoire of identities and communication strategies as resources in the process' (Kern *et al.* 2004: 254). FL learning online can, therefore, be seen as a highly complex endeavour.

Task 12.1 Identifying potential ICT use in relation to the programme of study (PoS) of the National Curriculum (NC) for MFL

The PoS of the NC for MFL (http://www.qca.org.uk/libraryAssets/media/MFL_KS3_PoS.pdf) includes few, if any, explicit references to ICT. This is, however, not a reflection of the role and potential of ICT in MFL teaching and learning. For each of the key concepts and processes delineated by the NC PoS, identify some examples of how ICT could be used effectively to support these aspects of FL teaching and learning.

For example, 2.2f 'initiate and sustain conversations': use instant messaging software to communicate in real time with native speakers in the context of an internet project.

ICT CAPABILITY AND EFFECTIVE PEDAGOGICAL PRACTICE

It is important to note that the effectiveness of technology in supporting face-to-face FL teaching is linked to the personal ICT capability of both learners and teachers.

The former will require you to familiarise yourself with the school-wide approaches to the development of ICT skills in learners and to ensure ICT-related activities in MFL relate to and build on those in other subjects across the curriculum.

Task 12.2 Developing pupils' ICT capability

1   Talk to the ICT co-ordinator at your school experience school. Find out what ICT skills pupils are expected to develop at Key Stages 3 and 4 and what might constitute evidence of ICT capability. See also the PoS for ICT for Key Stage 3, available at http://www.qca.org.uk/libraryAssets/media/ICT_KS3_PoS.pdf

2   How do the ICT skills relate to the scheme of work of the MFL department at your school experience school and what evidence of ICT capability could pupils show through their MFL work?

The latter requires, in addition to personal ICT skills, an awareness of the potential and characteristics of new technologies as well as about what constitutes effective technology-related pedagogical practice. In terms of relevant ICT skills and an awareness of examples of use, you can find a range of useful resources online including, for example:

- http://www.ict4lt.org/ The ICT4LT website offers a free collection of training modules for language teachers maintained by Graham Davies.
- http://www.languages-ict.org.uk/ from CILT (National Centre for Languages) and ALL (Association for Language Learning) provides a gateway to information and guidance for teachers of languages on using ICT in the classroom.

In addition, it is well worth considering joining a professional discussion forum such as 'Lingu@Net' available at http://www.mailtalk.ac.uk/lists/linguanet-forum.html which enables you to post any questions you might have about FL teaching and learning (with ICT). Thanks to a number of selfless 'activists', you stand a good chance of receiving a helpful and speedy response to any questions/queries posted. If you would rather not risk being inundated with a regular flurry of e-mails to your inbox, you might prefer to visit the online archive of the discussion group to pick up useful hints and tips and to get a feel for the topics that exercise the profession at any given point in time.

In a study commissioned by BECTA, the quango responsible for supporting the education sector in making effective use of ICT (http://www.becta.org.uk), Cox and Webb (2004: 6–7) identify the following as being central to effective technology-related pedagogical practice:

- Teachers need to understand the relationship between a range of ICT resources and the concepts, processes and skills in their subjects.
- Teachers need to use their subject expertise to obtain and select appropriate ICT resources which will help them meet the learning objectives of a particular lesson.

- Teachers need knowledge of the potential of ICT resources, not only in terms of their contribution to pupils' presentation skills but in terms of their facilities for challenging pupils' thinking and extending pupils' learning in a subject.
- Teachers need confidence in using a range of ICT resources, which can only be achieved through frequent practice.
- Teachers need to understand that some uses of ICT will change the nature and representations of knowledge and the way the subject is presented to and engages the pupils.
- Teachers need expertise in organising pupils when using ICT resources within the class – understanding when pupils should work on their own, how working in pairs and groups should be organised and when to use ICT for whole-class teaching.
- Teachers need to know how to prepare and plan lessons where ICT is used so that lessons challenge pupils' understanding and promote reflection and thinking.
- Teachers need to know which kinds of class organisation will be most effective for the learning tasks, e.g. individual/pair/group work or a whole-class presentation.

Task 12.3 Effective technology-related pedagogical practice

Carry out a self-assessment in relation to the issues identified by Cox and Webb above: on a scale of 1–5, with 1 being 'very good' and 5 being 'not at all', rate your personal state of readiness. Where do you need to improve?

You should consider keeping a personal ICT portfolio (from the start of your period of initial teacher education). It is very likely that you will be given the opportunity to work with a virtual learning environment (VLE) such as 'Moodle' or 'Blackboard'/ 'WebCT' as part of your course and increasingly VLEs feature an e-portfolio capability. Some courses also provide access to separate e-portfolio software. In addition to using the VLE for the purposes advised and required by your course, you might also give consideration to its use with pupils, not least as VLEs (or course/learning management systems (C/LMS), which provide various tools for learning and collaboration, are used more and more by schools. The 'London MLE', for example, offers the following tools (see http://fronter.info/londonmle/service.php) (Figure 12.2).

Task 12.4 Familiarise yourself with the functionality of VLEs and C/LMSs

Speak to the ICT co-ordinator in your school experience school and ask about the system used by the school. What are its functionality, strengths and weaknesses? How can it be and is it being used for MFL teaching and learning?

PERSONAL WORK	LEARNING	COLLABORATION	PUBLISHING	ADMINISTRATION
Environment (PLE). E-portfolio and personal working area.	Learning Management System (LMS). Customised learning, assessment and follow-up.	Intranet functionality for efficient collaboration and communication.	Learning content management system (LCMS). Production, management and publishing of content.	Solid administration tools for large scale installations.
• Today • Stickies • My calendar • Games • My contacts • Fronter Instant Messenger • My portfolio • My archive • My homepage • My public archive • E-mail client • To-do list • My blog • Weblog client • RSS reader • Calendar sync • Fronter sync	• Hand-ins • Individual folders • Statistics • Result matrix • Course import • Tests • Whiteboard • Learning path • Learning goals • Portfolio • Individual learning plans • Notes • Question database • Video • Search (repository) • Digital exam • Attendance registration • Survey • Grade book	• Frontpage • Messages • Shared calendar • Shared contacts • Chat • Discussion • Shared documents • Conversations • Debate • Brainstorm • Hot seat • Voting • Project archive • Framework plan • Activities • Time recording • Project archive	• Shared archive • File transfer • Links • News • Lists • Documents • Spelling check • Presentation pages • Statistics • Metadata • Version control • OpenEditSave • Search (metadata) • Article • Web publishing • Infopush • Export of today page • Search (semantic) • WebEq	• Room • Participants • Export • Organisation structure • Rights and roles • Global settings • Local settings • Reports • IMS sync • Database clean-up • Help • Language support • user-defined tool • Single Sign On • LDAP authentication • Design tool • Import configuration setup • Disc storage management

Figure 12.2 Functionality of 'Fronter'

VLEs, whether commercial or open source (e.g. 'Moodle' (http://moodle.org), 'Elgg' (http://elgg.net), 'Plone' (http://plone.org)), tend to have similar features and tools but can differ quite significantly in relation to their orientation to open content; are users being locked into the content provided within the system or is it open towards social networking features and, by implication, without the control of the teacher? It is likely that over time there will be convergence. Also popular in schools are so-called Wikis, websites allowing multimedia content and knowledge creation, which can be viewed and edited by all users; they lend themselves very well to collaborative project work and asynchronous communication, provided users are comfortable with the notion of shared authoring and editing. 'Wikipedia' (http://en.wikipedia.org), the multilingual, free content encyclopaedia project, has added considerably to the popularity of Wikis, particularly in the context of developing writing skills and of collaborative knowledge construction.

Addressing the following questions can yield useful and relevant evidence for an ICT portfolio:

- What ICT skills did I have at the start of the course?
- What have I learnt about ICT and what ICT skills have I developed during the course?
- How have I used ICT during my course, e.g. whole-class presentations, work on stand-alone machines, work in the computer room, production of

(online) worksheets, creation of a website, use of VLE/LMS, record keeping, etc.?
- How have my pupils (of all abilities) benefited?
- How have I used ICT to support the coverage of the NC PoS?
- What are the implications of ICT use for me as the teacher?
- When is it appropriate to use ICT, and when isn't it?
- How can ICT enhance MFL learning and teaching?

The following documents might be collected in hard or 'e'-copy:

- Webpages and ICT resources used for teaching;
- lesson plans featuring ICT use and their evaluation;
- evaluations of resources, software and web-based material;
- personal ICT skills audit;
- logs of personal ICT activities, e.g. a personal blog;
- ICT-related reflection activities completed;
- handouts, leaflets, printouts, annotated background reading;
- ICT-related resources developed throughout the year, e.g. webquests;
- pupils' work.

CHARACTERISTICS OF ICT-BASED RESOURCES

A realistic assessment of the potential and benefits of ICT is essential at all times. The overriding rationale for the use of ICT has to be determined by its effectiveness in helping teachers and learners meet MFL-related aims and learning objectives. ICT should not be viewed as an end in itself but as a means to an end. It should be used to support genuinely meaningful MFL learning activities.

ICT-based, and in particular computer-based, resources have specific characteristics, of which users need to be aware and which allow teachers and learners to do new things in new ways. These are, among others:

- interactivity, i.e. allowing users to create content, fill in and submit forms, receive feedback/scores etc, and communicative potential, i.e. to send and receive messages and attached files;
- collaborative potential;
- non-linearity and provisionality of information, i.e. hypertext-based pages through which there is often no sequential path and which can disappear as easily as they can be published;
- potential for distributed knowledge construction;
- multimodality, i.e. the combination of writing, the spoken word and images.

These characteristics allow ICT tools to perform a number of functions in MFL teaching and learning, e.g.:

- to access authentic material and real language used in context;
- to practise language skills;

- to communicate with TL speakers;
- to develop language learning skills;
- to develop cultural awareness.

In this chapter, we focus mainly on the branch 'applications and tools' of Figure 12.1 and recommend that you have a look, for example, at the discussion of the potential and characteristics of ICT (Chapters 7 and 8) in Allford and Pachler (2007).

PLANNING AND CLASSROOM ORGANISATION

Invariably, as in all MFL teaching, planning and classroom organisation are important considerations in ensuring the effective use of ICT. Most, if not all points raised in relation to planning and classroom organisation in earlier chapters apply and we will not reiterate them here. Similarly, many tried and tested approaches to MFL pedagogy can be adapted for ICT use. Nevertheless, the introduction of an additional, and inherently complex, variable in the ecosystem that is an MFL classroom increases the degree of unpredictability. While it might well lead to serendipitous learning, it might also become a potential barrier to learning unless you minimise the chances of something going wrong by careful planning. This should normally include a 'Plan B' in case the equipment malfunctions. Applications and programs not only have different technological features but also different temporal, spatial and organisational as well as pedagogical requirements which you need to be aware of. For example, is a tool/application/program to be used with the whole class, a group of pupils or are some pupils going to work independently? How do you gain access to the necessary equipment? How can you ensure it is fully operational?

As a general rule, we would argue that it is the curricular objectives that should determine the use of technology, not the other way round, i.e. technology should only be used if it can be seen to have a meaningful contribution to make to achieving the learning objectives identified on lesson plans and schemes of work, not just because it happens to be available.

Effective use can be seen to be characterised by cognitive engagement of learners and when the technology is used as a meditational tool that enables the learner to actively engage in meaning-making, knowledge-building and communication.

In our view, the particular value of new technologies lies in the potential for the agency for learning to be transferred to the learners and for them to become actively involved in the production of content in the process of FL learning. This change in agency from the teacher to the learner has considerable implications for traditional notions of classroom organisation, the role of the teacher and the learner as well as of individual, pair and group work.

Task 12.5 Classroom organisation and ICT use

Carry out a number of MFL lesson observations focusing on the implications of ICT use on classroom organisation. Note any issues.

Strategies for classroom organisation in the context of ICT use both in the classroom and the computer room can be different from the regular techniques you use as an MFL student teacher. Invariably, the methods employed to manage pupil learning and behaviour depend upon the nature of the technological aids used and whether the lesson takes place in the classroom or the computer room. Just as in lessons which do not feature ICT use, good pace, challenging activities and high teacher expectations are important.

Task 12.6 ICT and TL use

Observe a number of lessons in which different types of ICT are used. Note any issues affecting effective TL use by the teacher and pupils (positive and negative).

EVALUATING ICT RESOURCES

The choice of which ICT resource to use or which product to buy requires careful consideration, not least because of the considerable cost of many resources:

> The very nature of multimedia, vast, non-linear and readable only through the computer screen, means that it is difficult to assess the scope and quality of a title or source without spending considerable time on it. There is no equivalent to picking up and flicking through a book which will give an experienced teacher a clear view of its coverage and relevance.
>
> (McFarlane 1996: 4)

Research suggests that the choice of which resource to buy or use is often informed by the quality of support materials available to help you with classroom application such as activity sheets or suggestions for how the product fits into the curriculum.

Also, the creators of ICT-based resources make certain assumptions about the learning process, the teaching methodology and the knowledge, skills and understanding of the intended user group. Also, constraints in technical possibilities exist.

From this it follows that the ability to evaluate ICT-based resources is an important skill for you to have. The following questions should help you assess the value of a resource for MFL teaching:

- What assumptions are made about how pupils learn?
- What assumptions are made about pupils' cognitive abilities, i.e. what are the prerequisites for the use of this resource?
- Are the conceptual and linguistic/semantic assumptions clear and appropriate? Is the wording effective and appropriate?
- Are the scope and the aims of the resource explicit?
- Is the resource user-friendly and interactive?
- Does it have the potential for differentiated access?

- Has appropriate use been made of hypermedia: is the layout clear and consistent? Is the material well organised and nicely presented?
- Does the concept work and is functionality given, i.e. do all the 'buttons' work?
- Is the user able to pursue her own path through the material?
- Are examples of possible navigational structures available?
- Is there an 'About' page or a user guide?
- Is the authorship transparent and subject expertise given?
- Is the content accurate, reliable and up-to-date?
- Is the resource comparable with similar resources, e.g. what does it do a book doesn't/can't do?
- Is online help available and are error messages clear?
- Are there technical/compatibility problems?

In terms of how the resource can be integrated into MFL teaching and learning, you should ask yourself the following questions:

- Can links with existing learning objectives/schemes of work be easily established? Is there an appropriate indication as to the possible contexts of use?
- When do I use it? What aspects of the Programme of Study and the Attainment Targets of the National Curriculum does this resource cover?
- What skills/knowledge/understanding are being developed by using this resource?
- How do I use this resource? In what socio-cultural context is learning situated? What types of pupil–teacher, pupil–pupil and teacher–pupil interactions are facilitated? How flexible is it, i.e. does it stimulate individual work, pair work and/or group work?
- What are the implications for the role of the teacher?
- What specific TL do the learners need to be able to work with this resource?
- What ICT skills are prerequisite to the use of this resource?

These two lists of questions, while not comprehensive, are clearly too long to be given consideration in full for each resource. You might want to select the most appropriate questions for each resource and evaluate a specific resource against those questions in depth.

Task 12.7 Evaluation of ICT applications

1   Put the criteria above in order of your personal preference. What do you consider to be most important in ICT applications for MFL?
2   Then use this checklist for the evaluation of an ICT application. Also, ask your pupils what they think. Compare your views with those of your pupils.

DIGITAL VIDEO (DV)

Through the video recorder, and more recently the so-called personal video recorder (PVR) or digital video recorder (DVR), which allow users to record programs straight onto hard disc, two different types of material can be accessed: off-air recordings (in the TL) produced for non-educational purposes and language programmes produced specifically for educational purposes either stand-alone or accompanying/accompanied by printed material. Both types are readily available from national, satellite and foreign television stations and, increasingly, the internet.

An example of useful educational material are programmes broadcast by Teachers' TV (http://www.teachers.tv), albeit mainly for continuing professional development purposes; they cover a range of topics and issues such as assessment for learning, motivation, resource reviews etc. and can be viewed online or downloaded. An example of commercially produced DV material is 'Yabla', a video subscription service for language learning (http://home.yabla.com); it provides authentic online video through interactive captioning.

An example of material not explicitly produced for educational purposes are the many clips to be found on the video sharing and social networking site YouTube (http://www.youtube.com). This online repository, to which users can easily add, features a wide range of mostly amateur videoclips providing interesting insights into culturally diverse episodes and practices from everyday life. Users can also post comments in a threaded discussion and view the profiles of those who have posted or commented on clips. Importantly, YouTube allows users to easily embed videos in webpages. The clips feature real language use by real people, which does, of course, pose certain challenges for you, for example in terms not only of reliability and representativeness. According to Godwin-Jones (2007: 16), one problem results from the lack of prescribed or even recommended tags, which makes effective searching for appropriate material difficult. He also notes that there can be a problem in relation to the availability of particular clips due to the use of copyrighted audio and video material which can lead to certain clips being removed from the site. 'YouTube' uses the 'Flash' video format for its clips, which can be up to 10 minutes in length. It offers a small file size and uses a software application extension, a so-called plug-in, that is free and widely installed on computers.

One of the reasons for using video material in your MFL teaching is that it is often intrinsically motivating to pupils. It offers a degree of familiarity and with it security.

There is also an increasing range of software that enables the qualitative analysis and annotation of digital video and audio such as 'Transana' (http://www.transana.org/). This software package allows users to transcribe video and audio material, identify relevant episodes, organise them into meaningful categories and apply keywords. 'Victory Author' (http://tell.fll.purdue.edu/info/VA/) enables the creation and editing of video-based lessons around five exercise formats: subtitle, comprehension, role play, cloze dictation and reconstruction.

In terms of the exploitation of digital video for MFL learning, there is little, if any, difference to the analogue format and most, if not all, established pedagogical routines and approaches remain valid.

As Hill pointed out (1989: 3), recordings in the TL can provide useful examples of real life, which are potentially up-to-date and offer an intercultural perspective on life. Off-air recordings can bring the culture(s) of the target countries into the classroom.

As a teaching and learning resource, the DV offers useful listening material. The visual support allows pupils to make use of paralinguistic information and also to contextualise language use. The use of DV provides you with many options. Depending on the learning objectives and the language skills to be developed, sound can either be on or off, the picture can be on or off, frames can be frozen and passages fast-forwarded or rewound. Each of these uses can support a range of different learning processes. Digital video offers the user more control and flexibility. For example, video and audio tracks tend to be separate which offers the possibility to pupils to record their own audio track. Depending on the compression rate of the video, the audio and video quality can be better and it is easier to manipulate episodes and create extracts.

Simply playing an excerpt with strong visual clues can lead to passive understanding. Hill (ibid.: 8) argues that this passive understanding is a necessary precursor to oral work and that '[there] is also considerable evidence to suggest that learners will begin to speak when they are ready' (ibid.: 19).

Williams (see 1982: 69) recommends what he calls the 'witness activity' to stimulate a higher level of engagement. Learners are required to listen and observe and are quizzed on their non-verbal observations. This is intended to focus the pupils' interest on the context.

Swaffar and Vlatten (1997: 175) argue that 'identifying values implied by . . . pictorial messages . . . helps students recognize how pictorial messages are underscored and elaborated in a video's spoken language'. They also report research on children and adult foreign language learners that suggests that, 'when compared with students who have only print or auditory texts, learners supplied with video materials understand and remember more'.

Needless to say, certain DV resources lend themselves better to MFL teaching and learning than others. Television-based resources with relevance to MFL learning are:

- *News items* have a short life span but a high level of topicality. Watching news bulletins allows structured note taking and can serve as an excellent stimulus for discussions. Keywords can, for instance, be matched with newspaper headlines and comparisons between the presentation of a story in different media are possible.
- *Advertisements*, on the other hand, have a longer 'shelf-life'. They often represent, yet also distance, 'real life' through symbolism. Often little language is used and consequently the stimulus is essentially visual. The 'freeze-frame' is particularly useful, as is guessing the product by playing the sound-track only.
- *Drama*, notably soap opera, offers a wealth of transactional language. Short sequences can be used as stimuli for role plays by pausing at key moments of narration, by fast-forwarding or by switching off the sound. Prediction of events to come and the recapping of past events allow pupils to manipulate

tenses. Soap operas lend themselves to speculation about future events, which can lead to short dramatic performances by pupils. For drama work at a more basic level, scenes watched on screen can be copied.

Web-based DV resources, such as amateur video, can also be divided into different genres such as ethnographic pieces, comedy, entertainment, film, animation, how to, music, people, news, sport, travel, animals, etc., all of which can be relevant in some way to MFL teaching and learning.

Task 12.8 The relevance of web-based DV resources

Following the example of television resources above, consider the relative merits of web-based DV genres such as 'how to' clips or ethnographic pieces.

In addition to presenting brief segments of 30 seconds to 3 minutes of longer video 'text' or to choose shorter 'texts' such as commercials or newscast excerpts, Swaffar and Vlatten (1997: 177) argue the case for real-life video 'texts' of longer duration (between 10 minutes and one hour) on the grounds that they require pupils to produce their own language to generalise about what they have seen where shorter extracts focus pupils' attention on the precise language used in the video text. Shorter extracts, they argue, deprive pupils of redundant and contextual information such as story line.

Task 12.9 Using DV recordings

1   With a particular unit of work and its learning objectives in mind, record/select snippets of different programmes and devise a range of activities for each programme type.

2   In what way can any of the recordings/snippets be used to enhance this unit of work? What preparatory work needs to be undertaken in order to use the recordings successfully? What viewing tasks could pupils undertake and how would you follow them up?

Increasingly, newscasts and other source material, including transcripts and sometimes even activities for exploitation, are available as podcasts or videocasts or vodcasts. Put simply, they are audio or video files which are uploaded together with a Really Simple Syndication (RSS) file which notifies users through their podcatching software, such as 'iTunes', and alerts them to available downloads. In the language learning context, a quick websearch will throw up various pod- and vodcasts with a pedagogical orientation. However, in our experience it is pod- and vodcasts that have not been produced for a native speaker audience which yield more promise for language learning purposes. Television and radio stations make a wide variety of programmes available for download which lend themselves very well for listening for pleasure, particularly for more advanced learners. The Modern Foreign Language Environment on, for example, the Learning and Teaching Scotland website features a guide to podcasting in MFL teaching and learning, including to how to make basic recordings (http://www.ltscotland.org.uk/mfle/sharingpractice/podcasting).

Another important dimension of digital video is the use, by pupils, of a range of recording devices from camcorders to mobile phones to produce DV material. Recordings can be made by the teacher or by pupils.

In considering the production of a podcast as part of an MFL learning activity, the genres identified by the ufi/learndirect and kineo guide to podcasting (2007: 8–10) are useful: the monologue, the interview, the magazine show, the documentary, the audio tutorial and the marketing/promotional podcast. Which format is most suitable for a particular topic? The guide points out (ibid.: 10) that in addition to genre, frequency and length are important issues in podcasting and it considers the production of an interview-based podcast in more detail (ibid.: 12) noting that effective design makes a difference. It advises potential podcasters to think through carefully what they want to achieve in an interview and lists the following key steps in achieving it:

- Always write questions in advance – don't wing it, even if you know your subject well. Respect their time and know what you want to get from the session.
- Research your subject – are you aware of their views already? Do you want to cover points they've already expressed in other formats, or explore new ground?
- Think about the listener – what will be engaging? Are there points of controversy to explore? What are the absolute core messages that you must cover?
- Keep your question list to 5–7 questions, allowing opportunity to ask follow-up questions to pursue a topic further if a particular question merits deeper examination.
- Always submit your questions in advance and get confirmation that the subject is willing and able to address them.

Clearly, the need to ask the questions in the TL and ensure the podcast is comprehensible as well as engaging for a non-native speaker audience adds complexity to the task. The ufi/learndirect and kineo guide (2007: 12) suggests the following interview questions:

> Open questions are your best opportunity to engage a subject – here are five standard journalist questions you can nearly always ask to elicit answers that are useful to your listeners:
>
> What's the biggest lesson you've learned in X . . .?
> What's your key piece of advice on X . . .?
> How would you explain topic X to a newcomer?

What keeps you interested in X . . .?
What drives you mad about X . . .?

And the catch-all bonus question:
Is there anything we haven't covered that you want to get across about
X . . .?

If you are using podcasts as an outcome of an FL learning activity, you might well want to bear this advice in mind.

Pupils use a wide range of skills to produce their own information-based, documentary-type video clip such as a tour of their school in the TL. This requires a script and research. The case study in Box 12.1 is an example of such a project.

At a more advanced level, you can use DV and multimodal texts effectively in the context of cultural enquiry. In an interesting paper, Beers (2001: 1) argues that MFL teachers should be using ICT to address curricular objectives around inter-cultural sensitivity and tolerance rather than factual knowledge and she argues the case for ethnographic research methods to interpret complex, multimodal texts from the TL cultures. She identifies four skills (2001: 10–12) needed to carry out such research:

- thick observation: shedding yourself of prior static, product-based notions of culture for more process-based ones that recognise the fluidity of your identity in relation to the social context in which you interact;
- thick interpretation: determining the relations between each of the elements observed within the power structures of the larger cultural context;
- thick comparison: examine aspects of your identity in relation to the home and target cultures;
- thick description: compile selected observations and link them to a repre-sentative, though partial, account of the cultural event.

The paper presents a project based on the creation of a short digital video around cultural interpretations of an everyday object.

Digital storytelling operates in a similar vein; it combines narrative with digital media to create a short movie. We believe that the construction of narrative and its telling to an audience involves a range of important skills and can lead to effective FL learning. Normally, the process starts with the production of a script for which the storyteller assembles a range of media, including DV, photos, animations, music, audio files etc. to communicate the intended meaning. The BBC website hosts a range of interesting digital stories which can be used as examples for an FL project (http://www.bbc.co.uk/tellinglives/). The website of the Centre for Digital Story-telling has some useful resources on its website at http://www.storycenter.org/.

Box 12.1 A case study of a project based on the use of the camcorder

The 'German School Project' arose out of a need to 'kick start' a highly motivated and enthusiastic small group of Year 10 pupils at Whitton School, who had chosen German as their second foreign language GCSE option, having had one lesson per week in Years 8 and 9.

The overall objective of this project was to capitalise on pupils' enthusiasm and motivation and to stretch them intellectually as well as linguistically despite the deficit in their language skills over a conventional first foreign language German Year 10 group.

The aims of the project were:

- to practise, consolidate and extend Key Stage 3 language;
- to provide pupils with an opportunity to take charge of their learning and to 'own' their project, resuming responsibility for planning, execution, outcome and evaluation;
- progression from Key Stage 3 language situations to those more appropriate to Key Stage 4 despite of pupils' linguistic shortcomings;
- to utilise the individual interests and special talents within the group, e.g. technical and ICT skills.

An article in German about the German School in Richmond in the *Education Guardian* (see Kasten 1995) intrigued the pupils who, despite its proximity, had not been aware of the school's existence. This article provided the stimulus for the project.

The German School has approximately 600 German native-speaking pupils from the age of 5 to 19 and a mixture of English and German staff. It is very much a German environment and the working language at the school is German.

Once the go-ahead for the project had been given by both schools, the pupils' first task was to agree on a realistic programme for their visit to the German School. After lengthy discussions they settled for the production and presentation of a video for peers at their own school of:

1   the school environment at the German School (buildings and grounds);
2   two or three lessons in the lower school there;
3   interviews with three of four pairs of Year 3 pupils;
4   break time in the dining hall;
5   lunch in the dining hall.

The preparations involved

1   all technical equipment (camcorder, cassette recorder, boom microphone, tripod, camera etc.) to be booked, checked, loaded, etc.;
2   writing a commentary for filmed items;
3   writing cue-cards and link sequences between items;
4   interview question cards to be prepared using phrase books, dictionaries, coursebooks, etc.

The preparation of the interview cards involved the pupils in the recycling of all language items from Key Stage 3, starting with the topic of 'personal identification' and moving on to many more as they became more adventurous with their questions. Because the interviews were designed for young pupils (aged 8–9 years) at the German School, Whitton pupils' limited linguistic competence was appropriate for the audience.

The cue cards and link sequences required a more descriptive type of language. Pupils gathered the information for these from brochures and articles about the German School.

On the day of the visit the pupils were excited but quite nervous about their project. They were particularly worried about having to speak German all day and about how the German pupils would react to their linguistic efforts. But the day went very well.

The filming of a German lesson (pupils composing a poem about the topic 'spring'), a handicraft lesson (German Easter decorations) and a PE lesson (a German ballgame) turned out remarkably well on film – and Whitton pupils enjoyed and understood the lessons.

The most valuable part of the project turned out to be the interviews with the German pupils. Each pair of Whitton pupils interviewed a German boy and girl. It was most impressive how Whitton pupils adapted their questions to suit the individual pupils, displaying an impressive linguistic agility. At the end of the interviews the Whitton pupils 'pooled' their questions and interviewed an additional pair of German pupils using the questions that had worked best previously. This last interview consequently formed the basis of the follow-up work to the project.

The pupils found it challenging to produce items in the TL that were clearly spoken and easily understood. They also realised that there was a real difference between authentic language production and role plays and found that the most useful items turned out to be those that had been thoroughly discussed, carefully prepared and fully scripted.

Back at Whitton School, the pupils spent a considerable amount of their own time editing a final version of the videotape, having decided a running order and what to cut. The transcribing of the individual interviews was followed by the preparation of a worksheet for their peers in Year 7.

The next stage of the project was the presentation of the film and the worksheet to the Year 7 pupils.

The Year 10 pupils were surprised how much work was involved to turn their 'raw product' into something usable, but they rose to the challenge. After the project they were also much more appreciative of any language videos they watched.

In addition, they wrote many thank-you letters and faxes to various teachers and pupils at the German School and to Whitton's German assistant whose help was invaluable.

As an evaluation of their experience and the project, pupils wrote an account of the day in the past tense. They all wanted to repeat the activity and do everything much better!

The list of achievements – apart from the pupils' enjoyment of and pride in their work – is long and covers most of the NC PoS requirements, but particularly the sections on language skills, language learning skills and cultural awareness.

The photographs taken and other items of information material gathered at the German School were displayed in the languages corridor at Whitton and generated considerable interest from pupils, staff and parents.

SOCIAL SOFTWARE

One of the main advantages in terms of FL learning of the internet has been, and continues to be, the provision of access to authentic, up-to-date material. Of late, one of the significant shifts in the use of ICT has been that towards user-generated content, particularly in terms of the many social networking tools, including blogging and photo sharing, becoming available. *Social bookmarking* software, such as 'del.icio.us' (http://del.icio.us/) can be used as a tool for locating, organising and sharing internet resources. Social bookmarking tools are designed to allow users to store and share bookmarks on the web rather than on their computer, which means they can access them from anywhere. It also enables them to access bookmarks of other users. These features can be particularly useful in the context of project work, for example. Similarly useful for information retrieval and sharing can be *social networking sites* such as Facebook (http://www.facebook.com); they allow users to join networks based on location or other groupings, such as professional or political interests, and create and share online identities and resources and interact with members of these networks. One particularly attractive feature in the context of educational use is the strong privacy policy that offers the user a lot of control in deciding who can and cannot view their information. Facebook is based on a relationship model, on 'friends' and network membership. One of the drawbacks of using social networking sites is the fact that activities can lack substance; however, integration in an educational project can easily overcome this potential problem.

One advantage of Facebook if used as tool for resource sharing is its easy interoperability with other social networking tools such as Flickr (http://www.flickr.com), an *online photo management and sharing tool*, which offers a rich repository of resources for FL learning and teaching. Images lend themselves very well as stimulus for activities such as vocabulary learning, description, analysis, narrative, exemplification of cultural practices, etc.

A particular benefit of ICT for MFL teachers and learners is the ability to communicate with TL speakers. ICT allows both real-time (synchronous) and delayed-time (asynchronous) computer-mediated communication. In real time teachers and pupils can communicate with TL speakers through *instant messaging* programs such as 'Google Talk' and 'MSN' or 'Yahoo Messenger' as well as 'Skype' (http://www.skype.com), many of which also have voice-over IP, i.e. internet-based telephony, and video-sharing facilities. Chats are based on written text while videoconferencing combines text and picture. In research terms, the jury is still out the extent to which the video channel actually makes a noticeable difference in terms of learning.

The potential of *e-mail* for project and group work with partner schools in the TL is great and web-based partner-finding services are available. Webquests, online inquiry-based activities, are similarly an appropriate use of the internet in MFL teaching and learning. For a detailed discussion see Pachler (2007b). The case study in Box 12.2 describes an example of e-mail use.

Weblogs, or *blogs*, are tools that allow users to publish personal commentaries and diaries on the web. They are particularly interesting in the FL learning context as cultural artefacts in that they offer personal perspectives which are grounded in different social, generational, political and cultural traditions etc. and often lead to

Box 12.2 A case study of using e-mail links in MFL

Jonathan Day

At the Lord Grey School, we viewed our long-standing exchanges with partner schools in Germany, Spain and France as starting points for exploiting the use of e-mail. We started to work with our German and Spanish partners on various fronts, as a pilot in the first instance, with the aim of subsequently expanding good practice and including more staff and pupils.

We started by establishing a functional e-mail link with one teacher at our partner school in Spain.

We used this link to organise the school exchange, a traditional exchange where there are outward and return legs and where pupils are allocated partners with whom they stay when travelling abroad. We saved a huge amount on phone bills and were able to carry on a continuous dialogue through our almost daily e-mail contact.

Once the exchange had been set up administratively, the pupils were able to write to their partners in Spain in order to get to know each other before meeting face to face. A digital camera enables us to send pictures down the phone line.

Having established working routines on a small scale, it was clear that we could now begin to use e-mail for correspondence between larger numbers of A level pupils who, with the help of ICT, would be able to participate in an exchange without actually travelling abroad.

We piloted this system of correspondence with a dozen post-16 A level pupils who we paired off with peers in the Spanish and German schools. The results of these e-mail links were pleasing: exchanges were immediate, real and motivating, with pupils clamouring for replies from their partners abroad.

Having worked firstly on a small scale, we were subsequently able to involve more classes and other colleagues in the project. Our aim is for every pupil in the school to have a penfriend in a country where the language she is studying is spoken.

Further exploitation has been made by pupils at Key Stage 4 and at post-16 familiar with the system using it for their own research. For example, pupils sent questionnaires to Spanish classes on bullfighting and on tourism in Ibiza in order to collect information for A level coursework.

We have also set up a triangular link by putting our partner schools in Germany and Spain in touch with each other.

Some of the guidelines we drew up for developing successful e-mail links:

- keep a record of partners of each pupil;
- keep a record of who has sent/received mail and when;
- double up partners if somebody does not get a reply – it's important not to let people down, as they can feel left out/demotivated if their partner fails them for whatever reason. (If pupils miss a session through absence, they will often be prepared to catch up at a lunch or breaktime or bring in work done on disk at home.)
- explain to your pupils the implications of not keeping to their schedule;
- agree with your colleague abroad who will send first and what your topics will be;

- allow some flexibility, but structure your topics and link activities to your scheme of work – otherwise people run out of things to say;
- take advantage of seasons/times of the year/festivals and traditions as topics for description/discussion;
- current affairs and the way they are perceived/portrayed are good topics for A level pupils;
- vary the language used (by arrangement with your colleagues abroad), sometimes writing in the TL, sometimes in English, so that your pupils both read and write their foreign TL.

Implications:

It is clear that e-mail has enabled us to enhance and broaden the scope of the traditional school exchange involving more staff and pupils than may have been possible previously. We hope that there will be a greater uptake in numbers on exchange trips as a consequence.

Other curriculum areas have begun to show an interest in becoming involved too.

In our experience, successful projects require:

- time to familiarise staff and pupils with the equipment and systems;
- access to computers!;
- personal contacts with our colleagues abroad and goodwill, which is particularly useful/necessary when there is a technical problem or delay when your mail has not got through when expected;
- cheap phone time (we are lucky to have a very cheap system, but in any case, if you put all letters in a batch onto one file, then it takes next to no time to send the document).

Finally, some practical points:

- pupils themselves can be immensely helpful in sorting out technical problems that are beyond you (I am an MFL teacher, not an ICT teacher!);
- this is an ideal opportunity to teach and use classroom ICT language: you do *not* need to lapse back into English as your main means of communication;
- don't rush to make your e-mail exchange frequency too high as 'normal' teaching must still go on; it all takes time, even if electronic communications are almost instantaneous! Once every three weeks is probably a realistic frequency for sending mail at first;
- keep backups of all files – it's not good to lose somebody's work!

Using e-mail definitely adds an extra dimension to our school exchanges!

'discussions', i.e. cross-referencing, and community building between bloggers and their readers. Blogs lend themselves very well to the writing of reflective and learning diaries and to sharing them with peers and colleagues. Blogs are online journals and allow for multimedia content. RSS allows for readers to be alerted about new postings and delivers them via e-mail to users' inboxes. Many blogs allow readers to post feedback and comments on the blog page. They are increasingly used in the academic world as a tool for knowledge sharing and building across different communities of interest but also function as personalised discussion forums. They are very useful for capturing and disseminating user-generated content and lend themselves well to the development of reading and writing skills in the context of sharing personal ideas and opinions and interacting and communicating with others.

The TESL-EJ (Campbell 2005) offers a useful comparative review of different weblog applications for FL teaching and learning and distinguishes nine features that you might take into account when choosing which tool to use including a user-friendly, intuitive interface, a WYSIWIG text editor, ability to moderate comments and set access levels, customisability to the interface, built-in social networking features and aggregator, spell check function, multimedia content functionality. 'Blogger' (https://www.blogger.com) is one of the popular tools. Services geared to use in educational contexts include 'Blogs2Teach' (http://www.blogs2teach.net/) and 'Edublogs' (http://edublogs.org/). 'Hipcast' (http://www.audioblog.com) allows the posting of audio, video and podcasts to blogs.

Godwin-Jones (2006: 10–11) rightly notes that though blog writing has moved to the public domain, the so-called blogsphere, and blogs offer pupils ample opportunity to write in a public sphere, courseblogs are also very popular. In their discussion of a blog pedagogy, Fernheimer and Nelson (2005) argue against what they polemically call a 'cacophony' of individual pupil blogs and instead in favour of a class blog as 'a locus of civil discourse bound by social rues, but constituted by individual expression'. The ideal community, in their view, is 'agonistic, deliberate, and collaborative', one that functions as 'a public space in which people do not simply speak to each other but one in which they [also] listen' and one which prompts:

> students not only to express their positions, but also to acknowledge and then engage the positions and opinions others express. Ideally, students would then revise their positions, both argumentative and subjective, based on these 'real' and virtual classroom interactions, thus evolving the depth of their understanding, opinions, and constructions to account for the differences they encounter. For us, this classroom would encourage students to express their points of view freely and civilly, but civility would not be emphasized to the extent that it precluded 'true' argument, which we imagine as allowing and encouraging genuine dissent.

In other words, a space which is conducive to high level language use.

INTERACTIVE WHITEBOARD (IWBS)

Finally in this chapter, let us turn to IWBs. The introduction of IWBs, large, touch-sensitive screens onto which a computer screen can be displayed via a projector and through which a computer can be controlled, into British schools has been extensive and fast and was supported by the government. The government has produced a range of guidance material, e.g. DfES (2004). Critics wonder whether IWBs are really value for money and whether they have the potential to transform teaching and learning. Two main types of IWBs can be distinguished: boards with a hard magnetic surface, and soft boards; they are supported by specific software tools that need to be installed on the computer. IWBs can be used as presentation tools, e.g. to present pupils' work to the rest of the class or to use web-based resources in whole class teaching, but also for pedagogical practices such as analysing language, visualising concepts, illustrating explanations with video or audio files, manipulating information etc. The ability to move items on the screen supports a range of activities such as matching, labelling, categorising, sorting, gap filling, sequencing, etc. – all frequently used in MFL classrooms. Material can, of course, be stored digitally and reused as is or in a modified form in future lessons, which also supports recaps and revision activities. IWBs enable users – teachers and pupils – to embed a wide range of multimodal digital resources in their teaching and/or learning. For you as an MFL student teacher, IWBs offer great potential for making language and concepts less abstract and specific teaching points visually more salient through the use of colour, annotations, glosses, movement etc. One inherent danger in the nature of the IWB is a tendency to transmission-based, whole class teaching.

A report published by BECTA (2003: 1) presents findings from research in support of IWBs; it lists the following key benefits:

- encourages more varied, creative and seamless use of teaching materials;
- engages pupils to a greater extent than conventional whole-class teaching, increasing enjoyment and motivation;
- facilitates pupil participation through the ability to interact with materials on the board.

In an attempt to justify the expenditure, the government commissioned an evaluation of the educational and operational effectiveness of the project and to assess the impact of IWB use on teaching and learning, teacher/pupil motivation, pupils attendance and behaviour, standards in core subjects at KS3 and GCSE and the impact on teacher continuing professional development (CPD) (Moss *et al.* 2007: 5). The research found that IWBs are mainly used as data projectors, as a surface to generate dynamic display and to enhance presentation from the front of the class. The majority of texts used are the teachers' own but teachers appear to be struggling to incorporate design principles which establish clear reading paths for pupils; this difficulty also gets in the way of teachers designing resources that can be shared independently of their author. The research also shows that the introduction of IWBs does not in and of itself transform existing pedagogies and it concludes that the main emphasis should be on the appropriacy of pedagogical approaches not the use of the technology *per se*:

> To a large extent the kinds of changes the technology fosters depend on what teachers think it is for. There are three key themes that dominate thinking about the role of IWBs in changing pedagogy. These are: increased pace of delivery; increased use of multimodal resources, incorporating image, sound and movement in new ways; and a more interactive style of whole class teaching. The research suggests two important caveats to these anticipated benefits.

> First, it is possible to approach pace, multimodality and interactivity with either a surface or deep understanding of what they contribute to pedagogy. A surface approach rests at the level of the technical or physical attributes of the technology. From this perspective, making pedagogy interactive means using particular features of the IWB such as drop and drag, or moving between multiple screens during lesson time. A deep approach embeds the use of the technology more specifically in a broader pedagogic aim. This means assessing more precisely how particular features of the IWB can achieve a wider pedagogic purpose which is itself centred on increasing pupil understanding of key aspects of relevant subject knowledge.
>
> Second, the value of particular attributes of the technology and their capacity to achieve meaningful change depend on how these features fit with existing pedagogic approaches and priorities embedded in the particular subject domain and its existing practice. So fast pace in teaching is perceived as much more of a virtue in Maths than in other subject domains. This is also where the technology is most likely to be used to this effect. From this point of view, the introduction of IWBs to secondary schools may reinforce, or even distort, rather than reconfigure the dominant approach to pedagogy in particular subject areas.
>
> (ibid.: 6)

Moss *et al.* (ibid.: 7) also note that IWBs offer an opportunity to think about the strengths and weaknesses of whole class teaching. Discussion between colleagues about how IWBs can be used to support and transform existing practice, they argue, is important to ensure effective use of IWBs. A focus on interactivity as a technical process, for example, is not inherently beneficial and can lead to some relatively mundane activities being overvalued:

> Observations for this project suggest that developing good materials for use with the IWB is not just a matter of solving a range of technical or logistical problems but also means considering more fundamentally which kinds of texts can most usefully be shared in this way.
>
> (ibid.: 8)

Moss *et al.* (ibid.: 8) identify two potential drawbacks to the ways in which IWBs are currently being used. The technology can:

- Reinforce a transmission style of whole class teaching in which the contents of the board multiply and go faster, while pupils are increasingly reduced to a largely spectator role.
- Reduce interactivity to what happens at the board, not what happens in the classroom.

This, we argue, must be guarded against when using the IWB.

SUMMARY

In this chapter we discussed the role of ICT in MFL teaching and learning with a particular emphasis on introducing social networking applications and tools. ICT should not be seen as a possible replacement or challenge to your importance as an MFL student teacher. Indeed, the use of ICT makes your role more important but ICT use requires new pedagogical skills, such as the ability to evaluate multimodal resources.

ICT can play a key role in the development of listening, speaking, reading and writing skills as well as transferable skills such as independent learning and the use of reference material, and can prepare pupils for their (working) lives in modern society.

ICT should be used on the basis of its appropriateness in achieving MFL-related learning objectives, as a means to a end and not as an end in itself.

ICT can be used effectively inside and outside the MFL classroom and has great motivational potential for learners. It can meaningfully enhance and enrich pupils' MFL learning experience.

Last, but by no means least, ICT yields considerable potential for continuous professional development and networking.

FURTHER READING

Allford, D. and Pachler, N. (2007) *Language, Autonomy and the New Learning Environments.* Frankfurt a. M.: Peter Lang.

This book explores, with reference to relevant research findings, how digital technologies create new possibilities for FL teaching and learning, such as knowledge construction through computer-mediated interaction and learner autonomy in online networks.

Leask, M. and Pachler, N. (2005) (eds) *Teaching and Learning in the Secondary School using ICT*, 2nd edn. London: Routledge.

Two chapters in this book address the question of how ICT can be used for teaching and learning. It provides a starting point for exploring the possibilities that ICT offers to schools, teachers and pupils.

Language Learning & Technology, available at http://llt.msu.edu

Language Learning & Technology is a refereed journal which disseminates research related to technology and language education to foreign and second language educators.

13 The first appointment and professional development

INTRODUCTION

One aspect uppermost in many modern foreign languages (MFL) student teachers' minds, certainly during the latter stages of initial teacher education (ITE), is finding a first post. Therefore, initially, this chapter looks at some of the issues concerning applying for jobs and going for interviews.

The requirement for Newly Qualified Teachers (NQTs) to complete a period of probation, the induction year, is the focus of a subsequent section of this chapter. The role and nature of the statutory Career Entry and Development Profile (CEDP) – at the time of writing – are also discussed.

We also examine some issues concerning continuing professional development (CPD). CPD is important, as can be seen throughout this book, because MFL teaching is a continually changing, highly complex and demanding occupation, requiring knowledge, skills and understanding as well as competence in a wide range of different areas. Also, there are frequent changes in education policy and requirements, which normally necessitate some realignment of practice. The need for ongoing development is clearly recognised by the teaching profession. The willingness to engage in in-service education and training (INSET) and CPD, which can be carried out 'in-house' or outside school, is one of many indicators for success in MFL teaching and can also be seen as a prerequisite for promotion. Just as Standards exist for QTS, they are also in place for NQTs, Excellent Teachers, etc. and provide explicit reference points for target-setting in relation to career development.

OBJECTIVES

By the end of this chapter you should:

- understand the issues involved in finding your first MFL teaching post, such as writing letters of application or preparing and going for interview;
- understand the issues involved in starting your first teaching post, such as going for a preparatory visit, building on your CEDP, awareness of the induction standards, completing the induction year, team work with colleagues or interacting with parents;
- recognise the need for INSET, CPD and updating your knowledge and understanding throughout your teaching career;
- be aware of the importance of keeping a good record of evidence of your CPD activities;
- be aware of MFL-specific development and training opportunities with a particular emphasis on your first year of teaching as an NQT.

GETTING YOUR FIRST TEACHING POST

One considerable stress factor in the latter part of an ITE course tends to be the emotional upheaval and, of course, preparation, associated with applying for jobs and preparing for as well as going to interviews. Securing a first teaching post tends to include the following steps.

Step 1 Finding out about vacancies

The national educational press – particularly the *Times Educational Supplement* (TES) on Fridays and the education section of the *Guardian* on Tuesdays – contains adverts of vacancies around the country. Both the *TES* and the *Education Guardian* maintain a searchable database of vacancies on the internet; they can be found at http://www.tes.co.uk/ and http://www.educationunlimited.co.uk/ respectively. Local Authorities also tend to publish bulletins of vacancies periodically. On request, schools send out particulars of vacancies and, where appropriate, an application form. You may find your ITE institution also publicises posts (on boards and electronically) which are frequently sent in by schools.

Finding the right (first) school has always been important but can be considered to be much more crucial since the introduction of the induction year (which has to be passed and during which an NQT requires a planned, supported programme). Identifying appropriate vacancies among the large number of adverts regularly featured in the *TES* and the *Education Guardian* and elsewhere is not easy. NQTs often benefit greatly from a supportive environment, in which they can consolidate and build on what they have learnt during their period of ITE.

There are a number of personal and professional considerations, which govern the choice of school. They include:

- the characteristics and location of the school and the department: is it a boys', girls' or a co-educational school? What is the ethnic mix of the school? Is it a small or a large school? Where is it located: in a town or the country? Is it a community, specialist, comprehensive, foundation, grammar, independent school? Is it an 11–16 or an 11–18 school? If it has specialist status, what is its specialism? If it does not have specialist status, does the school have plans to achieve this? What range of languages is on offer?
- the information available on the school website and in the prospectus: where does the main focus lie? What does the school seem most proud of? What does the school's latest Ofsted report tell you about its achievements, strengths and weaker areas? What percentage of Key Stage 4 pupils take MFL at KS4 and what target for uptake in KS4 has the school set for itself?
- the roles and responsibilities sought: are there opportunities to take part in cross- and extra-curricular activities? Is there scope for promotion? What is the school's policy on CPD for staff?
- the facilities available at the school and the local community: are the information and communications technology (ICT) facilities at the school and in the department good? Depending on your out-of-school interests, are there cinemas, theatres, sports facilities in the vicinity?
- the infrastructure: how easy is it to get to the school on foot, by public transport, by car?
- proximity to friends and relatives: would you be able to keep in touch easily with your friends and family?
- the affordability of housing: how much will it cost to rent or buy?

Task 13.1 Choosing the right school

Consider the questions above in relation to a few vacancies you are interested in. Do your answers help you narrow down your choice?

Can you make a list of 'essentials' and 'desirables' which may help you choose a school? You might wish to find out more about the area in which the school is located on http://www.upmystreet.com/ or similar websites.

Step 2 Completing the application form and writing the covering letter

When applying for a vacancy in the majority of cases an application form needs to be completed and sent to the school together with a covering letter by a given deadline. Follow instructions to the letter: if they ask for a CV, include one; if not, do not.

A successful application hinges on a well-thought-out letter or supporting statement in which your personal philosophy and experience (of MFL teaching) in relation to the job specifications and other details provided by the school is set out. You should provide as much relevant detail as possible about personal strengths, achievements and past experience in a covering letter related to what the school is actually looking for. Your letter of application should attempt to address each of the items set out in the job specification directly. As different schools have different requirements and priorities, it is usually necessary to write a separate letter for each application rather than send out a 'standard' letter. Quality of use of English and presentation are two obvious criteria for judging letters of application. It is important to make sure the application form and the covering letter or supporting statement communicate your strengths in a manner that is informative but without seeming arrogant. In our opinion, the most crucial aspect of this supporting letter/statement is that it should ensure that you as an individual are clearly portrayed. The potential employer does not want to know what *everyone* on your ITE course does. They are interested in what *you* have achieved. The inclusion, therefore, of specific, concrete examples illustrating how you have successfully been effective in helping pupils learn MFL can be a deciding factor.

Many schools will draw up a shortlist on the basis of the information applicants provide about themselves and the apparently most suitable applicants are invited for interview.

Task 13.2 The covering letter

Here is a list of attributes that might be sought by a school in a MFL teacher:

- a well-qualified, able linguist offering preferably two languages, the first language to GCE A level, the second to at least GCSE level;
- a sound knowledge of the statutory requirements and recent developments in MFL teaching and learning;
- the ability to communicate effectively and work as a member of a team;
- high expectations of pupils and an enthusiasm for MFL teaching and learning;
- a commitment to equal opportunities in order to cater for the individual needs of pupils, e.g. those with special educational needs;
- a willingness to play an active part in the life of the MFL department, e.g. participation in extra-curricular activities and in the wider work of the school;
- an ability to develop the use of ICT in the department;
- a willingness to work hard and show commitment to the school.

1   How do you match up to these expectations?
2   Write a covering letter addressing these points and discuss it with a peer, a teacher you work with closely and/or your tutor.

Step 3 Preparing and going for an interview

Where at one time the interview day comprised a tour of the school and meeting a small panel of people, schools now generally employ more rigorous selection procedures which mostly include the teaching of sample lessons and may include the giving of presentations and sometimes the interviewing of candidates by pupils. Careful preparation for an interview, therefore, is essential, particularly so for the sample lesson, where you will need to be informed exactly what you are expected to teach and to whom.

Task 13.3 Preparing for the sample lesson

What information do you think you would need as a minimum in order to prepare as best as possible for the lesson you may be asked to teach during the interview day?
What essential items do you think you should take with you 'just in case'?

Just as schools are eager to choose the right candidate to suit their needs, you should use the interview process as an opportunity to find out what working at a given school would be like. Experience suggests that choosing a school carefully can make an important contribution to professional satisfaction. You might, for example, access the most recent Ofsted report on the school at http://www.ofsted.gov.uk to read up on inspection findings. In so doing, you need to bear in mind the purpose of and rationale behind the inspection process as well as the nature of the framework used and the validity and reliability of the judgements made. Areas identified in inspection reports might provide professional opportunities for NQTs and allow you to make a useful contribution to a department and/or school. It is, however, unwise to base all decisions about a potential school on an inspection report. All information you collate should be taken together.

It is very important to be perceptive to the ethos and policies of the school and the MFL department on the interview day. At the end of that day, and often without an opportunity for any deliberation, the successful applicant is required to make a decision about accepting the post. Only very rarely will she be able to consider a job offer overnight. For some MFL student teachers who have made a career change, this process can appear rather unusual.

In order to make this important decision easier, try to obtain as much relevant information during the day as possible. During the tour of the school on the interview day find out about the facilities available by observing, for instance, whether:

- there is a dedicated suite of MFL rooms decorated with stimulating and relevant displays;
- the department has an office with sufficient space to store resources, equipment and files, to work during non-contact time and to meet with colleagues;

- there is a data projector/interactive whiteboard, CD/cassette player and overhead projector in each classroom/for each member of staff in the department and, if not, you are aware how these facilities may be obtained;
- MFL staff have easy access to a TV and video recorder;
- there is access to a satellite receiver and the internet;
- there is a departmental handbook with schemes of work and appropriate policies;
- the department has its own computers with relevant software;
- the school has an induction programme for NQTs in place.

Also try to find out:

- about possible teaching rooms;
- if pupils are issued with coursebooks they can take home with them;
- whether the department has a range of resources supplementary to coursebooks and are they shared willingly (i.e. does the department adopt a genuinely collaborative approach);
- about recent inspection recommendations;
- what extra-curricular activities are offered;
- how your personal approach to MFL teaching compares to that prevalent in the department.

This information can offer a useful insight into what MFL teaching at the school might be like for you as an NQT and some of these may be more important for you than others. Of course, as you move around the school, both on any official 'tour' and e.g. during lunch, you should observe pupils carefully.

Task 13.4 Observing pupils on interview day

What do you think you could ascertain from observing the attitudes and behaviour of pupils during a day on interview or a pre-interview visit?
Ask yourself some key questions:
What attitudes do they appear to have towards the school/each other/(MFL) learning?
What sort of relationships are apparent between staff and pupils?
How do displays and the general impression of the school seem to contribute to pupils' attitudes? Do the pupils seem to show respect towards the displays and the school buildings?

In our experience, an atmosphere of mutual support and good working relationships with colleagues are not only desirable but essential. For this reason, schools often provide an opportunity during the interview day for members of the MFL department to meet candidates. Although often informal, these occasions tend to be used by members of staff at the school to assess whether candidates are likely to fit into the department. You should of course be working this out too!

As part of your interview preparation it is advisable to think of answers for questions, which the interview panel is likely to ask. These might include:

- Why did you want to become an MFL teacher?
- Please describe an MFL lesson you taught during your teaching experience, which you feel was particularly successful and say why.
- Can you please briefly describe your personal approach to MFL teaching?
- What, in your opinion, makes MFL teaching and learning stimulating for pupils?
- Can you describe some strategies for teaching in the target language (TL)?
- What role do you see ICT playing in MFL teaching and learning?
- Which resources do you consider essential for your teaching?
- What are your particular areas of interest and/or strengths, which you can offer to the MFL department and/or school?
- How important do you consider the role of the form tutor to be and what contribution do you feel you can make to the pastoral system of the school?
- What do you consider to be the most important aspects of the National Curriculum (NC) MFL Orders/of MFL teaching in the NC and the KS3 strategy?
- What, in your opinion, are the key implications of the primary languages entitlement?
- Give some specific examples of how you have effectively motivated pupils in your teaching so far.
- What do you perceive to be areas in need of development in your teaching? What strategies might you consider to address them?
- Where do you see yourself in five years' time?

There are of course nearly always surprises with some of the questions asked, so be prepared for the unpredictable. It is also to be expected that at some point you may be expected to respond at least in your main FL and perhaps your second foreign language too. This may not be in the formal interview, but perhaps in a meeting with members of the department. Useful information and support in matters relating to interviews and the writing of applications tends to be available from Careers Advisers. For information on getting a teaching post, see also Maguire and Morris-Lucas (2006).

Task 13.5 Preparing for an interview
1   How would you answer the possible interview questions above?
2   Discuss your answers with a peer, a teacher you work with closely and/or your tutor.
3   What are the current (MFL and more general) issues which you feel might be discussed at interview?

On the day of an interview it is important to make sure all open questions, including the starting salary, have been answered before accepting a job, even orally. Useful guidance on finding a job, including up-to-date information on pay, is available from teacher professional associations. It is the practice in some ITE institutions that they recommend student teachers take along a portfolio of their achievements which can be used during interviews to illustrate certain aspects of professional development. In our experience, and on the advice of Head Teachers, such material should not be a bulky file containing every piece of paper you have collected during the year, but a slim volume with a few key pieces of 'evidence' which can then be referred to as appropriate.

Task 13.6 Illustrating your expertise

If you were to take some key pieces of evidence with you to an interview, what would you choose to illustrate the following aspects of your work?

- how you successfully differentiated in a mixed ability group;
- a successful outcome to a series of lessons;
- how you helped a pupil/group of pupils using assessment for learning.

Which other aspects of your development would you choose to demonstrate in this way?

STARTING AS AN MFL TEACHER

Finding a teaching post and gaining qualified teacher status (QTS) signal the start of your CPD process. In the initial stages of your career as an MFL teacher, but particularly during the NQT year, priorities for professional development invariably focus on getting to know the school, its policies, procedures and curriculum as well as the many new colleagues who work there with responsibilities for the various aspects of school life. Most immediately there is, of course, the need to get to know the various groups of pupils and to become comfortable in the teaching situation. Only over time will the focus widen.

PREPARATORY VISIT

Newly appointed members of staff, and in particular NQTs, are often invited to spend a day or even a number of days at the new school before taking up their post. This enables you to get to know key colleagues in- and outside the department, to find out about the school procedures, departmental documentation including schemes of work, copies of relevant coursebooks and examination specifications, your timetable, meet the classes you are going to teach and/or to find answers to questions that have arisen since the interview. Experiencing the school 'at work' helps to prepare for the term ahead and more useful information is usually picked up on this type of day when the emotional intensity is much less then when being interviewed. In order to make the most of the preparatory visit it might be useful to make a checklist of the information or documents to be collected and the people to be met.

Task 13.7 Preparing a visit to the new school

Draw up a checklist of useful items to collect during your preliminary visit:

- *information*, such as contact telephone numbers or accommodation details;
- *documents*, for instance the scheme of work, staff and departmental hand-book, personal, social and health education (PSHE) documents for the work with your form group should you be allocated one, examination specifications, the timetable or events calendar, the proposed induction programme; and
- *resources*, for instance relevant coursebooks.

THE CAREER ENTRY AND DEVELOPMENT PROFILE

The Training and Development Agency's (TDAs) CEDP, available at http://www.tda.gov.uk/partners/induction/cedp.aspx plays an important role in your induction arrangement as an NQT. At the time of writing, the CEDP must be completed before QTS can be recommended.

You leave your course of ITE with a CEDP, which sets out your strengths and areas for further professional development in relation to the QTS Standards (see Chapter 2). The CEDP provides the starting point for planning your professional development and should be used as the basis for setting objectives and developing an action plan for the induction period.

INDUCTION YEAR

In 1999, the government introduced a statutory induction period, which applies to all NQTs and will usually be (the full-time equivalent of) one academic year in length, combining an individualised programme of monitoring and support, providing opportunities for you to develop further your knowledge and skills, with an assessment of your performance. The period of induction takes three terms full-time which equals six terms on a 0.5 FTE contract. In order to complete the induction period satisfactorily, you must meet the induction standards as well as continue to meet the Standards for the award of QTS on a consistent basis in an employment context. The induction standards, known as the core standards, have applied to all NQTs starting induction from September 2007 onwards (see http://www.tda.gov.uk/upload/resources/pdf/s/standards_core.pdf). There is guidance available to support your induction process as an NQT at online http://www.tda.gov.uk/Recruit/becomingateacher/inductionyear/inductionsupport.aspx.

Task 13.8 Preparing for induction

Have a look at the QTS Standards you work towards during your course and also at the Induction/Core Standards.

- How will you demonstrate you are continuing to meet the QTS Standards in a sustained way?
- How will you begin to address the extra demands outlined in the Core Standards?
- What sort of plans should you be making to enable you to have the opportunity to meet the particular expectations?
- What advice do you think you might need from your Induction Tutor?

The induction/core standards very much build on the standards for QTS and emphasise those aspects of MFL teaching difficult to develop during initial teacher education due to, for example, the relative brevity of time spent in any one placement school and the reduced teaching load you have as a student teacher, etc. They should not be viewed as a checklist but as a set of criteria, against which to discuss your progress and to set targets for further professional development beyond the induction year.

The induction tutor of a school oversees your NQT induction period but it is the headteacher who completes the report at the end of the year recommending whether or not all the required standards have been met.

During the induction period as an NQT you should have:

- a reduced timetable of 90 per cent of normal average teaching time with the release time being used for a coherent and relevant, individualised, induction programme, where the CEDP plays a significant initial role;
- support from a designated induction tutor, e.g. your head of department;
- your teaching observed and receive feedback in follow-up discussions;
- your professional progress reviewed;
- the opportunity to observe experienced teachers;
- a named contact beyond the school, e.g. in the Local Authority; and
- access to other targeted professional development activities in- or outside the school, which should be based on the CEDP and aimed to help you meet the required standards.

You will have three formal assessment meetings with either the headteacher or the induction tutor, recording your progress towards meeting the Standards.

As part of the formal assessment there should be written reports and judgements which are evidence-based with evidence coming from, for instance, lesson plans and evaluations, assessment data and record-keeping, information about liaison with others, e.g. colleagues and parents, self-assessment or a personal portfolio. As on your ITE course, it is to be recommended, therefore, that you assume responsibility for keeping records of your development and achievements and match these against the Standards.

The assessment procedures centre around a process of target-setting and review similar to those commonly applied in the period of ITE. You should not be left in any doubt as to the progress being made and the development targets to be addressed. If you feel you are not receiving adequate feedback or that communication is difficult, you should make your induction tutor aware of this, and, if necessary, your named contact beyond the school.

In the case of an NQT failing to complete the induction period satisfactorily, the NQT is no longer eligible to be employed as a teacher in a maintained school. No NQT may serve more than one induction period. The stakes, therefore, are high.

As part of the induction year, you normally also take part in the induction programme for all staff new to a school, including experienced teachers who have come from other schools. This induction programme often includes opportunities to get to know key colleagues and to become familiar with the organisation of life and work at the school as well as to share and discuss experiences and problems with settling in.

Off-site sessions, e.g. local authority-led programmes, provide an opportunity to meet other newly qualified MFL teachers with whom it might be possible to 'compare notes'. Meetings of this kind are useful for consolidating certain aspects of subject methodology as well as for networking with peers from different schools with different subject specialisms.

Secondary schools in England are required to identify on their calendar five days a year for staff development when only teachers attend and pupils stay at home. Each school decides how to organise these and the format may differ from school to school. Often, outside speakers are invited to talk to staff on whole school issues, such as for instance how to raise achievement, followed by departments being given time to discuss the subject specific implications, e.g. how can the department improve MFL GCSE results for boys? These INSET days can provide useful information about school procedures and relevant issues but also allow you as an NQT to get to know established members of staff from other departments.

Task 13.9 'Who is who' at the new school?

Recently, and particularly since the introduction of 'Remodelling the School Workforce' in 2003 there have been many new roles introduced in to schools.

During your induction programme try to find out the names of the members of staff listed in Figure 13.1. Introduce yourself to them and find out about their responsibilities.

WORKING IN A TEAM

It is likely that as an NQT you join a team of professionals who have worked together for a number of years, who have clearly defined roles and responsibilities and who follow well-established policies and procedures.

On joining the school, you will have to work towards establishing yourself and becoming an accepted member of the body of staff as a whole as well as a member of

Job title	Name(s)	Responsibilities
professional tutor (student teachers, NQTs etc.)		
school secretaries/ administrators		
teaching assistants		
Bursar/finance manager		
Heads of Year/House		
vocational co-ordinator		
Special Needs Co-ordinator		
site manager		
Deputy Heads: pastoral and curriculum		
Assistant Heads – responsibilities?		
Headteacher		
IT technicians		
assessment co-ordinator/ examinations officer		
Language support staff		
cover supervisor/ co-ordinator		

Figure 13.1 'Who is who' at the new school?

specific teams, for instance at departmental or pastoral level. You will have to earn the respect of colleagues and pupils and prove yourself by making meaningful contributions to the work of the school. In the main, experienced MFL teachers are very receptive to new ideas and inspiration from NQTs who, nevertheless, need to be aware that this is a two-way process. If as an NQT you are seen as 'know-it-all', you might find it hard to be accepted.

One possible approach is to start with the areas of priority of the departmental development plan. Building on existing personal strengths, you might take responsibility for specific issues identified as being in need of development. For example:

- a department might be keen to develop links with partner institutions abroad. If you have personal contacts with a school in the target country made while working there as a Foreign Language Assistant (FLA) these could be utilised to set up an e-pal link or to develop educational (internet-based) project work; or
- a department might be keen to extend links with the 'world of work'. If you have come into the profession with relevant work experience in business or industry, you might agree to build on these contacts and develop work-related MFL activities.

Various roles need to be assumed in team work and different responsibilities accepted. In order for teams to function well, all necessary roles and responsibilities need to be taken care of. It might, therefore, be useful for you to find out what roles you are suited for at a particular stage. Established self-perception inventories such as the one suggested by Belbin (2003) might be a useful starting point for finding out about personal strengths and weaknesses in relation to the roles required in a successful team.

INTERACTING WITH PARENTS

An important aspect of your work as an MFL teacher is learning about and consolidating how to interact with parents. The term 'parents' is used here to include carers.

Often communications with parents are channelled through Form Tutors or Heads of Year/House. It is important as an NQT to become familiar with, and follow the procedures in place at the school for contacting and interacting with parents.

Parents' evenings provide a fruitful opportunity to give direct feedback to parents. Because not all student teachers have the opportunity to gain first-hand experience of parents' evenings during their initial teacher education, your first parents' evening as an NQT can be the source of some anxiety. In order to make meeting parents as beneficial as possible, it is important to be well prepared. The anticipation of possible issues and the rehearsal of certain answers are useful strategies to which an induction tutor can contribute significantly (Wootton 1994: 6–7):

- Check your appearance.
- Greet parents formally.
- Whatever the circumstances, do appear to be concerned for the child and pleased that the parents have come.
- Never adopt a casual, off-hand, or flippant attitude towards the proceedings.
- If you have timed appointments keep *strictly* to your schedule.
- Make it clear to the parents that you know what you are talking about. Have some facts about the child at your fingertips.
- Don't invite obvious criticism by being behind with your marking.
- Always have *something* constructive and positive to say, even if your remarks must necessarily be heavily qualified.
- Try to advise the parents of something *they* can do.

Task 13.10 Interacting with parents

One of your responsibilities as an NQT will be to report to parents on pupils' achievement and attainment, both in writing and orally at parents' evenings.

As a preparation for this responsibility, consider the following scenarios. How would you react to:

- a parent who wants to know how they might help their child progress in MFL?
- a supportive single parent whose child's academic performance (including MFL) suffers from the recent divorce of her parents?
- a parent who wants to be convinced why his 14-year-old son should continue to study MFL?
- a parent who is concerned about her child having been put into the lowest attaining set?
- a parent who is concerned about a lack of/too much/difficult homework?
- a parent who feels her child is being picked on by you and given unfair detentions?

Prepare a line of argument and discuss it with a teacher in your placement department.

PERSONAL PORTFOLIO

The introduction of the induction period as well as the development by the TDA of qualifications and standards for various stages of teaching (see http://www.tda.gov.uk/teachers/professionalstandards.aspx for details) clearly demonstrates that qualified teacher status is increasingly being seen as a 'beginning' qualification only, i.e. successful completion of a period of initial teacher education is only the start in the course of your challenging and rewarding work as a teacher.

Job descriptions can provide a useful tool in the process of defining roles and responsibilities within MFL teams on the basis of personal strengths. They can also serve as an *aide-mémoire* and as the foundation for work on a portfolio of personal achievements and CPD, collecting evidence and documenting achievement when working towards the induction standards and/or in preparation for your next career move.

Your personal portfolio might include outstanding features of the teaching or course file or details of and handouts from INSET courses or conferences.

If stored systematically, such evidence can be useful and relevant at various stages in your teaching career such as when applying for jobs, when preparing for appraisal discussions or when applying for accreditation of prior learning (APL) as exemption from parts of a higher degree or professional qualification.

CPD

After the initial period of settling into a new post – becoming familiar with the policies and procedures of the department and the school and getting to know new classes – and after having established yourself and successfully completed the induction period, you may want to take on additional responsibilities and undergo CPD. Performance management can play an important role in this process and help with the identification of personal development needs. In most schools CPD is linked to the school and departmental development plans, which in turn often reflect issues identified in Ofsted inspections.

Performance management

Performance management came into force in 2000 and replaced appraisal, which was first introduced in the early 1990s but which was not always consistently implemented by schools. Maintained schools are required to have an agreed performance management policy in place requiring every teacher, apart from those in their induction year or on a contract of less than a year, to set and review objectives annually together with their line manager. Revised arrangements were published in 2006. For details, see http://www.tda.gov.uk/teachers/performance_management.aspx.

The purpose of performance management is the establishment of a shared commitment to high performance and it needs to be seen as inextricably linked to schools' target-setting and evaluation procedures. Performance management can also be seen as part of the government's attempt to increase teachers' accountability and be linked to the threshold arrangements for performance-related pay. Teachers can add their own comments to the report, which is confidential and 'should not be used as the basis for competency or disciplinary actions' (Duffy 2000: 30).

The process is not unlike that of the induction year and enables you to some extent to take responsibility for identifying factors, which have a positive and/or negative effect on your work and how the latter might be addressed.

The periodical review of objectives can be regarded as an important part of your career development process.

Developing a career plan

Once the development needs relating to the induction standards have been met, you can start to develop a career plan, although, of course, this can be something you have initial thoughts on from the beginning of your ITE programme. Personal career development needs to be carefully planned on the basis of your interests and strengths. It has already been noted that target-setting during your induction year and in the context of appraisal can play a useful part in identifying possible avenues for CPD.

The teaching profession offers wide scope for career development: as an MFL teacher you can, for instance, aspire to expertise in teaching skills, subject area management, curriculum development, pastoral responsibilities or work with pupils with special educational needs. It is up to you to consider and look for opportunities to gather experience in relevant areas such as primary MFL, working as a form tutor or taking on extra-curricular responsibilities such as organising exchanges.

The study for a higher degree such as a Master of Arts (MA)/Master of Education (MEd) or Doctor of Philosophy (PhD)/Education Doctorate (EdD) in an MFL-related or educational field is another way of developing professionally, particularly as you may have gained some Masters level credits as part of your ITE qualification. Many higher education institutions offer such courses on a part-time as well as a full-time basis. The nature of these courses can be quite distinct. It is, therefore, worthwhile to 'shop around' for a course that suits your personal requirements and caters for your particular specific areas of interest. The recent announcement by the government to introduce a 'Masters in Teaching and Learning', and the expectation that all teachers should complete it over the course of their career, placed renewed emphasis on CPD through the study at Masters level.

Participation in courses and conferences might be an effective way not only of improving and updating subject specific knowledge, skills and understanding but also to network with other professionals. Keeping in contact with colleagues from your ITE course might also be helpful at a professional as well as personal level.

Where they are in post, local authority advisers are possible external points of reference for support on curriculum development work and may well be involved in the assessment process during your induction year.

Ofsted inspections

Office for Standards in Education (Ofsted) inspection visits to schools aim at identifying strengths and weaknesses of the work of teachers in a whole school context with a view to improving the quality of education provided to pupils and the raising of standards.

A lot of emphasis is given now to schools' self-evaluation, but Ofsted inspectors, among other things, do also observe lessons. For details see http://www.teacher net.gov.uk/management/curriculumdelivery/ofstedinspections/.

Inspection findings should inform the MFL department's action planning as well as the classroom practice of individual MFL teachers. In addition to inspection reports of schools, the Ofsted website (http://www.ofsted.gov.uk/) also features a number of useful documents including the MFL subject reports. At the time of writing the most recent available was the report for 2002–03 published in 2004 (see http://www.ofsted.gov.uk/assets/3542.doc).

MFL-RELATED DEVELOPMENTS

One of the characteristics of teaching as a profession is the need for teachers to keep up to date with the developments in an ever changing educational world and their implications for classroom practice. CPD can be motivated by a number of factors.

As 'living organisms', MFL and their related disciplines invariably undergo changes, which require the constant updating your skills base. In the process of their use as communicative tools, MFL invariably change over time.

Ongoing research continues to push back existing boundaries of subject specialist knowledge and the understanding of the teaching and learning processes challenges you to keep up with developments in these fields, rather than risk 'stagnating' at a particular stage of your MFL professional development and methodological repertoire.

Rapid technological innovations over the past few decades have not only been greatly influencing teaching methodology but have also brought with them new linguistic conventions. Multimedia, internet-based and computer-assisted language learning material are increasingly used in the MFL classroom and for personal use.

Debates continue as to how best to integrate, exploit and develop such technology in the MFL classroom and how the roles of teacher and learner are changing as a consequence.

NQTs tend to be seen by experienced teachers as 'experts' in ICT and other fields. Depending on how ready you feel, you could seize such opportunities to become proactive and organise in-house training sessions for the rest of the department or provide input to departmental meetings. There is, however, a danger in taking on too many extra responsibilities too soon.

Many ITE courses now incorporate Masters level credits. Once qualified, further study to complete a full Masters course, particularly of a professional rather than an academic nature, may well be appropriate for you. It is important for you to maintain and refresh your knowledge of MFL teaching and learning developments whether you are planning further academic study or not. This is often most easily achieved by (active) membership of a professional association, ALL (Association for Language Learning http://www.all-languages.org.uk/) in the case of MFL teachers, and contact with such organisations as the National Centre for Languages (CILT) (http://www.cilt.org.uk). Belonging to an active e-mail discussion group or even checking some key websites regularly can mean you stay updated and informed.

In addition, regular reading of the national educational press such as the *TES*, which regularly publishes material related to MFL, or the *Education Guardian*, which has some very useful MFL resources and reading material on its website http://www.educationunlimited.co.uk/, as well as the exploration of resources can help in this respect.

Another very useful source for information and inspiration are specialist publications such as books, journals and occasional papers published by professional and other organisations such as the bi-annual *Language Learning Journal* (http://www.tandf.co.uk/journals/titles/09571736.asp) as well as publications and updates provided by CILT. In addition to MFL-specific literature, there is a wealth of literature on (Teaching) English as a Foreign Language (T/EFL) which can be helpful, particularly in terms of methodological considerations.

INTERNATIONAL DEVELOPMENTS

In addition to changes at a national level, there are continually developments at an international level. This makes it necessary for the aims and objectives of national educational policy and the intended learning outcomes associated with it to be reviewed from time to time. The implication for you as an MFL teacher is to keep up to date with these developments.

The identification in 1988 of a European Dimension as an aim in the education of young people by the member states of the then European Community (EC) has led to the formulation by the UK government of an international strategy for education, skills and children's services programmatically entitled 'Putting the world into world-class education' (available at http://www.globalgateway.org.uk/pdf/International-Strategy.pdf). There are many opportunities for you to take part in CPD, joint educational projects and teacher exchange programmes. The British

Council is the national agency dealing with the many action programmes for which funding is currently available to (MFL) teachers (see http://www.britishcouncil.org/learning-professional-development.htm for details). CILT also offers a number of TL-specific opportunities for you as a serving MFL teacher.

USING THE INTERNET FOR CONTINUING PROFESSIONAL DEVELOPMENT (CPD) AND ONLINE NETWORKING

Access to the internet affords you ample opportunity to develop professionally as well as to communicate with colleagues from near and far, nationally and internationally (see Chapter 12). One interesting way of networking with MFL professionals is to subscribe to an e-mail (discussion) list where MFL teachers exchange information and views about their teaching via e-mail, such as 'FLTeach', the Foreign Language Teaching Forum, available at http://www.cortland.edu/flteach/ or 'Lingu@Net' at http://www.linguanet.org.uk. The internet does, of course, also allow you to keep up with developments in the target countries, for example through online newspapers or information portals, and gives easy access to (authentic) materials, which can help you improve your own subject knowledge.

Task 13.11 Using the internet for CPD	
1	Find one website, which helps you improve your knowledge of language, one to deepen your knowledge of the target culture and one to develop your pedagogic skills.
2	Subscribe to an e-mail discussion forum. Check your account from time to time and read the messages you receive. What new insights are you gaining?
3	For your next assignment, look through some online journals or carry out an internet search for relevant background reading. Can you find any relevant articles and sources?

For a more detailed discussion of CPD in the early stages of your career, see Pachler and Field (2004).

SUMMARY

Finding your first teaching post cannot be left to chance. Various steps are involved. This chapter has shown that you need care and thoroughness in filling out application forms and in writing letters of application to increase the likelihood of being short-listed for a teaching post. It has also shown that preparatory work for the interview should enhance the chances of you being successful on the day.

As an NQT you are required to successfully complete a period of induction and this chapter has briefly outlined what this involves.

In an ever changing educational world, the ongoing updating of personal skills, understanding and knowledge is important and can be seen as your professional responsibility as a qualified MFL teacher. It is up to you to seek opportunities for development. In this chapter we have identified various opportunities and sources for CPD, including those making use of ICT.

FURTHER READING

Lamb, T. and Simpson, M. (2003) 'Escaping from the treadmill: practitioner research and professional autonomy', *Language Learning Journal*, 28: 55–63.

An article outlining the benefits to be gained from teachers' involvement in research projects.

Richards, J. and Rodgers, T. (2001) *Approaches and Methods in Language Teaching*, 2nd edn. Cambridge: Cambridge University Press.

This book covers a wide range of issues for the developing teacher of languages and enables an NQT to identify areas where she would benefit from further reading and research.

Williams, M. and Burden, R., (1997) *Psychology for language teachers: A Social Constructivist Approach*. Cambridge: Cambridge University Press.

A very interesting book for all MFL teachers which offers insights in to the 'why' of pupils' attitudes and behaviours.

14 Foreign language learning and second language acquisition research

Some implications for FL teaching and learning

INTRODUCTION

In recent years, particularly since the UK government claims to have become increasingly concerned with ensuring policy-making is evidence-informed (for a detailed discussion, see Pachler 2003), research findings have become ever more important in foreign language (FL) teaching. Moreover, the recent trend towards aligning (parts of) Postgraduate Certificate in Education (PGCE) courses with Masters level criteria has led to an increased emphasis on research-orientated approaches in initial teacher education.

Out of these developments a number of questions arise, such as: what types of evidence are considered valid and which research methods are fit for purpose, for example, research into the foundation disciplines of education, such as psychology, sociology or the history of education, or subject-specific research from the fields of foreign language learning (FLL) and second language acquisition (SLA)? Large-scale, longitudinal quantitative studies carried out by academics or small-scale, short-term, qualitative enquiries by (practitioner) researchers? What is the role of foreign language teachers in research? Increasingly, professional enquiry carried out by teachers (supported by higher educational institution (HEI) tutors) is being advocated (see Lamb and Simpson 2003; Macaro 2003a, 2003b) and it is argued that educational research literacy, i.e. the ability to carry out educational research, is an important part of a teacher's professionality. Many specialist schools, particularly those with training school status, are expected to be engaged in practitioner research and dissemination.

As space is limited, and as guidance on how to become educationally research literate abounds (see above and Pachler *et al.* 2007), we will focus here on some findings of recent research into FLL and SLA and consider possible implications for teaching. It is worth noting that in addition to empirical studies, this chapter also draws on literature reviews as well as more scholarly, i.e. conceptual work.

OBJECTIVES

By the end of this chapter you should:

- be aware of findings of recent research into FLL and SLA and possible implications for FL teaching;
- have realistic expectations in relation to what (FLL and SLA) research is available and its ability to offer answers (for pedagogical practice);
- have a heightened awareness of what types of evidence can be considered valid, which research methods are fit for purpose and what your role can be in research.

By and large we draw on work carried out by researchers, rather than teachers, not because we don't recognise the significance of practitioner knowledge but because it is not always easily available in published form. It tends to remain largely bound up in the educational settings in which it is generated, because teachers more often than not neither have the time nor the opportunity to disseminate their work more widely.

We also want to sound a word of caution in relation to possibly unrealistic expectations in relation to research and its ability to offer clear-cut answers. In engaging with research, particularly educational research and more specifically research in the fields of FLL and SLA, readers of research reports have to bear in mind that education and FL learning and teaching are highly complex fields influenced by many contextual factors and variables. Classrooms and schools are complex environments, or 'ecological' systems, where factors such as the physical environment, the time of day, the number of learners, the personal characteristics of the teacher and the learners, the proficiency of the learners, their age, their motivation, the time available, the teaching resources used, the status of the language in the educational institution and the society more widely etc. all have a potentially important impact on the learning experiences of pupils. It is very difficult, and often impossible to control these variables in a way that allows researchers to draw hard and fast conclusions which are transferable and generalisable to other contexts. Research findings, therefore, have to remain 'fuzzy' and the old adage 'apply with caution' (Hatch 1978) invariably applies.

Caution is particularly important in respect of the summary of key research findings presented in this chapter as necessarily, in order to be able to provide an overview of a range of studies across a number of topics, it is not possible to offer any meaningful background information, context and detail about the individual studies from which the recommendations presented here have been drawn. It is not possible, therefore, to validate the interpretations of the data made by researchers of the studies featured and in the literature reviews summarised. In our view, this does not, however, invalidate our attempt to provide an overview of some of the key research that exists and what relevance it might have for the FL classroom, provided you are fully aware of the limitations that exist, particularly as it is meant primarily as a springboard for you to follow up the work presented and examine the details yourself.

With Grabe (2004: 59–60) we would argue that, while there is unlikely to be a 'definitive research study', there is a danger in relying on the notion of 'doing what works' in that it can limit progress: 'Practitioner knowledge is typically not open to comparisons and competition from new ideas (except fashions and bandwagons), and it is easily abused when teaching practices become fossilized or politicized.' We concur that reliable evidence in support of instructional practices, even if it is invariably not perfect, can help minimise some of the negative consequences of relying on 'best practice' and allows you to test new ideas in your search for more effective outcomes: 'The ideal . . . is a merging of practitioner knowledge and persuasive research support: both are needed for effective instruction' (ibid.: 60). Lightbown (2003: 10) similarly argues that SLA research is an important source of ideas and 'can help shape teachers' expectations of themselves and their students, and provide valuable clues to effective pedagogical practice'. And, she rightly asserts: 'Pedagogical innovations must be implemented and adapted according to local conditions including the strengths of individual teachers and students, the available resources, the age of the learners, and the time available for teaching.'

The discipline of applied linguistics, within which we see both FLL and SLA located, also deals with mother tongue (L1) research; important considerations, therefore, when examining the usefulness of research, in particular in terms of its transferability to UK secondary classroom situations, among others are whether or not it has been carried out with L1 or L2 (English as a second language) learners, whether it concerns itself with language use in or outside the classroom, whether the language concerned is English as a foreign/second language or another language, the relationship between L1 and L2 and what the age of the subjects was.

TEACHER KNOWLEDGE AND TEACHER COGNITION AND LEARNING TO TEACH

Prior to our review of FLL and SLA research, we want to address the questions of how teachers learn (about) the content and practices of teaching.

In his review article tracing the conceptualisations of the above over time, Freeman (2002: 4) rightly reminds his readers that learning to teach is more than mastering specific content and methodologies for transmitting that content. Not only can, and should, content not be seen as fixed and given, but as constantly evolving and as being constructed by those involved in the teaching and learning process, but also such a view does not take into account the centrality of the multilayered sociocultural context at macro (national educational policy), meso (school policies) and micro level (factors pertaining to specific classes and pupils and individual teachers and their educational and experiential histories) in which learning to teach takes place:

the theory-practice gap is no longer an issue of lack of relevance or of faulty transfer of skills; rather it is one of connecting and integrating the social contexts of professional education with those of the classroom and the school.

(ibid.: 7)

In addition to the recognition of the importance of context, teacher thinking and decision-making, as cognitive as well as socially embedded and public activities, and the metalevel knowledge of teachers of their practical experience have become central. For Freeman (ibid.: 11), and we agree with him, the continued attempt of trying to find meaning in personal professional experience as well as that of more experienced teachers is key.

Borg (2003: 81) defines the term 'teacher cognition' as 'the unobservable cognitive dimension of teaching – what teachers know, believe, and think' and he posits that research into teacher cognition shows that 'teachers are active, thinking decision-makers who make instructional choices by drawing on complex, practically-oriented, personalised, and context-sensitive networks of knowledge, thoughts, and belief'.

A key issue for student teachers is to what extent their period of initial teacher education (ITE) is able to influence their cognition and to what extent prior beliefs remain dominant. With reference to research carried out with PGCE student teachers, Borg argues that extant factors from student teachers' own schooling are a strong influence on their practice but that ITE can, and does promote some change at least at the structural level, i.e. it leads to a clearer organisation – reordering, relabelling and sometimes reversal – of personal theories into thematic clusters of ideas and he recommends that student teachers should have opportunities early on in their course to confront their existing beliefs (ibid.: 90). We would strongly recommend to you to reflect on your own beliefs about learning, teaching and learning to teach from the start of your course.

Richards (1998: 117–18) notes that experienced teachers used more improvisation than inexperienced teachers which, according to him, suggests that they draw less on 'preactive decision making', by which he means planning, and more on 'interactive decision making'.

In a piece with Li and Tang, Richards (1998, in Borg 2003: 95) identified four areas of language teaching in which less experienced teachers differ from more experienced colleagues:

1   Thinking about the subject matter from the learner's perspective.
2   Having a deep understanding of the subject matter.
3   Knowing how to present subject matter in appropriate ways.
4   Knowing how to integrate language learning with broader curricular goals.

In our view, you need to be aware of this gap and you are strongly encouraged to try to bridge it as you work through the course.

SOME GENERALISATIONS AND HYPOTHESES FROM FLL AND SLA RESEARCH

We start the review of FLL and SLA research findings with a number of generalisations drawn from recent research. Three commentators in particular have tried to extract a number of such generalisations from available research: Lightbown (2003), Ellis (2005) and Chapelle (1998).

Lightbown starts off by asserting that adults and adolescents can 'acquire' a second language, i.e. that while it is true that learners learn things that were never the subject of explicit teaching, instruction can enhance language acquisition. The fact that FL instruction is not necessarily a futile endeavour seems to us to be a reassuring starting point! Another generalisation Lightbown makes is that the developmental stages of pupils' language learning, their so-called 'interlanguages', are often characterised by systematic errors that children make when learning the language as an L1 as well as others which are based on the learners' own L1. According to Lightbown, research shows that there are predictable sequences in L2 acquisition, i.e. that some structures have to be acquired before others. Grammar teaching, or form-focused instruction as it tends to be called in the research literature, may speed up pupils' progress through a sequence; the sequence itself, however, is not significantly changed by it. This suggests that pupils can only be taught what they are ready to learn. It also makes it clear that progress cannot simply be equated with greater accuracy: 'the developmental stages through which learners pass on their way to higher levels of proficiency include stages in which their performance, while systematic, is still far from target-like' (2003: 5). Lightbown warns against the conclusion that teachers should plan according to developmental sequences as there are only few detailed descriptions of such sequences in a small number of languages and as it is not feasible to determine the level of all pupils in a class. Even if these difficulties could be overcome, she sees a danger in teaching focusing too much on language features in isolation which has been discredited by research. The main conclusion Lightbown recommends to teachers from the developmental sequence generalisation is the realisation that progress need not necessarily manifest itself in terms of an increase in accuracy. Lightbown's next generalisation is that pattern practice and drill in isolation from meaningful language use does not make perfect. She also posits that knowing a language rule does not mean that pupils will be able to use it in communicative interaction. Research suggests that pupils do benefit from instruction that focuses their attention explicitly on language form (although that need not be rule learning); and learners need to notice certain features before they can acquire them and instruction may increase the likelihood of pupils noticing how the target language (TL) works. Lightbown also states that isolated explicit error correction is usually ineffective in changing language behaviour. She does note, though, that error feedback can be an effective approach to grammar teaching if it is focused on something the pupil is capable of learning, if the pupil is able to distinguish between feedback that is confirmatory of the content and feedback that provides information about linguistic accuracy or pragmatic appropriateness and if it is sustained over time. Furthermore, Lightbown posits that in instructional settings the age at which pupils start to learn a language is less important than the quality and intensity of instruction and the adequacy of time available. Lightbown also reminds us of the enormity of the task in hand for language learners in view of the complexity of language in terms of vocabulary, morphology, syntax and pronunciation as well as pragmatic and sociolinguistic features of language use, even for pupils with high levels of aptitude, i.e. individual pupil's strengths in the cognitive abilities required for language learning compared with other learners. Lightbown's final generalisation states that the pupils' ability to understand language in a meaningful context is greater than their ability to comprehend decontextualised language and to produce language of comparable complexity and accuracy; in other words their receptive language use will invariably exceed their productive ability and that presentation of language and language use in context is important.

Ellis is particularly concerned with the teaching of grammar and points out that there is no agreement among researchers whether the focus should be on the systematic teaching of grammatical features or on attention to linguistic features in the context of communicative activities or tasks. Like Lightbown, Ellis also identifies 10 generalisations.

First of all, he stresses the need for teachers to ensure that pupils develop both a rich repertoire of formulaic expressions and rule-based competence as research evidence shows that pupils first internalise prefabricated patterns and chunks of language which they later break down and analyse.

Second, Ellis reminds his readers that teachers need to ensure that pupils focus predominantly on meaning. Two types of meaning can be distinguished: semantic meaning, i.e. the meanings of lexical items or grammatical structures, and pragmatic meaning, i.e. the contextualised meanings that arise in communication. To be able to cater for the latter, Ellis argues, a task-based approach to language teaching is required which views language as a tool for communication whereas for the former language can be treated as an object of study.

Third, Ellis stresses that teachers need to ensure that pupils also focus on form, according to some researchers in particular on form-function mapping, i.e. the correlation between specific forms and the meaning(s) they realise in communication.

Fourth, Ellis reminds teachers to direct instruction predominantly at developing implicit knowledge of the L2, which is procedural and held unconsciously and available for use in real-time, while not neglecting explicit, declarative knowledge, which tends to include rules as well as metalanguage, i.e. terminology to label knowledge about grammar and other aspects of language. Ellis contends that 'explicit knowledge is arguably only of value if it can be shown that learners are able to utilize this type of knowledge in actual performance' (2005: 215). It can do that among other things by facilitating the development of implicit knowledge. He also reports that explicit grammatical knowledge can be seen to make it more likely that pupils attend to the structure in the input and make comparisons with their respective interlanguage. Depending on what role teachers afford to explicit knowledge, very different approaches to language teaching flow. A teacher who takes the view that explicit knowledge is of no or little value is likely to adopt a 'zero grammar' approach. If, on the other hand, a teacher who takes the view that it is of value, is likely to adopt the explicit presentation in a presentation, practice and production (PPP) model (see

Chapter 3 for a detailed discussion of the PPP model). If, however, a teacher adopts a middle position of affording explicit grammar teaching some importance, this can provide the basis of a consciousness-raising approach. It is the latter that Ellis sees best supported by research findings.

Fifth, Ellis points out that teachers need to take into account a pupil's 'built-in syllabus', i.e. the 'natural' order and sequence of acquisition followed by pupils in learning grammar as implicit knowledge (but see Lightbown's point above). Research suggests that the order and sequence of acquisition is the same for instructed and natural learners, but that instructed learners generally achieve higher levels of grammatical competence. Teachers can, therefore, take into account Ellis' fifth generalisation: (1) by adopting a zero grammar approach; (2) by ensuring that learners are developmentally ready to acquire a specific grammar point; and (3) focusing in their teaching on explicit rather than implicit knowledge as, according to Ellis, explicit knowledge is not 'subject to the same developmental constraints' as implicit knowledge.

Sixth, Ellis posits that successful FL learning requires extensive TL input; only with exposure to TL input that is 'comprehensible', i.e. that has been modified or is contextually supported, can pupils acquire language. As was discussed in Chapter 5, this can be achieved by optimising the use of the TL in the classroom and making it the medium as well as the object of teaching. As we have seen already, teachers can create opportunities for exposure to the TL outside the classroom, in particular in countries where the TL is spoken.

Seventh, Ellis reminds us that successful language learning also requires opportunities for output as it, among other things, requires pupils to engage in syntactic processing and to test out hypotheses as well as to automatise existing knowledge and to develop discourse skills. Task-based learning (TBL) can be seen to be a particularly advisable approach in this context; it focuses on activities which require pupils to use language with an emphasis on meaning to obtain certain objectives (see Skehan 2003) and it will be discussed in more detail below.

Ellis' eighth generalisation asserts that the opportunity to interact in the TL is central to developing proficiency in it. Among other things, interaction allows for the negotiation of meaning, which is considered to be a key process in language learning. Teachers, according to Ellis with reference to relevant research findings, therefore, should try to create contexts of language use where pupils have a reason to attend to language, they should provide opportunities for pupils to express their own personal meanings in the TL, they should help pupils participate in activities that are just beyond their current level of proficiency and they should offer a wide range of contexts. These key requirements for acquisition-rich classroom interaction are said to be more likely to occur in less rigid academic task and social participation structures, i.e. by less tightly sequenced subject matter and by less prescriptive allocation of roles and responsibilities of interactants. Again, Ellis views this as evidence in support of the use of tasks, as opposed to exercises, but recognises that a looser approach to interaction in the classroom is not easily achieved as teachers have to ensure classroom discourse is orderly. Because of classroom management considerations, Ellis argues, the so-called IRF (initiation, response, feedback) approach to controlling discourse topics is so widely used where the teacher initiates, the pupils respond and the teacher provides feedback. This highly structured approach, however, does not appear to provide ideal conditions for interaction in the TL which is why small group work, in which pupils interact among themselves, is so important. Once again, in order to be effective, small group work needs to be characterised by certain features and the avoidance of excessive use of the mother tongue in mainly monolingual groups is an important one. (For a detailed and very useful discussion of tasked-based learning, see Ellis 2003.)

Generalisation nine suggests that teachers need to take account of individual differences in pupils, in particular, their aptitude and motivation. Again, Ellis acknowledges the practical difficulties of identifying individual differences of all learners in large classes and he therefore suggests the adoption of a flexible approach to teaching which involves a variety of learning activities. He also points out the need to make pupils more aware of their own approaches to learning as well as to develop an awareness of alternative approaches. In particular it is suggested a balance is struck between analytical as well as experiential approaches. We will discuss the importance of learner and learning strategies and motivation from a research perspective later in this chapter.

Finally, Ellis reminds us that it is important to focus on free as well as controlled language production in assessing pupils' TL proficiency.

Chapelle (1998) sets out a model of SLA which is based on the notion that TL input is the key to successful language learning and attempts to describe, with reference to cognitive processes, what makes input comprehensible and how it is processed; the model delineates the following process from input to output: apperception (the noticing of salient features of input), comprehension (the understanding of semantic and syntactic features of input), intake (comprehended language) and integration (the development of the pupils' linguistic system). On the basis of this model, which notably excludes the social dimension of language learners, Chapelle formulates seven hypotheses about ideal conditions for language learning (with particular reference to computer-assisted contexts).

First of all, she notes that teachers need to make the linguistic characteristics of TL input noticeable. Then she posits that pupils need to receive support in comprehending semantic and syntactic aspects of linguistic input. She stresses the need for pupils to have opportunities to produce TL output and to notice errors in their own output. She also suggests that pupils need to correct their linguistic output. Furthermore, she believes that pupils need to engage in TL interaction whose structure can be modified for negotiation of meaning. And, finally, she thinks that pupils should engage in L2 tasks designed to maximise opportunities for good interaction.

In exploring the notion of 'good interaction', she draws on research which, among other things, sets out a number of task characteristics around the roles and relationships of participants in relation to each other and the information to be exchanged as well as requirements in terms of information exchange.

FL COMMUNICATION IN MULTILINGUAL CONTEXTS

In a recent think-piece, Kramsch (2006) moves the debate about communicative competence as a key aim of FL teaching and learning, and CLT (communicative language teaching) as the dominant pedagogical model (see Chapter 3, for a discussion of CLT) helpfully on by pointing out that we should be mindful of how the notion of communicative competence 'is being put to the service of instrumental goals' (ibid.: 250) by being interpreted in and by the educational world as 'the ability to exchange information speedily and effectively and to solve problems, complete assigned tasks, and produce measurable results' (ibid.: 250). She points out that in the move from predominantly monolingual to multilingual contexts, communication has become much more complex and breakdown in communication often is not due to 'a lack of linguistic comprehension, but because of a lack of understanding and trust of interlocutors' intentions' (ibid.: 250):

> The exacerbation of global social and economic inequalities and of ethnic identity issues, as well as the rise in importance of religion and ideology around the world have created historical and cultural gaps that a communicative approach to language teaching cannot bridge in itself.
>
> (ibid.: 250–1)

Kramsch stresses the need not only for knowledge about language and an ability to communicate meaning, but also for an understanding of meaning making itself in order to bridge these widening gaps. This, she cogently argues, has implications for language teaching and requires more sophisticated competences in what she calls 'the manipulation of symbolic systems' (ibid.: 251). By that she means discourse competence in a range of modalities (speech, writing, images) with an emphasis on the representation and interpretation of meaning. Pedagogically speaking, she argues for the need for complexity and a focus on alternatives in the production of meaning, the tolerance of ambiguity as well as an appreciation of form as meaning (ibid.: 251).

HOW TO MOTIVATE LANGUAGE LEARNERS

Dörnyei, in a number of publications, notably 1998 and 2001, takes the view that motivation is one of the most important factors in determining the rate and success of foreign language attainment:

> Without sufficient motivation, even individuals with the most remarkable abilities cannot accomplish long-term goals, and neither are appropriate curricula and good teaching enough to ensure student achievement. . . . high motivation can make up for considerable deficiencies both in one's language aptitude and learning conditions.
>
> (Dörnyei and Csizér 1998: 203–4)

Yet, as Macaro rightly points out (2003a: 89), motivation does not have obvious direct causes and it is even difficult to discern what the concept encompasses. He identifies the following 'determinants' for motivation, i.e. whether someone will be motivated to learn a foreign language (ibid.: 91):

- the usefulness of speaking another language;
- the influence of significant others such as parents or friends;
- the difficulty of the subject;
- its status compared to other subjects on the curriculum;
- world events;
- its 'genderedness';
- an individual's social and cultural background;
- contact with the target culture.

Dörnyei developed a framework which categorises motivational components into three main dimensions: language level (ethnolinguistic, cultural-affective and intel-lectual components and pragmatic values and attitudes), learner level (personality traits) and learning situation (course-, teacher- and group-specific components). On the basis of empirical work he (Dörnyei and Csizér 1998: 215) formulates the following 'ten commandments' for motivating language learners (but is keen to stress that degree of complexity involved in trying to conceptualise motivation:

1   Set a personal example with your own behaviour.
2   Create a pleasant, relaxed atmosphere in the classroom.
3   Present tasks properly.
4   Develop a good relationship with the learners.
5   Increase the learners' linguistic self-confidence.
6   Make the language classes interesting.
7   Promote learner autonomy.
8   Personalize the learning process.
9   Increase the learners' goal-orientedness.
10 Familiarize learners with the target language culture.

The issue of motivation, or rather lack of it, to learn foreign languages has dogged foreign language education for some time and the publication of the proposals follow-ing the Dearing Report in 2007 are a useful step in the direction of finding systemic solutions to challenges raised by certain imponderables of foreign language learning: that it is a difficult and complex process. One solution to lack of motivation suggested by the research literature is an emphasis on learning strategies and it is to these we turn next.

LEARNING STRATEGIES

In his review of learning strategies and use, Macaro (2006: 320–1) reports, among others, the following claims based on evidence-informed scholarship:

1   Strategy use appears to correlate with various aspects of language learning success although there is a lack of consensus about whether the range,

frequency and/or the nature of strategy use/strategies is the determinant factor.

2   There are group differences and individual differences in strategy use.

3   Strategy instruction/training appears to be effective in promoting successful learning if it is carried out over lengthy periods of time and if it includes a focus on metacognition, i.e. learning about learning.

Macaro also points out a number of problems in relation to learning strategies and use (ibid.: 325), not least the fact that there is no consensus about what learner strategies are, whether they consist of knowledge, intention, action or all three. He then goes on to describe and define learner strategies in terms of a goal, situation and mental action and asserts that strategies are the raw material of conscious cognitive processing and need to be distinguished from subconscious activity and processes.

Chamot, in her research review, defines learning strategies as 'procedures that facilitate a learning task' (2005: 112). In her view, strategies are often conscious but, through repeated use, can become automatised to some extent. She posits that learning strategies are important for two main reasons: (1) because they allow us to gain insights into the (meta)cognitive, social and affective processes involved in language learning; and (2) learning strategy instruction can help pupils become better language learners. Learning strategies are sensitive to the learning context as well as learner characteristics and their effectiveness depends as much on the frequency of use as it depends how they are used (ibid.: 115). Good language learners can be said to be better at matching strategies to task requirements, something less successful learners appear to lack (ibid.: 116). Chamot reports (ibid.: 115) various learning strategy research studies which identify the good language learner as someone who:

*   is mentally active;
*   monitors language comprehension and production;
*   practises communicating in the language;
*   makes use of prior linguistic and general knowledge;
*   uses various memorisation techniques;
*   asks questions for clarification.

On the basis of her overview of research studies in the field of learning strategies Chamot reports that the development of pupils' metacognition, i.e. 'their ability to understand and regulate their own thinking and learning' (ibid.: 124), is an aspect language teachers should consider very carefully. Metacognition, she also notes, can be considered to encompass both declarative as well as procedural knowledge, i.e. self-knowledge, world knowledge, task knowledge and strategy knowledge as well as knowledge how to plan for, monitor and evaluate learning. In terms of strategy training she proposes a recursive metacognitive model for learning in which teachers select learning strategies in the areas of planning, monitoring, problem-solving and evaluating on the basis of perceived need rather than covering them in a sequential manner (ibid.: 125).

THE IMPORTANCE OF PRONUNCIATION

Despite the importance afforded to the teaching of pronunciation in research, this aspect of FL teaching has become, and remains rather neglected. Jenkins (2004) notes that pronunciation teaching typically covers consonant and vowel sounds in isolation (segmental features) and in connected speech, word stress patterns, rhythm and intonation (suprasegmental features). She also reminds her readers of the importance of pronunciation in speakers' success or failure in communication in terms of conveying meaning in specific contexts, its links with a speaker's sense of identity, its contribution of signalling group membership, etc. Jenkins reports the moving away from an emphasis on native-like goals towards a stronger listener perspective in terms of intelligibility and comprehension of non-native speech. Setter and Jenkins (2005: 2) note that when a pronunciation feature gets in the way of the intelligibility of a word, non-native speakers (NNS) are particularly affected as they tend to focus on the acoustic signal rather than use contextual cues to resolve ambiguity. They suggest that teachers should consider replacing the notion of correctness with one of appropriateness. Jenkins (2004) also reports that the concept of 'accent reduction', which regards learners as subjects for speech pathology by trying to get them to lose all traces of their mother tongue accent; instead, she notes that a concept of 'accent addition' is being promoted. Jenkins (2000: 209–10) identifies the following five stages of pronunciation learning (for English as an International Language):

1   addition of core items to the learner's productive and receptive repertoire;
2   addition of a range of L2 target language accents to the learner's receptive repertoire;
3   addition of accommodation skills;
4   addition of non-core items to the learner's receptive repertoire;
5   addition of a range of L1 target language accents to the learner's receptive repertoire.

She estimates that learners who wish to acquire an accent that enables them both to preserve their mother tongue identity in their pronunciation of the TL and use intelligible pronunciation to NNS will restrict themselves to stages 1–3. If they also want to be able to understand the pronunciation of various native speaker (NS) accents, they are likely to go for all five stages. An important implication for FL teaching is the need to increase the availability of NNS renditions in listening activities.

It seems also relevant to point out the potential of ICT in terms of the identification and production of phonemes; of particular relevance in this context is voice recognition for independent pronunciation practice, i.e. learners listening to and repeating words and sequences, recording and listening to themselves and comparing themselves to the input provided etc., although there remain some issues around the ability of the software to deal effectively with NNS input (see e.g. Pachler 2002).

Jenkins (2004) also stresses the importance of pronunciation in terms of learners' identities and notes the fact that accent tends to lead to linguistic insecurity. Research also suggests that it relates significantly to social identity and the construction of self and other, particularly in international rather than national contexts of language use.

Setter and Jenkins (2005) report that while contrastive analysis was once thought to provide conclusive insights into what was difficult in TL compared with mother tongue pronunciation, research has shown that the syllable is a 'unit of immense importance' and the context of sounds in syllable need to be borne in mind. In line with the development of the notion of a constantly developing interlanguage researchers promote the idea of an interlanguage phonology according to which interference from the mother tongue is more prevalent in the initial stages of phonological acquisition to be replaced in importance over time by developmental factors similar to L1 phonological acquisition processes.

In term of implications for pronunciation teaching, Setter and Jenkins conclude that while pronunciation practice should be incorporated as early as possible, pronunciation should not be treated in isolation but instead as part of communication and discourse, i.e. on meaning making in communicative situations.

Macaro (2003a: 136) reinforces the importance of phonology as a desirable teaching focus in particular in relation to helping learners understand the relationships between the sounds of the TL and the written form. He advises teachers to encourage beginners to sound out phonemes and phonological units as a precursor to reading comprehension as it lessens the cognitive burden during reading (see the section on reading below). He also notes that by not focusing on pronunciation we not only deprive learners of sounding authentic but we might also deprive them of the ability to access reading texts by sounding out the phonemes of unknown words (ibid.: 209).

LEARNING AND TEACHING VOCABULARY

Knowledge of words and their meanings is important as words are central components of language production and use. Groot points out that learning a word is an 'incremental process that gradually develops with repeated exposure' and he distinguishes three stages of word acquisition (2000: 64):

1   Notice of the various properties of the new word: morphological and phonological, syntactic, semantic, stylistic, collocational, and so forth.
2   Storage in the internal lexicon in networks of relationships that correspond to the properties described in (1).
3   Consolidation of the storage described in (2) by means of further exposure to the word in a variety of contexts which illustrate its various properties. This results in a firmer embedding in the memory needed for long-term retention.

In order to be able to use vocabulary effectively in receptive and productive use, Groot argues (ibid.: 65), these three stages need to be implemented adequately. Also, he posits what he calls a 'stringent relationship' (ibid.: 65) between retention of vocabulary and the extent to which the various properties of words have been processed, i.e. the better the knowledge of the various properties of a new word the better it will be remembered. From that, he concludes that it is preferable to expose learners to new words in context rather than in isolation as only the context will enable the learner to fully understand the properties of a word. And, he concludes that it is better to ask learners to infer meaning of new words from context rather than giving them the meaning as deducing meaning requires greater cognitive effort. He does note, though, (ibid.: 64) that it is essential to have a thorough understanding of the context in order to be able to deduce the meaning of an unknown word.

One important distinction made in research on vocabulary learning is that between incidental and intentional learning and the consensus appears to be that while incidental vocabulary learning as a by-product of learning activities or of extensive reading certainly takes place, the systematic learning of vocabulary is also required particularly in FL learning contexts where there is limited exposure to the TL, not least as extensive reading is not a very prominent activity in typical FL classrooms in the UK. Read (2004) points out that pupils are normally conscious about the fact that lack of vocabulary knowledge can and does hamper effective communication in the TL. This is because 'lexical items carry the basic information load of the meaning [pupils] wish to comprehend and express' (ibid.: 146). He also argues, though, that FL teachers are often unsure about how best to teach vocabulary. And, he suggests that the tendency within communicative approaches to FL teaching to assume that vocabulary learning will take care of itself provided there is sufficient access to comprehensible input is not supported by research.

According to Hulstijn (2001: 275). 'It is the quality and frequency of the information processing activities (i.e., elaboration on aspects of a word's form and meaning, plus rehearsal) that determine retention of new information.' He suggests, therefore, that both incidental and intentional learning should be promoted. Considering the implications of Hulstijn's work, Read identifies two important implications for teaching: (1) the need to return to approaches such as regular rehearsal of words, rote learning, automatic word recognition; and (2) the grading of learning tasks according to their potential for vocabulary learning; here Read (2004: 148) identifies the following three factors: 'the learners' *need* to achieve, a requirement that they *search* for information on the meaning or form of the word, and *evaluation* of how the information obtained applied to the particular use of the word in question'.

Research on word frequency suggests that there is value in focusing on the relatively small proportion of words that are highly used bearing in mind there are differences across writing and speaking. Read notes that studies suggest that in English around 2,000 word families (rather than individual words) account for at least 80 per cent of running words in writing and for 95–99 per cent in speech. Other studies suggest 3,000 word families are needed for being able to deal effectively with everyday conversation. Some studies suggest that 80 per cent was the minimum threshold but that 98 per cent was required to be able to read independently. 'Thus, . . ., it appears that the vocabulary learning goals for minimum levels of both listening and reading comprehension need to be set somewhat higher than the 95 percent coverage that has been widely recommended until now' (Read 2004: 150). Macaro (2003a: 65) reports Nation's work (2001), which suggests that reading for pleasure in the TL requires understanding of 98 per cent of tokens in the text, which he rightly points out has serious pedagogical implications in terms of the selection of texts. Groot

(2000) also offers a very useful discussion of issues concerning word frequency. In his discussion, Read draws attention to what happens when learners engage with specific purpose vocabulary such as in academic writing where an academic word list combined with 'general purpose' vocabulary can make a significant difference in the percentage of the running words (up to 95 per cent in written texts), which suggests that there is value in explicit coverage of specialist terminology. Macaro also points out that to some extent so-called receptive skills, i.e. listening and reading, will require a higher amount of vocabulary than the productive skills of speaking and writing and that an overemphasis on oral interaction in FL teaching may result in lower vocabulary gain as spoken texts feature a higher percentage of high-frequency words. Pedagogical approaches suggested are for pupils to compile pupil- or discipline-specific dictionaries, glossing and the selection and recording of their own vocabulary based on individual needs or interest (although pupils tend not always to choose suitable words); some electronic tools such as Babylon allow for the easy compilation and distribution of such custom-made dictionaries (see Pachler 2001). Based on his review of available research, Read concludes that little research is available reporting on methods of presenting and practising vocabulary in the classroom.

One important question Macaro raises in his discussion of vocabulary teaching and learning is that of what it actually means to 'know' lexical items. He reports 'vocabulary knowledge criteria' from Paribakht and Wesche (1993) who, among others, identify the following criteria:

- The word is not familiar at all.
- The word is familiar but the meaning is not known.
- Learner gives correct synonym or translation.
- Learner uses word with semantic appropriateness in a sentence.
- Learner uses word with semantic appropriateness and grammatical accuracy in a sentence.

While different criteria can be found in the literature, this list goes to show that 'knowing' a word is far from straightforward and that it is important to be aware of different meanings individual words might have in different contexts. Macaro (2003a) suggests that FL teachers should not only look for in-depth knowledge of vocabulary, but also in particular increasingly sophisticated uses of function words, as well as topic coverage, when considering notions of progression.

LEARNING AND TEACHING LISTENING

Vandergrift (2004: 3) notes that listening is no longer considered to be a passive skill but an active one. According to him, approaches to listening instruction have evolved from 'listen to repeat' via 'question-and-answer' to 'real life listening in real time'. He also posits that listening instruction is expanding from 'listening to learn', with a focus on the product, to 'learning to listen', with a focus on the process.

In a recent systematic literature review, Macaro *et al.* (2005) stress the role of listening not just in formal education in general, but also in FL learning in particular.

They point out that listening plays an important part in what they call 'interaction-based acquisition' (ibid.: 6) by which they mean that, among other things, it is by listening to the TL that new vocabulary and the rule system are acquired. In their review the authors report on research which suggests that both top-down and bottom-up processing are important even if it is still unclear what the best balance between the two might be:

> Top-down processing is when *schemata* (or prior knowledge of a topic), as well as other strategies (logic, other knowledge of the world, such as speaking conventions), are applied to the incoming speech stream in order to offset the tendency to listen to every word, a virtual impossibility with fast flowing text. Bottom-up processing involves cognitive strategies for *perceiving* (for example, developing phonemic awareness) and *parsing* (segmenting the speech stream) of the linguistic input. This bottom-up processing is essential not only to identify key vocabulary and syntactical elements in the speech stream but also in order to confirm the initial conclusions made by the application of prior knowledge.
>
> (ibid.: 7)

In their section on findings (ibid.: 46–8), Macaro *et al.* explore the complex relationship between prior knowledge and comprehension in listening and conclude that there is a difference between prior knowledge facilitating listening comprehension and improving it.

Vandergrift (2004: 4–6) notes that beginners have limited prior language knowledge, can only process a limited amount automatically, and have a limited working memory; instead, they need to focus on detail and use compensatory strategies. He advocates the use of advance organisers provided they do not distract from the main focus of the text.

Based on Lund (1991), Macaro (2003a: 154) argues that there are major differences between reading and listening:

- the complete text is not available;
- the text exists in time not in space;
- the listener cannot control the pace of the text;
- listeners tend to try to integrate information from multiple sources simultaneously (parallel distributed processing);
- the sound system of the L2 can pose a significant problem;
- gaps in speech are different to gaps in writing;
- cognates may sound different in continuous speech;
- spoken texts have intonation, stress, regional accents, background noise and other variations of acoustic features.

When listening, more cognitive effort has to be placed on the decoding of a text in terms of noticing and then processing of acoustic information compared with reading where decoding tends to be an issue only where a word-recognition problem exists.

In addition to making allowances for the cognitive difficulties involved in listening, Macaro (2003a: 158) points to Lund's suggestion that listening to a spoken text twice allows the pupil to create context, generate hypotheses and identify gaps to focus on during the first exposure, whereas during the second listening pupils can infer meaning, confirm discarded hypotheses and fill gaps in detail missed the first time round. He also stresses the importance of prosodic features and clues, in particular intonation and stress.

For teaching and learning purposes, Macaro also emphasises the distinction between 'listening alone' or 'one-way listening' (ibid.: 152), i.e. where the listener has not got the opportunity to interrupt the speaker, and 'listening as interaction' or 'two-way listening' (ibid.: 171f.), where negotiation of meaning takes place between the speaker and the listener with a view to coming to a shared understanding of what is said and/or to have a satisfactory conversation. Interruptions, according to Long (1981), can be classified as:

- confirmation checks, where the listener is trying to ensure they have under-stood correctly;
- clarification requests, where the listener is asking for help with under-standing what was said;
- comprehension checks, where the speaker tries to assure herself that the listener has understood.

This reinforces the importance of the quality of the input, not the quantity of it; the focus should not be on talking at the learners, but on talking with them (Macaro, 2003a: 253).

Macaro also offers a very useful set of questions in relation to 'mediated listening' (ibid.: 176), in particular, in relation to the use of the pause button, with the help of which, he argues (ibid.: 177), one-way listening can be turned into two-way listening. These include:

- breaking down a long text into manageable chunks;
- allowing the hearer to ask for repetition;
- allowing the hearer to build hypotheses about what is to come;
- structuring listening texts into component parts, etc.

He also strongly supports the use of video and video captions in the TL (ibid.: 180) and endorses Chambers' recommendation (1996) to use predictive pre-listening activities as well as while-listening and post-listening activities focusing on different aspects of the listening process.

Vandergrift (2004: 9–10) draws a number of conclusion for listening instruction based on the review of some qualitative studies:

1 Limitations of working memory dictate that supports provided to the listener should relate directly to the text and the listening task.
2 Captions, annotations, and computer programs to slow down speech may be useful for developing word recognition skills and learning vocabulary.

3   Visual supports that are natural to the listening situation can provide important contextual information to help the listener.
4   Context is important to listening.
5   A strategies-based approach to listening instruction with beginner-level listeners builds confidence, raises awareness of the process of listening, and helps listeners to use effective combinations of metacognitive and cognitive strategies to understand texts in real time.

He also notes (ibid.: 10) that listening is too often associated with testing. Being asked to focus on the right answer creates high levels of anxiety which negatively affects the pupil's attention while it does not tell the teacher anything about the process of how pupils came to formulate their answers, which is what they need to know in order to be able to help pupils discover effective listening strategies.

LEARNING AND TEACHING SPEAKING

In their review of recent research in the teaching of speaking, McCarthy and O'Keeffe (2004: 27) note the shift away from native speakers as the dominant model for speaking. They also point out (ibid.: 29), that the value of scripted dialogues for enhancing conversation skills has been challenged as they do not really reflect the unpredictability, features and structures, such as discourse markers, incomplete utterances, vague language, ellipses and hedges, of real-life conversations and, therefore, offer learners only limited opportunities. With reference to Burns (2001), they note that two-part question-answer sequences, which often feature in coursebooks, are not very common in real conversations where replies to questions are usually followed up with a routine phrase. They also refer to Slade (1997), who found that social conversations are dominated by narrative genres such as narratives, anecdotes, exemplars and recounts, all of which are rarely presented in language learning material and teaching contexts.

McCarthy and O'Keeffe (2004: 30) also examine the value of the so-called 'IRF routine' (initiation, response, feedback), which is the dominant interactional pattern in language classes, and point out that, according to Kasper (2001), it fails to provide opportunities for addressing the complex demands of everyday conversations, for example as the learners often remain in a passive and the teacher in an active role.

Rather than relying on exchange structure analysis (IRF), which appears to be more beneficial for developing listening skills, McCarthy and O'Keeffe's review suggests the use of pre-task planning, (critical) discourse analysis ((C)DA) and conversation analysis (CA) as a productive way forward (2004: 30–32). They quote Burns (2001) who suggests that language tasks can be developed by a focus on turn-taking, i.e. a discussion of speaker roles, rights to turns etc, and turn types, i.e. an exploration of more or less preferred responses, repair strategies and reformulation. Such focus on the 'microstructures' of conversations, according to Burns (ibid.), 'can offer teachers the opportunity to highlight for students the appropriateness of utterances, how speakers negotiate certain situations . . . as well as providing a framework for the performance of speech acts' (McCarthy and O'Keeffe 2004: 33).

Burns, Gollin and Joyce (1997; in McCarthy and O'Keeffe 2004: 33) suggest the following analytical framework for teachers:

1   Transcribe the recording.
2   Give the background information to the text.
3   Analyse the text using an analytical approach.
4   Identify the significant teaching points which arise from the analysis.

Based on a review of literature on DA and CA, Dörnyei and Thurrell (1994) suggest the following headings for the selection of aspects of spoken language for teaching purposes (in McCarthy and O'Keeffe 2004: 34):

- conversational rules and structure (e.g. opening, topic shifting and closing);
- conversational strategies (e.g. paraphrase, asking for repetition and clarification);
- functions and meaning in conversation (e.g. illocutionary functions);
- social and cultural contexts (e.g. social norms and appropriateness).

Macaro (2003a: 19) stresses the dual function of speaking, i.e. to communicate meaning but also as a tool to think and organise.

Fluent speech is predicated on the speaker's ability to proceduralise declarative knowledge, i.e. to have overcome the need to explicitly and consciously focus on form. Macaro's reading of the available research evidence (ibid.: 186f.) suggests that input that is modified through interaction leads to improved oral production with there being more emphasis on the acquisition of lexis than grammatical patterns. Interaction and the production of output also gives the pupil an opportunity to 'notice' linguistic features, i.e. attend to them cognitively and establish connections with the long-term memory. However, there is a need for a balance between message and medium-focused interaction and, for pragmatic reasons such as large class sizes, the quality of teacher–whole class interaction is very important to compensate for lack of one-to-one interactions between the teacher and individual pupils as well as of pupil talk. Alternatively, an emphasis can be placed on pupil–pupil interaction with research showing that lower-proficiency pupils can gain a lot from working with higher proficiency pupils without the latter being disadvantaged (ibid.: 192). In relation to pupil–pupil activities, such as pair and group work, he particularly draws attention to the need for clear structuring of the language as well as the task: the language to be used by pupils needs to be clearly defined as should the pathways leading to completion of the task (ibid.: 193). Related questions are whether, when and how the teacher should intervene. Lynch (1997) argues that rather than intervening by correcting when monitoring, or at least to go for quality rather than quantity of corrections, or changing the focus or direction of the interaction, the teacher should intervene as late as possible to allow pupils to attempt their own communication repair and focus on initiating the process of negotiation of meaning and supporting the confirmation of clarification requests.

In her analysis of the quality of teacher-fronted interaction, Antòn (1999) distinguishes co-constructed or dialogic approach and a transmission-based approach to knowledge with the former comprising the following four features:

- eliciting problems and solutions when focusing on grammatical patterns; consciousness-raising of grammatical forms;
- feedback (to error) through awareness raising;
- turn allocation according to individual bidding;
- encouragement of pupils to identify and articulate their learning difficulties and to attempt new learning styles and strategies.

Another study demonstrating the importance of the quality, rather than the quantity of teacher interaction is Walsh (2002) who identifies a number of facilitative and obstructive features for learning potential. Positive teacher moves include direct error correction through explicit recasts, a personal dimension in content feedback, confirmation checks and the encouragement of clarification requests, extended waiting times, scaffolding and avoidance of teacher dominance in turn-taking. Obstructive features include teachers completing the turns for, or interrupting pupils as well as the use of IRF exchanges. The three-part IRF exchange (Sinclair and Coulthard 1975) is reported to account for as much as 70 per cent of all classroom talk (Wells 1993), and is considered to be constitutive of classroom discourse. Macaro also points to the pejorative effect of 'teacher echo' (2003a: 199).

LEARNING AND TEACHING READING

Grabe (2004: 46) develops 10 instructional implications for L2 reading instruction and curriculum design in his review of research:

1 Ensure word recognition fluency.
2 Emphasise vocabulary learning and create a vocabulary-rich environment.
3 Activate background knowledge in appropriate ways.
4 Ensure effective language knowledge and general comprehension skills.
5 Teach text structures and discourse organisation.
6 Promote the strategic reader rather than teach individual strategies.
7 Build reading fluency rate.
8 Promote extensive reading.
9 Develop intrinsic motivation for reading.
10 Plan a coherent curriculum for student learning.

Macaro (2003a: 118–19), rightly in our view, draws attention to the fact that compared with the other 'core' skills of foreign language learning, listening, speaking and writing, reading proficiency and overall text comprehension are comparatively difficult to gauge. He also explains the reading process as one whereby the reader engages in phonemic 'recoding', i.e. the sounding out of words, if she does not recognise a word and its meaning directly. At a whole text level, rather than advocating either a bottom-up (decoding of meaning by the reader encoded by the writer) or a top-down model (the inference of meaning on the basis of activating prior semantic, pragmatic, syntactic and discourse knowledge), he promotes an interactive model in which reading is:

a process which draws on various knowledge sources allowing for the fact that meaning does not reside in the text alone but is a co-construction of the writer's text and the reader's interpretation. Here there is a constant interaction between the surface structure of the text and the reader's own knowledge of the topic which that text is attempting to communicate. This model involves the reader in elaborating on the meaning of the text, inferring meaning but also at times stopping to pause and ponder over individual words and syntactic patterns and their relationships with other words and phrases in order to confirm hypotheses, strengthen connections and build up layers of interpretation.

(ibid.: 120–1)

Macaro points to the importance of contextual and prior knowledge as a combination of all clues surrounding the text, including schemata (individual constructs) or scripts (knowledge shared by certain socio-cultural contexts) (ibid.: 122) which help in text comprehension and 'fill in the gaps' even if the meaning of individual words is not clear; these include titles, pictures etc. He also stresses the importance of the need for effective strategies to make contextual and prior knowledge count. This clearly raises interesting questions for foreign language teachers about whether the emphasis on reading instruction should be on the teaching of lexical and syntactic knowledge, on so-called world knowledge, on strategy training or on a combination of them.

Another important aspect of reading discussed by Macaro (ibid.: 143) is the role of mental translations. He refers to a study by Kern (1994) which suggests that a certain critical threshold of language development needs to be crossed before they can be minimised and, thereby, reading rates can be increased. In his study, Kern identifies a number of benefits of mental translation including:

- support with the consolidation of meaning and clarification of contextual information;
- provision of an 'affective boost';
- help in the maintenance of concentration and in not losing track;
- clarification of the syntactic role of certain lexical items.

These findings suggest that up to a certain level of proficiency there is a role to be played for mental translation.

In relation to text comprehension, Grabe (2004: 51) recommends the following individual comprehension strategies:

- prior knowledge activation
- mental imagery
- graphic organisers
- text structure awareness
- comprehension monitoring
- question answering
- question generating
- mnemonic support practice
- summarisation.

He notes the importance of what he calls 'signalling systems', i.e. discourse structures, of texts, e.g. pronominal systems, other antecedent referencing, thematic signalling, transition words and structures, and syntactic foregrounding and backgrounding, which have functional purposes which need to be recognised by readers (ibid. 52).

In terms of reading strategies he recommends the promotion of the strategic reader, rather than to teach individual reading strategies and lists the following 10 approaches as an effective combination (ibid. 53–4):

1   KWL: Know, Want to know, Learned
2   ETR: Experience – Text – Relate
3   QAR: Question – Answer – Response
4   DR-TA: Directed Reading and Thinking Activities
5   Reciprocal Teaching
6   Collaborative Strategic Reading (CSR)
7   Direct Explanation
8   Questioning the Author
9   Transactional Strategies Instruction (TSI)
10 Concept-Oriented Reading Instruction (CORI)

LEARNING AND TEACHING WRITING

In her review article on writing in a foreign language, O'Brien (2004: 2) refers to Kern's (2000: 172) arguments in support of writing:

> it develops learners' ability to think explicitly about how to organise and express thoughts, feelings and ideas in ways compatible with imagined readers' expectations; it provides a platform for readers to text hypotheses about the new language; it provides time for learners to process meaning, reducing the anxiety often felt in oral production; it provides opportunities for creativity.

With reference to the literature, O'Brien reminds her readers that L2 processing is different from L1 processing and that, therefore, a specific pedagogical approach to the teaching of L2 reading and writing are required (2004: 6).

O'Brien (ibid.: 3) reports on a number of studies which aim to describe the processes of writing and enumerates planning, translating and formulating into language, revising as well as linguistic processes (grammatical, lexical, morphological, graphemic). In terms of process-based pedagogic approaches, awareness of successful writing strategy use and feedback from the teacher or peers are mentioned, as are purpose- and reader-specific tasks as well as focusing on meaning before accuracy and allowing sufficient time for drafting and redrafting (ibid.: 7). She notes that the perceived benefits from teacher and peer feedback vary: some pupils report that they gained a greater sense of ownership and audience from peers and a better grasp of macro-level organisation from the teacher (ibid.: 10). In terms of teacher feedback, the effectiveness of grammar correction is questioned and teachers are encouraged to give more explicit and positive comments as well as train pupils how to benefit from feedback by some researchers (ibid.: 11–13).

Way, Joiner and Seaman (2000) investigated the difference between three different writing task types: descriptive, narrative and expository (explanatory/argumentative). Their research shows that the descriptive task proved the easiest followed by the narrative task. This suggests a certain type of progression in writing tasks.

Macaro concludes from his examination of relevant research that:

> there appears to be little evidence that the traditional and prevailing approach to FL writing which involves learning to produce 'sentence level, error-free text within a progression of tasks and under conditions of careful guidance' (Heilenman 1991) is successful in achieving holistic competence (i.e. focus both on content and form) with L2 writers. Learners may well find greater satisfaction, freedom of expression and ultimately motivation if they are allowed to experiment with drafting and redrafting of their own language, not necessarily at the end of a topic of work.
>
> (2003a: 229)

He suggests that the focus should be on the process, not the product of writing, on planning, formulating, monitoring and checking (ibid.: 249). The finished product, he argues, gives a false impression of linearity and does not allow for an adequate analysis of the complexity of text production. He concludes that feedback from the teacher needs to focus on the difficulties and successes pupils experience as they write and should be problem-orientated. As with other skills, strategy training and metacognition, i.e. awareness of pupils about themselves as language learners, would appear essential (see separate section on learning strategies above). Correct models in and of themselves are insufficient. Macaro also comes out in support of the use of bilingual dictionaries for writing, provided they are used effectively.

LEARNING AND TEACHING GRAMMAR

One of the ongoing debates in foreign and second language research is on the relative importance of implicit and explicit approaches to the teaching of grammar. In view of the fact that it is dealt with already earlier in this chapter and in some detail earlier in this book (Chapter 7), as well as elsewhere (see e.g. Pachler with Bond 1999), we will deal with this important theme of SLA and FLL research rather briefly here.

Increasingly it is believed that drawing attention to vocabulary and syntax explicitly – rather than spending long periods of time on message-oriented exchanges at the expense of meaning-based interaction – can enhance implicit classroom-based learning (Macaro 2003a: 253–4). Focus on form as part of a meaning-based discourse, Macaro suggests (ibid.: 254), 'provides the optimum amount of spot-lighting of new TL models such that development of interlanguage can take place.' He also reports a feeling among researchers and commentators that a focus on language awareness in the early stages of foreign language learning can be beneficial (ibid.: 254).

Nassaji and Fotos (2004: 126) agree: they argue that recent research has demonstrated that there is a need for formal instruction in order for pupils to attain high levels of accuracy and they enumerate four reasons for the renewed interest in grammar (ibid.: 128–9):

1   According to their reading of relevant research, 'it is necessary for learners to notice target forms in input; otherwise they process input for meaning only and do not attend to specific forms, and consequently fail to process and acquire them.'

2   They point out that pupils move through developmental sequences, some of which are fixed, i.e. they cannot be changed by grammar teaching, whereas others can be influenced.

3   There is a significant amount of research which suggests that mainly meaning-focused approaches are inadequate.

4   There is evidence in support of explicit grammar instruction, i.e. presenting structures, describing and exemplifying them, and offering rules for their use, compared with implicit grammar instruction, i.e. communicative exposure to target forms.

Nevertheless, Nassaji and Fotos (ibid.: 129) are keen to point out that there exists a complex relationship between grammar teaching and learning of target forms, which tends not to be direct. Noticing, they argue (ibid.: 134), may be a necessary condition for acquisition, but it is not the only one.

They also report (ibid.: 129) that some researchers question traditional approaches to grammar teaching where language is viewed as an object of learning and presented in a decontextualised way in support for which there tends not to be research evidence. With reference to Larsen-Freeman (2003), they posit that learners must have 'opportunities to encounter, process, and use instructed forms in their various form-meaning relationships so that the forms can become part of their interlanguage behaviour' (Nassaji and Fotos 2004: 130).

With regard to possible approaches to grammar teaching, Nassaji and Fotos (ibid.: 131) argue for a 'focus on FORM', in which the teacher draws pupils' attention to grammatical forms in communicative contexts, rather than a 'focus on FORMS', the selection and teaching of discrete structures in isolation. Focus on form, they argue, can be achieved through process or through design, reactively or pre-emptively.

LEARNING AND TEACHING CULTURE

Paige et al. (2000: 4), in their comprehensive review of the literature on culture learning, note that culture can sometimes be viewed as relatively static, comprising classifiable and observable, and thereby 'teachable and learnable facts', focusing on behaviour, rather than underlying value orientations. In such a view of culture, the variability within given target culture communities, the role of the individual in the process of culture creation, and/or the interaction of language and culture in meaning making are not always recognised (Paige *et al.* 2000: 4). Other, more recent models view culture as more dynamic and changing, comprising variable behaviours and the construction of meaning through interaction and communication. Paige *et al.* propose the following definition of culture learning:

> Culture learning is the process of acquiring the culture-specific and culture-general knowledge, skills, and attitudes required for effective communication and interaction with individuals from other cultures. It is a dynamic, developmental, and ongoing process which engages the learner cognitively, behaviorally, and affectively.
>
> (ibid.: 4)

Implicit in this definition is a pedagogical approach which foregrounds notions such as 'interactional competence' *inter alia* comprising:

- learning about the self as a cultural being;
- learning about culture and its impact on human communication, behaviour, and identity;
- culture-general learning, i.e. learning about universal, cross-cultural phenomena such as cultural adjustment;
- culture-specific learning, i.e. learning about a particular culture, including its language;
- learning how to learn, i.e. becoming an effective language and culture learner.

This is at the expense of the memorisation of cultural facts and sociolinguistic conventions (ibid.: 4–5). Characteristic of such an approach is also the foregrounding of culture-general domains of learning as opposed to culture-specific ones and Paige *et al.* (ibid.: 5–6) list the following things in this context:

> the concept of culture, the nature of cultural adjustment and learning, the impact of culture on communication and interaction between individuals or groups, the stress associated with intense culture and language immersions (culture and language fatigue), coping strategies for dealing with stress, the role of emotions in cross-cultural, cross-linguistic interactions, and so forth. Culture-general skills include the capacity to display respect for and interest in the culture, the ability to be a self-sustaining culture learner and to draw on a variety of resources for that learning, tolerance and patience in cross-cultural situations, control of emotions and emotional resilience, and the like.

The authors also stress the importance of the affective, behavioural and cognitive domains of learning which they see supported by the following three learning processes (ibid.: 8):

1   the learners' exploration of their own culture;

2   the discovery of the relationship between language and culture;
3   the learning of the heuristics for analysing and comparing cultures.

Meta-level awareness and cross-cultural comparison, according to the authors of the review, can be seen to lie at the heart of such a culture pedagogy.

The emphasis on the importance of meta-level awareness also chimes with another recent review of literature on culture and language learning by Byram and Feng (2004), who note the problems of perceiving culture learning potentially as identity-threatening or as potentially leading to identity loss (ibid.: 152). The authors also stress the importance of experience as a basis for learning and teaching (ibid.: 152) and, with reference to Lantolf (1999: 29), problematise the feasibility of 'constructing and seeing the world through culturally different eyes' and the impact of decentring, i.e. reassessing that which is normally taken for granted (2004: 161). They also identify a move towards an ethnographic and critical perspective in culture teaching (ibid.: 154–5), the former of which – the ethnographic perspective – to them manifests itself in the processes of 'observing, participating, describing, analysing and interpreting' and where the emphasis is on negotiating relationships, rather than culturally appropriate and linguistically correct communication (ibid.: 156). The latter, i.e. the critical perspective, in their view, has resulted in a reappraisal of some key notions such as the role of native speakers, standard varieties and cultural identity and diversity (ibid.: 158–9). In addition, they point to the importance of context, whether 'intertextual', i.e. referring to a diachronic dimension, or external and internal, i.e. pertaining to the social or individual factors respectively (ibid.: 154). And, with reference to Doyé (1999), they refer to a pedagogical procedure which addresses the key domains of knowledge (cognitive), skills (pragmatic) and attitudes (attitudinal) by engaging learners in:

> exploring pre-knowledge, creating cognitive dissonance, replacing stereotypical images, exploiting related sources of information and non-verbal communication, comparing others with own and moving beyond the culture of the target languages.
>
> (Byram and Feng 2004: 161)

In view of the difficulty in defining that which is to be studied, i.e. the cultural content, participation in a cultural community becomes a more appealing concept than acquisition of a cultural system with the overarching metaphor being that of socialisation, i.e. the 'participation in the community and internalisation of its beliefs, values and behaviours' (ibid.: 163) with the role of the teacher being that of a mediator.

THE USE OF AUTHENTIC MATERIAL AND TEXTS

Groot (2000: 63) discusses the potential of exposure to authentic foreign language material with a view to bringing about the sort of incidental vocabulary learning seemingly important in mother tongue acquisition, but quickly comes to the conclusion that this is not very realistic for the following reasons:

- authentic 'texts' do not tend to have the purpose of illustrating aspects of language usage but instead wish to communicate meaning;
- new words tend not to be particularly salient in authentic texts;
- clues to the meaning of new words tend to feature in the wider, rather than the immediate context of authentic texts which might not form part of the specific extract chosen by the teacher;
- authentic texts tend to contain too many unknown words.

The final point is the most important for Groot.

Macaro also discusses the issue of what research has to say on the issue of the use of authentic texts. He recommends (2003a: 147) that the use of authentic texts with beginners should be kept to a minimum. One study referred to (Maxim 2002), carried out among beginner university language students, suggests that the reading of authentic fictional texts with recurring situations, accessible characters, culturally familiar genre and stereotypical behaviours and can be implemented with positive outcomes early on in an in-class group reading situation where pupils can share their prior knowledge and their reading strategies. The question remains how transferable these findings are for pre-university age pupils. Another study quoted by Macaro (Anderson 1996) suggests that the reading rate can be increased by:

- textual recognition (spotting similar words later in the text);
- chunking bits of text;
- line-by-line training (where the pupil is encouraged to avoid following the line with the finger but instead to maintain concentration by placing a pencil at the end of each line of text and moving it vertically down the text as she reads).

Reporting these, and other studies, Macaro (2003a: 148) draws the conclusion that while teachers should explore the possibilities afforded by authentic texts and continue to aim for their use with advanced pupils, the definition of 'authenticity' need/ should not be too narrowly defined such as 'written by and for native speakers'. Also, with the right kind of support, it might be possible to use authentic texts early on in the foreign language learning process in a measured way. Overall, Macaro comes to the conclusion (ibid.: 151) that it is mainly by making the reading process more 'visible', i.e. by discussing it at a process level with pupils, that progress can be made.

SUMMARY

In terms of a 'moral of the story', or an overall conclusion of this overview of pertinent SLA and FLL research findings, two things can be said. First, we once again want to refer to Macaro (2003a: 253) who notes the importance of principled eclecticism as opposed to what he calls 'highly delineated methods of teaching', i.e. on the basis of available research evidence he is of the view, as are we, that it is counterproductive to impose or rely on restricted practices in the classroom and that variety is the spice of life.

Second, this review and summary of some of the available research raise important questions about the extent to which UK government statutory requirements and non-statutory guidance and policy-making are, indeed, informed by research. For a discussion of the latter point see also King's contribution to the *Cambridge Journal of Education*'s Special Issue on Language Choice (2007).

FURTHER READING

Lightbown, P. and Spada, N. (1999) *How languages are learned*. Revised edition. Oxford Handbooks for Language Teachers. Oxford: OUP.

This book offers a very readable introduction to the study of language acquisition.

Macaro, E. (2003) *Teaching and Learning a Second Language: A Guide to Recent Research and its Applications*. London: Continuum.

This useful book synthesises relevant research findings for FL professionals and discusses their implications for teaching and learning.

Pachler, N., Evans, M. and Lawes, S. (2007) *Modern Foreign Languages: Teaching School Subjects 11–19*. London: Routledge.

This book provides FL teachers with ways of thinking about their specialism, how to teach it and how to engage with what pupils learn through it with reference to relevant research.

Epilogue

Modern foreign languages teaching and learning at 16 to 19

INTRODUCTION

Modern foreign languages (MFL) teachers have faced numerous challenges over the last decades pertaining to changes to their clientele, teaching methods and assessment processes. The Subject Criteria for MFL at GCE Advanced (A) and Advanced Subsidiary (AS), the guidelines used to draw up examination specifications, have changed frequently during that time, significantly at the beginning of 1997, again in 1999 (see QCA, ACCAC and CCEA 1999b) and subsequently in 2006 (QCA, 2006b). Specifications adhering to the 2006 criteria have been taught from 2007.

The earlier changes to the criteria came about at least partly in response to Lord Dearing completing his review of qualifications for 16–19-year-olds in 1996, which resulted in the development of a new-style GCE AS level qualification to be taken by students at the end of Year 12 leading to the GCE A level at the end of Year 13. This pattern of AS and A2 qualifications is now fully integrated in post-16 study, but the subject criteria have been amended in response to a variety of developments. The 14–19 phase of education has undergone a great deal of change and various pathways and frameworks have been suggested. The Tomlinson Report on 14–19 education (Tomlinson 2004) was generally well received by education practitioners, but was not taken up by the government of the day. The 14–19 'agenda' is, therefore, still very much alive and debate continues as to how best to prepare learners for their future lives and careers and how to address the perceived academic/vocational divide.

As noted in the Introduction to this book, most issues raised in this Epilogue are covered in detail in an accompanying volume entitled *Teaching and Learning Modern Foreign Languages at Advanced Level* (Pachler 1999b). Here we offer a summary and overview of pertinent questions with the main focus being on GCE AS and A2 level examination specifications with some reference also being made to alternative, vocational routes.

OBJECTIVES

By the end of this chapter you should:

- have an appreciation of the general requirements of GCE AS/A2 level compared to GCSE examinations;
- be aware of the main differences between GCSE and GCE AS/A2 levels from the point of view of both MFL teachers and learners;
- know about the main features of vocational MFL accreditation at post-16;
- have considered teaching and learning approaches at post-16.

THE POST-16 MFL CONTEXT

There are a number of excellent publications with some inspirational ideas for teaching post-16 learners. Teaching at this level can be a very rewarding experience, as most of the learners are very keen to make progress in the foreign language. The principles of teaching and learning at post 16 remain to a great extent very similar to those principles for teaching MFL to younger learners. There are, of course, changes in emphasis and some differences in approach, but what should not be the case is a switch at post-16 to dry, 'academic' teaching and learning, where engaging, active and motivating learning have been (consciously) rejected.

GCE ADVANCED AND ADVANCED SUBSIDIARY LEVEL EXAMINATIONS – RECENT TRENDS IN MFL EDUCATION AT 16–19

Pupils' success at meeting the demands of GCSE specifications does not always translate into a perception of success at preparing pupils for GCE AS/A2 level study. A 'gap', identified in the early 1990s, arguably still exists. John Thorogood and Lid King (1991: 2) commented as follows: 'Today's complaint is that there is a "gap" between the GCSE and the demands of "A" level courses in modern languages. Somehow, somewhere along the line, GCSE has "failed to prepare" the learner for the next stage up.'

The explanation for the perceived lack of preparation of MFL study pre-16 for the requirements of GCE AS/A2 level courses, therefore, seems to lie in the difference in demands made on learners by GCSE and AS/A2 level examinations. The number of students taking MFL post-16 has been declining for many years; and after MFL is no longer compulsory at KS4, many people fear this would deteriorate even more rapidly. However, figures for 2007 indicate that there was a small rise in MFL GCE A level entries in German and Spanish (BBC 2007a). Some would argue that this is perhaps because those students who wish to focus on foreign languages are more able to do so than previously. Statistics suggest that the positive trend concerning uptake and success rates at GCSE pre-16 was also prevalent at GCE AS/A2 level post-16 in the early 1990s. However, figures from 1993 onwards suggest a worrying decline in terms of uptake at post-16 in MFL (see Table E.1 but also Macaro 2008).

The decline in overall MFL A level uptake is due to a considerable decrease in the number of students choosing French – by far the largest group of MFL GCE A level learners. As can be seen from Table E.1, the number of students taking French has almost halved since 1992. For Spanish, on the other hand, a noticeable increase can be discerned.

Students who have opted to follow GCE AS/A2 level courses have become more diverse in ability and interests (see Coleman 1995; Fisher 2001). Their motivation and reasons for studying MFL have become more wide-ranging. Students taking GCE AS/A2 levels will not necessarily go on to study a modern foreign language at degree level. For many, the MFL may be an additional GCE AS/A2 level, supporting other scientific, technological or commercial subjects.

From 2008, GCE AS/A2 are bound by revised subject criteria, introduced in December 2006 (QCA 2006b). Awarding Bodies issued new specifications in line with these criteria during 2007, ready for the first GCE AS examinations in 2009 and A2 in 2010. The changes, applicable to all subjects, from previous subject criteria included:

- fewer units of study (from 6 units to 4 for MFL);
- fewer structured questions, and more open-ended questions which require extended essay responses (to 'stretch and challenge' candidates);
- more questions which require a synoptic overview of the subject;
- the introduction of a new A★ grade recognising very high achievement (from 2010).

With regard specifically to the changes to MFL criteria, coursework is now no longer a possibility for GCE AS/A2 MFL, so all assessment is via examination. Although the QCA criteria state that learners must still study aspects of contemporary society, cultural background and heritage of one or more of the target language (TL) countries or communities, this aspect is no longer specifically tested (the relevant assessment objective has been removed).

Table E.1 Number and results of GCE A level candidates in modern languages[a]

	French	German	Spanish
1992–93	25,215	9,548	3,767
1998–99	17,775	8,527	4,640
2006–07	14,477	6,303	6,951

Note: [a] Number of GCE A level candidates in French, German, Spanish and Italian (16, 17 and 18-year-olds).

Source: HEFCE (1999) and BBC (2007b).

The Advanced Subsidiary is a stand-alone qualification and is valued as half a GCE A level qualification. It normally consists of two units (assessed at the standard expected for a student half way through a GCE A level course) that contribute 50 per cent of the full GCE A level. The A2 is the second half of a full GCE A level qualification. It normally consists of two units (assessed at the standard expected for a student at the end of a full GCE A level course) that are worth 50 per cent of the full GCE A level qualification.

For A2, students combine knowledge, understanding and skills from across the GCE A level course through synoptic assessment.

From 2008 the following Assessment Objectives were specified for MFL AS/A2:

- **AO1** Understand and respond, in speech and writing, to spoken language
- **AO2** Understand and respond, in speech and writing, to written language.
- **AO3** Show knowledge of and apply accurately the grammar and syntax prescribed in the specification.

AS is assessed through two units, as is A2. At GCE AS level, the listening, reading and writing abilities of students are assessed in one unit and speaking in a second. The topics students study are assessed through both units. For A2, the pattern is similar. Awarding Bodies can differ in the precise format of the examinations, the topics to be covered and the weighting of papers.

DIFFERENCES IN DEMANDS OF GCSE AND GCE AS/A2 LEVEL EXAMINATIONS – AN OVERVIEW

Pupils following GCSE courses have been, in the main, required to operate at a transactional level within (quasi-)communicative contexts in relation to defined content, i.e. clear parameters concerning the range of topics and structures as well as, at Foundation Tier, vocabulary to be used. The revised GCSE criteria, offering more choice for pupils, should alter this situation somewhat. Pupils are still encouraged to work collaboratively through pair and group work, focusing on language use, which has communicative application.

A number of months elapse between sitting the GCSE examination and the start of the post-16 course. This break represents a discontinuity, which some departments try to overcome by setting preparatory work for prospective post-16 students. It also makes revision/consolidation of GCSE work at the beginning of Year 12 very important, particularly where students come from a range of 11–16 contexts (e.g. to a Sixth Form College or in a school where a consortium system post-16 applies). See Barnes (1996) for advice on starting work with post-16 MFL students.

At AS/A2 level there are considerably more demands on students in terms of language generation and productive skills, such as essay writing and oral presentations, as well as receptive skills, such as reading extensively, which demand much greater implicit and explicit knowledge of grammar as well as knowledge about register and vocabulary. Students are expected to produce discursive texts on social, political and economic topics related to the target culture(s) as well as general knowledge. There are also considerably more demands in terms of students' ability to work independently and autonomously. The need to reflect upon teaching and learning and to understand the extent to which the learning processes help to meet the demands of developing key skills also adds to the demands for teachers and learners. Furthermore, there is the requirement of building opportunities to develop four of the key skills into schemes of work, namely communication, IT, improving own learning as well as performance and working with others.

Students are expected to know the relevant vocabulary associated with chosen topics, although this lexis is not actually defined. It can be difficult for students to prioritise which items of vocabulary they need to know, be it actively or passively.

Approaches to the study of MFL at AS/A2 level are much less teacher-centred and demand a higher level of motivation from the student. The transition from dependence on the teacher to independence is a big challenge for students and MFL teachers alike.

Task E.1 Observing AS/A2 level classes

Observe some GCE AS/A2 level classes.

- What differences in teaching methods can you observe in comparison to pre-16 classes?
- What knowledge, skills and understanding are required of students?
- What types of activities are students asked to carry out? How do they differ from those at Key Stages 3 and 4?

Task E.2 Discussion with AS/A2 level students

Talk to a group of GCE AS/A2 level students in Year 12.

- Ask them what they have found difficult in the transition from GCSE to AS/A2 level.
- What aspects of the course did they feel well prepared for?

What implication does this information have on the planning of the initial phase of AS/A2 level courses?

THE AVAILABILITY OF DOCUMENTARY SUPPORT

The transition from GCSE to GCE AS/A2 level can be just as challenging for the MFL teacher as for students. Up to GCSE level, the MFL teacher is supported by the statutory framework and non-statutory guidance as well as, at Key Stage 4, by detailed examination specifications and past papers. Sample schemes of work for Key Stage 3 are available on the internet, which *inter alia* provide guidance on the presentation and practice of grammatical structures. There are requirements/guidelines on what needs to be taught, why and to a degree also how.

At GCE AS/A2 level there is noticeably less documentary support. Nevertheless, MFL teachers do have access to the Subject Criteria (QCA 2006b). They include aims and generic content for both GCE AS and A level as well as grade descriptions for each of the three Assessment Objectives

- understand and respond, in speech and writing, to spoken language;
- understand and respond, in speech and writing, to written language;
- show knowledge of and apply accurately the grammar and syntax prescribed in the specification.

The Subject Criteria also include lists detailing the aspects of grammar expected at GCE A2 and AS level.

There are also examination specifications issued by Awarding Bodies, which *inter alia* prescribe grammatical structures in line with the guidelines of the Subject Criteria. These specifications identify a wide range of broad topics without specifying the lexis to be covered and there tends to be only a brief indicative content for some topics across cultural study and/or literature work, although Awarding Bodies do now produce supportive, indicative materials, usually booklets of authentic resources, as well as specimen assessment material.

In addition, MFL teachers can, of course, use past papers in preparing students and familiarising them with task types used in examinations, as well as examiners' reports, available on the websites of Awarding Bodies. The latter often offer a wealth of specific advice helpful when teaching at advanced level.

Awarding Bodies have also drawn up guidance for the conduct of speaking exams which often can be conducted by a teacher examiner or, alternatively and dependent on the number of candidates, a visiting examiner, as opted for by the department. Awarding Bodies have also introduced the possibility of submitting digital recordings (rather than audio cassettes).

BRIDGING THE GAP FROM GCSE TO GCE AS/A2 LEVEL

Many MFL teachers are keen to teach at GCE AS/A2 level and often students embark upon their post-16 study with great enthusiasm. In order to avoid possible demotivation an awareness of the difficulties inherent in the transition from pre-16 to post-16 is important.

Given the differences in GCSE and GCE AS/A2 level, MFL teachers often dedicate a considerable amount of time to bridging the gap between GCSE and GCE AS/A2 level. Tables E.2 and E.3 give an overview of the differences in GCSE and GCE AS/A2 level examinations in terms of functions and topics. Tables E.2–E.4 have been drawn up on the basis of personal teaching experience and build on information

Table E.2 Bridging the gap to post-16: Functions

GCSE	Progression	A level
Listening Understand specific details. Extract relevant information. Identify themes for points of view. Draw conclusions and relate ideas expressed by others. Follow instructions.	State a personal reaction to a specific series of events.	Recognition of the mood and emotions being expressed. Understand and participate in personal conversations, group discussions and debates. To extract key information to enable summary and oral and written responses.
Speaking Respond to closed and structured questions. Elicit information. Convey factual information. Respond to visual stimuli. Elicit and convey agreement and disagreement. Request basic services and products.	Report on an event to more than one audience.	To express full meaning by conveying facts, mood and emotion. To respond to other speakers in an appropriate register and tone. To initiate and sustain extended conversations and discussions. To elicit further detail by focused questioning. To express and justify opinions.
Reading Understand instructions. Extract relevant information from authentic texts. Identify themes or points of view. Draw conclusions. Relate ideas and themes contained within a text.	Summarise the main arguments within a text, with support and guidance.	Recognition of mood, emotions and appropriate register. To understand and respond critically to extended fictional and non-fictional texts. To recognise and react to themes, arguments, images and ideas expressed within authentic texts. To analyse and respond to arguments and points of view.
Writing Respond to given stimuli. Convey information. Express simple feelings and opinions. Report on real events.	Respond by countering arguments presented in a short, authentic text.	To summarise information and to expand upon detail. To translate and transcribe. To express ideas in a creative way. To generate and manipulate original language forms to develop coherent arguments and creative texts. To handle grammar and syntax implicit in all of the above.

extrapolated from the GCSE criteria, the GCE AS/A2 level Subject Criteria and various examination specifications. The information contained in these tables does not purport to be exhaustive but is intended as a framework for devising a programme of work aimed at bridging the gap between GCSE and GCE AS/A2 level.

Task E.3 Bridging the gap to post-16 Functions

Table E.2 details the language functions generally required for GCSE and GCE A level.
Complete the centre column in a way that bridges the gap between GCSE and GCE A level requirements. Some examples have been provided for you.

Task E.4 Bridging the gap to post-16 Topics and issues

Table E.3 shows the progression from topics at GCSE to general issues at A level. In order to help students broaden their range of understanding you need to provide a focus for study. Complete the centre column in such a way that there is manageable progression. Some examples have been provided for you.

Because topics do not, on the whole, feature in examination specifications as a finite, prescribed list with clearly defined lexis (although some specifications do offer quite detailed subheadings for topics), coverage of content at GCE AS/A2 level is very complex. Departments need to judge carefully, for instance:

- how much time they ought to spend on any given topic;
- how many topics to cover in class and to what detail (the chosen specifications need to be studied in detail to ensure that at least the correct number of appropriate topics is covered for e.g. the speaking examination);
- whether to allow students to choose (some) topics according to personal interests;
- whether to prescribe topics according to the strengths of MFL teachers or the resources available;
- how much material to prescribe to students;
- how much to rely on the research and self study skills of students;
- most importantly, how much time to dedicate to transferable language skills and strategies, which students can use in a variety of situations and for a range of topics.

The focus on contemporary, up-to-date issues and stimulus material limits the amount of advance planning possible.

Task E.5 GCE AS/A2 level topics

1   Scrutinise a copy of the GCE AS/A2 level examination specification used at your school experience school. Alternatively, look at Table E.3. How well prepared do you feel in terms of subject knowledge to teach the various topics?

2   Discuss the programme of work students cover across Years 12 and 13 with the relevant MFL teacher(s) at your school experience school. Which topics do the students cover? Do all students study the same topics? Are students allowed to choose some topics? How are language skills and strategies integrated?

Table E.3 Bridging the gap to post-16: topics and issues

GCSE	Progression	A level
personal identification and the family	relationships with parents	the generation gap and youth culture
house and home		economic and social conditions
geographical surroundings and weather	local problems and issues	urbanism, ecology and the Third World, environment, geographical topic
travel and transport		communications (infrastructure and the media) and the energy crisis
holidays		cultural diversity, festivals and customs
accommodation		living conditions
food and drink		
shopping and services		consumerism, commercialism
		consumerism, environment
health and welfare	lifestyles of famous people	health promotion, addictions
free time		leisure provision and opportunities
education and future career		professional life, responsibilities and education systems, minority groups
money		economic and political systems

Task E.6 Planning a topic for AS/A2 level

Choose one topic prescribed by the GCE AS/A2 level examination specification used by your school experience school, for instance 'the media' or 'minority groups'.

1   Select key resources such as articles or recordings for this topic.

2   Then analyse the material you have chosen in terms of linguistic difficulty and decide on an appropriate sequence.

3   Plan a summary sheet for the topic, which is suitable as a revision checklist for students including details such as: title of resource, summary of content, key structures, key words and key skills.

> 4   Discuss your planning with the MFL teacher responsible for GCE AS/A2 level at your placement school.
>
> For details on macro- and micro-planning, see Meiring and Norman (1999a, 1999b).

THE TEACHING OF GRAMMAR

Students' grammatical proficiency has emerged as a focal point for discussion. Some higher education tutors have expressed concern about the lack of grammatical awareness of their new undergraduate students (see Sheppard 1993; McCulloch 1995, 1996). There are also GCE examiners' reports, which express concern about GCE AS/A2 level students' ability to generate grammatically correct language (see Metcalfe *et al.* 1995). In response it has been noted that the approaches to MFL teaching at degree level do not always reflect and build on the strengths of GCE AS/A2 level MFL students and that this might distort the perception of their level of preparedness (see Saunders *et al.* 1994: 10).

Klapper argues that the apparent conflict stems from a misinterpretation of communicative language teaching. He puts forward the view that true communication denotes a high level of development predicated on a solid grasp of structure and lexis (see Klapper 1997: 27).

The fact that grammatical requirements are explicit in the Subject Criteria for MFL makes planning for grammatical progression and coverage of specification requirements much easier and this prescription of grammatical content sits more comfortably with GCSE criteria as well as the non-statutory schemes of work for Key Stage 3, all of which feature increased explicit reference to grammar (see also Chapter 7). However, the gap between GCSE and GCE AS/A2 level in terms of understanding and application of grammar remains particularly difficult: part of the third Assessment Objective is to apply grammatical knowledge *accurately*. You need to build on existing knowledge and understanding, but should not put to one side aspects and concepts which do not follow coursebook models of presentation.

Because of the apparent differences of complexity of grammar use, it is very important for GCE AS/A2 level that you build on the tenets of the GCSE examination, namely of providing enjoyment and stimulation to pupils, promoting an ability to communicate and developing confidence and proficiency within a foreign cultural context.

In the light of the prescription of grammatical content, a systematic approach to linguistic structures throughout Years 12 and 13 seems all the more important. A consolidation of GCSE grammar during the first term of Year 12 (see Bond *et al.* 1993; Neather 2003) can lead to a systematic coverage of the required linguistic structures. A carefully formulated approach, where the teacher progressively adds grammatical knowledge to ease the transition from transactional language use to spontaneous TL use with the aim of enabling students to express opinions and ideas, can be seen to be consistent with the view that the language selected for the purpose of learning must be seen by the students to fulfil explicit and relevant objectives. Many commentators agree that progression in the understanding and application of grammatical structures is not a linear process (see Pachler 1999c; Jones 2000), which adds to the complexity of planning. Also, because of the paramount importance of the context in which the target language (TL) is encountered by students, i.e. mainly through authentic material at GCE AS/A2 level, grammatical progression is difficult to plan for.

Table E.4 gives an example how, for French, the 'grammar gap' between GCSE and GCE A level might be bridged.

Table E.4 Bridging the gap to post-16: grammar (French)

GCSE	GCE AS level	GCE A level
Nouns:		
gender, number and irregular forms contained within defined vocabulary list	nouns, unspecified but related to general issues	nouns, unspecified but related to general issues
Articles:		
all forms of direct, indirect and partitive articles	all forms including irregularities	all forms including irregularities
Adjectives:		
regular formation and position; irregular forms within a defined vocabulary list; possessive adjectives and recognition of comparatives and superlatives as lexical items	active knowledge of comparatives and superlatives, indefinite adjectives and position and formation of adverbs	position and agreement of all adjectives including interrogative adjectives; superlatives in concessive clauses
Pronouns:		
subject pronouns, recognition of object pronouns as lexical items; emphatic pronouns as lexical items and the recognition of interrogative and relative pronouns	active use of object pronouns, including correct positioning; use of disjunctive and relative pronouns	accurate use of direct and indirect object pronouns with correct past participle agreement; 'en' as a pronoun; use of demonstrative, indefinite and relative pronouns
Verbs and tenses:		
present indicative, perfect and immediate future; recognition of future, imperfect; past participle agreement with reflexive and 'être' verbs; active use of the imperative and the negative form of 'ne . . . pas'; recognition of the government of verbs and the present participle	active knowledge of imperfect, future, conditional, pluperfect, present subjunctive after 'il faut que'; all past participle agreements, government of verbs and the use of modal verbs; all negative forms including negatives with infinitives; recognition of the present subjunctive with expressions of fear, wishing, possibility and doubt	active knowledge of all tenses; use of the subjunctive in all tenses; all verbal agreements and inflections; use of the present participle and gerund; accurate use of verbs governing the use of the infinitive and all negative forms

(*Continued*)

GCSE	GCE AS level	GCE A level
Quantity: cardinal and ordinal numbers, dates and the time; basic expressions of quantity	fractions and dimensions	use of idiom and complicated structures; conjunctions requiring use of the subjunctive
Other: use of *'depuis'* and recognition of common structures	use of conjunctions and complicated structures	
Much of the grammar at this level is taught as lexical items and is implicit. The focus is on recognition and there is scope for the learning of paradigms and set phrases.	***At GCE A/S level most knowledge should be active and explicit; additional items are added to the GCSE repertoire.***	***At GCE A level all knowledge is assumed to be active to enable the generation and manipulation of language forms.***

Task E.7 Bridging the gap to post-16 Grammar

Where possible, compile a chart similar to the one in Figure E.4 for German or Spanish by drawing on examination specifications, schemes of work and the latest Subject Criteria for AS/A2 level.

CULTURAL AWARENESS AND GENERAL KNOWLEDGE

Knowledge about and understanding of the target culture(s) should not be seen as separate from work on the TL. The development of ideas and the ability to formulate opinions about the target culture(s) go hand in hand with the pupils' linguistic development. In examination specifications, candidates are often required to speak on a specific topic from a TL country or community. They will, therefore, need to have worked on up-to-date, authentic materials in order to be fully informed in their chosen area. Specifications indicate topics for AS which build on those covered at GCSE level (e.g. daily life, education, celebrity) and then move on at A2 to more challenging topics (e.g. environment, science and technology). Literature and culture remain part of the content to be studied at A2, often in the context of a historical period or the work of an author, for example.

The development of cultural awareness in students can be difficult, not only because the specifications may remain quite general about the actual content of some topics, but also because students' level of general knowledge and their knowledge about the target culture(s) tends to be limited at the beginning of Year 12.

Therefore, you need to assume responsibility, particularly early in the course, for the selection of activities aimed at developing a deeper insight into and understanding of the target culture(s) as well as developing the necessary lexis and grammatical knowledge and application. The selection of appropriate texts, authentic material and the choice of topics requires extremely detailed, yet at the same time broad subject knowledge on your behalf.

'Universal experiences of life' can be used to trigger meaningful intercultural comparisons. For examples of some useful techniques for teaching culture and literary topics see e.g. Chapter 8, Anderson (1996), Pachler (1999d) and Leah (2001).

INDEPENDENT LEARNING

Contact time with MFL teachers is limited. GCE AS/A2 level study usually involves up to six hours of 'contact time' per week and the same amount of independent study. Groups are often shared between different MFL teachers who, together, cover the specification requirements. It is important to ensure cohesion, continuity and progression.

The students need to assume responsibility for their learning from the very start of the course, but you should not take this ability for granted. Students have to develop new study skills such as time management, learning strategies, personal organisation, use of reference material and research skills. Despite the importance of learner independence, you need to oversee choices and decisions made by students throughout the period of study, but particularly at the initial stages.

Students need to be prepared to carry out the required preparatory as well as follow-up work and be proactive in order to maximise learning outcomes. For this reason, many teachers and commentators recommend the use of a learner diary as a focus for individual tutorial work with the teacher (see Field 1999a: 52; or Pachler and Field 1999: 72). As mentioned earlier, language learning strategies are a crucial component of independent learning. As with all learners of MFL, these strategies are not necessarily available immediately to all and may need to be exemplified, modelled and discussed. For examples of developing strategies generally, see Graham 1997; Jones 2001. There are also helpful publications available on particular aspects of advanced language learning, such as speaking (McLachlan 2001), listening (Wright 2004), reading (Grenfell 1995; Barnes 2000) and learning styles post-16 (Maubach and Morgan 2001). See also the two-part Special Issue on Learner Strategies of the *Language Learning Journal* in 2007 (35(1) and 35(2)).

Because of low numbers of MFL students in some schools and colleges, sometimes students in Years 12 and 13 are taught together for part of their contact time. This can complicate planning considerably, particularly as the requirements of AS and A2 demand very different linguistic skills (see the specifications offered by the Awarding Bodies) and students will obviously be at different stages in their linguistic development. Where students are taught in a consortium of neighbouring schools, regular information exchanges by all MFL teachers involved in course delivery is very important. The input from the various teachers must complement each other rather than repeat or even contradict.

The discussion in this section has shown that there are certain tensions between MFL teaching pre-16 and post-16 in GCE AS/A2 level contexts and that there are significant demands made on both the students as well as the MFL teacher at post-16. One demand you will face as a student teacher teaching at AS/A2 for the first time is to get used to the preparation and research required for some aspects of subject content knowledge. There may be areas where you do not feel particularly confident, e.g. a specific cultural or historical aspect of a TL country or a literary text or theme.

OTHER POST-16 ROUTES

Academic GCE AS/A2 level qualifications are not a suitable and/or desirable pathway for all MFL students at post-16, who want to (continue to) study a modern foreign language.

Alternatives include languages as part of a 14–19 diplomas. Diplomas, combining theoretical and practical learning, were introduced in 2008. Languages are an option within all of the first five Diplomas, sitting in the component of additional/specialist learning (CILT 2007).

Optional language units are also available within the advanced vocational certificate of education (VCE). Candidates may take one language unit as one of six units taken, while candidates for advanced VCE (double award) may take either or both language units among the 12 units taken for their award.

The units available are:

- Oral communication: speaking and listening
- Written communication: reading and writing

Depending on the Awarding Body, units are available in the following modern foreign languages: French, German, Italian, Japanese, Modern Greek, Russian and Spanish.

These possibilities can be seen as a progression route for those students at post-16 who are interested in continuing with their modern foreign language from Key Stage 4 outside the academic route. They are also suitable if students wish to begin to learn a new modern foreign language.

Vocational and/or occupational language units require from the MFL teacher knowledge of work-related vocabulary and technical terminology, an understanding of the processes involved in a given field of work, occupation or industry as well as different teaching strategies to be able to devise and deliver an appropriate programme of study and relevant assessment opportunities.

Task E.8 Planning activities for more vocationally-based programmes

With reference to the scenario of a simulated work experience as assistant to a conference organiser, think of a number of situations which allow learners to show competence.

For instance, learners might show that they are able to respond to an initial telephone enquiry by a prospective client giving details about the conference facilities available. Make notes of the situations you devise, for use in your teaching.

SUMMARY

In this Epilogue we examined some of the issues of academic as well as, to a lesser extent, vocational MFL teaching and learning at post-16.

The study of MFL at post-16 in one form or another can be seen to be a viable choice for students in post-compulsory education and it is one of our concerns as MFL teachers to continue to work towards learners maintaining their MFL study beyond 16.

We have shown that there are certain tensions concerning the transition from pre-16 to post-16 in the academic route caused by differences in course requirements at both levels. These require careful planning by and due attention from you as an MFL teacher.

The brief introduction to the vocational possibilities has shown that there are challenges associated with respective MFL provision at post-16 for MFL teachers such as the need to understand work-related terminology in the TL and to be knowledgeable about work-related processes in the target culture(s).

FURTHER READING

Graham, S. (1997) *Effective Language Learning: Positive Strategies for Advanced Level Language Teaching*. Clevedon: Multilingual Matters.

This book remains essential reading for teachers of MFL at post-16, looking in detail at the issues facing learners as they develop their language skills at this level.

Pachler, N. (ed.) (1999) *Teaching Modern Foreign Languages at Advanced Level*. London: Routledge.

A comprehensive guide to all the main aspects of teaching MFL at post-16 including practical advice as well as well-argued theories.

Shaw, G. (ed.) (2000) *Aiming High 2: Straight As*. London: CILT.

A collection of informative chapters focused on achieving the potential of A/AS learners covering a range of language skills and topics.

Appendix

Proformas

Lesson observation sheet			
Class:	Time:	Date:	Teacher:
Observation foci:		**Comments:**	
Time	**Description of action**	**Reflection**	

Figure A.1 Lesson observation proforma

Lesson plan			
Class:	Time:	Date:	Language:

Learning objectives	
Core	Extension

Previous learning outcomes

Lesson . . . out of . . . .

Resources required

Time	Activities		PoS ATL
	Teacher *Objectives*	**Pupils**	
	Plenary/summing up		

ICT

Homework

Evaluation

re pupil learning	re own teaching

Action to be taken for next lesson

Figure A.2 Lesson planning proforma

No.	Question	Response
1	Were my objectives for the lesson clear to me and did I achieve them?	
2	Did pupils know what they were trying to achieve at any given moment?	
3	Were my instructions clear?	
4	Were the material and lesson content appropriate for the group?	
5	Did I cater for the range of abilities in the group? How?	
6	Do I need to re-think the order and structure of my lesson?	
7	Did I cope effectively with disruptions?	
8	Did I use the target language appropriately?	
9	Did everyone get the opportunity to participate?	
10	Did I help the more reluctant and less able to join in?	
11	Did I ensure that everyone was on task consistently and monitor their work?	
12	Were pupils alert, confident, enthusiastic or apathetic, uncertain, obstructive?	
13	Do I know what individual pupils' strengths and weaknesses are?	
14	Did I diagnose and assess pupils' difficulties? Did I respond to them?	
15	Did I comment on work, praising effort, achievement and accuracy and give encouragement?	
16	Do I know if the pupils learnt anything?	
17	Did I include pair/group work?	
18	Did I make good use of resources?	
19	Do I know all the pupils' names?	
20	Did I cover cultural awareness adequately?	
21	Did I and the pupils enjoy the lesson?	

Figure A.3 Lesson evaluation proforma

Unit of work planning		
Year:	Number and length of lessons:	
End-of-unit goal		
Learning objectives		
Core	Extension	
Main language items/structures		
Core	Extension	
Main materials and resources		
Main activities		**PoS ATL**
Core:		
Reinforcement:		
Extension:		
Main homework		
Assessment opportunities		
Continuous:		
Summative:		

Figure A.4 Unit of work planning proforma

Bibliography

Adams, J. (2000) 'It all ended in tiers', in K. Field (ed.) *Issues in Modern Foreign Languages Teaching*. London: Routledge, pp. 194–211.

Ainslie, S. and Purcell, S. (2000) *Resource File 4: Mixed-Ability Teaching in Language Learning*. London: CILT.

Alger, C. (2006) ' "What went well, what didn't go so well": growth of reflection in pre-service teachers', *Reflective Practice* 7(3): 287.

Alison, J. (1993) 'Are they being served?' *TES National Curriculum Update*, 10 February, p. 15.

Alison, J. (1995) *Not Bothered? Motivating Reluctant Language Learners in Key Stage 4*. London: CILT.

Allford, D. (1999) 'Translation in the communicative classroom', in N. Pachler (ed.) *Teaching and Learning Modern Foreign Languages at Advanced Level*. London: Routledge, pp. 230–50.

Allford, D. (2000) 'Pictorial images and language teaching', *Language Learning Journal* 22. Rugby: ALL.

Allford, D. and Pachler, N. (2007) *Language, Autonomy and the New Learning Environments*. Oxford: Peter Lang.

Anderson, J. (1996) 'Communicating culture: approaches to teaching about German re-unification', in G. Shaw (ed.) *Aiming High: Approaches to Teaching A level*. London: CILT, pp. 58–69.

Antòn, M. (1999) 'The discourse of a learner-centred classroom: sociocultural perspectives on teacher-learner interaction in the second-language classroom', *The Modern Language Journal* 83(3): 303–18.

ARG (Assessment Reform Group) (1999) *Assessment for Learning beyond the Black Box*. Available at: www.assessment-reform-group.org.uk (accessed 20 June 2006).

Arthur, J., Davison, J. and Moss, J. (1998) *Subject Mentoring*. London: Routledge.

Atkinson, T. and Claxton, G. (eds) (2000) *The Intuitive Practitioner: On the Value of Not Always Knowing What One Is Doing*. Milton Keynes: Open University Press.

Barker, S., Brooks, V., March, K. and Swatton, P. (1996) *Initial Teacher Education in Secondary Schools: A Study of the Tangible and Intangible Costs and Benefits of Initial Teacher Education in Secondary Schools*. London: Association of Teachers and Lecturers.

Barnes, A. (1996) 'Getting them off to a good start: the lead-up to that first A level class', *German Teaching* 14: 23–28.

Barnes, A. (1997) 'Buyer Beware – evaluating MFL materials', *German Teaching* 16: 2–4.

Barnes, A. (1999) 'Assessment', in N. Pachler (ed.) *Teaching Modern Foreign Languages at Advanced Level*. London: Routledge, pp. 251–81.

Barnes, A. (2000) 'Developing advanced reading skills: learning to read intelligently', in G. Shaw (ed.) *Aiming High 2: Straight As*. London: CILT, pp. 26–36.

Barnes, A. (2005) 'A passion for languages: motivation and preparation to teach modern foreign languages in eight cohorts of beginning teachers', *Research Papers in Education* 20(4): 349–69.

Barnes, A. (2006) 'Confidence levels and concerns of beginning teachers of modern foreign languages', *Language Learning Journal* 34, Rugby: ALL, pp. 37–46.

Barnes, A. (2007) 'Communicative approaches to modern foreign language teaching and using the target language', in N. Pachler and A. Redondo (eds) *A Practical Guide to Teaching Modern Foreign Languages in the Secondary School*. London: Routledge, pp. 4–11.

Barnes, A. and Hunt, M. (2003) *Effective Assessment in MFL*. London: CILT.

Barton, A. (2002a) 'Learning styles: the gender effect', in A. Swarbrick (ed.) *Teaching Modern Foreign Languages in Secondary Schools: A Reader*. Buckingham: Open University Press, pp. 272–85.

Barton, A. (2002b) 'Teaching modern foreign languages to single-sex classes', *Language Learning Journal* 25, Rugby: ALL, pp. 8–14.

Bartrum, B. (2006) 'Attitudes to language learning: a comparative study of peer group influences', *Language Learning Journal* 33, Rugby: ALL, pp. 47–52.

Bauckham, I. (1995) 'A Vygotskyan perspective on foreign language teaching', *Languages Forum* (4): London: Institute of Education, pp. 29–31.

BBC (2007a) 'Increase in top grades at A level. 16.8'. Available at: http://news.bbc.co.uk/1/hi/education/6949084.stm (accessed 24 August 2007).

BBC (2007b) 'All Subjects A level grades 2007'. Available at: http://news.bbc.co.uk/1/shared/bsp/hi/education/07/exam_results/a_level/html/all_subjects.stm (accessed 24 August 2007).

Beaton, R. (1990) 'The many sorts of error', in B. Page (ed.) *What Do You Mean It's Wrong?* London: CILT, pp. 38–47.

BECTA (2003) *What the Research Says About Interactive Whiteboards*. Coventry. Available at: http://www.becta.org.uk/page_documents/research/wtrs_whiteboards.pdf (accessed 30 August 2007).

Beers, M. (2001) 'A media-based approach to developing ethnographic skills for second language teaching and learning', *Zeitschrift für Interkulturellen Fremdsprachenunterricht* [Online], 6(2), URL: http://zif.spz.tu-darmstadt.de/jg-06–2/beitrag/beers2.htm (accessed 30 August 2007).

Belbin, R. M. (2003) *Management Teams: Why They Succeed or Fail*, 2nd edn. Oxford: Butterworth-Heinemann.

Bennett, N. (1993) 'Knowledge bases for learning to teach', in N. Bennett and C. Carré (eds) *Learning to Teach*. London: Routledge, pp. 1–17.

Bennett, N. and Dunne, E. (1994) 'Managing groupwork', in B. Moon and A. Shelton-Mayes (eds) *Teaching and Learning in the Secondary School*. Milton Keynes: Open University Press, pp. 166–72.

Berwick, G. and Horsfall, P. (1996) *Making Effective Use of the Dictionary*. London: CILT.

Bialystok, E. and Hakuta, K. (1995) *In Other Words: The Science and Psychology of Second-Language Acquisition*. London: Basic Books.

Bimmel, P. (1993) 'Lernstrategien im Deutschunterricht', *Fremdsprache Deutsch. Zeitschrift für die Praxis des Deutschunterrichts* (8/1): 4–11.

Bishop, G. (2006) 'True independent learning – an androgogical approach: giving control to the learner over choice of material and design of the study session', *Language Learning Journal* 33, Rugby: ALL, pp. 40–6.

Black, P. (2005) 'How, and why, can assessment for learning be successful? Raising standards through formative assessment', paper presented at Language World, University of Kent at Canterbury, 1 July.

Black, P. and Jones, J. (2006) 'Formative assessment and the learning and teaching of MFL: sharing the language learning road map with the learners', *Language Learning Journal* 34, Rugby: ALL, pp. 4–9.

Black, P. and Wiliam, D. (1998) 'Inside the Black Box: raising standards through classroom assessment', *Phi Delta Kappa International*. Available at: http://www.pdkintl.org/kappan/kbla9810.htm (accessed 20 June 2006).

Black, P. and Wiliam, D. (2003) 'In praise of educational research: formative assessment', *British Educational Research Journal* 29: 623–38.

Black, P., Harrison, C., Lee, C., Marshall, B. and Wiliam, D. (2002) *Working Inside the Black Box: Assessment for Learning in the Classroom*. London: Kings College London Department of Education and Professional Studies.

Bond, J., Darby, J., Hyland, S., Stockdale, S. and Tebbutt, S. (1993) *Aus eigener Erfahrung: von GCSE bis 'A' level*. London: CILT and Goethe-Institut, pp. 83–103.

Booth, T., Ainscow, M., Black-Hawkins, K., Vaughan, M. and Shaw, L. (2000) *Index for Inclusion: Developing Learning and Participation in Schools*. Bristol: Centre for Studies on Inclusive Education in collaboration with the Centre for Educational Needs, University of Manchester and Centre for Educational Research, Canterbury Christ Church University College.

Borg, S. (2003) 'Teacher cognition in language teaching: a review of research on what language teachers think, know, believe and do', *Language Teaching* 36: 81–109.

Bramall, G. (2002) 'How do you work that out? A comparison of two question types in the GCSE reading tests', *Deutsch Lehren und Lernen* 26: 14–16.

Brandford, V. (2007) 'Use of Storylines to develop reading and writing skills in the modern foreign language', in N. Pachler and A. Redondo (eds) *Teaching Foreign Languages in the Secondary School: A Practical Guide*. London: Routledge, pp. 67–75.

Brandi, M.-L. and Strauss, D. (1985) *Training des Leseverstehens mit Hilfe von Sachtexten*. München: Goethe-Institut.

Bromfield, C. (2006) 'PGCE Secondary trainee teachers and effective behaviour management: an evaluation and commentary', *Support for Learning* 21(4): 188–93.

Brown, H. D. (1986) 'Learning a second culture', in J. M. Valdes (ed.) *Culture Bound: Bridging the Cultural Gaps in Language Teaching*. Cambridge: Cambridge University Press, pp. 33–48.

Buckby, M. (1980) *Action 1: Teacher's book*. Walton-on-Thames: Nelson.

Buckland, D. and Short, M. (1993) *Ideas and Strategies for Homework*. London: CILT.

Burn, A. (2005) 'Teaching and learning with digital video', in M. Leask and N. Pachler (eds) *Teaching and Learning in the Secondary School Using ICT*, 2nd edn. London: Routledge, pp. 100–14.

Burns, A. (2001) 'Analysing spoken discourse: implications for TESOL', in A. Burns and C. Coffin (eds) *Analysing English in a Global Context: A Reader*. London: Routledge, pp. 123–48.

Burns, A., Gollin, S. and Joyce, H. (1997) 'Authentic spoken texts in the language classroom', *Prospect* 12: 72–86.

Butler, M. and Kelly, P. (1999) 'Videoconferencing', in M. Leask and N. Pachler (eds) *Learning to Teach Using ICT in the Secondary School*. London: Routledge, pp. 95–108.

Butzkamm, W. (2003) 'We only learn language once. The role of the mother tongue in FL classrooms: death of a dogma', *Language Learning Journal* 28, Rugby: ALL, pp. 29–39.

Byram, M. (1989) *Cultural Studies in Foreign Language Education*. Clevedon: Multilingual Matters.

Byram, M. (1997) *Teaching and Assessing Intercultural Communicative Competence*. Clevedon: Multilingual Matters.

Byram, M. and Risager, K. (2002) 'Stereotypes, prejudice and tolerance', in A. Swarbrick (ed.) *Teaching Modern Foreign Languages in Secondary Schools: A Reader*. London: Routledge, pp. 81–94.

Byram, M. and Feng, A. (2004) 'Culture and language learning: teaching, research and scholarship', *Language Teaching* 37: 149–68.

Byram, M., Morgan, C. *et al.* (1994) *Teaching-and-Learning Language-and-Culture*. Clevedon: Multilingual Matters.

Cajkler, W. and Addelman, R. (2000) *The Practice of Foreign Language Teaching*, 2nd edn. London: David Fulton.

Calvert, M. (2007) 'Reflective practice through teacher research', in N. Pachler and A. Redondo (eds) *A Practical Guide to Teaching Modern Foreign Languages in the Secondary School*. London: Routledge, pp. 119–27.

Cambridgeshire (1994) *Discovering Dictionaries: Ideas for Modern Languages Teachers by Teachers*. Cambridge: Cambridgeshire County Council.

Campbell, A. (2005) 'Weblog applications for EFL/ESL classroom blogging: a comparative review', *TESL-EL 9(3)*. Available at http://tesl-ej.org/ej35/m1.html (accessed 30 August 2007).

Capel, S. and Pachler, N. (1997) 'Opportunities for continued professional development', in S. Capel, M. Leask and T. Turner (eds) *Starting to Teach in the Secondary School: A Companion for the Newly Qualified Teacher*. London: Routledge, pp. 257–69.

Carduner, J. (2003) 'Productive dictionary skills training: what do language learners find useful?' *Language Learning Journal 28*. Rugby: ALL, pp. 70–6.

Carter, R. (1997) *Investigating English Discourse*. London: Routledge.

Cassidy, S. (1999) 'IQ "has no impact" on exam success', *TES*, 18 June.

Central Bureau (1993) *European Awareness: Development Projects 1990/91. Report No 2*. London: Central Bureau, p. 4.

Chambers, G. (1996) 'Listening, why? How?' *Language Learning Journal* 7, Rugby: ALL, pp. 13–16.

Chambers, G. (1999) *Motivating Language Learners*. Clevedon: Multilingual Matters.

Chambers, G. (2005) 'Teaching modern foreign languages in single-sex classes in a co-educational context – review of a project in a North Yorkshire comprehensive school', *Language Learning Journal* 32. Rugby: ALL, pp. 45–54.

Chambers, G. (2007) 'Developing listening skills in the modern foreign language', in N. Pachler and A. Redondo (eds) *Teaching Foreign Languages in the Secondary School: A Practical Guide*. London: Routledge, pp. 50–7.

Chambers, G. and Pearson, S. (2004) 'Supported access to modern foreign language lessons', *Language Learning Journal* 29. Rugby: ALL, pp. 32–41.

Chamot, A. (2005) 'Language learning strategy instruction: current issues and research', *Annual Review of Applied Linguistics* 25: 112–30.

Chapelle, C. (1998) 'Multimedia CALL: lessons to be learnt from research on instructed SLA', *Language Learning & Technology* 2(1): 21–39. Available at: http://llt.msu.edu/vol2num1/article1/ (accessed 30 August 2007).

Channel Four Schools (1995) *Working Together: Teacher's Guide and Video: The Foreign Language Assistant in the Classroom and Strategies for Group Work*. Warwick.

Child, D. (1993) *Psychology and the Teacher*, 5th edn. London: Cassell.

CILT (2007) 14–19 Diplomas. Available at: http://www.cilt.org.uk/14–19/diplomas.htm (accessed 24 August 2007).

Clark, A. and Trafford, J. (1996) 'Return to gender: boys' girls' attitudes and achievements', *Language Learning Journal 14*. Rugby: ALL, pp. 40–9.

Coleman, J. (1995) 'The evolution of language learner motivation in British Universities, with some international comparisons', in R. Wakely *et al.* (eds) *Language Teaching and Learning in Higher Education: Issues and Perspectives*. London: CILT, pp. 1–16.

Coleman, J. (1996) *Studying Languages: A Survey of British and European Students: The Proficiency, Background, Attitudes and Motivations of Students in the UK and Europe*. London: CILT.

Convery, A. and Coyle, D. (1993) *Differentiation: Taking the Initiative*. London: CILT.

Cornell, A. (1996) 'Grammar – grinding or grounding?' *German Teaching* 13: 26–9.

Cox, M. and Webb, M. (eds) (2004) *An Investigation of the Research Evidence Relating to ICT Pedagogy. Version 1*. Coventry: BECTA.

Coyle, D. (1999) 'The next stage? Is there a future for the present? The legacy of the communicative approach', *Francophonie* 19: 13–16.

Coyle, D. (2002) 'Towards a reconceptualisation of the MFL curriculum', in A. Swarbrick (ed.) *Teaching Modern Foreign Languages in Secondary Schools: A Reader*. London: Routledge, pp. 156–72.

Cremin, H., Thomas, G. and Vincett, K. (2005) 'Working with teaching assistants: three models evaluated', *Research Papers in Education* 20(4): 413–32.

Crozier, M., Gidley, R., Lertoria, T., Murphy, D., Slater, S. and Wardle, M. (2003) 'Starters and plenaries – a practical resource', *Deutsch: Lehren und Lernen* 28: 11–14.

Crystal, D. (2003) *The Cambridge Encyclopaedia of Language*, 2nd edn. Cambridge: Cambridge University Press.

Cunningsworth, A. (1995) *Choosing Your Coursebook*. Oxford: Heinemann.

Dahlhaus, B. (1994) *Fertigkeit Hören*. Berlin: Langenscheidt.

Dakin, J. (1976) *The Language Laboratory and Language Learning*. Harlow: Longman.

Dam, L. (1990) 'Learner autonomy in practice', in I. Gathercole (ed.) *Autonomy in Language Learning*. London: CILT, pp. 16–37.

Dam, L. (1995) *Learner Autonomy 3: From Theory to Classroom Practice*. Dublin: Authentik.

Davies, B. (2004) 'The gender gap in modern languages: a comparison of attitude and performance in Year 7 and Year 10', *Language Learning Journal* 29, Rugby: ALL, pp. 53–8.

Davison, J. (2000) 'Managing classroom behaviour', in S. Capel, M. Leask and T. Turner (eds) *Learning to Teach in the Secondary School*, 2nd edn. London: Routledge, pp. 120–32.

Deane, M. (1992) 'Teaching modern languages to pupils with special educational needs? With pleasure!' *Language Learning Journal* 6, Rugby: ALL, pp. 43–7.

Dearing, R. (1996) *Review of Qualifications for 16 to 19 Year-Olds*. London: SCAA.

Dearing, R. and King, L. (2006) *Languages Review: A Consultation Report*. London: DfES. Available at: http://www.teachernet.gov.uk/_doc/10690/6869_DfES_Language_Review.pdf (accessed 30 August 2007).

Dearing, R. and King, L. (2007) *Languages Review*. Available at: http://www.teachernet.gov.uk/_doc/10690/6869_DfES_Language_Review.pdf (accessed 30 August 2007).

DeKeyser, R. (2005) 'What makes learning second-language grammar difficult? A review of issues', *Language Learning* 55, Supplement 1, pp. 1–25.

Denscombe, M. (1980) 'Keeping 'em quiet: the significance of noise for the practical activity of teaching', in P. Woods (ed.) *Teacher Strategies*. London: Croom Helm.

Denton, C. and Postlethwaite, K. (1985) *Able Children: Identifying Them in the Classroom*. Windsor: NFER-Nelson.

DES (1989) *Discipline in Schools: Report of the Committee of Enquiry Chaired by Lord Elton* (The Elton Report). London: HMSO.

DES/Welsh Office (1990) *Modern Foreign Languages for Ages 11–16*. London: HMSO.

DES/Welsh Office (1991) *Modern Foreign Languages in the National Curriculum*. London: HMSO.

DfE/Welsh Office (1994) *Code of Practice on the Identification and Assessment of Special Educational Needs*. London: HMSO.

DfEE (1998a) *Health and Safety of Pupils on Educational Visits*. Suffolk: DfEE Publications.

DfEE (1998b) *National Literacy Strategy. Framework for Teaching*. London: HMSO.

DfEE (1998c) *The National Literacy Strategy*. London: HMSO.

DfEE/QCA (1999) *Modern Foreign Languages: The National Curriculum for England*. London: HMSO.

DfES (2001) *The SEN Code of Practice*. London: DfES. Available at http://www.teacher net.gov.uk/_doc/3724/SENCodeOfPractice.pdf (accessed 30 August 2007).

DfES (2002a) *Languages for All: Languages for Life*. London: DfES. Available at: http://www.dfes.gov.uk/languagesstrategy/pdf/DfESLanguagesStrategy.pdf (accessed 30 August 2007).

DfES (2002b) *Key Stage 3 Strategy: Framework for Teaching MFL*. London: DfES. Available at: http://www.standards.dfes.gov.uk/secondary/keystage3/respub/mflframework/ (accessed 30 August 2007).

DfES (2004) *Use of Interactive Whiteboards in Modern Foreign Languages: Embedding ICT @ Secondary*. London: DfES. Available at: http://publications.teachernet.gov.uk/eOrdering-Download/1283–2005PDF-EN-01.pdf (accessed 30 August 2007).

DfES (2005) *Developing the Global Dimension in the School Curriculum*. London: DfES. Available at: http://www.dfid.gov.uk/pubs/files/dev-global-dim.pdf (accessed 30 August 2007).

Dickson, P. (1996) *Using the Target Language: A View from the Classroom*. Slough: NFER.

Dobson, A. (1998) *Mfl Inspected: Reflections on Inspection Findings 1996–97*. London: CILT.

Dörnyei, Z. (2001) *Teaching and Researching Motivation*. London: Longman.

Dörnyei, Z. and Csizér, K. (1998) 'Ten commandments for motivating language learners: results of an empirical study', *Language Teaching Research* 2(3): 203–29.

Dörnyei, Z. and Thurrell, S. (1994) 'Teaching conversational skills intensively: course content and rationale', *ELT Journal* 48: 40–9.

Doyé, P. (1999) *The Intercultural Dimension: Foreign Language Education in the Primary School*. Berlin: Cornelsen.

Driscoll, P. (1999) 'Modern languages in the primary school: a fresh start', in P. Driscoll and D. Frost (eds) *Teaching Modern Foreign Languages in the Primary School*. London: Routledge-Falmer, pp. 9–26.

Duffy, M. (2000) 'Just more hoops to jump through?' *TES*, Friday, 2 June, pp. 29–30.

Dunne, E. (1993) 'Theory into practice', in N. Bennett and C. Carré (eds) *Learning to Teach*. London: Routledge, pp. 105–19.

Ellis, G. and Sinclair, B. (1989) *Learning to Learn English: A Course in Learner Training*. Cambridge: Cambridge University Press.

Ellis, R. (1986) *Understanding Second Language Acquisition*. Oxford: Oxford University Press.

Ellis, R. (1994) *The Study of Second Language Acquisition*. Oxford: Oxford University Press.

Ellis, R. (1997) *SLA research and Language Teaching*. Oxford: Oxford University Press.

Ellis, R. (2003) *Task-based Language Learning and Teaching*. Oxford: Oxford University Press.

Ellis, R. (2005) 'Principles of instructed language learning', *System* 33: 209–24.

Everett, V. (2005) 'You can get the grammar needed for GCSE on to one side of A4 . . . but it takes two years to get good at using it', *Language Learning Journal* 32, Rugby: ALL, pp. 68–73.

Fawkes, S. (2001) *CILT Briefings 1: Using Authentic Materials in Key Stages 3 and 4*, London: CILT.

Fernández-Toro, M. (2005) 'The role of paired listening in L2 listening instruction', *Language Learning Journal* 31, Rugby: ALL, pp. 3–8.

Fernheimer, J. and Nelson, T. (2005) 'Bridging the composition divide: blog pedagogy and the potential for agonistic classrooms', *Currents in Electronic Literacy* 9. Available at: http://www.cwrl.utexas.edu/currents/fall05/fernheimernelson.html (accessed 30 August 2007).

Field, K. (1999a) 'GCSE and A/AS level teaching and learning: similarities and differences', in N. Pachler (ed.) *Teaching Modern Foreign Languages at Advanced Level*. London: Routledge, pp. 33–59.

Field, K. (1999b) 'Developing productive language skills – speaking and writing', in N. Pachler (ed.) *Teaching Modern Foreign Languages at Advanced Level*. London: Routledge, pp. 184–208.

Field, K. (2000) 'Why are girls better at modern foreign languages than boys?', in K. Field (ed.) *Issues in the Teaching of Modern Foreign Languages*. London: Routledge, pp. 134–45.

Field, K., Holden, P. and Lawlor, H. (2000) *Effective Subject Leadership*. London: Routledge.

Field, S. (2007) 'Presenting new vocabulary and structures', in N. Pachler and A. Redondo (eds) *A Practical Guide to Teaching Modern Foreign Languages in the Secondary School*. London: Routledge, pp. 23–34.

Fisher, L. (2001) 'Modern Foreign Languages recruitment post 16: the pupils' perspective', *Language Learning Journal* 23, Rugby: ALL.

Fisher, L. and Evans, M. (2000) 'The school exchange visit: effects on attitudes and proficiency in language learning', *Language Learning Journal* 22, Rugby: ALL, pp. 11–16.

Fleming, F. and Walls, G. (1998) 'What pupils do: the role of strategic planning in modern foreign language learning', *Language Learning Journal* 18, Rugby: ALL, pp. 1–21.

Forth, I. and Naysmith, J. (1995) ' "The good the bad and the ugly": some problems with grammar rules', *Language Learning Journal* 11, Rugby: ALL, pp. 78–81.

Freeman, D. (2002) 'The hidden side of the work: teacher knowledge and learning to teach: a perspective from North American educational research on teacher education in English language teaching', *Language Teaching* 35: 1–13.

Furlong, J. and Maynard, T. (1995) *Mentoring Student Teachers: The Growth of Professional Knowledge*. London: Routledge.

Furlong, J., Whitty, G., Miles, S., Barton, L. and Barrett, E. (1996) 'From integration to partnership: changing structures in initial teacher education', in R. McBride (ed.) *Teacher Education Policy: Some Issues Arising from Research and Practice*. London: Falmer Press, pp. 22–35.

Gardner, H. (1983) *Frames of Mind*. New York: Basic Books.

George, D. (1993) 'Meeting the challenge of the able child', *Topic 10*. Windsor: NFER-Nelson.

Godwin-Jones, R. (2006) 'Tag clouds in the blogsphere: electronic literacy and social networking', *Language Learning & Technology* 10(2): 8–15. Available at http://llt.msu.edu/vol10num2/emerging/ (accessed 30 August 2007).

Godwin-Jones, R. (2007) 'Digital video update: YouTube, Flash, High-Definition', *Language Learning & Technology* 11(1): 16–21. Available at http://llt.msu.edu/vol11num1/emerging/ (accessed 30 August 2007).

Goleman, D. (1996) *Emotional Intelligence: Why It Can Matter More Than IQ*. London: Bloomsbury.

Grabe, W. (2004) 'Research on teaching reading', *Annual Review of Applied Linguistics* 24: 44–69.

Graham, S. (1997) *Effective Language Learning: Positive Strategies for Advanced Level Language Teaching*. Clevedon: Multilingual Matters.

Graham, S. (2002) 'Experiences of learning French: a snapshot at years 11, 12 and 13', *Language Learning Journal* 25, Rugby: ALL, pp. 15–20.

Graham, S. (2003) 'Learner strategies and advanced level listening comprehension', *Language Learning Journal* 28, Rugby: ALL, pp. 64–9.

Graham, S. (2004) 'Giving up on Modern Foreign Languages? Students' perceptions of learning French', *The Modern Language Journal* 88(2): 171–91.

Graham, S. (2007) 'Developing speaking skills in the modern foreign language', in N. Pachler and A. Redondo (eds) *Teaching Foreign Languages in the Secondary School: A Practical Guide.* London: Routledge, pp. 58–66.

Grauberg, W. (1997) *The Elements of Foreign Language Teaching.* Clevedon: Multilingual Matters.

Green, P. and Hecht, K. (1992) 'Implicit and explicit grammar: an empirical study', *Applied Linguistics* 13: 168–84.

Grell, J. and Grell, M. (1985) *Unterrichtsrezepte.* Basel: Beltz Verlag.

Grenfell, M. (ed.) (1995) *Reflections on Reading: From GCSE to A Level.* London: CILT.

Grenfell, M. (1998) *Training Teachers in Practice.* Clevedon: Multilingual Matters.

Grenfell, M. (2000) 'Modern Languages – beyond Nuffield and into the 21st century', *Language Learning Journal* 22, Rugby: ALL, pp. 23–9.

Groot, P. (2000) 'Computer assisted second language vocabulary acquisition', *Language Learning & Technology* 4(1): 60–81. Available at: http://llt.msu.edu/vol4num1/groot/default.html (accessed 30 August 2007).

Hallam, S. and Deathe, K. (2002) 'Ability grouping: year group differences in self-concept and attitudes of secondary school pupils', *Westminster Studies in Education* 25(1): 7–17.

Halliwell, S. (1991a) *Grammar Matters.* London: CILT.

Halliwell, S. (1991b) *Yes – But Will They Behave? Managing the Interactive Classroom.* London: CILT.

Han, Y. and Ellis, R. (1998) 'Implicit knowledge, explicit knowledge and general language proficiency', *Language Teaching Research* 2(1), pp. 1–23.

Hargreaves, A. and Evans, R. (1997) *Beyond Education Reform: Bringing Teachers Back In.* Buckingham: Open University Press.

Harris, D. (1994) 'Learning from experience', *Languages Forum* 2/3: 33–5.

Harris, V. (1997) *Teaching Learners How to Learn: Strategy Training in the ML Classroom.* London: CILT.

Harris, V. (2002) 'Treading a tightrope: supporting boys to achieve in MFL', in A. Swarbrick (ed.) *Teaching Modern Foreign Languages in Secondary Schools: A Reader*, London: Routledge, pp. 187–202.

Hatch, E. (1978) 'Apply with caution', *Studies in Second Language Acquisition* 2: 123–43.

Hawkins, E. (1984) *Awareness of Language.* Cambridge: Cambridge University Press.

Hawkins, E. (1987) *Modern Languages in the Curriculum*, rev. edn. Cambridge: Cambridge University Press.

Hawkins, E. (1994) 'Percept before precept', in L. King and P. Boaks (eds) *Grammar! A Conference Report.* London: CILT, pp. 109–23.

Heafford, M. (1990) 'Teachers may teach, but do learners learn?' *Language Learning Journal* 11, Rugby: ALL, pp. 88–90.

HEFCE (1999) Letter to Vice-Chancellors. 17 December.

Heilbronn, R. (2004) 'The national Strategy for KS3 and its application to modern foreign language teaching', *Language Learning Journal* 30, Rugby: ALL, pp. 42–9.

Heilbronn, R. (2007) 'Planning modern foreign language lessons', in N. Pachler and A. Redondo (eds) *Teaching Foreign Languages in the Secondary School: A Practical Guide.* London: Routledge, pp. 12–22.

Heilenman, L. (1991) 'Writing in foreign language classrooms: processes and reality', in J. Alatis (ed.) *Georgetown University Round Table on Languages and Linguistics*. Washington, DC: Georgetown University Press, pp. 273–88.

Hewer, S. (1997) *Text Manipulation: Computer-Based Activities to Improve Knowledge and Use of the Target Language*. London: CILT.

Hill, B. (1989) *Making the Most of Video*. London: CILT.

Hill, J. (2004) 'Developing reading skills during Key Stage 3', *Deutsch Lehren und Lernen* 30: 12–14.

HMI (1992) *The Education of Very Able Children in Maintained Schools*. London: HMSO.

HMI (1993) *Special Needs Issues: A Survey by HMI*. London: HMSO.

Hood, P. (2000) 'Logging on to learning: ICT, modern languages and real communicative classrooms?' In S. Green (ed.) *New Perspectives on Teaching and Learning Modern Languages*. Clevedon: Multilingual Matters, pp. 124–37.

Hornsey, A. (1993) 'The written word in oral language teaching', *Languages Forum* 1: 15.

Hornsey, A. (1994) 'Authenticity in foreign language learning', *Languages Forum* 2/3: 6–7.

Horsfall, P. and Evans, M. (1995) *Dictionary Skills: French/German/Spanish*. Leamington Spa: Language Centre Publications.

Hulstijn, J. H. (2001) 'Intentional and incidental second language vocabulary learning: a reappraisal of elaboration, rehearsal and automaticity', in P. Robinson (ed.) *Cognition and Second Language Instruction*. Cambridge: Cambridge University Press, pp. 258–86.

Hunt, M. (2007) 'KS2–KS3 transfer', in N. Pachler and A. Redondo (eds) *A Practical Guide to Teaching Modern Foreign Languages in the Secondary School*, London: Routledge, pp. 102–9.

Hunt, M., Barnes, A., Powell, B., Muijs, D. and Lindsay, G. (2005) 'Primary Modern Foreign Languages: an overview of recent research, key issues and challenges for educational policy and practice', *Research Papers in Education* 20(4): 371–87.

Hurren, C. (1992) *Departmental Planning and Schemes of Work*. London: CILT.

Jackson, A. (2004) 'Pupil responsibility for learning in the KS3 French classroom', *Francophonie* 30: 16–21.

Jenkins, J. (2000) *The Phonology of English as an International Language*. Oxford: Oxford University Press.

Jenkins, J. (2004) 'Research in teaching pronunciation and intonation', *Annual Review of Applied Linguistics* 24: 109–25.

Johnstone, R. (1988) 'Communicative methodology: second generation', in P. Kingston (ed.) *Languages Breaking Barriers*. London: Joint Council of Language Associations, pp. 12–21.

Jones, B. (1992) *Being Creative*. London: CILT.

Jones, B. (1995) *Exploring Otherness: An Approach to Cultural Awareness*. London: CILT.

Jones, B. (2000) 'Developing cultural awareness', in K. Field (ed.) *Issues in Modern Foreign Languages Teaching*. London: Routledge, pp 158–70.

Jones, B. (2001) *Developing Learning Strategies*, London: CILT.

Jones, B. and Jones, G. (2000) *Boys' Performance in Modern Foreign Languages: Listening to Learners*. London: CILT/QCA/Homerton College.

Jones, J. (2000a) 'Teaching and learning modern foreign languages and able pupils', in K. Field. (ed.) *Issues in the Teaching of Modern Foreign Languages*. London: Routledge, pp. 105–21.

Jones, J. (2000b) 'Teaching grammar in the mfl classroom', in K. Field (ed.) *Issues in Modern Foreign Language Teaching*. London: Routledge, pp. 146–61.

Jones, J. and Black, P. (2006) 'Formative assessment and the learning and teaching of MFL: sharing the language learning road map with the learners', *Language Learning Journal* 34, Rugby: ALL, pp. 4–9.

Jones, N. (2007) 'Assessment and the National Languages Strategy', *Cambridge Journal of Education* 37(1): 17–33.

Kagan, S. (1988) *Co-operative Learning: Resources for Teachers*. Riverside, CA: University of California.

Kasper, G. (2001) 'Four perspectives on L2 pragmatic development', *Applied Linguistics* 22:. 502–30.

Kasten, J. (1995) 'Eine Insel in der Hauptstadt', *Education Guardian*, 21 March, p. 15.

Kavanagh, B. and Upton, L. (1994) *Creative Use of Texts*. London: CILT.

Kay, J. (1978) *Un kilo de chansons*. Cheltenham: Mary Glasgow Publications.

Kern, R. (1994) 'The role of mental translation in second language reading', *Studies in Second Language Acquisition* 16(4): 441–61.

Kern, R. (2000) *Literacy and Language Teaching*. Oxford: Oxford University Press.

Kern, R., Ware, P. and Warschauer, M. (2004) 'Crossing frontiers: new directions in online pedagogy and research', *Annual Review of Applied Linguistics* 24: 243–60. Also available at http://www.gse.uci.edu/faculty/markw/frontiers.pdf.

King, L. (ed.) (1991) 'Graded objectives and the National Curriculum', *GOML News* 15. London: CILT.

King, L. (2007) 'Shadows on the wall: a policy viewpoint and personal view', *Cambridge Journal of Education* 37(1): 129–37.

Kingman, J. (1988) *Report on the Committee of Enquiry into the Teaching of English Language*. London: HMSO.

Klapper, J. (1997) 'Language Learning at school and university: the great grammar debate continues', *Language Learning Journal* 16, Rugby: ALL, pp. 22–7.

Klapper, J. (2003) 'Taking communication to task? A critical view of recent trends in language teaching', *Language Learning Journal* 27, Rugby: ALL, pp. 33–42.

Kolb, D., Rubin, I. and McIntyre, J. (1974) *Organisational Psychology: An Experiential Approach*. Hemel Hempstead: Prentice Hall.

Kramsch, C. (2006) 'From communicative competence to symbolic competence', *Modern Language Journal* 90(2): 249–52.

Kramsch, C. and Thorne, S. (2002) 'Foreign language learning as global communicative practice', in D. Block and D. Cameron (eds) *Globalization and Language Teaching*. London: Routledge, pp. 83–100.

Kyriacou, C. (1986) *Effective Teaching in Schools*. Hemel Hempstead: Basil Blackwell.

Kyriacou, C. (1991) *Essential Teaching Skills*. Hemel Hempstead: Basil Blackwell.

Lamb, T. and Simpson, M. (2003) 'Escaping from the treadmill: practitioner research and professional autonomy', *Language Learning Journal* 28. Rugby: ALL, pp. 55–63.

Langran, J. and Purcell, S. (1994) *Language Games and Activities*. London: CILT.

Lantolf, J. (1999) 'Second culture acquisition: cognitive considerations', in E. Hinkel (ed.) *Culture in Second Language Teaching*. Cambridge: Cambridge University Press.

Larsen-Freeman, D. (2003) *Teaching Language: From Grammar to Grammaring*. Boston: Heinle & Heinle.

Leah, G. (2001) 'An approach to teaching literature under AS and A2 specifications', *Deutsch: Lehren und Lernen* 23: 14–17.

Leask, M. and Pachler, N. (eds) (2005) *Learning to Teach Using ICT in the Secondary School*. London: Routledge.

Lee, J. (2002) 'The invisible child: an MFL improvement and development programme in the London Borough of Barking and Dagenham', in A. Swarbrick (ed.) *Teaching Modern Foreign Languages in Secondary Schools: A Reader*. London: Routledge, pp. 255–71.

Lee, J., Buckland, D. and Shaw, G. (1998) *The Invisible Child: The Responses and Attitudes to the Learning of MFL Shown by Year 9 Pupils of Average Ability*. London: CILT.

Lightbown, P. (2003) 'SLA research in the classroom/SLA research for the classroom', *Language Learning Journal* 28, Rugby: ALL, pp. 4–13.

Lightbown, P. and Spada, N. (1993) *How Languages Are Learnt*. Oxford: Oxford University Press.

Lin, M. and Mackay, C. (2003) *Thinking through Modern Foreign Languages*. London: Chris Kington Publications.

Little, D., Devitt, S. and Singleton, D. (1989) *Learning Foreign Languages from Authentic Texts*. Dublin: Authentik.

Littlewood, W. (1981) *Communicative Language Teaching*. Cambridge: Cambridge University Press.

Long, M. (1981) 'Input, interaction and foreign language acquisition', in H. Winitz (ed.) *Native Language and Foreign Language Acquisition*. New York: Annals of the New York Academy of Sciences 379, pp. 259–78.

Lund, R. (1991) 'A comparison of second language listening and reading comprehension', *Modern Language Journal* 75(2): 196–204.

Lynch, T. (1997) 'Nudge, nudge: teacher interventions in task-based learner talk', *ELT Journal* 51(4): 317–25.

Macaro, E. (1997) *Target Language, Collaborative Learning and Autonomy*. Clevedon: Multilingual Matters.

Macaro, E. (2000) 'Issues in target language teaching', in K. Field (ed.) *Issues in Modern Foreign Languages Teaching*. London: Routledge, pp. 175–93.

Macaro, E. (2001a) *Learning Strategies in Foreign and Second Language Classrooms*. London: Continuum.

Macaro, E. (2001b) 'Analysing student teachers' codeswitching in foreign language classrooms: theories and decision making', *The Modern Language Journal* 85(4): 531–48.

Macaro, E. (2003a) *Teaching and Learning a Second Language: A Guide to Recent Research and Its Applications*. London: Continuum.

Macaro, E. (2003b) 'Second language teachers as second language researchers', *Language Learning Journal* 27, Rugby: ALL, pp. 43–51.

Macaro, E. (2006) 'Strategies for language learning and for language use: revising the theoretical framework', *The Modern Language Journal* 90(3): 320–37.

Macaro, E. (2008) 'The decline in language learning in England: getting the facts right and getting real', in *Language Learning Journal 36(1)*, pp. 101–108.

Macaro, E., Vanderplank, R. and Graham, S. (2005) 'A systematic review of the role of prior knowledge in unidirectional listening comprehension', *Research Evidence in Education Library*. London: EPPI-Centre, Social Science Research Unit, Institute of Education, University of London. Available at: http://eppi.ioe.ac.uk/EPPIWebContent/reel/review_groups/MFL/mfl_rv2/MFL_rv2.pdf (accessed 30 June 2006).

McBride, N. and Seaga, K. (2000) *Target Culture, Target Language?* London: CILT.

McCarthy, M. and O'Keeffe, A. (2004) 'Research in the teaching of speaking', *Annual Review of Applied Linguistics* 24: 26–43.

McCulloch, D. (1995) 'Where has all the grammar gone? An "accusative" search', *German Teaching* 12, Rugby: ALL, pp. 13–18.

McCulloch, D. (1996) 'What follows the revolution?' In G. Shaw and S. Myles (eds) *German Grammar Teaching in Crisis?* Occasional Papers 4. London: Association for Modern German Studies, pp. 13–17.

MacDonald, C. (1993) *Using the Target Language*. Cheltenham: MGP/ALL.

McFarlane, A. (1996) 'Blessings in disguise', *TES Computers Update*. 28 June, p. 4.

McKeown, S. (2004) *Meeting SEN in the Curriculum: Modern Foreign Languages*. London: David Fulton.

McLachlan, A. (2001) *Advancing Oral Skills*. London: CILT.

McLachlan, A. (2002) *New Pathfinder 1: Raising the Standard: Addressing the Needs of Gifted and Talented Pupils*. London: CILT.

Macrory, G. (2000) 'Learning to teach grammar in the Modern Foreign Languages classroom', *Research in Education* 1: 1–11.

Maguire, C. and Morris-Lucas, C. (2006) *Getting a Teaching Job 2007*. Teaching Task Group. Association of Graduate Careers Advisory Services. Available at: http://www.derby.ac.uk/careers/handouts/gettingateachingjob2007.pdf (accessed 18 July 2007).

Maubach, A. and Morgan, C. (2001) 'The relationship between gender and learning styles among A level modern languages students', *Language Learning Journal* 23, Rugby: ALL.

Maxim, H. (2002) 'A study into the feasibility and effects of reading extended authentic discourse in the beginning German language classroom', *Modern Language Journal* 86(1): 20–35.

Meijer, D. with Jenkins, E.-M. (1998) 'Landeskundliche Inhalte – die Qual der Wahl? Kriterienkatalog zur Beurteilung von Lehrwerken', *Fremdsprache Deutsch* 18(1): 18–25.

Meiring, L. and Norman, N. (1999a) 'Planning a programme of work', in N. Pachler (ed.) *Teaching Modern Foreign Languages at Advanced Level*. London: Routledge, pp. 119–38.

Meiring, L. and Norman, N. (1999b) 'Planning an integrated topic', in N. Pachler (ed.) *Teaching Modern Foreign Languages at Advanced Level*. London: Routledge, pp. 139–59.

Meiring, L. and Norman, N. (2001) 'Grammar in MFL teaching revisited', *Language Learning Journal* 23, Rugby: ALL, pp. 58–66.

Meiring, L. and Norman, N. (2002) 'Back on target: repositioning the status of target language in MFL teaching and learning', *Language Learning Journal* 26, Rugby: ALL, pp. 27–35.

Meiring, L. and Norman, N. (2007) 'Grammar in the modern foreign language classroom', in N. Pachler and A. Redondo (eds) *Teaching Foreign Languages in the Secondary School: A Practical Guide*. London: Routledge, pp. 76–86.

Metcalfe, P., Laurillard, D. and Gates, P. (1995) 'The decline of written accuracy in pupils' use of French verbs', *Language Learning Journal* 12, Rugby: ALL, pp. 47–59.

Miller, A. (1995) *Creativity*. Cheltenham: Mary Glasgow Publications and Association for Language Learning.

Miller, A. (2000) 'Word and text: when vocabulary is part of the bigger picture', *Francophonie* 21: 20–4.

Miller, A. (2002) 'Communicative grammar teaching', in A. Swarbrick (ed.) *Teaching Modern Foreign Languages in Secondary Schools: A Reader*. London: Routledge, pp. 141–55.

Mitchell, I. and Swarbrick, A. (1994) *Developing Skills for Independent Reading*. London: CILT.

Mitchell, R. (1988) *Communicative Language Teaching in Practice*. London: CILT.

Mitchell, R. (1994) 'The communicative approach to language teaching: an introduction', in A. Swarbrick (ed.) *Teaching Modern Languages*. London: Routledge, pp. 33–42.

Mitchell, R. (2000) 'Applied linguistics and evidence-based classroom practice: the case of foreign language grammar pedagogy', *Applied Linguistics* 21(3): 281–303.

Mitchell, R. (2003) 'Rethinking the concept of progression in the National Curriculum for Modern Foreign Languages: a research perspective', *Language Learning Journal* 27, Rugby: ALL, pp. 15–23.

Morgan, C. (2006) 'Appropriate language assessment in content and language integrated learning', *Language Learning Journal* 33, Rugby: ALL, pp. 59–67.

Morgan, C. and Neil, P. (2001) *Teaching Modern Foreign Languages*. London: Kogan Page.

Morley, J. and Truscott, S. (2006) 'Incorporating peer assessment in to tandem learning', *Language Learning Journal*, 33: 53–8.

Moss, G., Jewitt, C., Levacic, R., Armstrong, V., Cardini, A. and Castle, F. (2007) *The Interactive Whiteboards, Pedagogy and Pupil Performance Evaluation: An Evaluation of the Schools Whiteboard Expansion (SWE) Project: London Challenge*. London. DfES Research Report 816. London. Available at: http://www.dfes.gov.uk/research/data/uploadfiles/RR816.pdf (accessed 30 August 2007).

Mutton, T. (2007) 'Developing modern foreign language skills through formative assessment', in N. Pachler and A. Redondo (eds) *A Practical Guide to Teaching Modern Foreign Languages in the Secondary School*. London: Routledge, pp. 35–47.

NALA and Central Bureau (1992) *The Foreign Language Assistant: A Guide to Good Practice*. London: Central Bureau.

Nassaji, H. and Fotos, S. (2004) 'Current developments in research on the teaching of grammar', *Annual Review of Applied Linguistics* 24: 126–45.

Nation, I. (2001) *Learning Vocabulary in Another Language*. Cambridge: Cambridge University Press.

NCC (1989) *Special Educational Needs in the National Curriculum*. York: NCC.

NCC (1992a) *Modern Foreign Languages Non-Statutory Guidance*. York: NCC.

NCC (1992b) *Target Practice: Developing Pupils' Use of the Target Language*. York: NCC.

NCC (1993) *Modern Foreign Languages and Special Educational Needs: A New Commitment*. York: NCC.

Neather, T. (2003) *Getting to Grips with Grammar*. London: CILT.

Neather, T., Woods, C., Rodrigues, I., Davis, M. and Dunne, E. (1995) *Target Language Testing in Modern Foreign Languages: A Report of a Project on the Testing of Reading and Listening Without the Use of English*. London: SCAA.

Neil, P. (1996) 'German in the classroom: what the pupils think', *Language Learning Journal* 13, Rugby: ALL, pp. 10–15.

Neil, P. (1997) *Reflections on the Target Language*. London: CILT.

Neill, S. (1993) *Body Language for Competent Teachers*. London: Routledge.

Neuner, G. and Hunfeld, H. (1993) *Methoden des fremdsprachlichen Deutschunterrichts: Eine Einführung*. Berlin: Langenscheidt.

Norman, N. (1995) 'Initial teacher education in France, Germany and England and Wales', *Links 12*. London: CILT, pp. 5–7.

Noss, R. and Pachler, N. (1999) 'The challenge of new technologies: doing old things in a new way, or doing new things?' In P. Mortimore (ed.) *Understanding Pedagogy and Its Impact on Learning*. London: Sage, pp. 195–211.

Nuffield Languages Inquiry (2000) *Languages: The Next Generation: Final Report and Recommendations*. London. Available at: http://languages.nuffieldfoundation.org/filelibrary/pdf/languages_finalreport.pdf (accessed 30 August 2007).

Nunan, D. (1989) *Designing Tasks for the Communicative Classroom*. Cambridge: Cambridge University Press.

Nunan, D. and Lamb, C. (1996) *The Self-Directed Teacher: Managing the Learning Process*. Cambridge: Cambridge University Press.

O'Brien, T. (2004) 'Writing in a foreign language: teaching and learning', *Language Teaching* 37: 1–28.

Ofsted (2004) *OFSTED Subject Reports 2002/03: Modern Foreign Languages in Secondary Schools*. London. Available at: http://www.ofsted.gov.uk/assets/3542.doc (accessed 30 June 2006).

Oliver, M. (1994) 'Question-and-answer revisited: introducing reflexive verbs in German', *Languages Forum* 2/3: 16–18.

Oxford, R. (1987) *Language Learning Strategies: What Every Teacher Should Know*. Boston: Heinle & Heinle.

Pachler, N. (1999a) 'Teaching and learning grammar', in N. Pachler (ed.) *Teaching Modern Foreign Languages at Advanced Level*. London: Routledge, pp. 93–115.

Pachler, N. (1999b) 'Teaching and learning culture', in N. Pachler (ed.) *Teaching Modern Foreign Languages at Advanced Level*. London: Routledge, pp. 76–92.

Pachler, N. (1999c) 'Using the internet as a teaching and learning tool', in M. Leask and

N. Pachler (eds) *Learning to Teach Using ICT in the Secondary School*. London: Routledge, pp. 51–70.

Pachler, N. (1999d) 'The new A/AS level', in N. Pachler (ed.) *Teaching Modern Foreign Languages at Advanced Level*. London: Routledge, pp. 22–30.

Pachler, N. (2000a) 'Re-examining communicative language teaching', in K. Field (ed.) *Issues in Modern Foreign Language Teaching*. London: RoutledgeFalmer, pp. 26–41.

Pachler, N. (2000b) 'Secondary education', in M. Byram (ed.) *Encyclopedia of Language Teaching and Learning*. London: Routledge, pp. 510–15.

Pachler, N. (2001) 'Electronic reference tools for foreign language learners, teachers and users: offline vocabulary look-up programs', *Language Learning Journal* 24, Rugby: ALL, pp. 24–9.

Pachler, N. (2002) 'Speech technologies and foreign language teaching and learning', *Language Learning Journal* 26, Rugby: ALL, pp. 54–61.

Pachler, N. (2003) 'Foreign language teaching as an evidence-based profession?' *Language Learning Journal* 27, Rugby: ALL, pp. 4–14.

Pachler, N. (2007a) 'Choices in language education: principles and policies', *Cambridge Journal of Education* 37(1): 1–15.

Pachler, N. (2007b) 'Internet-based approaches to modern foreign language teaching and learning', in N. Pachler and A. Redondo (eds) *Teaching Modern Foreign Languages in the Secondary School: A Practical Guide*, London: Routledge, pp. 93–9.

Pachler, N. with Bond, J. (1999) 'Teaching and learning grammar', in N. Pachler (ed.) *Teaching Modern Foreign Languages at Advanced Level*. London: Routledge, pp. 93–115.

Pachler, N. and Field, K. (1999) 'Learner independence', in N. Pachler (ed.) *Teaching Modern Foreign Languages at Advanced Level*. London: Routledge, pp. 60–75.

Pachler, N. and Field, K. (2004) 'Continuing Professional Development', in S. Capel, R. Heilbronn, M. Leask and T. Turner (eds) *Starting to Teach in the Secondary School*, rev. edn. London: RoutledgeFalmer, pp. 233–46.

Pachler, N. and Redondo, A. (eds) (2005) 'Support for Learning: Special Issue on Inclusive Approaches to Teaching Foreign Languages', *British Journal of Learning Support* 20(3). NASEN.

Pachler, N. and Redondo, A. (2007) *Teaching Foreign Languages in the Secondary School: A Practical Guide*. London: Routledge.

Pachler, N. with Reimann, T. (1999) 'Reaching beyond the classroom', in N. Pachler (ed.) *Teaching Modern Foreign Languages at Advanced Level*. London: Routledge, pp. 282–97.

Pachler, N., Evans, M. and Lawes, S. (2007) *Modern Foreign Languages: Teaching School Subjects 11–19*. London: Routledge.

Page, B. (1989) 'Language learning – objectives and forms of assessment: GOML submission to the National Curriculum Working Group', in L. King (ed.) *Graded Objectives and TVEI*. GOML News 14. London: CILT.

Page, B. (1990) 'Why do I have to get it right anyway?' in B. Page (ed.) *What Do You Mean It's Wrong?* London: CILT, pp. 102–6.

Page, B. (ed.) (1992) *Letting Go: Taking Hold. a Guide to Independent Language Learning by Teachers for Teachers*. London: CILT.

Page, B. and Hewett, D. (1987) *Languages Step by Step: Graded Objectives in the UK*. London: CILT.

Page, R. (1997) *Working with Your Foreign Language Assistant*. Cheltenham: Mary Glasgow Publications/Association for Language Learning.

Paige, M., Jorstad, H., Siaya, L., Klein, F. and Colby, J. (2000) *Culture Learning in Language Education: A Review of the Literature*. St Paul, MN: Centre for Advanced Research in Language Acquisition (CARLA), University of Minnesota. Available at: http://www.education.umn.edu/EdPA/People/paigCV.pdf (accessed 30 August 2007).

Paribakht, T. and Wesche, M. (1993) 'Reading comprehension and second language development in a comprehension-based ESL programme', *TESL Canada Journal* 11: 9–27.

Parkinson, B. (1992) 'Observing foreign language lessons', *Language Learning Journal* 5, Rugby: ALL, pp. 20–4.

Pearson, S., Chambers, G. and Hall, K. (2003) 'Video material as a support to developing effective collaboration between teachers and teaching assistants', *Support for Learning* 18(2): 83–7.

Pillette, M. (1996) *Developing Dictionary Skills in French*. Glasgow: Collins Educational.

Poole, B. (2002) 'The potential impact of the National Literacy Strategy on MFL learning', in A. Swarbrick (ed.) *Teaching Modern Foreign Languages in Secondary Schools: A Reader*. London: Routledge, pp. 203–21.

Powell, B. (1999) 'Developing receptive language skills – listening and reading', in N. Pachler (ed.) *Teaching Modern Foreign Languages at Advanced Level*. London: Routledge, pp. 160–83.

Powell, B. and Barnes, A. (1996) *Developing Advanced Reading Skills*. Cheltenham: MGP/Stanley Thornes.

Powell, B., Barnes, A. and Graham, S. (1996) *Using the Target Language to Test Modern Foreign Language Skills: A Report on Research Conducted in 12 Secondary Schools*. Warwick: University of Warwick.

Pugh, N. and Murphy, B. (1993) *Steps towards Achievement*. Colchester: Essex Development and Advisory Service.

QCA (2000a) *Schemes of Work: Secondary Modern Foreign Languages*. London. Also available at: http://www.ncaction.org.uk/subjects/MFL/ (accessed 30 August 2007).

QCA (2000b) *GCSE Criteria for Modern Foreign Languages*. London. Available at: http://www.qca.org.uk/downloads/5708_modern_foreign_lang.pd(1).pdf (accessed 30 August 2007).

QCA (2006a) *A Review of GCSE Coursework*. London: QCA.

QCA (2006b) *GCE Advanced Subsidiary and Advanced Level Specifications Subject Criteria for Modern Foreign Languages*. London: QCA. Available at: http://test.qca.org.uk/downloads/qca-06–2860_gce_as_a_level_sc_for_mfl.pdf (accessed 30 August 2007).

QCA (2007a) *GCSE Subject Criteria for Modern Foreign Languages*. London: QCA. Available at: http://www.qca.org.uk/qca_11999.aspx (accessed 30 August 2007).

QCA (2007b) *Modern foreign languages. Programme of Study: Key Stage 3*. London: QCA. Available at: http://www.qca.org.uk/libraryAssets/media/MFL_KS3_PoS.pdf (accessed 30 August 2007).

QCA (2007c) GCSE *Consultation Criteria for Modern Foreign Languages*. London: QCA. Also available at: http://www.qca.org.uk/qca_11999.aspx (accessed 30 August 2007).

QCA, ACCAC and CCEA (1999a) *Subject Criteria for Modern Foreign Languages: GCE Advanced Subsidiary and Advanced Level Specifications*. London: QCA.

QCA, ACCAC and CCEA (1999b) *GCE Advanced Subsidiary and Advanced Level Specifications Subject Criteria for Modern Foreign Languages*. London: QCA.

Rampillon, U. ([1989] 1994) *Lerntechniken im Fremdsprachenunterricht*. 2nd edn. München: Hueber.

Read, J. (2004) 'Research in teaching vocabulary', *Annual Review of Applied Linguistics* 24: 146–61.

Redondo, A. (2000) 'Mixed ability grouping in modern foreign languages teaching', in K. Field (ed.) *Issues in Modern Foreign Languages Teaching*. London: Routledge, pp. 122–33.

Redondo, A. (2007) 'Working with other adults', in N. Pachler and A. Redondo (eds) *A Practical Guide to Teaching Modern Foreign Languages in the Secondary School*, London: Routledge, pp. 4–11.

Rendall, H. (2003) 'Developing neural pathways: making the most of computers', *Scottish Languages Review* 8. Available at http://www.scilt.stir.ac.uk/SLR/Issue8/Heather.htm (accessed 3 June 2007).

Richards, J. (1998) 'What's the use of lesson plans?' in J. Richards (ed.) *Beyond Training*. Cambridge: Cambridge University Press, pp. 103–21.

Richards, J. and Rodgers, T. ([1986] 2001) *Approaches and Methods in Language Teaching*, 2nd edn. Cambridge: Cambridge University Press.

Richards, J., Li, B. and Tang, A. (1998) 'Exploring pedagogical reasoning skills', in J. Richards (ed.) *Beyond Training*. Cambridge: Cambridge University Press, pp. 242–59.

Rivers, W. (1975) *Teaching French: A Practical Guide*. Illinois: National Textbook Company.

Roberts, C., Byram, N., Barro, A., Jordan, S. and Street, B. (2000) *Language Learners as Ethnographers*. Clevedon: Multilingual Matters.

Roberts, J. (1998) *Language Teacher Education*. London: Arnold.

Roberts, T. (1992) *Towards a Learning Theory in Modern Languages*. London: Institute of Education. Occasional Paper No. 2.

Robertson, J. (1989) *Effective Classroom Control: Understanding Pupil/Teacher Relationships*. London: Hodder and Stoughton.

Rogers, C. (1982) *A Social Psychology of Schooling: The Expectancy Process*. London: Routledge and Kegan Paul.

Rowles, D., Carty, M. and McLachlan, A. (1998) *The Foreign Language Assistant: A Guide to Good Practice*. London: CILT.

Rumley, G. and Sharpe, K. (1993) 'Generalisable game activities in modern language learning', *Language Learning Journal* 8, Rugby: ALL, pp. 35–8.

Rutherford, W. (1987) *Second Language Grammar: Learning and Teaching*. London: Longman.

Saunders, K., Martin, G. and Richards, B. (1994) 'The standards debate – responses to Richard Sheppard', *German Teaching* 9. Rugby: ALL, pp. 10–14.

Setter, J. and Jenkins, J. (2005) 'Pronunciation', *Language Teaching* 38: 1–17.

Sharpe, K. (2001) *Modern Foreign Languages in the Primary School: The What, Why and How of Early MFL Teaching*. London: RoutledgeFalmer.

Shaw, P. (1994) 'Reluctant learners – you can do it!' in P. McLagan (ed.) *Steps to Learning. Modern Languages for Pupils with Special Educational Needs*. London: CILT, pp. 35–9.

Sheppard, R. (1993) 'Getting down to brass syntax: German teaching and the Great Standards Debate', *German Teaching* 8, Rugby: ALL, pp. 2–9.

Sinclair, J. and Coulthard, M. (1975) *Towards an Analysis of Discourse: The English Used by Teachers and Pupils*. London: Oxford University Press.

Skehan, P. (2003) 'Task-based instruction', *Language Teaching* 36: 1–14.

Slade, D. (1997) 'Stories and gossip in English: the macro-structure of casual talk', *Prospect* 12: 72–86.

Snow, D. and Byram, M. (1997) *Crossing Frontiers: The School Study Visit Abroad*. London: CILT.

Stobart, G. and Gipps, C, (1997) *Assessment: A Teacher's Guide to the Issues*. 3rd edn, London, Hodder & Stoughton.

Stobart, G. and Stoll, L. (2005) 'The Key Stage 3 Strategy: what kind of reform is this?' *Cambridge Journal of Education* 35(2): 225–38.

Swaffar, J. and Vlatten, A. (1997) 'A sequential model for video viewing in the foreign language curriculum', *The Modern Language Journal* 81(2): 175–84.

Swarbrick, A. (1998) *More Reading for Pleasure in a Foreign Language*. London: CILT.

Tabberer, R. (1996) *Teachers Make a Difference*. Slough: NFER.

Taylor, A. (2000) 'Boy-free zone?' *Language Learning Journal* 21, Rugby: ALL, pp. 3–7.

Taylor, W. (1994) 'Classroom variables', in B. Moon and A. Shelton-Mayes (eds) *Teaching and Learning in the Secondary School*. Milton Keynes: Open University Press, pp. 161–5.

TES (2007) 'Still in the dark about personalised learning', 8 June, p. 12.

Thorne, S. (2003) 'Artifacts and cultures-of-use in intercultural communication', *Language Learning & Technology* 7(2): 38–67. Available at: http://llt.msu.edu/vol7num2/pdf/thorne.pdf (accessed 30 August 2007).

Thorogood, J. and King, L. (1991) *Bridging the Gap: GCSE to A Level*. London: CILT.

Tierney, D. and Humphreys, F. (1992) *Improve Your Image: The Effective Use of the OHP*. London: CILT.

Tomlinson, M. (2004) *Final Report of the Working Group on 14–19 Reform*. London: DfES. Available at: http://www.14–19reform.gov.uk (accessed 30 August 2007).

Turner, J. (2001) 'Breaking the ice on exchanges: a tried and tested exercise to bring German and English exchange partners together', *Deutsch Lehren und Lernen* 23: 3–6.

Turner, K. (1995) *Listening in a Foreign Language: A Skill We Take for Granted?* London: CILT.

Turner, K. (1996) 'The National Curriculum and syllabus design', *Language Learning Journal* 14, Rugby: ALL, pp. 14–18.

Turner, K. (2001) 'The National Literacy Strategy – what's in it for modern language teachers', *Language Learning Journal* 24, Rugby: ALL, pp. 37–42.

Turner, T. (2000) 'Differentiation, progression and pupil grouping', in S. Capel, M. Leask and T. Turner (eds) *Learning to Teach in the Secondary School: A Companion to School Experience*. London: Routledge, pp. 134–50.

Turner, T. with Field, K. and Arthur, J. (1997) 'Working with your mentor', in S. Capel, M. Leask, and T. Turner (eds) *Starting to Teach in the Secondary School: A Companion for the Newly Qualified Teacher*. London: Routledge, pp. 26–39.

ufi/learndirect and kineo (2007) *Podcasting Reviewed*. Available at: http://www.ufi.com/home/section5/10_goodPracticeGuides/goodPracticeGuides.asp (accessed 30 August 2007).

Vandergrift, L. (2004) 'Listening to learn or learning to listen?' *Annual Review of Applied Linguistics* 24: 3–25.

Wajnryb, R. (1992) *Classroom Observation Tasks: A Resource Book for Language Teachers and Trainers*. Cambridge: Cambridge University Press.

Walsh, S. (2002) 'Construction and obstruction: talk and learner involvement in the EFL classroom', *Language Teaching Research* 6(1): 3–24.

Warnock, M. (1978) *Report on the Committee of Enquiry into the Education of Handicapped Children and Young People*. London: HMSO.

Watkins, C. (1999) *Managing Classroom Behaviour: From Research to Diagnosis*. London: Institute of Education in association with the Association of Teachers and Lecturers.

Way, D., Joiner, E. and Seaman, M. (2000) 'Writing in the secondary foreign language classroom: the effects of prompts and tasks on novice learners of French', *The Modern Language Journal* 84(2): 171–84.

Weeden, P., Winter, J. and Broadfoot, P. (2002) *Assessment: What's in It for Schools?* London: Routledge/Falmer.

Wells, G. (1993) 'Reevaluating the IRF sequence: a proposal for the articulation of theories of activity and discourse for the analysis of teaching and learning in the classroom', *Linguistics in Education* 5: 1–37.

Westgate, D., Batey, J., Brownlee, J. and Butler, M. (1985) 'Some characteristics of interaction in foreign language classrooms', *British Educational Research Journal* 11(3): 271–81.

White, J. (2004) 'Howard Gardner: the myth of multiple intelligences', lecture at the Institute of Education, University of London. November 17. Available at http://www.ioe.ac.uk/schools/mst/LTU/phil/HowardGardner_171104.pdf (accessed 30 August 2007).

Wiliam, D. and Black, P. (1996) 'Meanings and consequences: a basis for distinguishing formative and summative functions of assessment?' *British Educational Research Journal* 22(5): 537–48.

Wiliam, D. and Black, P. (2002) 'Feedback is the best nourishment', *Times Educational Supplement* 4 October, pp. 8–9.

Wilkins, D. (1976) *Notional Syllabuses*. Oxford: Oxford University Press.

Wilkinson, J. (1994) 'Self-access learning by German for business students: what role the tutor?' In S. Myles (ed.) *German for Special Purposes*. Studies and Occasional Papers 2 Association for Modern German: London, pp. 12–26.

Williams, E. (1982) 'The "witness" activity: group interaction through video', in M. Geddes and G. Sturtridge (eds) *Video in the Language Classroom*. London: Heinemann, pp. 69–73.

Williams, M., Burden, R. and Lanvers, U. (2002) ' "French is the Language of Love and Stuff": student perceptions of issues related to motivation in learning a foreign language', *British Educational Research Journal* 28(4): 503–28.

Williams, M., Burden, R., Poulet, G. and Maun, I. (2004) 'Learners' perceptions of their successes and failures in foreign language learning', *Language Learning Journal* 30, Rugby: ALL, pp. 19–29.

Wingate, U. (2004) 'Dictionary use – the need to teach strategies', *Language Learning Journal* 29, Rugby: ALL, pp. 5–11.

Wootton, M. (1994) *Meeting Parents: Practical Advice for the New Teacher*. Upminster: Nightingale Teaching Consultancy.

Wragg, T. (ed.) (1984) *Classroom Teaching Skills*. London: Croom Helm.

Wright, H. (2004) *Learning through Listening*. London: CILT.

Wright, M. and Brown, P. (2006) 'Reading in a modern foreign language: exploring the potential benefits of reading strategy instruction', *Language Learning Journal* 33, Rugby: ALL, pp. 22–33.

Wringe, C. (1989) *The Effective Teaching of Modern Languages*. London: Longman.

Wringe, C. (1994) 'Ineffective lessons – reasons and remedies: jottings from the tutor's notepad', *Language Learning Journal* 10, Rugby: ALL, pp. 11–14.

Yaxley, B. (1994) *Developing Teachers' Theories of Teaching: A Touchstone Approach*. Brighton: Falmer Press.

Index

Note: References with *tbl* direct you to tables and *tsk* to tasks